AF693508

Physician Policies:
A Practical Guide to Governance Issues

Physician Policies:
A Practical Guide to Governance Issues

Marshall M. Baker, FACMPE
Kenneth M. Hekman, MBA, FACMPE

Medical Group Management Association
104 Inverness Terrace East
Englewood, CO 80112-5306
877.275.6462
mgma.com

MGMA®
Defining Your Profession

Medical Group Management Association® (MGMA®) publications are intended to provide current and accurate information and are designed to assist readers in becoming more familiar with the subject matter covered. Such publications are distributed with the understanding that MGMA does not render any legal, accounting, or other professional advice that may be construed as specifically applicable to individual situations. No representations or warranties are made concerning the application of legal or other principles discussed by the authors to any specific factual situation, nor is any prediction made concerning how any particular judge, government official, or other person will interpret or apply such principles. Specific factual situations should be discussed with professional advisers.

Editorial/Production Managers: Marilee Aust-Lewis and Craig Wiberg, MLS, ME
Editorial and Production: Glacier Publishing Services, Inc.
Cover Design: Ian Serff, Serff Creative Group, Inc.

Library of Congress Cataloging-in-Publication Data

Baker, Marshall M.
Physician policies : a practical guide to governance issues / Marshall M. Baker and Kenneth M. Hekman.
p. ; cm.
Includes bibliographical references.
Summary: "Applicable for nearly any size physician practice, this manual is the practice manager's one-stop resource for operational challenges regarding physicians. It helps the administrator set succinct, comprehensive policies and procedures for managing physicians on a day-to-day basis--adhering to the practice's philosophy while ensuring efficient, consistent, and quality patient care"--Provided by publisher.
ISBN 978-1-56829-386-8
I. Hekman, Kenneth M. II. Medical Group Management Association. III. Title.
[DNLM: 1. Practice Management, Medical--organization & administration--United States. 2. Guidelines as Topic--United States. 3. Policy Making--United States. W 80]

610.68--dc23
2011038952

Item 8260
ISBN: 978-1-56829-386-8

Copyright © 2012 Medical Group Management Association

All rights reserved. No part of this publication may be reproduced, stored in a retrieval system, or transmitted, in any form or by any means, electronic, mechanical, photocopying, recording, or otherwise, without the prior written permission of the copyright owner.

CPT codes copyright 2012 American Medical Association. All Rights Reserved. CPT is a trademark of the AMA. No fee schedules, basic units, relative values or related listings are included in CPT. The AMA assumes no liability for the data contained herein. Applicable FARS/DFARS Restrictions apply to Government Use.

Printed in the United States of America
10 9 8 7 6 5 4 3 2 1

Contents

Foreword

An organization that lacks clear, current, consistent, and consistently enforced policies is an organization destined for chaos. Policies are one of the most basic management tools available to managers and leaders of any organization. They are the vehicle for communicating expectations to employees and for permitting governance to meet its fiduciary responsibilities.

The purpose of this book is to offer medical practice leaders a comprehensive compendium of sample policies, designed specifically to meet the unique needs of medical practices and covering all major aspects of practice operations. Whether you lead a small single-specialty group, a larger physician-owned practice, or a major physician services enterprise within an integrated delivery system, you will find this volume invaluable. The authors are widely recognized for their expertise in all facets of the management of physician services, and they have done a superb job of laying out the philosophy and rationale for policies in each area, and then providing specific sample policies that can be adapted to your specific organization.

But creating a comprehensive set of organizational policies is only the first step. For a policy manual to be useful, it must become a living document that employees and physicians can turn to for clarification whenever a question arises about how an issue or problem should be handled. When I visit a practice, I will often ask to see the current policy manual. If the staff knows immediately where to find it — and the policies show that they have been recently reviewed to ensure that they are current — that is usually a sign of a high-performing organization. Conversely, if the policy manual is simply gathering dust on a shelf, that often is a symptom of a troubled organization.

You will find this book to be a valuable adjunct to your professional library, and a reference to which you will return many times during your career. Use it to make your own organization's policy manual a valuable tool for leading your practice to world-class performance.

William F. Jessee, MD, FACMPE
MGMA President and CEO
Englewood, Colorado

Acknowledgments

As with any idea, task, or project, success doesn't happen in a vacuum and this book is no exception. Working with a team of MGMA members and experts helped shape this book into what it is today and we are most appreciative of the team endeavor.

Physician Policies: A Practical Guide to Governance Issues was the brainchild of several MGMA staff members, who found that our members were consistently — and often desperately — searching for physician policies to implement inside their organizations. However, the only resource we had on hand was the sold-out 1996 edition of MGMA's *Governing Policies Manual for Medical Practices.* Certainly not everything in healthcare changes drastically in 15+ years, but policies do need to be reviewed and updated from time to time. We turned to the author of the original book, Alys Novak, only to remember that she has since retired. Therefore, we had to set our sights on those who are current in the industry — those who personally create, implement, and defend their own physician policies and practices.

The editors of this book would like to thank the following individuals for their expertise, talents, and mighty contributions to this text. It is with much appreciation and gratitude that we recognize these professionals for sharing their insight and knowledge:

- **Marshall M. Baker, FACMPE:** Marshall provided advice and context, reviewed chapters, suggested updates to many policies, and provided numerous samples and examples;
- **Kenneth M. Hekman, MBA, FACMPE:** Ken wrote each the Philosophies surrounding the book's three separate sections, and he also wrote the philosophies for several chapters;
- **Alys Novak, MBA:** Many of this manual's policies are based on the timeless policies she wrote in the 1996 edition of MGMA's *Governing Policies Manual for Medical Practices*;

- **Courtney Price, PhD:** Several of this manual's policies are based on the evergreen policies found in the *HR Policies and Procedures Manual for Medical Practices* she and Alys cowrote in 2007; and
- Last but not least, no MGMA book would be complete without a review by our extraordinary MGMA member volunteers who took the time to read and review each of this book's chapters:

  George Brown, FACHE
  Director, Clinic Operations
  Scott & White Healthcare
  Round Rock, Texas

  Meredith Fratantonio, MBA
  Chief Operations Officer
  Firelands Physician Group
  Sandusky, Ohio

  Paul Scimeca, CMPE
  VP Physician Practice and Community Health
  Glens Falls Hospital
  Glens Falls, N.Y.

  Kathleen "Katie" Utech
  Practice Administrator
  Health Visions, Inc., Sherman Health
  Elgin, Ill.

Because this manual is designed for a national audience, the editors and MGMA cannot express enough caution and prudence as you work your way through this book. It is important to note that this manual may not adhere to the legal requirements of your specific specialty, locality, commonwealth, or state. Rather, an attempt has been made to consider the impact of federal laws and nationwide trends. It is therefore recommended that before implementing any policy in your organization, you take the proper precautions of having legal counsel review and approve these policies. Only your legal representative can ensure that your practice is following the legal and fiscal requirements specific to your locale.

Introduction: Setting the Stage for Effective Physician Policies

Most of us have a love–hate relationship with policies. We appreciate the order they can lend to a complex organization, but we also chafe under the accountability that comes with them. We may be more inclined to write policies that others must comply with than to draft rules that apply to us.

The potential for conflict can be accentuated when dealing with physician policies. Physicians are taught to think for themselves. They gather the results of diagnostic tests and weigh the evidence to establish a differential diagnosis for each patient. Treatment plans are likewise selected from the broadest array of thoughtful options based on medical research, best practices, and experience. The medical decision-making process requires independent thinking, which is why medical education is such a long and arduous journey.

Practicing medicine in America is increasingly becoming a group effort rather than an individual discipline. Physicians who think for themselves in medical decision-making are called upon to collaborate with other independent thinkers, as together they seek to improve clinical outcomes at lower costs. The Patient Protection and Affordable Care Act of 2010 affirmed and emphasized the call to collaborate. Public policymakers recognized the downside of independent thinking. They documented the costs of fragmentation and disjointed communication in the American healthcare system. They heard the cries for better patient safety, reduced variance in adhering to best practices, and consistent standards for health providers. The response was a grand new policy for the country's healthcare system. While the details will take years to unfold, the philosophical message of the legislation is clear: healthcare institutions, including physician groups, will be held accountable for improving outcomes and lowering costs.

While the national healthcare drama is unfolding, medical group executives and managers have more practical challenges to attend to. They must set the stage for good decision-making, day in and day out, within their own organizations. Medical group leaders need to establish the tone for collaboration, balanced with the freedom for independent judgment. They need to offer a framework of standards that point to the most efficient use of limited resources without choking the freedom to think independently as a medical practitioner. They need to create an environment marked by trust, fairness, and consistency while also fostering individual creativity to solve problems and improve services. It is a daunting challenge.

Sound policies can help. Policies can lend order to chaos and structure to complexity. They can offer a degree of consistency for organizations otherwise characterized by their independence. Policies can be powerful tools in the hands of skillful leaders.

Policies can also be misused and abused. I conducted a strategic consultation for a three-physician practice several years ago that demonstrated the misuse and abuse of policies. The office manager presented two boxes of written policies for our review. Many of the policies were outdated and contradictory. The following sign was posted on the bulletin board in the staff kitchen:

OUR POLICY IS TO FOLLOW THE POLICIES. WHERE THERE IS NO POLICY, OUR POLICY IS TO CREATE A POLICY.

I thought it might have been a joke, but a simple inquiry was met with a terse affirmation. Their overarching "policy on policies" was a true reflection of their philosophy. It infused their culture. The practice was not benefiting from its volumes of policies. In fact, the office manager was frustrated by her inability to keep them updated, and the staff found it impossible to comprehend, much less comply, with the compendium of minute details.

Policies can be tools or weapons. Wise leaders must discern the difference. This book is designed to present policies as tools along with guidance about how to use them well.

Why Policies Matter

Policies play a key role in organizations. They offer several indispensable functions.

- **Policies guide decision-making processes, particularly for recurring situations.** Personnel policies illustrate this function well. Imagine what might happen if there was no policy for vacations. Every employee could take as much time as he or she wanted, whenever he or she wanted. The result would be chaos. Policies guiding physician behavior work the same way. They offer guidance and order for recurring decisions about call coverage, time off, distribution of revenues and expenses, and so much more.
- **Policies offer standards for efficient operations, safety, and effectiveness.** Efficient practices look for ways to simplify clinicians' patient encounters. They may equip and supply each exam room exactly the same, for example, so physicians don't waste time looking for essential items during patient visits. Recommended screenings, such as mammograms or colonoscopies, serve as cost-effective population-wide policies to detect cancer in the early and most treatable stages. Standardizing clinical approaches to specific chronic illnesses can increase the effectiveness of disease management and reduce overall costs of care.

Policies about clinical care may be the key to providing better value in the era of accountable care.

Policies also allow for standardization across locations. Standardization is particularly important for large organizations with multiple sites. Standardized policies streamline patient flow and staff expectations, allowing physicians to be equally efficient in every setting. Physicians and staff know what to expect because the standards and policies transcend local differences. They apply equally to all corners of the organization.

- **Policies are tools for building trust, consensus, and consistency.** Organizational development specialists tell us that trust is a foundational element for healthy organizations. Trust is a key to effective teamwork, and policies set the foundations for trust to grow and nurture a well-functioning organizational culture. They become the boundaries for acceptable behavior. When everyone works consistently within those boundaries, trust grows and the organization fulfills its opportunity to thrive.

  Medical group managers work hard to build consensus among independent-minded physicians. The metaphor of "herding cats" resonates with even the most accomplished medical group manager at some point in his or her career. Effective managers sometimes draft policies as a first step to building consensus around difficult issues. If the group can buy into a written policy impacting professional behavior, its consensus about other operational issues can follow, increasing the efficiency and effectiveness of the organization as a whole.

  Sound policies allow managers to avoid unnecessary conflicts. When groups develop consensus about important decisions in advance of those decisions, they have a solid baseline for consistent decision-making. Developing policies in a crisis can compound the crisis, but policies developed in anticipation of a crisis can help the organization steer clear of the conflict altogether.

- **Policies set the stage for accountability.** Organizations prove the adage, "Good fences make for good neighbors." Relationships are essential for functioning organizations, but relationships can be messy. Policies provide infrastructure for holding each other accountable. They represent the fences, and when people breach the fences, they can expect to be held accountable. The words "policy" and "policing" have common roots. They both hint of good citizenship and good governance.

Policies help to ensure fairness in compensation and benefits. Fairness may be a first cousin of trust, even if it is more elusive. Fairness is in the eye of the beholder, but open dialogue about policies can build consensus about issues that involve justice, equity, and equanimity. The mark of a sound physician compensation policy has been described, tongue-in-cheek, as one that is perceived to be "equally unfair." Injustice and inequity can undermine managers' efforts to build an effective organizational culture. Policies can be tools for countering the destructive effects of unfairness in relationships.

Policies are similar to procedures, and the terms are often referenced in the same breath. They are usually catalogued in a policy and procedure manual, but policies are distinct from procedures. Policies contain principles of conduct, while procedures represent a series of actions based on those principles of conduct. The difference can be illustrated by these parallel terms:

Policies	Procedures
Guidelines	Practices
Plans	Methods
Rules	Tactics
Strategies	Techniques

Policies are tools of leadership, while procedures are tools of management. Policies guide governance, while procedures guide implementation and operations. Each must be consistent with the other to be effective, but they are distinct in their functions.

Characteristics of Effective Policies

Not all policies are created equal. Some organizations have more "unwritten policies" than written ones. Written policies can be as widely varied as the personalities of their authors, and since many policies are written with input from several people, it can be challenging to keep the intended message of each policy clear.

The goals of effective policies are similar to the ideals of sound governance in global politics. The United Nations defines good governance this way:

> *Good governance promotes equity, participation, pluralism, transparency, accountability and the rule of law, in a manner that is effective, efficient and enduring.*[1]

Qualities of good governance — and good policies — in a medical group might be restated in the following terms. Effective policies should be:

- Written;
- Simple and clear;
- Consistent with legal and internal requirements;
- Not a burden;
- Representative of those they are designed to serve;
- Enforceable; and
- Designed for the common good of the organization.

Let's examine each of these characteristics more closely.

- **Written.** Perhaps this should be obvious, but in many cases, it is not. If policies are to govern behavior, they must be communicated clearly and effectively to all. If policies are only expressed verbally, they are subject to interpretation based on the context of the communication and the biases of the listener. Written policies affirm that the communication is the same for all readers. Written policies become the boundaries that govern behavior and the reference points for accountability.

  In every organization, unwritten policies can have a great deal of influence over behavior. This condition is a natural quality of human organizations, but sometimes the influence of unwritten policies or politics can be in conflict with written policies. Wise managers watch for conflicts between written and unwritten

1 United Nations Website, "Global Issues." www.un.org/en/globalissues/governance (accessed July 15, 2011).

policies. Those conflicts provide opportunities to clarify intentions and refine communications as well as to hold people accountable.

A classic example I encountered was a medical group of senior physicians that adopted the following mission statement (a foundational policy): "Dedicated to cutting-edge medical excellence and growth." Meanwhile, the behavior of the physicians nearing the end of their careers pointed to an unwritten policy of "hanging on until retirement." Their behavior was distinctly different from their declared purpose. Their tools were antiquated, and their reticence to take business risks said more about their organizational culture and philosophy than their mission statement.

- **Simple and clear.** Confusing policies don't help anyone. Governmental regulations might fill hundreds of pages to guide the implementation of complex legislation, but policies for governing a medical group need to be easily understood the first time they are read. If physician compensation policies describe incentives that physicians cannot link to their behavior, the policies cannot be effective in driving productivity and growth.

  Policies may need to govern performance for people at all levels of the educational and intellectual spectrum. Personnel policies, for example, should apply to entry-level staff as well as seasoned professionals. They need to be comprehensible and understandable by all, regardless of education and experience. In working across cultures around the globe, I have learned that clear communication comes from using words that a typical eighth grader would understand. Written policies are not the place to demonstrate intellectual superiority or verbal prowess. Good writing is simple so people can understand it.

- **Consistent with legal and internal requirements.** Policies must be consistent with laws. Personnel policies must follow labor laws, and physician compensation policies must comply with Stark laws. All organizations should require a legal review of all written policies to ensure their consistency with legal expectations and regulatory events, but every policy writer should be aware of basic business laws that pertain to the issue the policy is designed to address.

  Policies should also be internally consistent with other departments, divisions, and business segments. A large hospital with employed physicians should use comparable policies to govern the staff in physician offices as well as those in the acute-care hospital. If pay scales or benefits are significantly different in the two settings, managers may find employees wanting to defect from one division to another, disrupting continuity and efficiency.

- **Not a burden.** Policies should be designed to be tools for sound organizational development and operations, but having too many of them can diminish their effectiveness. Highly detailed policies about obscure decisions are difficult to take seriously. They can undermine the validity of all established policies and erode confidence about the usefulness of the best ones. Policies should be designed to guide decision-making and support the values of the organization. Effective policies do no more and no less.

Remember that policies are different from procedures. An organization might have many procedures based on a few policies. Personnel procedures will include timekeeping, payroll processes, vacation schedules, and protocols for requesting time off, but all these procedures will be governed by policies that are consistent with labor laws and market forces.

- **Representative of those they are designed to serve.** Policies are a reflection of the values of the owners and leaders of the organization, so the owners and leaders must be represented in their creation and refinement. Policy development should be an exercise in building consensus among peers rather than a rigid command-and-control declaration from the top. Healthy organizations use a democratic approach to establishing policies rather than an autocratic method. The American colonists rallied around the declaration that "taxation without representation is tyranny." In a similar manner, policy development without representation can cause tyranny within organizations.
- **Enforceable.** Effective policies govern behavior within the organization, so they must be enforceable if they are to be effective. Policies become part of the fabric of trust that binds people together in an organization. Therefore, they must be applicable to everyone in the organization or the fabric of trust will be threatened. Leaders and owners must be the enforcers, but they are not above the policies they designed for the good of the whole organization. If their individual or corporate behavior is inconsistent with the agreed principles of conduct and they are not held accountable, their credibility and effectiveness as leaders will plummet.
- **Designed for the common good of the organization.** Policies are, by definition, intended to be equitable. They are applicable to everyone. Policies for one department should be good for all departments. Their purpose is to unify the organization by their equitable applicability. If one department (or one physician) declares, either verbally or nonverbally, that the policy does not apply to it, the policy loses its authority. It has no teeth.

  Policies should be designed for the common good. They should offer boundaries that preserve the interests of the organization over the interests of any of its members. It should be abundantly clear that if individuals cross those boundaries, it threatens the common good of the whole organization. That is what policies are for — to preserve the good of the whole.

How Policies Shape Organizational Culture

What comes first: organizational culture or policies? It is hard to say. Maybe it doesn't matter. Policies and organizational culture go hand in hand. They feed each other. Policies set the tone for the work environment. Overbearing policies tend to raise the level of fear. They destroy risk-taking behaviors essential for innovation and entrepreneurship. Ambiguous and unenforced policies tend to confuse people. When policies lose their relevance, people make their own policies. They do what they want. The results in both extremes can be dysfunctional and harmful. They undermine the purposes and potential of the organization. They contribute to turnover and discontinuity.

Sound policies, on the other hand, can set a tone of respect and expectation, order and synergy. They can point the way to the common good of the organization and grease the operational gears. When policies and leaders speak with the same respected voice, they guide wise decisions, encourage orderly progress, and inspire individual performance consistent with the group's goals. Policies set the stage for extraordinary achievements by ordinary people.

Policies help employees, vendors, patients, and clients understand "how we do things around here." They embody the philosophy and personality of the organization's leadership, but policies can also shape the philosophy of the organization and extend its legacy across generations of designated leaders.

Lands' End, the retailing giant, has had a long-standing policy to ensure customer satisfaction. Guaranteed. Period. It has guided the company's leaders and employees so effectively through decades of growing competition that they trademarked the phrase. The simple guarantee is an integral part of the company's legacy. It promises to shape the organizational culture for decades to come. It attracts employees and customers alike because it embodies "how they do things around there."

Better-performing organizations, including medical groups, develop mission, vision, and values statements as foundational policies to shape their culture. Each component of these foundational policies requires thoughtful discussion and consensus:

- A well-formed mission statement establishes the identity of the organization. It answers the question, "Who are we?" If traveling is a metaphor for organizational development, a mission statement is like the organization's vehicle of choice. Management guru Peter Drucker rightfully recognized that this simple question of identity rarely has a simple answer. Physicians, for example, can do much more than diagnose and treat sick people. They can play vital roles in preventing illness, encouraging wellness, and managing chronic disease cost-effectively community-wide.
- A vision statement answers the question, "Where are we heading?" A vision statement is like a destination on a map. While a mission statement might remain relatively unchanged, vision statements should become obsolete with accomplishment. They should require renewal every few years based on changes in the market dynamics and careful assessments of internal strategic directions. Organizations on a virtual cycle of continuous improvement outlive their visions. They need new ones periodically.
- Values statements answer the question, "How will we conduct ourselves along the way?" Written values are like road signs, speed limits, lane markers, and other rules of the road guiding the organization safely toward its destination. Written values statements provide a baseline for governing behavior and holding each other accountable.

Mission, vision, and values statements may be foundational, but they only represent the skeleton of a complete organization. Governing and operational policies embody the muscle and connecting tissue for the bones. They hold the organization together and prepare it to move forward. They give the foundational statements vibrancy and substance, enabling it to be more than a collection of wishful ambitions and principles.

Effective policies must therefore be completely consistent with the mission, vision, and values of the organization. Governing and operational policies are interdependent with the foundational policies. Governing policies must support the organization's identity and ambitions. Operational policies should be in sync with the core values that govern decision-making. Likewise, developing governing and operational policies without a clear articulation of the mission, vision, and values would be like putting the cart before the horse (or the trailer before the truck, to update the metaphor). The mission, vision, and values represent the first word on how the organization's culture will unfold. Governing and operational policies are the sequel, but they are all part of the same story and should flow together with continuity and consistency.

When policies are designed according to the principles outlined here, they can have a profoundly positive effect on organizational culture. The following tangible results have their roots in the intangible soil of policies:

- Sound operational policies build consistency, which leads to efficiency. Sound physician compensation policies highlight behaviors that keep each physician focused on the functions that reward him or her personally while simultaneously keeping the corporate overhead under control. When physicians stay on task, they can see more patients, increasing their personal productivity and the overall profitability of the practice.
- Sound policies fuel a sense of fairness and cohesiveness, enabling colleagues and coworkers to focus on professional services rather than employee conflicts. Human interactions can never be completely devoid of the risk of conflict, but by developing fair policies and applying them consistently in a spirit of cohesiveness, managers can minimize the time and emotion wasted on mending coworker relationships after interpersonal conflicts.
- Wise policies function like pre-made decisions, developed by consensus of the leadership team. Written policies can govern in absentia, effectively and consistently even when the manager is absent. Decisions covered by policies don't require additional deliberation by the leadership team. The frontline staff can discern what is expected of them by consulting the written policies. They don't need to disrupt a manager the moment a decision is needed. They can find the pre-made decision in the policies and reserve management time and input for the exceptional decisions. Sound policies place the power to make decisions in the hands of those on the front lines. That power enables employees to be effective decisionmakers as they engage others on the phone and in the office and communicate with collaborating healthcare organizations. That power affirms their importance to the organization and helps them properly represent the core values of their leaders with every interaction.

How Organizational Culture Shapes Policies

The interdependence between organizational culture and policies is subtle. They shape each other almost without recognizing that it is happening. We have looked at how policies shape culture; now we will examine how culture shapes policies.

Organizational culture does not exist in a vacuum. It is a reflection of the collective philosophies of the leaders and managers. In a sense, there is no such thing as organizational culture. It is nothing more than the impact, the results of how leaders and managers think and act day to day. Their behavior weaves a fabric that sets expectations for future daily interactions. The more consistent those interactions are, the stronger the fabric becomes. Leadership behavior becomes predictable. Employees can anticipate what managers will think or do in various circumstances. That predictability is the essence of organizational culture. It reflects the philosophies of leaders and managers about how to make decisions in predictable patterns.

Policies are tools for holding people accountable. They represent power. Some organizations build an environment where power is reserved for those in leadership positions. Others share power too readily without expecting accountability. The tone of written policies tends to fall somewhere in between those two extremes. Where it falls between those extremes is usually a reflection of the leadership team's philosophy about power and their natural leadership style:

- Managers who enjoy the power of holding others accountable might take delight in creating policies that affirm their power with a tone that resembles a drill sergeant. They might also use policies as weapons to "punish" noncompliant employees. Autocratic managers act more like police officers than sensitive humanitarians.
- On the other extreme are managers who refuse to accept responsibility for directing others. They may believe that those on the front lines know best, and that leaving them alone to discern the best way of accomplishing their work is the best policy. Laissez-faire managers act more like best friends than responsible directors.
- Balanced managers are comfortable sharing power without abrogating their responsibility to hold employees accountable. They tend to have fewer policies and spend less time enforcing them. They grant responsibility and accountability for decision-making to their employees and stand with them to redeem mistakes by turning errors into learning opportunities. The managers combine the roles of sensitive humanitarians and responsible directors.

Managers also have a responsibility to lead change in the organization. Change is inevitable as fresh competition comes on the scene, new technologies emerge, and rising customer or patient expectations reshape the market. The healthcare industry is constantly changing. Change is an integral part of every organization's culture, and policies can be used as tools for implementing change at the organizational level.

The pace and process of change is also impacted by organizational culture. Risk-averse managers are prone to analyze information carefully and thoroughly before implementing change. If the changes require modification of policies, the cautious manager will anticipate every question, dot every *i* and cross every *t* before presenting proposed policy changes to the governing body. Managers who are more comfortable with risk might go forward with operational changes, followed by changes to the written policies that document the philosophy behind the operational change. They might be more inclined to ask for forgiveness than permission when implementing organizational changes.

Organizational culture can also drive the process of reviewing and updating policies. Some managers might prefer to establish policies and leave them alone until there is a compelling reason to implement a change. Others will insist on an annual review simply to become personally familiar with them once again. Policies that are central to operational efficiency and strategic achievement should at least be given priority for regular review processes. Changes in relevant laws should also stimulate changes to policies. For example, changes to employment laws should immediately impact human resources policies.

We have said from the outset that governing and operational policies should result from consensus of those who lead and govern the organization. Consensus-building requires trust, which is sometimes a scarce commodity in organizations. Trust is another component of organizational culture. If trust is low, every policy discussion can turn contentious. If trust has been developed and nurtured, leaders and managers have much less difficulty creating sound policies and changing them in a timely manner in the face of new strategic or legal imperatives.

Policies often convey a certain tone about who is most important in the organization. If the medical group exists to serve its member physicians, the policies will carry a distinctive physician-centric tone. If medical services are oriented more toward patients in both philosophy and behavior, the policies are likely to reflect the value that patients' needs take priority over the needs of employees. The choice of who takes priority is also a reflection of the organizational culture.

In a similar vein, policies can point to desired behaviors and offer incentives for achieving those behaviors. Managers can use policies to encourage employees to perform in ways that achieve the common good. They can communicate what behaviors should be primary in the workplace. Incentives might take many forms, including bonus payments, extra time off, meals or theater tickets, or simply public affirmation of a job well done. Written policies are not necessary to affirm particular behaviors or performance, but they can support the philosophy that individual performance impacts organizational achievement.

Limitations of Policies

Policies may be valuable tools in the hands of a skilled administrator, but they also have limitations. They cannot be a substitute for wise personal interactions between managers and employees. They cannot be a cookbook for management. Their consistency cannot make up for a manager's inconsistent behavior. If a manager's behavior appears to be contrary to written policies, employees will mimic the behavior rather than the policies. Simply stated, good policies cannot make up for bad management.

Governing and operational policies are also not substitutes for strategic planning. The strategic planning process is another management tool for guiding the organization and leading its achievements, but it is distinct from policy development. Policies must reflect strategy rather than drive it. Organizational strategies should be derived from a clear understanding of what the market expects of the organization, and how the organization intends to meet those expectations. Policies should be derived from a clear understanding of how the organization will meet the market's needs, rather than the other way around.

Policies are also not sufficient to change individual behavior. If one physician is acting contrary to the common good of the organization, he or she will not change with the enactment of a new policy. Individual misbehavior must be addressed directly. Likewise, if an employee disregards current policies, creating new ones won't solve the problem. Individuals must be managed as individuals. Policies offer guidance for individual performance within the context of the organization.

How This Book Is Organized

This book offers models of policies in three parts. These parts were selected because they represent three types of policies essential to well-functioning medical groups:

I. **Employment.** Defined physician recruitment policies are instrumental in fostering long-term and productive physician–practice relationships. The policies in Chapter 1 lay the foundation to ensuring successful physician recruitment and retention.

Physician compensation policies are central to collegiality, profitability, and the overall strategy of the medical group. Compensation is often cited as the main reason why physicians leave a group. Physician compensation policies are essential, so we deal with these in Part I (Chapter 3). Physician benefits (Chapter 2) are a close second to compensation policies and drive physician satisfaction, retention, and collegiality.

II. **Clinical Practice.** Clinical practice policies are likely to play an increasingly central role in the era of accountable, high-quality patient care. Likewise, patient relations policies are emerging as an integral part of accountable physician performance. In Part II, we explore policies that address clinical competency, quality improvement, and patient-centric practices.

III. **Professionalism.** The policies in Part III cover the standards and expectations that promote collegiality, physician citizenship, and fruitful internal and external relationships. This section provides the framework for articulating your practice's mission, vision, and values statements, as well as the code of conduct and code of ethics that shape your practice's organizational culture.

Policies and Management Behavior

By now it should be crystal clear that managerial polices and managerial behaviors need to be completely consistent. When leaders act contrary to their own policies, when they follow unwritten policies in conflict with written expectations, they destroy their personal integrity and the credibility of their written policies. Employees will trust their eyes and ears more than the written words in the policy manual. They will rely on the observed behavior as the real policy. Managers lead more by example than by written policy.

In my earliest training as a manager, I was given this simple advice: "Whatever kind of manager you wish to be, be consistent. If you are going to be a good manager, be consistently good. If you are going to be a bad manager, be consistently bad. Inconsistency causes more chaos than consistency, even if the consistency is predictably bad." Policies give managers an opportunity to be consistent in the best way. They provide methods for people to be genuine and filled with integrity. They offer managers the challenge to "practice what you preach." Policies are powerful tools, but they should be used carefully.

—Kenneth M. Hekman, MBA, FACMPE

PART I

Employment

CHAPTER 1

Recruitment

Policy 1.1

Recruitment Policy

Please note: Any dollar figures provided are examples only.

Approval for Position

Submit new physician requests to the governing body. The rationale behind the request should be created by the division/department/specialty area with an attempt to achieve consensus within the division/department/specialty area to support recruiting an additional physician/specialist, including:

1. Financial analysis for the position with a pro forma identifying projected revenues and costs directly resulting from the addition of a new physician; and
2. Clinical rationale for the requested new physician, including forecasted referral patterns and identification of existing referral patterns for the specialty (if applicable).

Following approval from the governing body, the recruitment process can be initiated.

Recruiting and Selection Procedure

1. First, assess the current candidate pool. Are there existing physicians in the market, or physicians known to the physicians of the Practice?
2. If there are no identified candidates, a recruiting firm will be identified (following review of at least two (2) proposals).
3. A lead physician for the recruiting will be identified, usually the department chair/division chief. The lead physician will work with the physician recruitment coordinator. A budget will be established to cover travel, materials, advertising, entertainment, mailings, telephone expenses, etc.
4. When candidates are identified, the lead physician and the physician recruiting coordinator will meet with physicians in the department/division to review the candidates' credentials/application. A key consideration, beyond assessment of the individual's professional skills, is attempting to identify/understand the individual's "fit" within the department/division and the Practice.
5. Secondary reference checks (primary reference checks are conducted by the search firm) are the responsibility of department/division members. When a search firm is not retained, the department/division will assume responsibility for primary reference checking.
6. With the file complete, the lead physician will make a formal presentation to the governing body, and a decision will be rendered regarding whether to offer association to the candidate.
7. The board will be notified when a physician has returned a signed contract, and the employment agreement will be ratified with a fully executable copy sent to the candidate.
8. A $3,000.00 (three thousand dollars) "finder's fee" will be paid to any Practice physician and/or spouse or Practice employee upon signature and actual recruitment of a new physician. An additional $2,000.00 (two thousand dollars) will be paid to the "finder" if the physician remains a minimum of three (3) years.

Physician Recruiter Procedure

1. **In-House Recruitment.** The physician recruiter will obtain and review physician candidates from physician databases and personal contacts. Letters will be mailed to candidates who seem viable. Within one (1) week of the mailing, telephone contacts will be made to determine a candidate's interest. If a candidate's interest is positive, requested information and reference checks are completed.
2. **Recruitment via Recruitment Firm.** A recruiting coordinator will be the primary contact for the search firm. The firm will present identified candidates for review.
3. **Interview.** Once a candidate has been identified, following critical review of credentials and reference checking, the physician candidate will be invited for an interview. The physician candidate will be notified of authorized visit and dates will be confirmed. The administrative assistant/physician recruiter will be advised to proceed with finalizing visit and arranging the itinerary. The Practice will be responsible for expenses associated with travel, hotel, and meals during the site visit. Additional requested expenses (e.g., babysitting, child travel) will be approved on a case-by-case basis by the chief executive officer (CEO) or medical director. Expenses for more than one (1) visit will be considered on a case-by-case basis.

Mentor Program Procedure

1. Upon arrival at the Practice, each physician will be assigned a mentor physician.
2. Mentor physicians will serve as advocates and resource persons for the newly recruited physician. The medical director will assign the mentor.
3. The mentor program period shall commence on hiring and extend for a period not to exceed six (6) months.
4. The mentoring physician will have daily contact with the new physician during his or her initial two (2) weeks for the purpose of problem solving and support.
5. The mentor physician will assign clinical personnel to orient the new physician to area hospital(s), including clinical departments, laboratory, diagnostic imaging, pharmacy, administration, health information (clinical records), and, where applicable, obstetrical units, surgery, Post-Anesthesia Care Unit (PACU), and emergency room.
6. The mentor physician will assign clinical personnel to review with the new physician the Practice's policies and protocols concerning telephones and patient scheduling information and review all forms, including diagnostic testing, therapy services, and payers (commercial and governmental).
7. The mentor physician will be responsible for coordinating a formal evaluation of performance of the new physician at three (3) months and six (6) months. The evaluation could include feedback from the department chair, division chief, medical director, mentor physician, and senior leadership.
8. The new physician is requested to attend at least three (3) board of directors meetings within the first year of employment.
9. The mentor physician will be responsible for providing the new physician with general information on customer service, patient relations, communication skills, and community relations.

The goal of this program is to provide new physicians, their spouses, and their families with the appropriate support and direction to create an environment that is pleasant, challenging, and rewarding. This program will support new associates, helping them develop as productive members who are committed to the Practice, which will enhance a long-term relationship.

Policy 1.2 Relocation Policy

Physicians may receive, upon submission of original receipts, payment or reimbursement for costs associated with relocation from __________ to __________. Such payment/reimbursement is intended for the purpose of moving household goods, "house hunting" trips, and temporary housing. Payment/reimbursement shall not exceed actual costs that have been preapproved by the Practice in accordance with applicable legal guidelines.

Policy 1.3

Physician Employment Contracts and Agreements Policy

NOTE: State law requirements can and do differ. This sample agreement must be tailored to conform to legal and regulatory requirements in a particular jurisdiction.

Sample: Physician Employment Agreement

THIS EMPLOYMENT AGREEMENT is entered into as of this [DAY] day of [MONTH], [YEAR], by and between __________, MD (the "Physician") and __________ (the "Practice"), a [LIMITED LIABILITY COMPANY, PROFESSIONAL CORPORATION, ETC.].

Recitals

A. The Practice is rendering professional medical services to the general public through one or more of its Physicians;

B. The Physician is duly licensed to practice medicine in [CITY], [STATE], or if not licensed, the Physician understands and agrees that he or she will be so licensed and credentialed (including satisfactory progress toward hospital privileges and payer credentialing) before any compensation will be payable under this Agreement;

C. The Practice has agreed to employ the Physician, and the Physician has agreed to enter into such employment; and

D. The Practice and the Physician desire to formalize their contractual arrangement for the employment of the Physician in his or her professional capacity and in the rendering of services on behalf of the Practice.

AGREEMENT

NOW, THEREFORE, in consideration of the mutual agreements combined herein, and for other good and valuable consideration, the sufficiency of which is hereby acknowledged, the parties hereby agree as follows:

1. **Employment.** The Practice hereby employs the Physician, and the Physician hereby accepts employment on the terms and conditions set forth herein.
2. **Term.** The term of this Employment Agreement shall commence on [START DATE] and continue until terminated as provided in Section 10 of this Agreement. Notwithstanding termination of employment, this Agreement shall remain in effect until all the parties' rights and obligations have been satisfied, terminated, or have expired, as provided herein. The Physician's date of employment is [START DATE].
3. **Title and Duties.**
    a. The Physician shall serve the Practice as a doctor of medicine or osteopathy in the specialty of [SPECIALTY].
    b. The Physician agrees to accept and abide by the professional standards of the Practice in all areas of the Practice. The Physician further agrees to actively participate in peer evaluations and review activities as required by the Practice and/or contracts that are entered into by the Practice for the provision of healthcare.
    c. The Physician agrees to conform to such policies and procedures as may be instituted from time to time by the Practice pursuant to the Practice's Operating Agreement, bylaws, or other governing documents (the "Agreement") and any other policies and procedures approved by the Practice's board of managers. The Physician further agrees to participate in case management review of the Physician's patients as may be required by the Practice.

Sample continues next page

Sample: Physician Employment Agreement (continued)

d. The Physician agrees to attend and participate in all meetings required by the Practice unless prevented by unforeseen circumstances. Such meetings shall include, without limitation, medical staff meetings, committee meetings of which the Physician is a member, and peer review meetings.

e. The Physician agrees to accept as patients any individuals whom the Practice has appropriately assigned to him or her or referred to him or her by another Practice physician without regard to the health status of such individuals, unless the Physician is not qualified to provide the required services.

f. The Physician agrees to perform medically necessary institutional visits (including emergency room and inpatient) for Practice patients for whom he or she has medical care management responsibilities under any care program managed by the Practice.

g. The Physician shall, in the manner required by the Practice, report to the Practice the professional services performed by the Physician on behalf of the Practice to enable the Practice to provide timely billing and other required service reporting, as may be required under any service agreement of the Practice. Accounting for the Physician's professional services and collection of accounts receivable accruing by virtue of services performed on behalf of the Practice shall be the responsibility of the Practice; however, the Physician agrees to assist in such collection efforts as needed.

h. The Physician shall practice medicine exclusively for the Practice and shall devote his or her full time and efforts to the practice of medicine. Any and all agreements relating to the practice of medicine (specifically agreements with payers, hospitals, and health plans, as well as medical directorships and any agreement for the purchase/lease of equipment or supplies) shall be entered into by the Practice and not in the individual name of the Physician. Any violation of this paragraph shall be grounds for immediate termination of employment, and any amounts then owing by the Practice to the Physician may be withheld as an outset against damages to the Practice for such violation, in addition to other damages or remedies available at law or in equity.

   Further, the Physician shall keep the Practice's executive administrator and board of managers fully informed of any and all agreements entered into by the Physician (whether for remuneration or not) related to all other professional activity, including research, honoraria, teaching, and administration.

i. The Physician agrees to maintain professional licenses and specialty certifications as set forth in Section 9 of this Agreement through successful completion of continuing medical education requirements.

j. In addition to the duties set forth herein, and elsewhere in this Agreement, the Physician agrees to perform such other duties as the Practice may reasonably direct.

4. **Scheduling and On-Call Time.** The Physician shall practice medicine for the Practice within such time limitations as set by the Practice in consultation with his or her colleagues in the division of __________.

5. **Records and Files.** The Physician shall keep and maintain complete documentation and medical records for each patient receiving professional services during the employment period. The medical records shall be the property of the Practice.

Sample continues next page

Sample: Physician Employment Agreement (continued)

6. **Fees.** Except as provided in this Agreement, and unless otherwise determined by the Practice's board of managers (the "Board"), all revenues that result from the professional or other services of the Physician rendered on behalf of the Practice, or from outside professional activities, shall be for the benefit of and be the sole property of the Practice. The Physician has no right, title, or interest in or to accounts receivable or funds otherwise resulting from the rendition by the Physician of such services or from such activities. Solely the Practice shall determine the fees charged for professional services rendered by the Physician on behalf of the Practice after consultation with the Physician.
7. **Compensation.**
    a. The Physician shall be compensated in accordance with the Practice's Compensation Plan. For all services rendered by the Physician under this Agreement, the Practice shall pay the Physician 85 percent of the Compensation Plan Result. During the first 24 months of employment, the Physician shall receive the Compensation Plan Result or an annual salary of $[X], payable in accordance with the Practice's payroll policy, whichever is greater. The Physician's compensation beginning the 25th month of employment will be based solely on 85 percent of the Compensation Plan Result.
    b. Calculation of the Physician's Compensation Plan Result will include allocations for salary, payroll taxes, fringe benefit insurance premiums, retirement plan contribution, and professional development expenses paid on the Physician's behalf by the Practice.
    c. The Physician acknowledges that the Practice's Compensation Plan may change from time to time, as approved by the membership. The Physician will be treated the same as all other employed physicians under the terms and conditions of the most recently approved Compensation Plan.
    d. All compensation paid under this Section 7 shall be less all appropriate income taxes, FICA, FUTA, SUTA, and other taxes properly chargeable against the Physician's compensation.
    e. All Compensation Plan calculations shall be cumulative.
8. **Benefits.**
    a. **Professional Liability Insurance.** The Practice shall maintain at its expense such professional liability insurance coverage as it shall deem appropriate, covering the acts or omissions of the Physician in the course of employment.
    b. **Retirement Plan.** Subject to the satisfaction of the eligibility requirements, the Physician may participate in the Practice's qualified pension, profit-sharing, or other deferred-compensation plan or any combination thereof, if any.
    c. **Time Off.** The Physician shall receive time off in accordance with the Practice's policies. Such time off includes vacation, parental leave, sick leave, and time used for attendance at professional meetings. When taken as vacation time, time off is to be scheduled in consultation with the Practice and in recognition of the current demands of the Practice's business. The Physician shall accrue time off at the rate of two point zero eight (2.08) days per calendar month, to a total of twenty-five (25) days per calendar year. Up to [X] days of time off may be carried forward from year to year to a maximum cumulative amount of [Y] days.
    d. **Leave of Absence.** The Practice may grant the Physician a leave of absence at such time or times and upon such terms and conditions as the Practice, in its discretion, may determine.
    e. **Professional Development.** The Physician shall be entitled to payment directly by the Practice or reimbursement, upon submission of satisfactory documentation,

Sample continues next page

Sample: Physician Employment Agreement (continued)

of expenses incurred for continuing education, educational materials, dues to professional organizations, and any other such expenses that would meet Internal Revenue Service guidelines, to a maximum of __________ hundred dollars ($__________) per year, accruing at the rate of $__________ per calendar month.

f. **Fringe Benefits.** The Physician shall be entitled to receive the same physician fringe benefits and insurance coverages made available to all other Practice physicians.

g. **Relocation Allowance.** If the Practice paid a relocation allowance to the Physician at the time of employment and the Physician terminates employment at any time during his or her first two (2) years of employment, the Physician shall reimburse the Practice for this relocation allowance.

9. **Professional Certification and Licenses.** The Practice agrees to pay the usual fee to [CITY], [STATE], for the Physician to obtain his or her initial license to practice medicine in [STATE], if he or she is not licensed at this time.

The Physician warrants that he or she is certified in [STATE], that he or she is and will remain board eligible or board certified in his or her noted specialty, that he or she is licensed to practice medicine in [STATE], and that there are no undisclosed medical or criminal charges pending against him or her. During the term of this Agreement, the Physician shall:

a. Maintain a valid and unrestricted license to practice medicine;

b. Maintain a valid and unrestricted permit from the federal Drug Enforcement Administration (DEA) to prescribe and possess pharmaceuticals;

c. Maintain unrestricted Practice privileges and medical staff membership with any healthcare facilities as the Practice may reasonably require to serve its patients or intended patients;

d. Maintain valid and unrestricted rights to participate as a Physician in Medicare, Medicaid, and the Workers' Compensation program of [STATE];

e. Maintain membership in such county, state, or national medical associations as the Board may require;

f. Practice without negligence or misconduct;

g. Be able to be insured under the same terms and conditions as all other physicians for professional liability insurance and through the same insurance carrier as all other Practice physicians;

h. Meet the Practice's criteria for quality of care to its clients; and

i. Immediately advise the Practice in writing of any proceedings or threatened proceedings that will or could result in any impairment of the obligations identified in this section.

10. **Termination.**

a. **Termination for Cause.** Subject to compliance with the procedures set forth in the Agreement, the Practice may terminate the Physician's employment hereunder for "Cause" (definition follows) upon fourteen (14) days' prior written notice to the Physician. In the event of termination for Cause, all obligations of the Practice under this Agreement will immediately cease, and no payments of any kind, including but not limited to the payment of the basic compensation (except for the payment of such base salary and fringe benefits accrued through the date of termination), will thereafter be made in respect of the remaining term of this Agreement. As used herein with respect to termination by the Practice, "Cause" shall mean failure to meet any of the requirements of Sections 3 or 10 of this Agreement or any other conduct constituting "just cause" for termination under [STATE] common law.

Sample continues next page

Sample: Physician Employment Agreement (continued)

b. **Termination without Cause.** Subject to compliance with the procedures set forth in the Agreement, the Practice may terminate the Physician's employment hereunder without Cause upon ninety (90) days' prior written notice to the Physician. In the event of termination of the Physician by the Practice without Cause, the Practice shall satisfy its remaining obligations under this Agreement by the payment of the Physician's base salary and fringe benefits for the remainder of the term of employment through the effective date of termination of employment.

c. **Payment in Lieu of Notice.** The Practice may, in lieu of affording a period of notice specified in Sections 10a or 10b, pay the Physician his or her salary and fringe benefits as set forth and for the periods described in Sections 10a or 10b attributable to such period.

d. **Resignation.** Should the Physician wish to resign from his or her position with the Practice during the term of this Agreement, the Physician shall give ninety (90) days' written notice to the Practice specifying the date on which such resignation is to become effective. In the event of resignation, the Practice shall have no further obligations to the Physician under this Agreement other than to pay the Physician his or her base salary and fringe benefits up through the effective date of the resignation.

e. **Death.** This Agreement, the Physician's employment hereunder, and the Practice's obligations hereunder shall terminate forthwith upon the death of the Physician. Notwithstanding the foregoing, the Physician's heirs or representatives shall be entitled to receive the Physician's salary earned or accrued up and through the date of his or her death.

f. **Disability.** This Agreement, the Physician's employment hereunder, and the Practice's obligations hereunder shall terminate should the Physician become disabled as the result of a physical or mental impairment and is unable to perform the essential functions of his or her duties with reasonable accommodation. Notwithstanding the foregoing, the Physician shall be entitled to receive the Physician's salary and fringe benefits earned or accrued through the date of commencement of such disability. To the extent that the Physician's disability can be reasonably accommodated by providing a leave of absence, such leave of absence may be paid or unpaid, as determined by the Board in its discretion. This subsection 10f shall be construed in accordance with any and all applicable state and federal laws. Physician's rights and obligations shall thereafter be governed by the applicable shareholder and related agreements, which shall supersede this Agreement in all respects.

g. **Physician-Shareholder.** This Agreement shall immediately terminate should the Physician become a shareholder of the Practice, in which case the Practice shall have no further obligations to the Physician under this Agreement other than to pay the Physician his or her base salary and fringe benefits up through the date of such event.

h. **Assignment of Third-Party Reimbursement Contracts.** Upon termination pursuant to Sections 10a, 10b, 10d, or 10f hereof, the Physician shall in good faith negotiate to assign to the Practice any rights or benefits enjoyed by the Physician pursuant to any third-party reimbursement contracts to which the Physician is a party.

i. **Survival of Terms.** The provisions of Sections 10 through 16 of this Agreement shall survive any termination or expiration of the term of this Agreement or the Physician's employment hereunder.

Sample continues next page

Sample: Physician Employment Agreement (continued)

11. **Post-Termination Understanding.** Upon termination of the Physician's employment with the Practice for any reason, the Physician agrees never to disclose any confidential information of the Practice, and the Physician agrees not to practice as a physician within the territory [TO BE DEFINED CONSISTENT WITH APPLICABLE STATE LAW] for a period of ____ years from and after the date of termination of his or her employment, whether such association be as an employee or as an independent physician or subsequently as a member of the Practice. The parties agree that a reasonable estimate of damages for the Physician's breach of this Agreement shall be [DEFINE DAMAGES PAYABLE CONSISTENT WITH APPLICABLE STATE LAW]. The Physician agrees not to solicit, accept, or assist in the employment of any person, directly or indirectly, who has been an employee of the Practice at any time within the previous year, for a period of one (1) year after the Physician terminates his or her employment with the Practice. It is the parties' intention that this noncompetition section be enforced by both an injunction and by an action for damages, and that should a court of competent jurisdiction find any part of it to be unenforceable for any reason, that it be modified and enforced to the maximum extent permitted by law.
12. **Confidentiality.**
    a. The Physician acknowledges that by association with the Practice and the Practice's other professional physicians, the Physician will gain access to confidential and proprietary information of the Practice and will be introduced to numerous patients of the Practice. The Physician acknowledges that the Practice's business and future success depends on preservation of trade secrets and other confidential, proprietary information concerning the Practice, its shareholders, and its professional physicians ("Secrets"). These Secrets include, without limitation: treating methods; patient charts and treatment records, lists, and needs; market surveys and plans; pricing methods; proposal terms; contract renewal dates; information about the qualifications of other physicians; and other such business information. The Physician also expects to accumulate new information of a similar type through his or her own work. The Physician agrees that all such nonpublic information belongs solely to the Practice. For the duration of his or her employment and indefinitely thereafter, the Physician agrees to keep such information confidential and to use it only to benefit the Practice's business. He or she further agrees to return all patient charts and other Practice documents, whether on paper, electronic, or other medium, including copies thereof, and any equipment or other tangible things that reflect confidential information immediately upon termination of his or her employment.
    b. The Physician covenants that this confidentiality provision shall supplement, rather than replace, any other rights or remedies the Practice may have under applicable law for the protection of its properties and trade secrets.
13. **Business Opportunities and Professional Engagements.**
    a. The Physician agrees that he or she will during the term of his or her employment with the Practice promptly and fully disclose to the Practice any business opportunity coming to the Physician's attention, or conceived or developed in whole or in part by the Physician, that relates to the Practice's business or anticipated business. Except with respect to other devices (as defined in Section 14a of this Agreement) invented by the Physician, which the Physician may freely exploit, the Physician will not at any time exploit such business opportunities for his or her own gain or that of any person or entity other than the Practice. Notwithstanding the foregoing, the performance by the Physician of panel exams, independent medical exams, or academic activities that have been approved by the Practice in advance, as well as charitable activities, shall not be considered usurpation of corporate business opportunities.

Sample continues next page

Sample: Physician Employment Agreement (continued)

b. Notwithstanding subsection 13a of this Agreement, the Physician shall be entitled to payment of honoraria paid to the Physician in connection with his or her participation at professional conferences and other gatherings to which the Physician is invited to speak, in accordance with the Practice's Operating Agreement or bylaws, as applicable, and its Compensation Plan.

14. **Intellectual Properties.**

a. **Corporate Ownership.** All ownership, copyright, patent, trade secrecy, and other rights in all works, programs, manuals, ideas, improvements, discoveries, processes, or other properties ("Intellectual Properties") made or conceived by the Physician during the term of his or her employment by the Practice which are within the scope of Physician's employment shall be the sole property of the Practice, whether or not developed independently by the Physician or jointly with others, whether developed or conceived during regular work hours or at the Practice's facilities, and whether the Practice uses, registers, or markets such properties; provided, however, that any such rights and properties in any device invented by the Physician during the term of his or her employment shall, as between the Physician and the Practice, be the rights and properties of the Physician. In accordance with the Practice's policy and [STATE] law, this Agreement does not apply to, and the Physician has no obligation to assign to the Practice any Intellectual Properties for which no Practice trade secrets, and no equipment, supplies, or facilities of the Practice were used, and which was developed entirely on the Physician's own time, unless: (i) the Intellectual Properties relate directly to the Practice's business; (ii) the Intellectual Properties relate to the Practice's existing or demonstrably anticipated research or development work; or (iii) the Intellectual Properties result from the Physician's work for the Practice. Notwithstanding the foregoing, the Physician shall retain all rights, title, and interest, including copyrights, in and to any outside writing, whether technical or fiction, as long as such activities do not impact the Physician's abilities to carry out his or her duties hereunder. Attached hereto as Exhibit A is a list and description of all Intellectual Properties that the Physician has owned or has developed prior to being employed by the Practice. Any such Intellectual Properties so listed and not otherwise expressly assigned in writing by the Physician to the Practice will be excluded from the terms of this Agreement.

b. **Disclosure Duty.** To determine whether the Physician has an obligation to assign particular Intellectual Properties to the Practice, the Physician shall promptly make full written disclosure to an officer of the Practice other than the Physician of all Intellectual Properties that he or she developed, or on which he or she is working during the term of his or her employment.

c. **Assistance.** The Physician will assist the Practice as it may request during and after the term of his or her employment to further evidence, perfect, and/or enforce the Practice's rights in and ownership of the covered Intellectual Properties. The Physician's obligation in this respect includes, without limitation, execution of additional instruments of conveyance and assistance to the Practice with applications for patents, copyright, or other registrations.

d. **Infringement Warranty.** The Physician warrants that, to the best of his or her knowledge, any and all items, technology, and Intellectual Properties of any nature developed or provided by the Physician, or which in any way benefit the Practice will be original to the Physician and will not infringe in any respect on the rights or property of others. The Physician will not, without prior written approval of the Practice, use any equipment, supplies, facilities, or proprietary information of any other party. The Physician warrants that he or she is entirely free to contract for employment with the Practice and to perform his or her duties under this Agreement without any conflict with other commitments, agreements, understandings, or

Sample continues next page

Sample: Physician Employment Agreement (continued)

duties to prior employers or others. The Physician will indemnify the Practice for all losses, claims, attorneys' fees, and other expenses that may arise from any breach of this warranty.

15. **Certain Remedies.**
    a. The harm to the Practice from any breach of the Physician's obligations under or related to this Agreement may be difficult to determine and may be wholly or partially irreparable. Thus, the Practice may enforce such obligations by seeking an injunction in addition to seeking other appropriate relief. If any bond from the Practice is required in connection with such enforcement, the parties agree that a reasonable value of such bond shall be $[X]. The Physician further agrees that any profits made in violation of this Agreement shall be held in constructive trust for the Practice.
16. **Miscellaneous.**
    a. **Amendments and Waivers.** Only a written instrument signed by both parties may amend this Agreement. No breach of any agreement, warranty, or representation shall be deemed waived unless expressly waived in writing and signed by the party who might assert such breach. No failure or delay by either party in exercising any right under this Agreement shall operate as a waiver of such right, nor shall any single or partial exercise of any right preclude any other or further exercise of such right or the exercise of any other right.
    b. **Assignment Prohibited.** The Physician may not assign any of his or her rights nor delegate any of his or her duties hereunder. The Practice may assign this Agreement and delegate its duties hereunder in connection with any merger, consolidation, or sale of assets, or to any of its affiliates at any time owned by, or under common ownership with, the Practice.
    c. **Governing Law and Venue.** This Agreement, including all matters of construction, validity, and performance, shall be governed by, construed, and enforced in accordance with the laws of [STATE], as applied to contracts made and executed and to be fully performed in such state by citizens of such state, without regard to its conflict of law rules. The parties agree that the exclusive jurisdiction and venue for any action brought between the parties under this Agreement shall be the state and federal courts sitting in or for [COUNTY], [CITY], [STATE], and each party hereby agrees and submits itself to the exclusive jurisdiction and venue of such courts for such purpose.
    d. **Savings Clause.** If any provision of this Agreement is held to be invalid or unenforceable to any extent in any context, it shall nevertheless be enforced to the fullest extent allowed by law in that and other contexts, and the validity and force of the remainder of this Agreement shall not be affected thereby. If any provision of this Agreement violates applicable federal or [STATE] law, then this Agreement shall be automatically amended to the extent necessary to comply with the law or regulation.
    e. **Notices.** All notices and other communications called for or required by this Agreement shall be made in writing to the parties at their respective addresses listed at the end of this Agreement, or to such other address as a party may subsequently specify and shall be deemed to have been received (i) upon delivery in person, (ii) upon the passage of seventy-two (72) hours following post by first-class registered or certified mail, return receipt requested, with postage prepaid, (iii) upon the passage of twenty-four (24) hours following post by overnight receipted courier service, or (iv) upon transmittal by confirmed telex or facsimile provided that, if sent by facsimile, a copy of such notice shall be concurrently sent by U.S. certified mail, return receipt requested, and postage prepaid, with an indication that the original was sent by facsimile and the date of its transmittal.

Sample continues next page

Sample: Physician Employment Agreement (continued)

Notice to Physician:
Notice to Practice:
Chairman, Managers
____________________________ [PRACTICE NAME], LLC
With a copy to: (legal counsel)

f. **Complete Agreement.** This Agreement comprises the entire agreement between the parties. It supersedes and merges within it all prior agreements and understandings between the parties, whether written or oral, express or implied. In interpreting and construing this Agreement, the fact that any particular party may have drafted this Agreement or any provision hereof shall not be given any weight or relevance.

g. **Counterparts.** This Agreement may be signed in several counterparts, each of which shall be an original, but all of which together shall constitute the same instrument.

h. **Costs and Expenses of Enforcement.** If suit is brought to interpret or enforce any term or provision of this Agreement, or if any dispute between the parties is settled by agreement of the parties, the prevailing party in either case shall, in addition to any other relief to which such party may be entitled, be awarded against the other party such prevailing party's attorneys' fees and costs reasonably and actually incurred.

i. **Representation.** The Physician acknowledges that the firm [NAME OF PRACTICE'S LEGAL COUNSEL/FIRM] is representing only the Practice and that the Physician is entitled to seek separate legal counsel regarding this Agreement and related documents. By his or her signature hereto, the Physician consents to any conflicts of interests arising now or hereafter as a result of this arrangement.

j. **Limited Offer.** This Agreement must be signed and returned to the Practice on/before [DATE]; otherwise the entire offer and this Agreement become null and void.

By the following signature, the Physician acknowledges that he or she has read and understood this Agreement, that its terms have been fully and fairly negotiated by himself or herself and the Practice, and that he or she signs it voluntarily.

Executed by the parties as of the date first written in the Agreement.

____________________________ [PRACTICE NAME], LLC

By: ____________________________, Chairman, Board of Managers

____________________________ [PHYSICIAN NAME], MD

NOTE: State law requirements can and do differ. This sample agreement must be tailored to conform to legal and regulatory requirements in a particular jurisdiction.

Sample: Employment Contract

THIS EMPLOYMENT CONTRACT ("this Agreement") is entered into effective the [DAY] day of [MONTH], [YEAR], between __________ (the "Practice") and __________, MD ("the Physician").

The Practice is a __________ that provides [SPECIALTY] services at sites including __________, __________, and __________ in [CITY], [STATE]. The Practice also provides pain management services at __________ in [CITY], [STATE]. The Physician is a(n) [SPECIALTY], duly licensed by the State of [STATE]. The Practice desires to obtain the services of the Physician, and the Physician desires to be employed by the Practice.

THEREFORE, in consideration of the mutual promises contained in this Agreement, the Practice hereby employs the Physician, and the Physician hereby accepts employment upon the following terms and conditions:

1. **Term.** The Physician's initial term of employment is confirmed upon the execution of this Agreement and shall continue for two (2) years from the date of execution or until terminated in accordance with this Agreement. The provisions of this Agreement (specifically including but not limited to the provisions relating to termination of employment) shall apply notwithstanding anything to the contrary in any employee manual, correspondence, or other document prepared or published by or on behalf of the Practice either previously or in the future, other than an executed amendment to this Agreement.
2. **Duties, Qualifications, Extent of Services, and Requirements.** Except as otherwise expressly authorized by the Practice's board of directors, the Physician shall devote the Physician's full working time and best professional skill to the performance of such duties and responsibilities as may be assigned to the Physician from time to time by the Practice, in its sole discretion. The Physician agrees to be and to remain (a) duly and properly licensed and qualified as a practicing [SPECIALTY] under the laws of [STATE] and all other applicable laws, rules, and regulations and (b) either "board certified" or "board eligible" according to the [APPROPRIATE CREDENTIALING ASSOCIATION]. (Without limiting the generality of the preceding sentence, the Physician agrees to obtain continuing medical education (CME) sufficient in amount and content to meet or exceed [APPROPRIATE CREDENTIALING ASSOCIATION] guidelines.) The Physician agrees to obtain and maintain unqualified privileges to the Practice and any other medical facility designated by the Practice. The Physician agrees that the Physician's qualifications and duties will include but not necessarily be limited to those adopted from time to time by the Practice's board of directors and which are uniformly applicable to all of the Practice's employed physicians on a nondiscriminatory basis, which qualifications and duties the Practice may reasonably alter and amend at any time and from time to time in a manner consistent with the terms of this Agreement.

   The Physician agrees to discharge the Physician's responsibilities faithfully, diligently, and in a timely manner and agrees to abide by (a) all the Practice policies relating to its employees generally; (b) all Practice policies relating specifically to the Practice's physician employees; (c) all rules, regulations, and policies promulgated by the Practice's board of directors; (d) all applicable laws, rules, regulations, policies, and procedures promulgated by any government entity; and (e) all medical staff bylaws and similar provisions adopted by the Practice and any governing body of any other medical facility where the Practice provides services. The Physician acknowledges that the Practice reserves the right to alter and amend its rules, regulations, and policies at any time and from time to time.

Sample continues next page

Sample: Employment Contract (continued)

In addition to the Physician's professional responsibilities, the Physician agrees to fulfill administrative duties reasonably assigned to the Physician by the Practice. All such functions and duties shall be reasonably and equitably taken into account in determining the overall professional and other employment responsibilities assigned to the Physician in relation to others similarly situated.

The Physician shall abide by and comply with the Practice's bylaws, the provisions, and requirements of all contracts between the Practice and any third parties with which the Practice contracts in furtherance of carrying out its business, and any rules and regulations promulgated by the Practice, including the requirement to be publicly and privately supportive of and for the Practice and any hospital or facility at or in which the Practice conducts its business. Failure to abide by and adhere to the terms of this Agreement or any rules and regulations established by the Practice or any other rules, regulations, policies, or procedures incorporated herein shall subject the Physician to discipline, fine, and/or termination. The Physician also agrees to abide by and be bound by all policies, procedures, and rules that are hereby incorporated into this Agreement, promulgated by any medical staff or department located at or functioning in conjunction with any hospital or other facility at which the Practice has elected to provide professional services. The Physician further agrees to fully cooperate and participate in any managed care contracting arrangements entered into by the Practice and cooperate and assist the Practice with any and all business development measures taken by the Practice. Similarly, if at any time any such agreement between the Practice and a third party requires that the Practice cease providing professional services through the Physician, upon the written request of the Practice, the Physician shall resign effective immediately, and if the Physician does not resign, the Practice shall terminate the Physician's employment immediately. In addition, the Physician agrees that upon the written request by the Practice, the Physician will honor, abide by, and execute any document reasonably required to implement and all uniform nondiscriminatory requirements imposed upon the Practice and its physicians in contracts with third parties.

3. **Fees and Payments.** The Physician agrees that all fees and payments received as a result of professional services rendered to or for the benefit of patients by the Physician, together with all other fees and payments generated as a result of the Physician's work for or on behalf of the Practice, shall be the property of the Practice. Accordingly, the Physician acknowledges that the Physician has no ownership interest in or personal claim upon any such fees or payments whether collected during or after the termination of the Physician's employment. The compensation and benefits received by the Physician or payable to the Physician under this Agreement shall fully satisfy all the Physician's claims upon the Practice for compensation in respect to the Physician's professional and other services.

   The Physician may engage in or produce, and receive and retain income from, activities or work products that are not inconsistent with the Physician's duties under Section 2 of this Agreement, under Section 10 of this Agreement, or under any other provision of or amendment to this Agreement, upon the condition that such activities are not based upon or derived from the Physician's employment by and activities for the Practice; are not based upon or derived from and do not utilize any information, data, or anything else belonging to the Practice; and do not have any adverse impact upon the Physician's availability and performance as a full-time employee of the Practice. Specifically, but without limitation, the Physician and the Practice agree that the Physician will be able to earn and retain witness fees, report fees, speaker fees, teaching fees, and similar income generated solely by the Physician's individual and personal efforts outside the scope of his work on behalf of the Practice, provided that

Sample continues next page

Sample: Employment Contract (continued)

such outside activities do not materially interfere with the Physician's performance of his or her duties and responsibilities for the Practice.

If the Physician receives income that the Physician believes he or she is entitled to retain as his or her own, the Physician agrees to provide to the Practice, quarterly or more frequently, a written report stating that such income has been received and briefly describing the type and source of the income (but not the amount). The Practice shall be entitled to request and receive additional or more detailed information about such income in order to resolve any questions about the proper classification of it. This income reporting and classification process will be administered in a uniform and nondiscriminatory manner.

Except as provided previously, if the Physician engages in any income-producing activity or creates any work product not in conflict with Section 2, Section 10, or any other provision of this Agreement or any amendment, but such activity or work product nevertheless is to a substantial and material degree based upon, derived from, or utilizing any information, data, equipment, personnel, or resources of the Practice, then the Practice shall be paid as received by the Physician a portion of the income derived from the activity or work product. Such portion shall be determined on a commercially reasonable basis by the Practice's board of directors or a duly appointed subcommittee thereof, whose determination of both whether any income-producing activity or work product is within the scope of this provision, and what is a fair and reasonable apportionment of income between the Physician and the Practice shall be final and binding upon the Physician. In making such determination, the Practice's board of directors, or the subcommittee so appointed for this purpose, shall take into account the relative contributions of and benefits to the respective parties, including without limitation contributions of the Physician and the Practice of time, effort, opportunity, data, equipment, personnel, and resources to the conduct of the income-producing activity or the generation of any income-producing work product. For the purposes of this provision, the Practice acknowledges that the Physician's prior professional experience alone would not be a basis for the Practice's having any claim to any work product or income generated by such activities.

As an example of the preceding provisions of this Section 3, if on his or her own time the Physician conducts sponsored (paid) research and uses the Practice's personnel and other resources in connection with the research, the resulting profit shall be accounted for, and the Practice will be entitled to reimbursement for its expenses incurred in connection with the research and shall also be entitled to participate in the profit in a manner determined in accordance with Section 4 of this Agreement.

4. **Compensation.** For all services rendered by the Physician during the term of this Agreement, the Practice shall, for the first year of employment, pay the Physician an annual salary of $[X] that shall be paid in equal monthly payments. The Practice shall, for the second year of employment, pay the Physician an annual salary of $[X] that shall be paid in equal monthly payments.
5. **Employment-Related Policies and Authority.** The Physician acknowledges that the Practice's board of directors will adopt and may change from time to time and at any time policies, medical groups, and procedures regarding the following subjects (among others):
    a. Payment of or reimbursement for expenses incurred for subscriptions, dues, and association fees;
    b. Payment of or reimbursement for expenses incurred for, and time off for attendance at, professional meetings (or CME, continuing medical education);
    c. Required CME; and,

Sample continues next page

Sample: Employment Contract (continued)

d. Vacations, sick time off and similar personal time off, and coordination of absences from work. However, during the terms of this Agreement, the paid time off will be as follows:

(1) First year __________ weeks
(2) Second year__________ weeks

Without the prior express written consent from the Practice or an executive officer of the Practice acting pursuant to authority granted by the Practice, the Physician shall have no apparent or implied authority to:

(a) Pledge the credit of the Practice or any of its other employees;

(b) Bind the Practice under any contract, agreement, note, mortgage, or otherwise;

(c) Release or discharge any debt due the Practice unless the Practice has received the full amount thereof;

(d) Sell, mortgage, transfer, or otherwise dispose of any assets of the Practice; or

(e) Individually contract with any patient, third party, or customer of the Practice.

6. **Insurance and Fringe Benefits.** The Practice shall furnish the Physician with professional liability insurance during the term of the Physician's employment. Such professional liability insurance shall be provided in such amounts, with such deductibles, in such forms or policies, and by such insurers as the Practice shall determine from time to time in the Practice's sole discretion. If the Physician is terminated for cause, the Physician will purchase, at the Physician's sole expense, an extended reporting endorsement ("tail" endorsement). If the Physician does not purchase such a policy or extended coverage, the Practice may in its sole discretion elect to purchase such a policy or extended coverage and charge the cost of such policy to the Physician. In addition, the Physician shall have the right to participate in all other fringe benefits made generally available by the Practice for its physician employees on the same basis as and pursuant to the same criteria applied to the Practice's other physician employees. The Physician agrees to cooperate with the Practice regarding — and to execute and deliver to the Practice such applications and forms as the Practice reasonably requests (either during or after the Physician's employment with the Practice) in connection with the purchase by the Practice of life, health, disability, worker's compensation, or professional or other liability insurance — insuring the Physician or the Physician's acts and omissions. The Physician acknowledges that the Practice may alter, amend, and/or discontinue any such fringe benefits at any time and from time to time. The Physician also acknowledges that any such benefits program may impose eligibility, insurability, minimum working time, and similar requirements and conditions as a result of which the Physician may not be covered by any particular program.

7. **Disability, Retirement, Death, Possible Benefits, and Coordination.** Upon the disability, retirement, death, or termination of employment of the Physician, neither the Physician nor the Physician's estate shall be entitled to any further compensation from the Practice except such compensation, if any, as may be provided for in a separate written resolution or plan adopted by the Practice and applicable to all shareholders or all physician employees of the Practice, as applicable. The Physician acknowledges the right of the Practice to alter, amend, and terminate any such resolution or plan at any time and from time to time.

   The Practice's board of directors is authorized to make in good faith such determinations as are required to administer any such resolution or plan, including coordinating any benefits because of multiple events (e.g., disability and then death)

Sample continues next page

Sample: Employment Contract (continued)

occurring to any one individual. Also, if at any time the Practice becomes obligated to make payments simultaneously to two or more employees on account of disability, retirement, death, or termination of employment, the Practice's monthly payments pursuant thereto to each employee may be adjusted by dividing the agreed benefit payable to each employee by the number of employees then receiving benefits. The number of months of benefit payments shall be extended accordingly to preclude any total loss of benefits to any employee.

8. **Termination of Employment.** The Physician and the Practice shall have the right to terminate this agreement at any time by mutual agreement in writing. The Practice and the Physician agree that the Practice may terminate the Physician's employment at any time, with or without cause, but only if such action is approved by a two-thirds or greater vote of its entire board of directors, and then only upon three (3) months' notice to the Physician. (If the Physician's employment is terminated for any reason effective as of any particular future date, the Practice reserves the right to require that the Physician immediately cease providing services on behalf of the Practice, but such cessation of services at the request of the Practice shall not affect the Physician's right to compensation and benefits, if such right exists, through the termination date.) The Physician shall have the right to terminate this Agreement as of the last day of any month by giving written notice at least three (3) months prior to the proposed termination. Upon such termination, neither the Practice nor the Physician shall have any further rights or obligations under the terms of this Agreement (except that the Physician may be entitled to post-termination benefits as referred to in Section 7, if applicable, and certain provisions of this Agreement shall survive such termination as provided in Section 10).
9. **Patient Charts.** The Practice and the Physician acknowledge that the patient charts of the individuals to whom the Practice provides services normally are the property of and remain with the Practice, the hospital, or other facility at which the services are provided, as applicable. However, to the extent (if any) to which the Practice or the Physician retains possession and control of such patient charts upon the termination of the Physician's employment, all patient charts shall remain with or be returned to the Practice. The Practice agrees, however, that it will reproduce and forward by mail all such retained patient charts (i.e., the charts, if any, over which the Practice retains possession and control) of a patient who makes a request in substantially the following form:

   Please forward all medical records in your possession that concern me to Dr. ____________________ at the earliest possible date after receipt of this request.

   ____________________ [Patient's Name] __________ [Date]

   The Practice further agrees that such requests will be honored immediately, but all reasonable costs for the reproduction and mailing of any such documents and records shall be borne by the Physician to whom they are forwarded.
10. **Noncompetition.**
   [Note: State laws vary widely on the enforceability of noncompetition agreements. This is only an example, which must be tailored to the requirements of a particular jurisdiction.]
   a. As used in this Agreement, the term "Termination Date" means the date on which the Physician's employment with the Practice is terminated for any reason. As used in this Agreement, the term "Noncompete Period" means the period of time beginning on the Termination Date and continuing for [X] months after the Termination Date. The Physician agrees that both during employment and during the Noncompete Period, the Physician will not enter into, engage in, or be employed

Sample continues next page

Sample: Employment Contract (continued)

by any person, firm, institution, association, corporation, or other entity engaged in the professional practice provided by the Practice or the rendering of such services in or at (i) the following locations where the Practice is providing such services or treatment to patients on an exclusive or largely exclusive basis: (a) __________ Medical Center in [CITY], [STATE]; (b) __________ Hospital in [CITY], [STATE]; and (c) __________ Surgical Center in [CITY], [STATE]; (ii) any hospital or medical facility where the Practice is providing such services to patients on an exclusive or largely exclusive basis at the time of termination of the Physician's employment with the Practice; or (iii) any hospital or medical facility with which the Practice is in active negotiations, at the time of termination of the Physician's employment with the Practice, for the right to provide such services or treatment to patients on an exclusive or largely exclusive basis. The Physician agrees that the Practice may attach hereto as Schedule I and update from time to time a list of hospitals and/or medical facilities, in addition to those specifically identified in Section 10a(i), that come within the scope of the prohibition of this Section 10a. Schedule I and any amendments to Schedule I shall be the same for all employment contracts for all shareholder employees of the Practice. The Physician shall promptly provide a copy of Schedule I and any amendment to Schedule I when available.

b. In order to protect the reputation and contractual rights of the Practice, if the Physician's employment with the Practice terminates for any reason, the Physician will immediately resign and surrender all medical staff privileges at each Practice site and at any other hospital or other medical facility at which the Practice is then providing services or treatment to patients exclusively or largely exclusively. Such resignation shall be in the form of that attached hereto as Schedule II. **[Note: Discuss if this mandatory resignation provision is relevant to the Practice.]** The Physician agrees that because the Physician's abilities and skills are readily usable in most or all geographic areas throughout the United States, the foregoing restriction does not impose any undue hardships upon the Physician or unreasonably restrict the Physician with respect to practicing the Physician's profession elsewhere should the Physician terminate the Physician's employment with the Practice. It is recognized by the Physician that the Physician's breach of the provisions of this Section 10b will result in irreparable injury to the Practice, which will entitle the Practice to an injunction restraining and enjoining the Physician from committing or continuing any such breach.

c. It is agreed that in the event of a breach by the Physician of the covenants contained in Section 10a hereof, the Practice will suffer irreparable harm, and in addition, the determination of actual damages will be very difficult and time consuming. [DEFINE APPROPRIATE LIQUIDATED DAMAGES AMOUNT UNDER APPLICABLE STATE LAW.] It is understood and agreed between the parties that these liquidated damages are not intended to be payable in return for the Physician's breach of the covenants contained in Section 10a and do not exclude the Practice's right to enforce said covenant by injunctive relief in a court of equity. This liquidated damages provision is included in this Agreement only for the purpose of calculating damages in the event of litigation in addition to recovery of damages for breach of the covenants contained in Section 10a instead of an action for injunction and shall not be deemed or considered to be evidence that the Practice has an adequate remedy at law for a breach of the covenants contained in Section 10a. It is understood and agreed between the parties to this Agreement that in the event of a suit in equity by the Practice against the Physician regarding said covenant, and the court shall refuse for any reason to enforce the covenants contained in Section 10a by injunction, such suit in equity shall

Sample continues next page

Sample: Employment Contract (continued)

not be a bar to a later suit, or to a separate or alternative claim in the same suit, to recover the liquidated damages herein agreed upon. It is also understood and agreed that the liquidated damages provided for in this Section 10c are to quantify the damages that would be suffered by the Practice as a result of the Physician's individual breach of Section 10a while not acting in aid of, in combination with, or in concert with other physicians, and not the damages the Practice would suffer if the Physician also breaches Section 10a by acting in aid of, in combination with, or in concert with other physicians. Therefore, it is understood that if the Physician breaches the covenants contained in Section 10a by not only acting individually but also acting in aid of, in combination with, or in concert with other physicians, the Practice shall be entitled to recover from the Physician, in addition to the liquidated damages provided for previously, such additional damages, if any, that the Practice suffers as a result of the Physician acting in violation of such covenants in aid of, in combination with, or in concert with other physicians.

d. In addition, and in order to protect the contractual rights of the Practice, the Physician agrees to honor and not to solicit any termination or nonrenewal of any agreement or contract held by the Practice, including but not limited to any agreement for the exclusive or largely exclusive provision of services by the Practice and between the Practice and any other hospital or medical facility with which the Practice has an agreement or contract at the time of the Physician's termination of employment; the governing body of any other medical facility at which the Practice is providing any services or treatments to patients; or any other third party such as a health insurance carrier. The restriction set out in the preceding sentence shall apply during the term of the Physician's employment, during the Noncompete Period, and also thereafter during the remainder of any unexpired specific term of any such agreement or contract which specific term was in effect as of the Termination Date. In addition, the Physician agrees not to solicit the termination of or otherwise interfere with the valid economic relationships between the Practice and third parties such as the third parties referred to previously in this subparagraph. For example, the Physician agrees that the Physician will not solicit the termination of or otherwise interfere with a relationship between the Practice and a site pursuant to which the Practice provides exclusively or largely exclusively the services to patients at that site, even if such relationship is not embodied in a written agreement that is in effect at the relevant time. In addition, the Physician agrees that the Physician will not solicit the termination of or otherwise interfere with the actual prospective economic advantages of the Practice, including but not limited to the continuation of customary medical practice arrangements and actual opportunities to enter into new arrangements for medical practice at new sites. The restriction set out in this Section 10d shall apply during the term of the Physician's employment and during the Noncompete Period. This restriction shall also continue after the Noncompete Period to the extent and for the duration permitted by law.

e. It is agreed that in the event of a breach by the Physician of the covenants contained in Section 10d hereof, the determination of actual damages will be very difficult and time consuming. The parties hereto stipulate and agree that a reasonable forecast of the probable loss to the Practice in the event of a breach of Section 10d of this Agreement by the Physician that results in [APPLICABLE DAMAGES UNDER STATE LAW], as liquidated damages and not as penalty. In the event of a breach by the Physician of the covenants contained in Section 10d with respect to an opportunity to enter into a new arrangement for medical practice

Sample continues next page

Sample: Employment Contract (continued)

at a new site that results in the loss of the Practice's opportunity to enter into such new arrangement, such liquidated damages shall be equal to __________ the gross revenue reasonably anticipated to be received by the Practice as a result of such new arrangement if the Practice had been successful in implementing such arrangement and such arrangement had continued for one (1) full calendar year for the Practice.

f. The Physician acknowledges that the covenants and agreements set forth in this Section 10 (the "Covenants") are offered as an inducement to the Practice to enter into this Agreement, without which this Agreement would not have been made, and that the Physician has received sufficient consideration for execution of this Agreement and the Covenants. The Physician acknowledges that such consideration includes the benefit of this Employment Agreement, which the Practice would not have been willing to enter into without the protection of the Covenants.

The Physician presents to the Practice that he or she has sufficient training and skills to be able to obtain similar employment in locations where the restrictions imposed by this covenant do not apply so that the enforcement of this covenant would not prevent the Physician from earning a satisfactory living and an income substantially comparable to that which the Physician will earn under this Agreement.

Furthermore, the Physician specifically agrees that there may be substantial similarities between the provisions of services by the Practice, and that the two medical groups are significantly interrelated and that the knowledge and skills required are largely transferable between the medical groups. The Physician therefore acknowledges and agrees that the Covenants not to compete with the Practice in the services provided are reasonable and protect the legitimate business interests of the Practice, even though the Physician may concentrate the Physician's medical group primarily or exclusively in the same services provided by the Practice.

g. The Physician further acknowledges that in addition to the Physician and in addition to others employed by the Practice, other individuals in and other individuals with immediate access to the geographical area and medical facilities described in this Section 10 possess skills and training equivalent to the skills and training of the Physician, and that the citizens or residents of the geographical area covered hereby would not be denied access to adequate skilled medical care should the Covenants be enforced against the Physician, and that enforcement of the Covenants will not create any substantial question of potential harm to the public health or create or tend to create a monopoly for services in the Practice.

h. The Physician further acknowledges that the Practice has over many years developed and nurtured the contractual and economic relationships protected by Section 10d hereof at great effort and expense to the Practice and its individual physicians. Such rights and relationships constitute extremely valuable property and rights of the Practice, and not of any individual employee, shareholder, or physician, and the loss of any such contracts, rights, or relationships by the Practice or the interference with any such contracts, rights, or relationships by the Physician would cause severe economic and professional damage to the Practice. During the term of his employment with the Practice, the Physician has and will continue to benefit from the contracts, rights, and relationships of the Practice and may develop personal or professional relationships in connection therewith that the Physician could use to the substantial economic and professional detriment of the Practice. The Physician therefore acknowledges that the provisions in Section 10 of this Agreement are reasonable and necessary to protect the Practice's legitimate business relationships and expectations and

Sample continues next page

Sample: Employment Contract (continued)

should be enforced against the Physician and against any other employee of the Practice who signs an employment agreement containing comparable provisions, to the full extent anticipated by the parties, as evidenced by this Agreement. The Physician further acknowledges that by reason of the contemporaneous amendment of all Employment Contracts, this Section 10 and all of the Covenants also provide substantial protection to the economic benefits that the Physician realizes as a shareholder of the Practice.

11. **Nondisclosure.** The Physician acknowledges and stipulates that during the term of this Agreement, the Physician will have access to Confidential Information (as defined in Section 11b) and that the use or disclosure of the Confidential Information by the Physician, except as expressly authorized by the Practice, may cause serious damage to the Practice and is prohibited. The Physician therefore agrees as follows:
    a. During the term of this Agreement and thereafter, the Physician shall not, except as required in connection with the performance of the Physician's duties hereunder, without the prior written consent of the Practice, directly or indirectly:
        (1) Divulge, furnish, copy, take, use, or make accessible to any individual or entity, in any manner, any of the Confidential Information of the Practice (as defined in Section 11b), either to gain an advantage over the Practice or to the Practice's disadvantage;
        (2) Take any action that might reasonably or foreseeably be expected to compromise the confidentiality or proprietary nature of any of the Confidential Information; or
        (3) Fail to follow the reasonable suggestions made by the Practice from time to time regarding the confidential and proprietary nature of the Confidential Information.
    b. "Confidential Information" shall mean all confidential and proprietary materials, information, and ideas of the Practice, including, without limitation, accounting and financial information, marketing and pricing information and materials, and other matters reasonably considered confidential by the Practice.
    c. All Confidential Information and copies or reproductions thereof shall be promptly returned to the Practice upon request.
12. **Remedies.** The parties to this Agreement recognize that irreparable damage will result to the Practice in the event of a breach of the terms of Sections 10 or 11 of this Agreement by the Physician. The Practice and the Physician therefore agree that in the event of a breach or threatened breach by the Physician of any of the provisions of Section 10 or Section 11 of this Agreement, the Practice shall be entitled, in addition to any other remedies and damages available by law or under this Agreement, to an injunction to restrain and enjoin the Physician from violating the covenants contained in such sections. In the event of litigation between the Practice and the Physician arising out of or in connection with this Agreement, the prevailing party shall be entitled to recover its reasonable attorneys' fees and expenses from the other party.
13. **Miscellaneous.**
    a. Except as may be modified or supplemented by any exhibits or addenda attached hereto, or executed contemporaneously herewith and intended to become a part hereof, this Agreement sets forth the entire understanding between the parties, and all prior or contemporaneous written or oral agreements with respect to the subject matter hereof are merged herein. Specifically, the Physician has no expectations as an employee of the Practice other than as reflected in such written agreement. This Agreement cannot be amended except by a writing signed by both parties. No waiver of any term or provision shall be deemed to be a waiver of any subsequent breach of any term or provision hereof.

Sample continues next page

Sample: Employment Contract (continued)

b. This Agreement shall be governed by and construed in accordance with the laws of the State of [STATE].

c. This Agreement shall be binding upon and inure to the benefit of the parties hereto, their respective representatives, successors, and assigns, provided, however, that this is an agreement for the personal services of the Physician, and these services may only be provided by the Physician.

d. Upon written demand of either party, any controversy or claim arising out of, in connection with, or related to this Agreement or the breach thereof, including any breach or alleged breach by the Physician of the terms of Sections 10 or 11 of this Agreement, shall be settled by arbitration in the City of [CITY], State of [STATE], administered by the American Arbitration Association under its Employment Dispute Resolution Rules, as modified by this Agreement. Judgment on the award rendered by the arbitrator shall be final, and judgment may be entered thereon in any court having jurisdiction thereof. The State Uniform Arbitration Act, as contained in Chapter __________, Article __________ of the General Statutes, shall apply to this agreement to arbitrate.

No demand for arbitration by either party shall deprive the General Courts of Justice of the State of [STATE] of jurisdiction to grant and to enforce temporary restraining orders or preliminary injunctive relief to enjoin breaches or threatened breaches by the Physician of Section 10 or Section 11 of this Agreement. In the event of such breach or threatened breach by the Physician, the Practice shall be entitled to obtain a temporary restraining order and preliminary injunction from the General Courts of Justice, and no demand for arbitration by the Physician shall be effective until after such court has entered a preliminary injunction or otherwise ruled on the Practice's motion for preliminary injunctive relief. Thereafter, either party may demand arbitration in accordance with this Section 13d, and in that event, any injunction entered by the court shall remain in full force and effect pending a final determination on the merits by the arbitrator.

The Practice may, at its sole option and discretion, waive the jurisdiction of the General Courts of Justice and immediately submit any such controversy to arbitration. The Physician agrees that, and in that event, the arbitrator is authorized to award temporary injunctive relief for a period of no more than (thirty) 30 days to enjoin violations of Sections 10 or 11 of this Agreement. The Physician shall then have ten (10) days after notice of such temporary relief to file an answering statement to the Practice's claims, and prior to the expiration of any temporary relief, hearing shall be held on the Practice's request for preliminary injunctive relief, and the arbitrator shall either vacate the temporary relief or continue such relief until final determination on the merits. Judgment on any such temporary or preliminary award or relief may be immediately entered by any court having jurisdiction thereof.

e. Each part, article, section, paragraph, subparagraph, sentence, phrase, clause, term, provision, and condition of this Agreement (all referred to herein as the "provisions" of this Agreement) is independent and severable. The unenforceability of any one or more of the provisions of this Agreement shall not alter the enforceability of any other provision of this Agreement. Wherever possible, all provisions shall be interpreted so as not to be unenforceable, and any court of competent jurisdiction is authorized and directed by the parties to enforce any otherwise unenforceable provision in part, to modify it, to partially enforce it, or otherwise to enforce that provision only in a manner and to an extent that renders the provision valid or enforceable. The intent of the parties is

Sample continues next page

Sample: Employment Contract (continued)

that this Agreement be enforceable and enforced to the maximum extent possible after excising (or deeming excised) all invalid or unenforceable provisions, whether or not the remaining provisions are grammatically correct. For example, if it is determined that any part of Section 10 is unenforceable because it would otherwise impose too broad a restriction upon the Physician, the remainder of Section 10 shall be enforceable.

f. The Physician agrees that the Practice may assign this Agreement to any professional entity (such as a professional corporation) into which or with which the Practice is merged, consolidated, or otherwise combined. The Practice may also assign this Agreement to any entity to which the Practice transfers and conveys all or substantially all of the Practice's assets. If any such assignment occurs, the assignee shall be substituted for the Practice in all respects under this Agreement and shall receive all benefits of and assume all obligations of the Practice under this Agreement. If such an assignment occurs, the assignee shall be entitled to enforce all provisions of this Agreement, including but not limited to Sections 10 and 11, but the scope of the restrictions upon the Physician shall not be broadened by the assignment.

g. The provisions of this Agreement shall survive the Physician's termination of employment with the Practice to the extent reasonably necessary to provide the intended benefit. For example, the provisions of Sections 10 and 11 and the last sentence of Section 2 shall survive such termination.

h. All examples and illustrations given in this Agreement are nonexclusive and shall not be interpreted as limiting the scope or application of this Agreement.

IN WITNESS WHEREOF, the parties have executed this Agreement effective the day and year written at the beginning of this Agreement.

PRACTICE

By: ____________________ (PRESIDENT)

Date: ____________________

PHYSICIAN

____________________ [PHYSICIAN NAME], MD

SCHEDULE I

Hospitals and medical facilities at which the Practice provides services on an exclusive or largely exclusive basis:

1. ____________________ Medical Center in [CITY], [STATE]
2. ____________________ Hospital in [CITY], [STATE]
3. ____________________ Surgical Center in [CITY], [STATE]

Issue date: ____________________

Sample: Letter of Resignation of Medical Staff Privileges

SCHEDULE II

__________________ (Date)

__________________ , Chief Executive Officer
[HOSPITAL OR MEDICAL FACILITY]
[STREET ADDRESS]
[CITY], [STATE] [ZIP]

Re: Letter of Resignation of Medical Staff Privileges

Dear Sir or Madam:

This correspondence will serve as notification of my resignation of any and all medical staff privileges that have been granted to me as a member of the medical staff of [FACILITY/HOSPITAL NAME].

The [MONTH], [DAY], [YEAR], effective date corresponds with the termination of my employment with _________.

Sincerely,

__________________ [Signature]

__________________ Medical Group

Policy 1.4 Part-Time Physician Policy

The Practice must have adequate physician staffing to meet the needs of its patients at all locations and all hours of service. To supplement its full-time physicians, it will occasionally authorize the medical director to employ part-time physicians.

Such physician staffing must concur with personnel policies related to part-time employment, including matters related to compensation, benefits, Practice insurance, and performance expectations. Such staffing also must correlate with noncompetition requirements for physicians.

Such physicians will not be eligible for shareholder/member/colleague status.

Such physicians may have another professional practice or other activities as reviewed/approved by the medical director.

Such physicians will sign a contract specifying the details of the relationship.

See Appendix for Employment Contract for Part-Time or Partially Retired Physicians.

Procedure

1. The medical director and the department chair/division chief will identify the need for part-time physician assistance and develop a position description/plan of service, including location, hours, and type of specialty/skill needed. Compensation, in line with the annual budget, will be determined. This recommendation will be submitted for executive committee review and board approval.
2. The administrator or human resources manager will assist the medical director in recruiting candidates for the position.
3. The medical director and, if applicable, the department chair/division chief will interview the candidates and select a finalist. All appropriate information, such as position description, compensation, performance expectations, noncompete restrictions, etc., will be shared with the candidates to ensure full knowledge of expectations.
4. The human resources specialist will check credentials and references. If satisfactory, the Practice will make an offer to the physician.
5. Upon acceptance of the offer, the human resources specialist will complete any necessary paperwork, and the medical director will arrange for appropriate orientation.

Responsibility

The medical director, administrator, and human resources manager shall take necessary actions to ensure compliance with this policy.

Policy 1.5

Locum Tenens Policy

The Practice has the authority to approve the use of locum tenens physicians under the following guidelines:

1. Prolonged physician illness;
2. Single-physician departments requiring coverage during time off;
3. Departments that are short staffed, have been unable to meet the needs of patient services, and are in the process of recruiting; and
4. Coverage for a department or facility so that the physicians may be able to attend a specific Practice-approved function or event.

Policy 1.6

Retention Programs Policy

Human resources remain our most important asset in the workplace. Improving all physicians' performance is essential to the profitability and growth of the Practice. While customer service and information technology drive most organizations today, no advances can be made without very competent and motivated physicians.

Training and development opportunities contribute to physician growth and benefit the physician and organization. With the current trends to reduce expenses, more emphasis is being placed on training and retaining top talent.

Types of Development Programs

Training encompasses the entire range of planned, programmed, or coordinated learning experiences that are used to help physicians acquire new knowledge, skills, or abilities. Continuing education relates directly to physicians' current and future performance. Development programs are designed to enlarge a physician's capacity to successfully take on more responsibilities or to better manage current ones.

Retention and Motivation

The ability to retain and motivate the most talented physicians is directly related to the Practice's success. The cost of recruiting and training new physicians is easily double that of a departing physician's salary. Because of the shortages of qualified applicants in many healthcare fields, retaining top talent is crucial to the group's success. The Practice should establish a culture that promotes physician involvement and encourages top talent to stay with the Practice. The goal should be to become an "employer of choice" in the community.

Elements of retaining and motivating top talent:

1. **Physician Engagement**

   Organizations with engaged physicians are successful, productive, and cost-effective.

   a. The Practice will provide its physicians with everything and anything, within reason, that physicians need to perform their jobs successfully.

   b. Physicians will have all the materials they need readily accessible to be as productive as possible. The Practice supervisors will ensure that new physician hires have the necessary resources to start working in their new positions immediately and to continue their work throughout the year.

   c. The Practice will clearly communicate to all employees what is expected of them, the Practice's vision, the Practice's values, and how the Practice measures success.

   d. The Practice will make an effort to get to know each physician's personality and behavioral traits and provide physician-specific rewards to encourage productivity, engagement, motivation, and retention.

2. **CME Programs**

   a. The Practice will provide physicians with continuing medical education (CME) program opportunities, so they might advance their careers and perform at their highest potential.

b. CME programs will be offered within the constraint of the Practice's needs for higher-level skills and the availability of resources to support those efforts.

3. **Competitive Rewards and Incentives**

   The goal of incentive and reward programs is to positively reinforce the desired on-the-job behavior, improve physician morale, and contribute to physician retention. Examples of rewards and incentives that the Practice will entertain include:

   - Allowing top performers to work flexible hours;
   - Providing physicians with more prestigious titles, when appropriate;
   - Posting special achievement and thank-you letters;
   - Creating a "wall of fame" featuring top physicians' photos;
   - Recognizing contributions by assigning a special parking spot;
   - Sending news releases to the local media detailing physicians' accomplishments and awards; and
   - Featuring top performers in the Practice's printed marketing materials.

Policy 1.7

Orientation Policy

The Practice will provide new physicians with a "New Physician Checklist" (see pages 31–34) to ensure that all topics are covered. This checklist can be used as a tool for training supervisors on their roles and for ensuring that new physicians are properly instructed about their essential functions. All orientation procedures should give new physicians a warm and friendly welcome and encourage them to think positively about the Practice and their employment experience.

Orientation Checklist

New physicians, established physicians new to the Practice, and even those colleagues traveling to new Practice locations need to be oriented to the Practice, the medical community, and/or the specific location, as the case may be. The Practice administrator and/or department chair/division chief should review the following, as applicable, with any new physician:

☐ Contract provisions, especially the Compliance Plan

☐ Group's structure

☐ Performance evaluation

☐ Protocols

☐ Communication

☐ Basic performance expectations

☐ Visit (or minimally, call) the Practice location and meet with the executive committee representative before arriving.

☐ Accounts receivable management

- Charge capture
- Coding

- ☐ Practice operations
  - Case/room assignments
  - Supplies
  - Narcotics
  - Peripheral sites, if any
  - Parking
  - Food service
- ☐ Customer service rules
  - Introductions should be done by supervising colleague, but this is not always possible, so take responsibility.
  - Introduction to key personnel
  - Physician as "representative of the Practice": on time (or early!); no venting in public; best behavior; be proactive, positive, and professional. Anything you do reflects on everyone else.
- ☐ Additional notes
  - It is *always okay* to call a colleague if a question comes up, even in the middle of the night. Oversight and introductions for the first week at a minimum (obviously longer where proctoring or other requirements are present).

Supervisor Checklist for Orientation

- ☐ Introductions to:
  - Department;
  - Other employees; and
  - Facilities, such as coatroom, lavatory, lunchroom, etc.
- ☐ General instructions on:
  - Break times and lunch periods;
  - Reporting times and absences;
  - Performance management system;
  - Parking facilities;
  - Provisionary status; and
  - Policy on personal telephone calls, faxes, e-mails, and Internet use.
- ☐ Position instruction about:
  - The importance of the employee's position in providing effective patient care;
  - Essential functions;
  - Performance standards;
  - Position procedures; and
  - Planning, monitoring, and measuring position performance.
- ☐ Safety and health instructions on:
  - Position health and safety precautions;
  - Use of equipment or protective devices;
  - Fire protection procedures, including the proper usage of alarm boxes, fire extinguishers, etc.;
  - Smoking regulations; and
  - Emergency evacuation routes.

Sample: New Physician Checklist 1

- ☐ Recruitment packet with maps and Practice information
- ☐ [STATE] medical license information, including electronic fingerprinting
- ☐ Colleagueship agreement
- ☐ Contract __________(DATE SENT) __________(DATE RETURNED)
- ☐ Medical license(s)
- ☐ Drug Enforcement Administration (DEA) number
- ☐ National Provider Identifier: number, user ID, password
- ☐ Board certificate or letter
- ☐ Driver's license
- ☐ Social Security card
- ☐ Continuing education units (unless resident)
- ☐ Procedure logs with complication rates for 12 of the previous 24 months of practice
- ☐ Electronic health record (EHR), practice management system (PMS), telephone/voice mail, e-mail access, patient portal, etc. training
- ☐ Tuberculosis testing
- ☐ Photos (at least four passport-type photos)
- ☐ Other special legal paperwork (military discharge, other)
- ☐ Claims history report from previous carriers
- ☐ Current insurance certificate
- ☐ Nametag/ID ____________ (DATE ORDERED) ____________ (DATE PICKED UP)
- ☐ The following items entered into the administrative system:
  - Medical license
  - DEA number
  - Birthdate
  - Performance evaluation
  - Ownership status
  - Anniversary dates (at least one year)
- ☐ Welcome basket
- ☐ Compliance binder and other handouts
- ☐ Business cards __________(DATE REQUESTED) ____________(DATE COMPLETED)
- ☐ Corporation name and number
- ☐ Website username, password, and e-mail address
- ☐ Patient portal instructions and password
- ☐ Corporation info ________(DATE DISCUSSED) ____________(DATE OBTAINED)
- ☐ Staff bylaws for facility, as applicable
- ☐ E-mail [INSERT APPROPRIATE STAFF CONTACT] with contact information, including address and Social Security number
- ☐ Insurance/benefits information packet with memo

Sample: New Physician Checklist 2

DESCRIPTION	COMMENTS	DATE COMPLETED
AGREEMENTS		
Employment agreement		
Hospital contract		
Health insurance application		
LICENSES		
State board of medicine		
State board of pharmacy		
Drug Enforcement Agency		
Hospital privileges		
State medical society		
INSURANCE CONTRACTS		
Medicare		
Medicaid		
Cigna		
United Healthcare		
Blue Cross		
MISCELLANEOUS		
Update provider table in practice management system		
Photograph		
Cellular phone service		
SUPPLIES/EQUIPMENT		
Appointment cards		
Prescription cards		
Controlled substance cards		
Update letterhead		
Order start-up supplies		
Order furniture		
Order equipment		
Order tables		
Order charts, dividers, and medication forms		
Petty cash money		

Sample continues next page

Sample: New Physician Checklist 2 (continued)

DESCRIPTION	COMMENTS	DATE COMPLETED
DÉCOR		
Signage • Door sign • Lobby and building directory		
Pictures		
Patient magazines		
ADVERTISING		
Arrange talks with local community groups		
Newspaper advertising		
Patient target mailing list		
New physician mailing letter to referral physicians		
Hospital advertisement		
Press release		
Plan office open house		
Yellow Pages listings • Yellowbook • Dex		
White Pages listings		
Update Web page and other social media sites		
IT		
Order computers for office staff		
Set up computer accounts		
Set up computers		
Set up printer ports		
Order fax machine		
Order printer		
Order copier		
Obtain transcription services		
Inpatient hospital monitoring system		
Phones for office • New extension • Send new extension list • Add name to display		
Program phones		

Sample continues next page

Sample: New Physician Checklist 2 (continued)

DESCRIPTION	COMMENTS	DATE COMPLETED
PERSONNEL		
Determine number and type of FTEs to work for new physician (PA, RN, MA, etc.)		
Establish job description and wages		
Post job openings on job Websites • Interview • Check references and licensure • Hire		
ORIENTATION		
Orientation schedule/plan given		
New employee forms (W-4, I-9, physician information)		
Benefit plan orientation • Forms completed		
Payroll schedule discussed		
Building keys or electronic key cards • Form completed • Keys and/or key card given		
Policy and procedure agreement signed		
Physician form given • Time-off request form • Cafeteria plan • Conference form		
HIPAA training		
HIPAA procedure book		
Physician confidentiality agreement signed		
Site/facility tour and introduction to coworkers		

Sample: Employment Checklist for New Physician

Physician: __________, MD
Expected Employment Date: __________

	Requirement	Comments	Date Completed
1	Signed contract		
2	Residence address/local address		
3	Curriculum vitae		
4	Bio		
5	Orientation arranged		
6	Assign mentor		
7	Personnel file		
8	W-4 (income tax)		
9	W-9 (insurance purposes)		
10	I-9 (personal information)		
11	Meet administration		
12	Add to the Practice mailing list		
13	Documentation from current malpractice carrier		
14	Enroll in excess insurance		
15	Explanation of malpractice group suits		
16	Add to paycheck system		
17	Enroll in employee health insurance plan		
18	Enroll in pension program		
19	DEA certificate		
20	Practice admission privileges		
21	Inform the Practice's physician referral services		
22	Documentation of annual physical		
23	Copies of diplomas		
24	Internship		
25	Residency		
26	Fellowship (if applicable)		
27	State license		
28	Board certificate		
29	CME credits		
30	Order business cards		
31	Add to practice management system and electronic health record		
32	Enter medical codes and group		

Sample continues next page

Sample: Employment Checklist for New Physician (continued)

	Requirement	Comments	Date Completed
33	Network services		
34	Set up e-mail address		
35	MD's insurance table		
36	Add to participating list		
37	IDX • Appointment template • Remote access • Outside e-mail address		
38	Paperless training		
39	Review billing reconciliation		
40	Notify cell phone carrier		
41	Phone carrier/directory assistance		
42	Telephone system		
43	Assign long distance calling code		
44	E-mail to staff • Introduction • Front desk and secretaries, in case of patient calls		
45	Define paper mail routing		
46	Desk space		
47	Assign consult/exam rooms		
48	Assign MA		
49	Appointment protocol		
50	Training on public folders		
51	Add to letterhead		
52	Specialist supplies		
53	Signage • Internal • External		
54	Beeper/cell phone texting		
55	Answering service		
56	Keys and security		
57	Provide NPI # or enroll online		
58	OSHA training		
59	Welcome reception		
60	Add bio and photo to Website and social media sites		

Sample continues next page

Sample: Employment Checklist for New Physician (continued)

Local Address	Phone Numbers
Home Phone:	Public Phone:
Home Fax:	Public Fax:
Cell Phone:	Private Phone:
Pager:	Private Fax:
	DOB:
	State License #:
	DEA#:
	SS#:
	TAX ID:
Awaiting Medicare number from doctor (application sent)	
Notes:	

Policy 1.8

Credentialing Policy

Credentialing the Practice's healthcare providers ensures up-to-date privileges and acceptance with hospitals and payers. The Practice employs a credentialing specialist to follow specific guidelines outlined by hospitals and payers.

Position Description: Credentialing Specialist

The credentialing specialist provides general support to the daily operations of the Practice through the credentialing of healthcare providers for hospital appointment as well as insurance companies. The credentialing specialist works for the Practice's administration, the physicians, and the executive director.

Reports to

Practice manager

Position Requirements

High school education with one (1) to two (2) years of office experience. Knowledge of telephone messages, typing, filing, communication, and organizational skills.

Duties

- Completes/maintains physician hospital credentials and re-appointments. Does the same for nurse practitioners.
- Completes/maintains physician insurance company credentials and re-credentialing. Does the same for nurse practitioners. Includes periodic review of insurance company provider directories for accuracy.
- Maintains physician CVs and physician CME hours.
- Reviews all physician licenses, DEA certification, and Bureau of Narcotics and Dangerous Drugs (BNDD) registration. Coordinates renewals of these, as well.
- Completes physicians' professional liability insurance applications. Does the same for nurse practitioners.
- Provides secretarial support, including typing, composing, and proofreading correspondence as well as indexing and filing documents. Develops and implements office documents/forms used in daily activities.
- Maintains strictest confidentiality.
- Assists in training other associates.
- Performs related work as required.

Tools

Microsoft® (MS) Office (MS Word, MS Excel, MS Access, MS Outlook), Med-Multi App, CAQH, Internet, telephone system/paging system, e-mail client.

Policy 1.9

Provider ID Policy

National Provider Identifier (NPI) and National Provider System (NPS)

In order to simplify claims transactions, the Health Insurance Portability and Accountability Act of 1996 (HIPAA) calls for the development of an identifying number to be given to all providers. (In addition, the legislation calls for all health plans, employers, and, eventually, all individuals to receive unique numbers.) As well as developing the NPI, the Health Care Financing Administration (HCFA) was mandated to create the NPS, a database of provider information that payers and others with a legitimate business use for the information could access.

HCFA published the notice of proposed rulemaking (NPRM) for the NPI in the *Federal Register* on May 7, 1998. According to the proposed regulation, every healthcare provider is issued an identifying number and is required to have enumerated data entered into the NPS. The following are the major regulatory provisions:

- NPI expected to be a 10-digit numeric identifier (last digit a check digit) with no embedded intelligence;

- Providers are to be enumerated in stages, with those currently billing Medicare and Medicaid to be first to receive their NPIs;
- Data for NPS will include demographic as well as business information; and
- Access to the NPS will be on two levels. On the first level, enumerators would have access to all the data in the NPS. The public, which includes providers, health plans, clearinghouses, and software vendors, would comprise the second level and have access to selected data.

National Employer Identifier (NEI)

Health and Human Services (HHS) published the NPRM for the NEI on June 16, 1998. Every employer is issued an identifying number for the purposes of conducting electronic health transactions. The following are the major provisions:

- The NEI is to be the current Employer Identification Number (EIN), which is issued and maintained by the Internal Revenue Service;
- Employers are not required to use the NEI, though HCFA believes employers will want to take advantage of this standardization; and
- HHS estimates the savings, taking in to account start-up costs, to total $1.5 billion over the first five (5) years of implementation.

The NEI final rule was released in the fourth quarter of 2000.

National Payer Identifier (PAYERID)

- The PAYERID will have nine digits, including a check digit. For those entities requiring many different numbers, they will be issued in the form of a six-digit base number, two-digit suffix, and a check digit.
- HCFA will create a PAYERID database, populated initially from HCFA files of Medicare contractors, Medigap insurers, and Medicaid state agencies. The rest of the database will be comprised of health insurance companies, health maintenance organizations, and self-administered plans obtained from payer associations.
- The PAYERID database will be a relational structure with multiple occurrences for address sets and other data.
- A PAYERID registrar will manage the issuance of numbers.

This PAYERID will impact group practices as electronic billing systems must be upgraded to accept this new identifier.

National Individual Identifier (NII)

Although only in its formative stage, the NII is already the most contentious of all the administrative simplification provisions. HCFA had plans to release a notice of intent (NOI) outlining various options for the NII. In an effort to begin this process of soliciting public input, HHS released a white paper on July 7, 1998, outlining issues and options for the development of the NII. It was expected that the NOI would draw heavily from this white paper. The paper outlined seven potential identifier candidates:

1. The present individual Social Security Number (SSN) or a number based on the SSN;

2. An American Society for Testing and Materials sample "universal healthcare identifier" of up to 29 characters;
3. A biometric identifier such a retinal pattern analysis, DNA analysis, or fingerprints;
4. An identifier created from personal immutable properties that cannot change, like a mother's maiden name or birthdate; and
5. A randomly generated number from a civil registration system.

The other two options for individual identifiers will not require a unique universal identifier. One would utilize existing medical record numbers with a practitioner prefix, and the other would draw from a master patient index similar to those used by large healthcare organizations to track medical records.

CHAPTER 2

Benefits

Policy 2.1	Benefits and Eligibility
Policy 2.2	Time Off (Illness, Injury, Vacation, Professional Development)
Policy 2.3	Leave without Pay
Policy 2.4	Holiday and Paid Time Off
Policy 2.5	Insurance
Policy 2.6	Disability
Policy 2.7	Professional Liability Insurance
Policy 2.8	Interruption of Service
Policy 2.9	Bereavement Leave
Policy 2.10	Military Leave
Policy 2.11	Phones and Pagers
Policy 2.12	Cars and Mileage Reimbursement
Policy 2.13	Retirement and Semi-Retirement
Policy 2.14	Retirement Planning
Policy 2.15	Succession Planning
Policy 2.16	Professional Development/Education

Benefits Philosophy

Employee benefits used to be called fringe benefits. They were on the edges, out of view, less visible than compensation. Benefit structures have become an integral part of employment packages, often adding 25 percent to 50 percent to the value of annual compensation for middle-income earners. They include required payroll taxes as well as a growing range of insurances, provisions for time off, and support services designed to engender security and loyalty.

Physician benefit structures have the same core purposes, but as demand for physicians increases, benefits can become a distinguishing feature between competing offers. There are core expectations about what is to be included, but a boundless range of creative possibilities for how they are offered and administered. Both the content and the administration of physician benefit structures can impact the quality of life within the organization. They can become tools for shaping organizational culture.

Basic Considerations

Physician benefits policies, like compensation policies, may be included in employment contracts or they may be integrated into corporate employee policy manuals. Larger medical groups may have a formal employee policy manual just for physicians, offering benefits that may be different from those offered to support staff. Retirement plans may have their own separate manuals detailing how physicians can save for retirement through a combination of pre-tax contributions matched by employer contributions. The manuals may also outline how funds can be invested, the vesting schedule, and how they can be withdrawn upon resignation or retirement.

Organizations may offer different benefits for specific types of employees. Physicians and executives may have access to certain benefits that may not be available to support staff, recognizing the need to attract and retain specialized talent in a competitive marketplace. Physicians and executives may have car allowances, for example, to enable them to work in multiple worksites with ease. They may also have different time-off policies to allow for continuing education and to balance the responsibilities of intense workloads and call coverage. Classifications should be developed with careful legal advice to avoid running afoul of federal or state restrictions. Administrators need to be aware of the classification differences and two specific implications they may have for organizational culture. First, the privileges can have the effect of widening the social gap and threatening trust between the "haves" and the "have-nots." Second, administrators must implement the benefit plans consistently within each classification or risk internal jealousies and conflicts.

Some benefits, such as retirement plans, are subject to federal restrictions about how much difference can exist between high earners and their support staff. The details change as laws change, so policy writers should obtain current legal advice when structuring benefits policies. The social policy behind these restrictions is that employees deserve equal protection from social disasters brought about by illness and external economic crisis, and that benefits for those in power — executives and high-earning physicians — should be shared with their employees as well. The laws reflect a deep American value expressed in the Preamble to our Constitution to "promote the common welfare."

Physician-owned groups may also design benefits policies with tax considerations in mind. Tax advisers may demonstrate cost-effective approaches to providing benefits pre-tax rather than post-tax. Tax-wise strategies might apply to the use of cars, cell phones, disability insurance, and healthcare expenses not covered by insurance. Complex tax laws are constantly changing, so it is important for administrators to seek advice from certifed public accountants and tax lawyers to keep up with the changes.

Purpose

Benefits policies have a few basic purposes. They are designed to offer support, comfort, and security to employees, enabling them to be free to concentrate on their work and careers without worrying about basic social needs.

Benefits policies have become part of the social fabric of the American employment scene. The labor movement that began more than 100 years ago had its roots in the exploitation of workers. As workers united to demand better working conditions, employers gradually developed new philosophies that included protections for workers both on the job and at home. Social Security benefits emerged during the Roosevelt administration to protect the most vulnerable elderly and infirm segments of society. Social Security was to be paid for by a combination of employer and employee contributions, setting the stage for introducing more complex social benefits throughout the rest of the century. After World War II, employers introduced health insurance benefits as a way to attract able-bodied workers from a smaller employment pool. Insurance and other benefits were treated as tax-deductible costs of doing business while simultaneously attracting discerning employees with services that provided security and comfort for their growing families. Benefits policies became win-win propositions for both employers and employees.

While employers' costs for benefits have increased, employees have come to expect them — even to take them for granted. Benefits are now an integral part of employment offers along with competitive salaries and desirable working conditions. In the highly competitive world of physician services, benefits have become creative bargaining chips in the hands of recruiting executives. American physicians now face a constant stream of offerings that include not only handsome salaries but also benefits ranging from signing bonuses to medical school debt retirement in exchange for a multiyear commitment to stay in the community. Benefits that distinguished employers a few decades ago are now considered traditional expectations. Cutting-edge employers are constantly searching for new distinctions to attract and retain talented physicians.

Benefits play another role in building loyalty, especially for those who commit their full-time efforts to the organization over a long period of time. Most organizations reserve their full range of benefit options for full-time employees only. Part-time employees may have access to some benefits, or they may have the option of purchasing benefits, but they are frequently not treated the same as full-time employees. Likewise, retirement plans often have vesting schedules, allowing employees to retain a greater portion of employer-paid contributions with each year of employment. Loyalty has its rewards.

Components

Competition for physicians is fueling dynamic changes in the field of benefits policies. Nonetheless, the following components should be foundational for every physician organization:

- **Insurances.** Health insurance has become a first-line expectation in physician employment. Most organizations provide insurance for both physicians and their families to protect them from the economic risks of illness. Other insurance policies may include life insurance, disability insurance, and dental and vision insurance. Professional liability insurance is a virtual requirement for practicing physicians. Some employers treat professional liability insurance as an employee benefit for physicians, while others treat it as a separate line item of overhead cost.
- **Time Off.** The rigors of being a physician are legendary. Medical school and residency training require long hours, sometimes marked by intense concentration and stress. Physicians need time off to recuperate and refresh, not only for their own sakes, but also for the sake of patient safety. Benefits policies need to address consistent rules for vacations, continuing education, sick time, holidays, and other special leaves of absence.
- **Credentials.** Physicians face legal requirements unique to the profession and distinct from other employees. In addition to maintaining a medical license in the state in which they practice, most physicians also need to maintain a controlled substance license and board certification in their specialty. Beyond the basics, many physicians also find benefit by staying active in a variety of professional associations for continuing education offerings and collegiality with their peers.

Conclusion

Physician benefit policies fortify professional loyalty and commitment by providing a measure of security, support, and comfort to physicians and their families. A solid benefit structure frees physicians to do what they do best in caring for their patients without nagging concerns about the economic risks of illness, time off, and sustaining professional credentials. Sound benefits need to be part of the package that enables physicians to perform at their highest levels.

Policy 2.1

Benefits and Eligibility Policy

The policy of the Practice is to provide full-time physicians with adequate economic and personal security benefits as part of their employment. Benefits have been designed to meet this goal in a fair and equitable manner consistent with the Practice's objectives. The Practice protects the interests of benefits plan participants and beneficiaries by making full disclosure to physicians and administration of the physician benefits program.

The director of human resources (HR), in conjunction with senior management, is responsible for managing the benefits program as well as reviewing the current program and making recommendations to the governing body for approval of changes. Physician preferences are surveyed at least annually to ensure that current interests are considered. Proposed changes will be presented to the medical staff prior to any decisions to change the current program.

Procedure

1. HR is responsible for providing physicians with a summary description of benefits, including eligibility for participation.
2. In the event that a benefit is added or withdrawn, physicians are notified well in advance of any proposed change.
3. When allowed by the law, physicians may elect not to participate.
4. The plan description provides details regarding when a change is allowed and the process to effect such change.
5. Complete copies of the plan description are available upon request.

Sample: Summary of Physician Benefits

Benefit	When Eligible	You Receive
Time off (vacation, professional development, illness/ injury)	Upon employment	A maximum of twenty-five (25) business days, accruing at the rate of 2.08 days per month. The accrual and maximum accrual increases to thirty (30) days, accruing at the rate of 2.5 days per month beginning the 37th month of employment, and the maximum accrual increases to a total of thirty-six (36) days, accruing at the rate of three (3) days per month, beginning the 61st month of employment.

Sample continues next page

Sample: Summary of Physician Benefits (continued)

Benefit	When Eligible	You Receive
Holidays	Upon employment	The Practice recognizes and will be closed on the following holidays: • New Year's Day; • Memorial Day; • Independence Day; • Labor Day; • Thanksgiving Day; • The Friday after Thanksgiving; • The afternoon of Christmas Eve; and • Christmas Day.
Professional liability insurance	Upon employment	The Practice will pay the premium.
Long-term disability insurance (specialty specific)	Upon employment	The Practice pays the premium. Coverage begins on the 91st day of disability.
Health insurance	Upon employment	Family coverage — the Practice pays [X] percent of the premium.
Dental insurance	Upon employment	The Practice pays the premium for the physician.
Life insurance and accidental death and dismemberment insurance	1st of month following ninety (90) days of employment	The Practice pays 100 percent of the premium on the physician's life. Benefit is equal to two (2) times annual compensation (W-2) to a maximum of $500,000.
Supplemental life insurance	1st of the month following eligibility	Physician pays the premium for any desired additional coverage.
Retirement plan	Physician is eligible to participate on the first of January or July, following twelve (12) continuous months of employment.	Plan provides for contribution (payroll deduction) by the physician and a matching amount from the Practice.
Deferred compensation plan	Upon employment	Annual election — post-income tax contribution to a nonqualified deferred compensation plan.
Bereavement	Upon employment	Up to five (5) days for the death of an immediate family member.
Jury duty pay	Upon employment	The difference between jury duty pay and the physician's base pay for scheduled hours not worked.
Flex benefit plan Section 125	1st of the month following thirty (30) days of employment	Annual election for the payment of noninsurance-covered medical expenses, dependent-care expenses, and other allowable expenses.

Professional Development

The Practice shall pay on behalf of the physician, or reimburse upon submission of original receipts, costs associated with professional development (educational program expenses, registration, travel, lodging, meals), professional memberships, and professional subscriptions a maximum of $6,000 per calendar year, accruing at the rate of $500 per month. Should there be any unused funds in the physician's account at the end of the calendar year, 50 percent of such unused balance may be carried forward to the next calendar year.

Complete plan descriptions for the benefits programs of the Practice (insurance, retirement, Section 125) are available from HR. The Practice shall pay the physician's annual dues to the county and state medical societies, as well as annual membership dues to a maximum of two (2) hospitals.

Unless provided for elsewhere, at termination of employment, there shall be no payout for accrued but unused time off or professional development balances. The Practice contracts with [CELLULAR SERVICE PROVIDER] for service and provides monthly service as a benefit. The practice shall purchase/lease a cellular phone for the physician.

Policy 2.2 Time Off Policy (Illness, Injury, Vacation, Professional Development)[1]

Policy considerations include:

- Who recommends the policy?
  - HR or practice executive
- Who approves the policy?
  - Governing body
- Who establishes the written policies and procedures?
  - HR
- Who communicates the policies and procedures to physicians (written and verbal)?
  - HR or practice executive
- Who manages the policy?
  - HR

Requesting Time Off

Physicians should complete a leave request form (see page 49) at least sixty (60) days in advance of the requested dates to allow adequate time for blocking schedules, reassigning call duties (when applicable), and rescheduling appointments. Because illness/injury cannot usually be predicted, any absence because of illness/injury should be reported immediately to allow as much time as possible for patient rescheduling, as well as adjustments to the call schedule. Holidays do not require a request form.

1 Printed in *HR Policies and Procedures Manual for Medical Practices, 4th Edition*, by Courtney Price, PhD, and Alys Novak, MBA (Englewood, CO: Medical Group Management Association, 2007).

Personal Leave of Absence

The Practice may in its sole discretion grant physicians unpaid personal leaves of absence. Such requests must be submitted at least ninety (90) days in advance of the requested date(s).

Procedure

1. Unpaid personal leaves of absence may be granted to full- and regular part-time physicians who have completed at least twelve (12) continuous months of employment.
2. Management makes every effort to grant a leave of absence request when it is properly justified and in the best interests of the physician and the medical practice.
3. A formal leave request form must be completed by the physician, which includes an explanation for the requested leave of absence (see page 49). The leave request form is submitted to the medical director and/or the Practice administrator.
4. The medical director (or Practice administrator), in consultation with the other physicians in the specialty/service/division/department, will determine the ability of the Practice to grant the request. The Practice administrator makes the final decision concerning the request.
5. Requests for a leave of absence are granted for family and medical leaves governed by the Family and Medical Leave Act (FMLA) and for active and reserve military duty.
6. Extensions of a personal leave of absence for more than thirty (30) days are granted only in extenuating circumstances.
7. Request for the extension of an approved personal leave must be submitted at least thirty (30) days prior to the original start of the leave period.
8. A physician who returns to work at the conclusion of a family and medical leave or personal leave of absence is restored to his or her former position or to a comparable position at the same rate of pay.
9. If the physician fails to return to work at the conclusion of an approved leave of absence, the leave is cancelled and employment is terminated with an effective date of termination being the last day worked.
10. Under all circumstances, leave of absence requests are set at a maximum of one (1) per twelve- (12-) month period.
11. As provided for in the individual plan descriptions, benefits may continue during the leave of absence; however, there shall be no accrual of benefit amounts during the period of absence. To ensure continuation of insurance coverage during a leave of absence, and in accordance with the plan descriptions/policies, the physician may pay the premiums during an approved leave of absence.

Sample: Leave Request Form

Physician Name: ____________________ Date: __________
Department: ____________________ Date of Employment: __________

Type of Leave Requested

- ☐ FMLA
- ☐ Vacation
- ☐ Illness/injury
  - Projected return to work date: __________
- ☐ Court
- ☐ Disability
  - Projected return to work date: __________
- ☐ Military
  - Projected return to work date: __________
- ☐ Personal leave of absence
  - Projected return to work date: __________
- ☐ Other (explain) __________

Dates Requested

1st choice: From (month, date, year) __________ to (month, date, year) __________
2nd choice: From (month, date, year) __________ to (month, date, year) __________

Requesting physician's signature: ______________________________

- ☐ Approved
- ☐ Disapproved

If disapproved, explanation for denial: ____

____

Signature: ______________________________
Date: ______________________________
Notes: ____

____

Policy 2.3

Leave without Pay Policy[2]

Extended Leave Policy

The Extended Leave Policy would allow the following for any physician-shareholder with the Practice. For the purposes of this policy, "extended leave" means leave time without any scheduled hours for the physician.

2 Printed in *HR Policies and Procedures Manual for Medical Practices, 4th Edition,* by Courtney Price, PhD, and Alys Novak, MBA (Englewood, CO: Medical Group Management Association, 2007).

Procedure

1. Requests may be submitted after the physician has completed twenty-four (24) continuous months of employment.
2. Time off is granted at the discretion of the governing body.
3. Requests must be for time off after all accrued time has been used.
4. The request must be submitted to the Practice administrator at least twelve (12) months in advance of the requested leave date.
5. The requests must be for a minimum of six (6) months and a maximum of twelve (12) months.
6. Compensation: There would be no salary or other compensation during the leave period.
7. Benefits: In accordance with the plan description and policy eligibility criteria, insurance benefits may continue in effect. Premium payments would be the responsibility of the physician.
8. Any commitments for repayment of loans, ownership purchases, or other obligations to the Practice will be required to be paid during the leave period.
9. Any "early cancellation" or other premium amounts for professional liability insurance, including tail coverage, during the period of absence will be the responsibility of the physician.
10. If the physician becomes disabled during the leave, he or she will be entitled to disability insurance proceeds in accordance with the policy's provisions.

Family and Medical Leave Act (FMLA)

The Practice complies with FMLA.

Procedure

1. A physician may request leave from work for the purposes of:
   - A birth, adoption, or foster-care placement of a child;
   - Care for a spouse, child, or parent with a serious health condition; or
   - A serious health condition that renders the physician unable to perform his or her employment duties.
2. To be eligible for leave under FMLA, a physician must have been employed for more than twelve (12) consecutive months and must have worked at least 1,250 hours in the preceding twelve (12) months.
3. A leave of absence request must be completed for leaves, whether paid or unpaid. A physician intending to take leave is required to give advance notice in a reasonable and practical manner. In situations involving leave for a serious health condition, every reasonable effort to schedule medical treatment so that it does not unduly disrupt practice operations should be made before a leave is considered.
4. A physician requesting medical leave must provide medical certification that indicates a serious health condition exists and that provides other information as requested. A serious health condition means an illness, injury, impairment, or condition that will not allow the physician to perform the duties normally associated with his or her specialty and practice.

5. Eligible physicians are entitled to the following mandatory leaves of absence under the law:
   - A physician may take as many as twelve (12) weeks of leave in a twelve- (12-) month period for the birth of the physician's natural child or the placement of a child with the physician for adoption or foster care;
   - Leave following birth or adoption is time off of work for physicians who are physically able to return to work but choose to stay home and care for a newborn or adopted child; and
   - Pregnancy leave is characterized by a physical disability because of childbirth or a related medical condition.
6. A physician must use accrued time off during a medical leave and before the requested time-leave period is effective.
7. Leaves are without pay.
8. During the period of leave, in accordance with the insurance policies' provisions, participants in the group health insurance plan may continue coverage; however, the physician will be responsible for the payment of the premium to continue such coverage.
9. Any physician benefit that accrued before a family or medical leave began will be "frozen" and held in reserve. No further benefit will accrue during the leave period.
10. Physicians returning to work at the end of the leave period are returned to their same position or an equivalent position.

Policy 2.4

Holiday and Paid Time Off Policy[3]

Holidays

It is the policy of the Practice to observe certain holidays each year as established by the group's management. Each holiday observed by the practice is a day off with pay for most physicians. The following holidays are observed by the medical practice annually:

- New Year's Day;
- Memorial Day;
- Independence Day;
- Labor Day;
- Thanksgiving Day;
- Day after Thanksgiving Day;
- Christmas Day;
- Physician's birthday; and
- Two (2) floating holidays.

3 Printed in *HR Policies and Procedures Manual for Medical Practices, 4th Edition,* by Courtney Price, PhD, and Alys Novak, MBA (Englewood, CO: Medical Group Management Association, 2007).

Procedure

1. If there are any changes, HR will notify all physicians.
2. Full-time physicians receive their regular rate of pay for each holiday. Part-time physicians receive holiday pay only for holidays on which they normally would be scheduled to work and only for their regularly scheduled number of hours.
3. Temporary physicians are not eligible to receive holiday pay.
4. To receive holiday pay, an eligible physician must be at work or on authorized absence on the workdays immediately preceding and following the day on which the holiday is observed. If a physician submits a request for sick leave on these days, the physician must render a physician's statement supporting this request. Management reserves the right to approve or disapprove the sick leave request.
5. A holiday that occurs on a Saturday will be observed on the preceding Friday. A holiday that occurs on a Sunday will be observed on the following Monday.
6. If the holiday occurs while a physician is away from the practice for vacation or professional development, that day will not be included as a time-off day nor charged against the physician's accrued balance.
7. The Practice recognizes that some physicians may wish to observe certain days not included in the group's holiday schedule, such as religious holidays. In these instances, a physician should request a floating holiday. Management makes every effort to accommodate these requests if such absences do not result in an undue business hardship on the medical practice.
8. A holiday is granted to each physician on his or her birthday. If not taken on the physician's actual birthday, the birthday holiday must be taken in the month in which the birthday occurs.

Paid Time Off

The Practice provides paid time off (PTO) to compensate for holidays, vacations, short-term illnesses, and personal time off.

Procedure

1. PTO may be used for holidays, vacations, short-term illnesses, or personal needs. Physicians cannot borrow or lend PTO but can donate PTO using an approved process.
2. Physicians must request PTO at least two (2) weeks in advance by requesting such leave in writing. Before approving PTO requests, supervisors consider medical practice workload needs.
3. PTO is accumulated by full- and part-time physicians from the day they are hired. With the exception of agency-recognized holidays, physicians may not use PTO until they complete the ninety- (90-) day provisionary period.
4. Full-time physicians may accrue twelve (12) hours of PTO each calendar month of employment during their first twelve (12) months of employment; during the physician's 13th and 59th months of employment, the physician will accrue at the rate of sixteen (16) hours each month; during the physician's 60th and 120th months of employment, the physician will accrue at the rate of twenty (20) hours per month. Beginning with the 121st month of employment, the physician will accrue at a rate of twenty-four (24) hours per month.

Policy 2.5

Insurance Policy

The Practice furnishes an insurance program that includes the following.

Health Insurance

Individual medical insurance is provided for all members of the Practice. The insurance plan also provides a Prescription Drug Benefit. Family coverage is available by payroll deduction. The details of coverage, copay amounts, deductibles, and limits on coverage are outlined in the policy description, a copy of which is provided to each physician.

Dental Insurance

Individual dental insurance is provided for all members of the Practice. Family coverage is available by payroll deduction. The details of coverage, copay amounts, deductibles, and limits on coverage are outlined in the policy description, a copy of which is provided to each physician.

Disability Insurance

The Practice maintains a group disability policy. It is to be noted that this is a "Your Specialty" policy. The premium for these policies is paid by the Practice. The details of coverage, waiting periods, calculation of benefit, and limits on coverage are outlined in the policy description, a copy of which is provided to each physician.

Life Insurance

The benefit for group term life insurance is $250,000. The premium for these policies is paid by the Practice. The details of coverage, waiting periods, calculation of benefit, and limits on coverage are outlined in the policy description, a copy of which is provided to each physician.

Long-Term Care

The Practice maintains a long-term care policy for the physicians and their spouses. There is a ninety- (90-) day cumulative elimination period. The details of coverage are outlined in the policy description, a copy of which is made available to all physicians.

Policy 2.6

Disability Policy[4]

The policy of the Practice is to provide short- and long-term disability insurance coverage in conjunction with benefits available through government sources.

4 Printed in *HR Policies and Procedures Manual for Medical Practices, 4th Edition,* by Courtney Price, PhD, and Alys Novak, MBA (Englewood, CO: Medical Group Management Association, 2007).

Procedure

1. Full- and part-time physicians are eligible for disability leave. Temporary physicians are not eligible.
2. Physicians are eligible for disability leave when they are physically unable to perform the duties of their position or another position within the medical practice due to injury or occupational disease incurred in the course of their employment. When such disability determination has been made, the insurance company the Practice has selected for disability insurance coverage will be notified.
3. Disability benefits are not awarded when the disability is an aggravation of a known medical condition that existed prior to employment with the medical practice. Such benefits are not awarded when the disability is the result of aggravation of a preexisting disability arising from another employment for which the physician has received a permanent partial award, nor are benefits awarded when the physician receives a civil judgment or settlement for permanent disability arising from a nonindustrial injury.
4. Every physician who sustains an injury in the course of his or her employment must notify the immediate supervisor within the time period specified by local law.
5. If the physician fails to report an injury, he or she may lose one day's disability leave for each day's failure to report.
6. Physicians on disability leave may be required to be examined periodically by their personal physician. Compliance with this requirement is a condition for continuing disability leave with pay.
7. Disability leaves are not granted beyond a physician's mandatory retirement date.

Short-Term Disability

Short-term disability insurance (total and permanent) is provided at no cost to the physician beginning the first of the month coinciding with the physician's first day of employment:

- During the first month of a disability, 100 percent of the physician's salary is paid by the Practice; and
- During the second and third months of a disability, the short-term disability insurance pays 66⅔ percent of the physician's salary up to a maximum of $2,500 per week after a thirty- (30-) day waiting period.

Long-Term Disability

Long-term disability insurance (total and permanent) is provided at no cost to the physician beginning the first of the month coinciding with the physician's first day of employment. Individual "Your Specialty" disability policies (i.e., policy pays if you are unable to perform the duties of your specialty) for the maximum protection available at this time, utilizing a ninety- (90-) day waiting period, are provided to all of the physician-shareholders of the Practice.

The Practice maintains each physician-shareholder at full salary level for ninety (90) days following the onset of disability. Thereafter, the individual and group disability coverage should become effective and salary will cease.

The premium for these policies is paid for by the Practice as a benefit to the physicians.

Policy 2.7

Professional Liability Insurance Policy

Medical professional liability (MPL) insurance or medical malpractice insurance is necessary for asset protection from a patient claiming injury due to alleged negligence by a physician. The alleged deviation from the accepted standard of care can be due to an act of omission or an act of commission. This insurance, like other insurances, involves payment of a premium in exchange for defense and the payment of claims up to the liability limit for a certain period of time. The insurer spreads the risk, pays the losses, saves reserves, and invests them for a profit margin. An MPL policy pays for:

- The cost of investigating and defending any claims against the insured. There are, in general, no limits for these costs, although some policies may have an upper limit; and
- The indemnity cost of any legal settlement or a judgment against the insured up to the policy limit.

Procedure

1. The Practice will furnish and maintain malpractice and public liability insurance for protection of the physician for the performance of his or her duties on behalf of the Practice in reasonable amounts and in accordance with the customary professional standards in effect within the Practice's practice area.
2. As a condition to such coverage, the physician must meet the eligibility requirements for coverage as set by the carrier used by the practice for the other professional physicians of the practice.
3. Coverage for the medical practice NOT on behalf of the Practice or the Practice's patients is not included.

Coverage through a Hospital as Medical Staff

Obtaining MPL insurance through a hospital as a member of its medical staff is a complicated issue from a legal regulatory standpoint. Significant risks exist for hospitals in this area, unless these actions are specifically protected by safe harbors under the anti-kickback laws and exceptions under the Stark law. In general, if a hospital has a self-insurance trust, it may not write policies for nonemployed physicians, such as medical staff members. This action would require, among other problems, an insurance license. If the hospital is covered by an offshore or domestic "captive" insurance arrangement, it may consider covering nonemployed physicians. However, this may also constitute solicitation of insurance unless the arrangement is structured properly. The hospital then takes on the risk of the insured physician and must be careful that it does not violate its bond agreements. To then avoid Stark law violations, it has to charge the physician fair market value of the cost of the policy. To avoid these regulatory traps and the enormous premium increases of high-risk specialties, such as obstetrics and trauma surgery, physicians have increasingly resorted to full-time employment contracts with the hospital.

Summary

Whereas it may not be practical for a physician to review and comprehend all the legal language in a professional liability policy, it behooves the physician to ask some basic questions. These questions should include (1) type of policy, (2) limits of coverage, (3) exclusions, (4) cancellation clauses, (5) company ratings, and especially (6) tail coverage. If a claim is filed against the physician, the expense of hiring an attorney at personal expense to review the judgment of the insurers' legal counsel may be worth considering.

Tail Coverage

The physician agrees to maintain at his or her own expense insurance for claims made after he or she terminates employment with the Practice for acts or omissions by him or her during his or her employment. Regardless of the reason for termination of employment, the Practice has the right to purchase tail (prior acts) coverage, charge the amount of the premium to the physician, and deduct it from any amounts of compensation due to him or her under this agreement unless the physician presents satisfactory evidence of continuing coverage after his or her employment with the Practice ends.

Procedure

1. The physician and the Practice agree that, in the event that the physician's employment is terminated for any reason whatsoever or upon expiration and nonrenewal of this agreement, the Practice shall be responsible for paying such premiums through the date of termination only, and upon such termination and nonrenewal, the physician shall be responsible for purchasing and paying the cost of a "claims made" professional liability policy covering the period of employment (also called "extended period" or "tail" or "prior acts" coverage), and the Practice shall have no responsibility to the physician, the physician's surviving spouse or descendants, or the physician's estate for purchasing or paying the cost of such coverage.
2. The physician shall provide the Practice with evidence of the physician's full payment of the premiums for such tail coverage, also referenced as prior acts coverage. The physician may also be covered by his or her new employer, commonly called "nose coverage." However, if such coverage for prior acts is not purchased, the Practice shall have the right to hold any compensation or other amounts due to the physician in escrow until the physician provides to the Practice evidence of the full payment of the premium for such tail coverage.
3. If the physician fails to pay the full premium for such tail (prior acts) coverage as may be available, then the Practice shall have the right to pay the premiums for such tail coverage and to immediately offset the expense against the compensation or other amounts due from the Practice to the physician hereunder.
4. If there is legal action as a result of the physician's noncompliance with these provisions, the Practice shall recover all costs and fees connected with establishing such tail (prior acts) coverage from the physician.

Policy 2.8

Interruption of Service Policy

An "Interruption of Service" shall be defined as any working day during which the physician fails to perform, for any reason, the duties set forth in the Physician Employment Agreement (see Policy 1.3). This policy does not apply to time away from the practice for approved time off.

Procedure

1. **Compensation during Interruption of Service.** The physician's compensation for any month including the Interruption of Service shall be withheld to be offset against expenses arising during the Interruption of Service. Any remaining sums will be paid when the physician returns to work at the Practice on a full-time basis.
2. **Return to Work.** In the event that the physician fails to return to work on a full-time basis within ninety (90) days of the beginning date of the Interruption of Service, this Agreement may be terminated by the Practice and no further compensation provided.

Policy 2.9

Bereavement Leave Policy

Bereavement leave is typically granted to physicians in the event of an immediate family member's death. The leave is usually for a maximum of five (5) consecutive working days. Additional leave may be arranged by using available paid time off (PTO). Bereavement leave for anyone other than immediate family must be taken by using PTO and must be approved by the immediate supervisor. Proof of death may be requested.

Immediate family is defined as spouse/significant other, child, parent, or grandparent. In the case of married children, immediate family includes the married child's spouse as well as any children of the marriage.

Policy 2.10

Military Leave Policy

Military leave, in peacetime, is mainly for training duty in the National Guard or reserves. Federal law prohibits employers from forcing physicians to use personal vacation leave for such mandatory duty. Employers are expected to accommodate requests for military leave or calls to active duty. A military leave policy helps physicians discharge their military obligations and gives employers an opportunity to demonstrate their patriotism.

If a physician enlists, is drafted, or is called to active duty, the statute states that physicians may spend as many as five (5) years on active duty. After discharge, the physician must apply for his or her previous position within ninety (90) days of his or her release from active duty, and the employer is required to reinstate the physician at a comparable job level (although there may be some exceptions). For more information on military leave, please review information on the Department of Labor Website.

The policy of the Practice is to grant military leave to eligible physicians who are required to attend annual military training encampment with the U.S. government or any political subdivision thereof or physicians who are called to active military duty.

Procedure

1. Physicians, except temporary physicians, are eligible for military training leave.
2. A single fifteen (15) calendar-day period of military training leave is granted annually.
3. In the event that the military training leave is optional, the physician is allowed vacation time for this purpose.
4. If the amount of pay, subject to income-tax provisions, received for military training is greater than the pay that would be earned by the physician, such leave is considered leave without pay. If the military pay, subject to income-tax provisions, received by the physician is less than he or she would earn from the medical practice, the practice pays the physician the difference between the military pay and his or her regular pay.
5. If a physician is inducted into active military service or the Armed Forces of the United States or is called from a Reserve or National Guard unit into active duty, or if emergency duty is declared by the proper authority of the state, then the physician is placed on military leave without pay.
6. Military leave without pay is granted for the duration of active military service, not to exceed five (5) years, plus ninety (90) days from the date of discharge. Extensions are granted if a physician is required to serve a longer period of time involuntarily because of war or national emergency.
7. Vacation and sick leave credits are not earned during military leave without pay.
8. Physicians must submit applications for return from military leave without pay within ninety (90) days of the date of discharge from military service.
9. A return from military leave without pay is conditional upon submitting a certificate of satisfactory completion of military service.
10. Failure to apply for a return to employment from military leave without pay within the time limit previously stated is considered a resignation.
11. A written request form must be submitted to the physician's supervisor at least two (2) weeks in advance, indicating the starting and ending dates of the military training leave. To receive this benefit, the physician must furnish a copy of his or her military orders signed by an authorized military officer.
12. The length of military training leave granted to a physician depends on his or her military orders, not to exceed fifteen (15) calendar days annually.
13. If a physician is disabled while on military training leave or military leave with pay and rendered incapable of performing the duties of the position previously

occupied, the physician is offered the best available position for which he or she qualifies, providing the physician reapplies within the previously stated time limit.

Policy 2.11

Phones and Pagers Policy

The physician is expected to maintain and carry a cellular phone as necessary to manage expected contact with patients and other physicians. For all practical purposes, the Practice will cover any expenses accrued by the physician that are associated with being in practice, including cellular phones and monthly service charges that are directly related to practice communication. The Practice may provide the physician with a cellular phone and participate in a cellular phone calling plan or program on behalf of the physician.

Policy 2.12

Cars and Mileage Reimbursement Policy

The physician is expected to have and properly maintain an automobile or other transportation suitable for the physician to fulfill his or her duties, including the provision of call coverage. As a result, the physician may lease an automobile and pay for its maintenance and upkeep at the Practice's expense. Any personal usage of the automobile shall then be treated as additional income to physician. On a monthly basis, the physician shall keep and submit to the Practice adequate records showing business and personal use of any such automobile.

Automobile Use

The Practice will reimburse the physician for an automobile to be used in the performance of the physician's duties under the following conditions:

1. The physician shall pay all expenses attributable to the use of the physician's assigned corporate automobile and shall carry and pay for automobile liability insurance of no less than one hundred thousand dollars ($100,000) for the injury or death of one person; three hundred thousand dollars ($300,000) for injury or death arising from one accident; and fifty thousand dollars ($50,000) for property damage; and
2. The physician shall be responsible for carrying excess liability insurance ("umbrella") coverage of one million dollars ($1,000,000), and the Practice may reimburse the physician for these insurance costs.

Mileage Reimbursement

1. The Practice will reimburse the physician for any mileage accrued by the physician in driving from his or her primary practice office location to other practice locations where he or she is assigned from time to time or to hospitals where the

physician admits patients and/or provides services. No reimbursement shall be made for mileage accrued by the physician driving between his or her home and primary practice location.

2. Reimbursement will be at the currently approved mileage rate as set by the Internal Revenue Service (IRS).
3. Should the IRS or the [STATE] Department of Revenue disallow all or any part of the automobile expenses incurred by the physician or reimbursed to the physician as a deductible expense, the amount of such disallowed costs and expenses shall be deemed additional taxable compensation paid by the Practice to the physician.

Policy 2.13 Retirement and Semi-Retirement Policy[5]

Traditionally, retirement has been thought of as the end of a person's career. Today, however, retirement is seen more as a transition to a new stage of life. More and more, people are starting new careers after their "retirement." This trend reflects the fact that people are living longer, want to continue working, and need to supplement their income.

Prior to 1979, many organizations had retirement policies that made retirement mandatory at age 65. The Age Discrimination in Employment Act Amendments of 1978, and as amended in 1987, now prohibit involuntary retirement.

The prescribed age at which retirement benefits begin is outlined in both the provisions of an organization's policies, benefit structure, and/or established by state/commonwealth statute/law. Practices can use age sixty-five (65) as the "normal" retirement age. The difference is that no physician may be forced to retire at any age. As of 1987, the age cap of seventy (70) was eliminated.

In some practices, the normal time for retirement is determined by adding the person's age to his or her length of service. This calculation establishes a minimum number of points for retirement (often either eighty (80) or eighty-five (85) points). For example, a physician may be eligible for full retirement benefits when he or she reaches age fifty-five (55) with twenty-five years of service (eighty (80) points).

Some employers offer early retirement packages to encourage physicians to retire earlier than they would otherwise. The early retirement provisions normally include a "buyout" concept — an offer of cash inducements for early retirement. Usually, physicians have a certain time period during which to decide whether to accept or reject the offer. This approach allows the employer to downsize in a way that does not discriminate. However, the Older Workers Benefit Protection Act prohibits age discrimination in physician benefits and establishes minimum standards for waivers of claims. Compliance with these requirements is critical in a buyout or other retirement option.

5 Printed in *HR Policies and Procedures Manual for Medical Practices, 4th Edition,* by Courtney Price, PhD, and Alys Novak, MBA (Englewood, CO: Medical Group Management Association, 2007).

Another retirement option is semi-retirement. Under this approach, a physician reduces his or her normal working hours to a predetermined lower number of hours per week. These can be configured as a reduced number of days per week or hours per day.

A final option is full retirement, but with the retired physician continuing to work for the employer as an independent contractor. This arrangement can be beneficial for both the employer and the physician. Some physicians lose their productivity and enthusiasm for the job before reaching retirement age. Early retirement allows practices to recruit new physicians while simultaneously protecting their older physicians' pensions and other benefits.

Retirement plan provisions outline the details of how the physician may receive his or her retirement benefits. Most retirement plans are "defined contribution" plans, whereby the physician and/or the Practice "define" the contribution to be made. The other common type of retirement plan is a "defined benefit" plan, where the "benefit" is defined. The Practice's governing body shall establish through its benefits program retirement plan(s) and the specific details regarding eligibility to participate, funding, withdrawal of benefits, etc.

Complete information about the Practice's retirement program is available from human resources.

The medical director and department chairs shall consult with the retirees in terms of a transition from patient care and other responsibilities. Options may include early retirement and/or partial retirement, especially when a disability may be involved.

Pension Plan

A noncontributory Pension Plan provides a benefit to eligible members based on annual base pay and vesting-service requirements. Each year, the Practice will credit the physician's account with an amount equal to two (2) percent of the physician's base pay up to a specified maximum. An account is established for each eligible member, and the Practice adds to the account each year. The account is portable, and members may take the vested portion at the time of retirement or termination.

Definition of Terms

Break in Service: A plan year in which a physician completes less than 501 hours of service.

Compensation: All amounts reported on the physician's W-2 form each calendar (or plan) year should be recognized as compensation under the provisions of the plan.

Hours of Service: Each hour for which the physician is paid or entitled to payment for the performance of duties for the Practice or its affiliates.

Plan Year: The twelve- (12-) month period beginning on January 1 every year and ending on December 31 of the same year.

Vesting Schedule/Years of Vesting Service: The physician shall vest at zero (0) percent during his or her first fifty-nine (59) months of employment. Beginning with the 60th month of employment, the physician shall be 100 percent vested.

Vesting Service: A physician will be credited with one (1) year of vesting service for each year during which the physician has completed a minimum of 1,000 hours.

All physicians are eligible on the first day of appointment to staff.

Procedure

1. Vesting credit earned prior to December 31 will count toward the vesting requirements under the Pension Plan that became effective on January 1 of the next year.
2. Physicians who transfer from residency to staff status at the Practice shall receive vesting credit for years during residency.
3. The Practice physicians appointed to staff after age sixty (60) and working less than the five- (5-) year vesting requirements are automatically 100-percent vested at the time of retirement or termination.
4. At the time of retirement or termination, the eligible physician may select his or her preferred payment option.
5. Physicians planning to retire need to contact the staff services department at least three (3) months prior to their anticipated retirement date. Staff services will schedule a follow-up meeting to review the entire retirement benefits package.

Forms of Retirement

- **Normal Retirement.** A physician may retire on or after his or her normal retirement (the first of the month following or coinciding with age sixty-five (65).) Upon retirement, a physician may receive his or her account balance or may select a benefit payout as defined within the Pension Plan Document.
- **Early Retirement.** A physician may elect early retirement if he or she is at least age fifty-five (55) and has completed at least five (5) years of service. Upon retirement, a physician may receive his or her account balance or may select a benefit payout as defined within the Pension Plan Document.
- **Retirement Options.** Within a reasonable time prior to the commencement of retirement payments to a physician, the retirement committee shall give the physician a written notice of his or her right to elect not to receive his or her account balance and of his or her right to make an election; for example, 100-percent survivor annuity or 50-percent survivor annuity.

Retirement Savings Plan

All physicians are immediately eligible to participate in a contributory Retirement Savings Plan that enables the physician, along with the Practice, to provide income for retirement. The physician's decision is a one-time irrevocable decision, made at the time of joining the staff, to participate.

The contribution schedule will depend on the physician's base pay and the Social Security taxable wage base. The Practice's contributions shall equal 2.5 percent of the member's base pay less than the Social Security taxable wage base and 5 percent of the member's base pay greater than the Social Security taxable wage base. Physicians' contributions are made with before-tax dollars.

Definition of Terms

Compensation: Basic earnings paid by the Practice exclusive of maintenance, bonuses, membership units, and other forms of supplemental compensation, premiums, pay for overtime, or any other kind of extra or additional compensation.

Vesting Schedule: Members are 100-percent vested in money they contribute to the Plan. The Practice's contributions are vested based on the physician's length of service: less than 3 years, 0 percent; 3 years, 50 percent; 4 years, 75 percent; 5 years, 100 percent.

Vesting Service: A physician will be credited with one (1) year of vesting service for each year during which the physician has completed a minimum of 1,000 hours.

Your Retirement Savings Plan is portable. You can receive the vested portion of your account balance when you retire or leave the Practice for any other reason.

If you die, your beneficiary will receive the full value of your account. Under current tax law, your account balance will be subject to income and other applicable taxes when you receive it.

Semi-Retirement Policy for a Shareholder

Procedure

1. The option of semi-retirement in any form requires governing body approval.
2. **Notice.** Any shareholder considering semi-retirement must give written notice to the Practice board of directors [X] years prior to the expected effective date of semi-retirement. A written agreement defining the terms of semi-retirement must be executed at least ninety (90) days prior to the intended effective date.
3. **Minimum Age and Years of Service.** In order to be considered for semi-retirement, a physician must have a minimum of [X] years of service with the Practice, and the sum of a physician's age in years plus his or her full years of service must equal at least seventy (70). For example, if a physician starts with the practice at age thirty-five (35), the earliest he or she may semi-retire is age fifty-three (53). If a physician is age forty (40) when he or she starts at the practice, semi-retirement will first be an option at age fifty-five (55).
4. **Severance Pay.** Severance pay will be fixed on the last day of the calendar quarter preceding the effective date of semi-retirement. For example, if semi-retirement begins on January 1, severance pay will be fixed as of December 31. Severance pay will be payable in three (3) annual installments with the first installment payable six (6) months after the effective date of semi-retirement, the second payment twelve (12) months later, and the third payment twelve (12) months after the second installment. For example, if the effective date of semi-retirement is January 1, 2013, the first installment will be on July 1, 2013, the second on July 1, 2014, and the third on July 1, 2015. No interest will be paid by the Practice on severance pay.

5. **Compensation and Benefits.** The governing body will negotiate a contract annually with the retiring physician, which stipulates specific responsibilities, base pay, and production bonus. However, for the physician who gives up call in its entirety, his or her base pay shall be 67 percent of his or her base pay as of the date formal notice of semi-retirement is given to the board and paid time off (vacation, continuing medical education (CME), etc.) shall be reduced by 25 percent. Any and all bonuses will be at the discretion of the governing body.
6. **Ownership.** The semi-retiring physician shall sell his or her ownership shares to the practice as of the effective date of semi-retirement. Payments shall be made in the same manner as for severance pay. If necessary, the Buy/Sell Agreement will be changed to be in compliance with this policy.

Policy 2.14

Retirement Planning Policy

Continued Employment of Partially Retired Physicians

In an effort to address the needs of physician-shareholders who are in the process of slowing down their practices in preparation for retirement, the following plan has been implemented.

This plan is available to physician-shareholders with at least twenty (20) years of experience with the Practice and/or who have reached the minimum age of sixty (60).

All physicians who have reached age sixty-five (65) will be reviewed each year by the Practice governing body. The governing body will decide on a yearly basis to renew Option 1 or Option 2 for each physician falling into this category.

Option 1

Option 1 is simply to remain a shareholder in the Practice and remain a participant in the then-current Income Distribution Plan (IDP). (As one's production declines, one's income would decline commensurably under this option.) All shareholder privileges would remain (e.g., full voting privilege, ancillary services, profit sharing, participation in Practice committees and board).

Physicians who wish to slow down but continue to work more than 1,000 hours per year are subject to the then-existing IDP and call schedules of the department.

Paid benefits will include:

- Medical insurance coverage for family and physician if not qualified for Medicare;
- Dental/vision assistance plan;

- Life insurance;
- Disability insurance;
- Retirement plan, if the physician meets qualification of hours;
- Vacation/holidays;
- Continuing medical education/dues and licenses, as per individual department policy; and
- Flex benefits.

Option 2

Option 2 is made available for individuals who meet the age and/or experience requirements previously stated and who wish to reduce their practice activities to less than 1,000 hours per year, and/or whose individual productivity is less than expenses. This reduction in activities includes elimination from call rotation. The decision to continue hospital work is left to the discretion of the department.

For the benefit of working less than full time, and being removed from night/weekend call schedules, the person in this category would receive 5 percent less than the department average. That is, if the departmental average is 45 percent (compensation to net revenue), said individual would be calculated at 40 percent of his or her net revenue. The 5-percent differential would be calculated monthly.

Individuals who choose Option 2 will relinquish their shareholder status and will be provided an Associate Physician Contract, which will delineate the terms of the agreement.

Slowdown of Practice

Each specialty and department, including branch offices, is unique in its practice patterns, call demands, and the technology skills required. Every individual is unique in his or her response to the demands of medical practice and to the aging process. It is not possible, therefore, to have rules that must be followed throughout the Practice. Instead, each department is meant to use the following guidelines as it develops its own plan.

Guidelines

1. Slowing down can be a means of gradually moving into retirement. It implies a decrease in workload, including the possibility of going part time, and a decrease in income. It may or may not include doing fewer technically difficult procedures. These decisions remain individual ones. Each department's plan will be designed to allow individuals to make these decisions with minimum impact on patient care. It is recognized that this could mean more work for others in the department or recruitment of a new partner or locums with a financial impact. However, for those physicians who make the Practice a career, their opportunity to slow down will also come.

2. Slowing down may include decreased requirements for taking calls. This will vary with the specialty and size of the department. The individual may not desire it. It may not be possible for the organization because of patient-care needs.
3. The seniority benefit of increased availability of vacation time will be honored. This does not imply decreased call time unless agreed to in the department's plan.
4. It may be in the best interests of all concerned for a physician who is slowing down to have a negotiated compensation arrangement rather than the usual compensation plan.
5. If the need exists for the organization to utilize physicians to develop new programs or expand existing ones, initial consideration will be given to physicians already at the Practice, including those who desire to slow down. These positions may be salaried.
6. Opportunities for individual funding for the slowdown period and retirement years will be an ongoing benefits committee agenda item.
7. After a physician reaches age forty-five (45), an aspect of the periodic interviews between that physician and the medical director or president will be discussion of plans for slowing down and retirement.
8. A physician who wishes to be less than full time will formally request this through the chairman of his or her department to the section head committee and finally the board of directors.

Departmental Responsibilities

1. With the help of administration, each department will chart the number of physicians, their current age, and any individual thoughts about salary or late retirement.
2. This chart will be updated annually along with projected needs for new physicians as workload increases because an individual is slowing down and/or because of patient needs.
3. Each department will develop a program based on the guidelines of the group to deal with slowdown and retirement. This will be agreed upon by all current members and explained to all physicians who later join the Practice.
4. In the event that agreement cannot be achieved within a department, the section head committee will mediate.

Sample: Pre-Retirement/Slowdown Policy

WHEREAS Medical Group Physicians, LLC (hereafter referred to as "the Practice"), is a limited liability company organized to render professional medical services within [STATE]; and WHEREAS the Practice desires to adopt a "Slowdown Policy" and define the procedure by which a physician-member of the Practice may qualify for "slowdown";

BE IT RESOLVED:

Slowdown

1. A physician who satisfies the following criteria may apply for "slowdown":
   a. Member of the Practice;
   b. Age fifty-five (55) or older;
   c. Fifteen (15) years of association with the Practice; and
   d. Provides the Practice's board of managers with a minimum of twelve (12) months' notice of his or her intention to slow down.
2. Satisfying the previous conditions, slowdown will be granted by the board of managers.
3. The term of "slowdown" shall be for a minimum of twelve (12) and a maximum of twenty-four (24) months; after which the physician will be required to:
   a. Terminate association and retire; or
   b. Sell his or her ownership interest in the Practice and become a physician employee; with such employment, working hours, and compensation as set by the board of managers on a year-to-year basis.
4. The compensation to be received during slowdown will be per the written agreement between the physician and the Practice but will require a minimum allocation for expenses of the Practice. Further, his or her compensation may be reduced in accordance with the Practice's Compensation Plan.

Policy 2.15

Succession Planning Policy

Senior Physician Status

A senior physician is defined as a physician who:

- Continues to maintain an active practice, which may include providing inpatient care and performing surgery within his or her personal skill level and under the review of the executive committee;
- Agrees to not perform certain procedures or surgeries as determined by the board of directors;
- Does not accept any new patients sixty (60) days prior to retirement except those specifically referred to him or her or that request him or her;
- Does not participate in group call rotation but may elect to continue taking calls for personal patients. In his or her absence, or if he or she elects to not take calls for his or her personal patients, the group will cover his or her personal patients, and he or she shall not be required to reciprocate call coverage. In the event that the senior physician has a post-op patient in the hospital, he or she shall be on call during the period the patient remains in the hospital;

- Works less than five (5) days per week and/or takes more than six (6) weeks off including CME meetings. The actual time to be worked shall be at the physician's discretion subject to the compensation arrangement. The physician shall adhere to a regular schedule and provide adequate notice of schedule changes to allow the group to allocate physicians; and
- Has been approved and deemed by the board as a "senior physician."
  - Senior status is available eighteen (18) months prior to retirement. At the completion of the senior status period, the physician shall retire in accordance with the Employment Agreement, Stock Transfer Agreement, and other corporate documents.

The board may withdraw senior status at any time. Upon such withdrawal, the physician may return immediately to full-time employment or give ninety (90) days' notice of his or her intent to retire completely.

The board shall limit "senior physician" status to three (3) physicians at any time or two (2) physicians per call group.

The board shall not be required to grant "senior physician" status if requested.

A senior physician shall be compensated based on the following concepts:

- The physician under senior status is expected to maintain a level of production equal to or greater than that produced by the lowest level of production of any full-time physician-shareholder. If the senior physician maintains that level of production, then he or she will continue to be paid on the same basis and calculation as is currently in effect for all physician-shareholders.
- The physician shall continue to have an expense account equal to other physician-shareholders, and the accounting shall be the same, except any overage remaining in the expense account at termination shall be prorated to reflect actual months worked in the fiscal year. Before any expense account overage is dispersed as additional salary, the overage may be adjusted to recoup any production shortages discussed as follows.
- If the senior physician's total compensation from salary and bonus is less than $__________.00 (or the then-current IRS threshold for maximum compensation), the senior physician's retirement contribution will be calculated with the normal plan's formulas. The formulas will not be restated for him or her to achieve the maximum contribution unless the formulas need to be restated for all physician-shareholders to receive the maximum contribution. The senior physician can make a 401K contribution from his or her normal compensation to achieve the maximum contribution, but the group will not pay a bonus to achieve the maximum contribution.
- Any surgery fees for patients referred to other physicians shall be split between the senior physician and the surgeon. If the senior physician refers the case, provides pre- and post-op care, and serves as the assistant (if needed), then the total net fee shall be split fifty-fifty (50/50). If the senior physician refers the case, and the surgeon performs the surgery and provides all post-op care, then the surgeon's net fee shall be split 75 percent to the surgeon and 25 percent to the senior physician. The assistant fee is credited to the physician providing the service.

- A physician or senior physician shall be eligible for all bonuses paid during the period, and his or her percentage of the bonus shall be based on his or her actual percentage of the total production during the time period. If the physician's production tracking for his or her regular salary reflects a shortage, then the bonus shall be used to offset the shortage before any bonus is paid.
- If the group's financial statements reflect a profit at retirement, then the group may elect to pay all physicians a bonus to reduce the profit, or the profit may be allowed to remain in the Practice, in which case, the retiring physician's stock valuation shall reflect the profit.
- If the senior physician's quarterly production is less than the lowest level of production of any full-time physician-shareholder during that same quarter, then his or her compensation shall be changed to be calculated on a monthly basis. For this policy, it is agreed that 50 percent of the net production is allocated to overhead and 50 percent to physician salary, malpractice insurance, retirement contributions, and other benefits as funded from the expense account. For this policy, it is agreed that 8.5 percent of net production shall be allocated to malpractice insurance, retirement contributions, and other benefits as funded from the expense account. The board of directors may adjust these percentages at any time if the same percentages are applied to all full-time physician-shareholders.
- If the senior physician is switched to a monthly compensation formula, then the quarterly overhead contribution (50 percent) and the quarterly physician benefit component (8.5 percent) of the lowest full-time physician-shareholder shall be calculated. These two amounts shall be divided by three (3) to get a monthly amount. The senior physician shall be paid a salary equal to his or her net production minus the overhead contribution amount and minus the physician benefit amount attributable to the lowest full-time physician-shareholder. The senior physician's salary shall be calculated each month, but the same contribution amounts for a quarter shall be used and then the contribution amounts will be recalculated for the next quarter. In order to provide adequate time for preparation of the data, the senior physician's monthly salary amount will be based on the previous month's net production. Any overage or underage of salary paid shall be recouped from the next month's salary and/or any salary continuation paid upon retirement.
- In the event that a senior physician is changed to a monthly salary calculation as previously defined, if the executive committee approves, a fixed monthly salary can be negotiated that allows the physician to maintain a level minimum income, thus allowing the option to take an extended period of time off. If this is approved, the monthly calculation shall be computed as previously noted, but the physician shall be paid at the agreed-upon level. The physician will be allowed to be overdrawn against the monthly calculation for up to three (3) months of the agreed-upon salary. In the event a physician terminates while in a deficit situation as a result of overdrawing the salary, then the deficit shall be recouped against his or her salary continuation agreement as outlined in his or her Employment Agreement.
- The senior physician's final check shall be on the 15th of the month following his or her retirement, for production during the previous month. If the final calculation results in a shortage, then salary continuation or any expense account overage shall be adjusted to recapture the shortage.

- It is the executive committee's responsibility to monitor the senior physician's production and overhead contribution and advise the board of directors if his or her production is inadequate to continue as senior physician.
- The senior physician continues to be subject to his or her Employment Agreement, the Stock Transfer Agreement, and all other corporate documents. The senior physician, if he or she remains a shareholder during that period, shall participate in any personal guarantees or indemnifications required of other physician-shareholders.

Notification Letters to Patients

Sample Letter 1: Physician Retirement

[DATE]

Dear Patient,

This letter is to inform you that after practicing as a(n) __________ [SPECIALTY] for [X] years, I have made the decision to retire effective [RETIREMENT DATE].

I would like to express my gratitude to you for the trust and confidence you have placed in me as a physician. It has been a true privilege to provide care for you. I also sincerely appreciate your referrals of friends and family members over the years.

Your care will continue uninterrupted by my fellow physicians at the Practice. These very capable physicians will have your records and will be able to continue your treatment uninterrupted.

Thank you for trusting me to help you with your healthcare needs.

Sincerely,
__________, MD

Sample Letter 2: Physician Relocation

[DATE]

Dear Patient,

To begin, I would like to thank you for the trust you have given me over the years as your physician. Taking care of you and your family has been an honor for my staff and for me. Your wellness and health are priorities for us. I'm writing today to inform you that I am leaving __________ [PRACTICE NAME] effective __________ [DATE].

If you would like to follow me to my new location, __________[NEW PRACTICE NAME], please complete a medical release form. The staff will forward your records to me at my new location prior to your appointment.

If you would like to continue as a patient at __________ [PRACTICE NAME], I would ask that you schedule an appointment with either Dr. __________ or Dr. __________.

Please call and talk with us about any of your concerns. Thank you again for allowing me to serve as your physician.

Sincerely,
__________, MD

Sample Letter 3: Physician Relocation

[DATE]

Dear Patient:

To begin, I would like to thank you for the trust you have given me as your ______________ [SPECIALTY]. Taking care of you has truly been an honor for me. Your wellness and health have always been and will continue to be a priority for my staff and for me. Regrettably, I'm writing today to inform you that I have decided to take another practice opportunity, and as such, I am relocating my practice as of __________ [DATE]. I will be relocating to __________ [NEW PRACTICE NAME].

While this transition is ongoing, I can be reached at __________ [CONTACT NUMBER]. After __________ [DATE], you may reach me at my new office number, __________ [CONTACT NUMBER]. I am happy to speak with you at any time if you should have questions about your care, medical records, or any other healthcare matter where I can assist you.

Your medical records will continue to be housed in the practice of my former colleague, __________, MD. If you should desire to transfer your records to another physician, you can simply call the office at __________ [CONTACT NUMBER], and the staff will be happy to assist you.

To assist you in this transition, I have sought out several local physicians who are available to continue your care. Their names are listed below, as well as a national resource for __________ [SPECIALTY].

- [enter practice name]
  [enter practice address]
  [enter phone number]
- [enter practice name]
  [enter practice address]
  [enter phone number]
- [enter practice name]
  [enter practice address]
  [enter phone number]
- American Society of [enter specialty]
  [enter address]
  [enter phone number]

Thank you again for allowing me to serve as your __________ [SPECIALTY]. I will miss my many patients and friends, and wish you all the best.

Sincerely,
__________, MD

Sample Letter 4: Practice Notification of Physician Relocation

[DATE]

Dear Patient:

__________ [PHYSICIAN NAME], MD, will be leaving __________ [PRACTICE NAME] as of __________ [DATE]. He will be reestablishing his private __________ [SPECIALTY] practice as of __________ [DATE]. If your specialist at __________ [PRACTICE NAME] is Dr. __________ [PHYSICIAN NAME], you have the choice of remaining with Dr. __________ [PHYSICIAN NAME], or you may change to another specialist within __________ [PRACTICE NAME].

If you choose to remain a patient of Dr. __________ [PHYSICIAN NAME], you will need to sign a release for your medical records. A records release form is enclosed for your convenience. Please return the release to our office as soon as possible so that we may transfer your records without delay.

Dr. __________ [PHYSICIAN NAME]'s phone number will be __________ [CONTACT NUMBER], and his address will be __________ [CONTACT ADDRESS].

Sincerely,
__________, MD

Sample Letter 5: Physician Relocation

[DATE]

Dear Patient,

I am writing to tell you of a difficult decision that I have made. I have decided to move to __________ [NEW LOCATION NAME] and begin practicing at __________ [PRACTICE NAME] starting __________ [DATE].

I have decided to make this move after careful consideration. I spent many years obtaining special training in __________ [SPECIALTY]. I need to be in a larger community where I can better put these skills to use to help more people.

I look forward to this new challenge, but it is difficult to leave the patients that I have worked with over the last few years.

My partners at __________ [PRACTICE NAME] are ready to care for my patients until another physician is hired to take over my practice. __________ [PRACTICE NAME] is actively looking for a physician to replace me.

In the meantime, if you need care, please call my nurse __________ [NURSE NAME] at __________ [CONTACT NUMBER] and you will be scheduled with one of the other providers at __________ [PRACTICE NAME]. Your medications can be refilled by calling your pharmacy.

If you prefer to see me at __________ [NEW PRACTICE NAME], I encourage you to make those arrangements on your own. Copies of your medical records will be provided to you as necessary.

I am very sorry for any inconvenience to you. The office will do all they can to make the adjustment as smooth as possible.

Sincerely,
__________, MD

Sample Letter 6: Referring Physicians

[DATE]

[REFERRING PHYSICIAN]
[ADDRESS]
[CITY], [STATE] [ZIP]

Dear Dr. ________________,

This letter is to inform you that after practicing as a(n) _________ [SPECIALTY] for [X] years, I have made the decision to retire effective _________ [DATE].

I would like to express my gratitude to you for the trust and confidence you have placed in me. It has been a true privilege to be your colleague and care for your patients; I sincerely appreciate your referrals to my practice.

Your patient's care will continue uninterrupted by my associates at the Practice. These very capable physicians will have your patient's records and will be able to maintain treatment.

Thank you for entrusting the care of your patients to me over the last [X] years. I wish the best to you and your families.

Sincerely,
_________, MD

Policy 2.16 Professional Development/Education Policy

The board will annually approve a professional development plan and budget that meets the Practice's mission of providing the highest level of patient care.

Procedure

1. Each year at budget time, the medical director and administrator will recommend a professional development budget based on input from department chairs and will include allowances for attendance at professional meetings.
2. Each physician will submit professional development requests to department chairs for individual approval.
3. Following the professional development program, the physician will complete reimbursement forms available from HR and have them signed by the department chair and will complete all travel/expense requirements.
4. The department chair and medical director shall review all professional development requests to ensure that adequate staffing is available at all times.

Responsibility

The medical director, administrator, department chairs, and HR office shall take necessary actions to ensure compliance with this policy.

Away Time

A maximum of eighteen (18) days away per calendar year shall be provided for participant travel and nonparticipant leave.

1. **Type/Description**
   a. **Professional Business Obligation:** required as part of a contract or affiliation, or the Practice work requirement. Professional Business Obligation is that which is required by a contract, affiliation, or the Practice work assignment (e.g., a research or educational project for which the physician is receiving salary support), which includes meetings of study participants.
      - Source of travel reimbursement: sponsoring organization/program
      - Away-time limit does not apply.
      - Examples: research grant–related travel; lectures/committee work; required internal training

   b. **Participant:** activities in support of other organizations or medical profession(s). A participant is an attendee who is the primary author of a scientific paper or other scientific presentation (exhibits or invited discussants), invited and published panelist, moderator, officer, or professional society officer.
      - Source of travel reimbursement: the Practice or sponsoring organization
      - Away-time limit applies.
      - Examples: professional society meeting as presenter or officer; examiner for board examinations; site visitor for review committee or granting agencies

   c. **Nonparticipant:** personal professional development time. A nonparticipant is an attendee at a scientific meeting who does not meet the participant criteria. Reimbursement for nonparticipants is limited to an annual maximum as set forth in the Professional Development Allowance (PDA).
      - Source of travel reimbursement: professional development allowance
      - Away-time limit applies.
      - Examples: seminars, conferences to enhance attendee knowledge

   d. Types of travel for consideration:
      - The Practice travel supported by salary;
      - Research grant-related travel;
      - Committee work and lectures; and
      - Legal defense of the Practice cases.

2. **Staff Eligibility**
   a. Full-time physicians are eligible for full travel benefits. Regular part-time physicians are eligible for prorated travel benefits. A regular part-time physician is one who works at least 75 percent of the time or a minimum of thirty (30) hours per week. Part-time physicians working less than 75 percent of the time are eligible for prorated travel benefits.

b. Eligibility for participants' benefits shall be limited to one (1) author per publication, unless the presenter is in training, in which case a senior professional staff member may accompany him or her.
c. Saturdays, Sundays, and institutional holidays are not counted in the eighteen (18) travel-day allowance, provided reimbursement is not requested for these days, and provided the physician is not scheduled to work or required to be on call during the time away.
d. Travel time is calculated on the basis of air travel and included in the total meeting-time allotment. Travel time in excess of that required for air transportation will be charged against vacation time.
e. Request for professional travel and professional development time for chairs and medical directors must be approved by the chair of the board of directors. The chair/medical director or his or her designee is responsible for determining the appropriateness of each request and adherence to this policy.

Guidelines for Professional Time Exceeding the Eighteen (18) Away-Days Maximum

Periodically, physicians will require exceptional time to support national organizations or a medical profession(s) that, in combination with other obligations/opportunities, may require more than eighteen (18) away days. The affected physicians should prioritize their time, identify professional obligations and commitments, and develop an Education/Away Time Plan to manage within the eighteen (18) away-days allowance. Physicians are required to prepare a plan for professional time away for the entire year. This plan for the entire year should be reviewed and approved by the chair/medical director prior to its start.

Upon review of the Education/Away Time Plan, only the following honors may be considered for exception to the eighteen (18) away-days maximum:

- Appointment as professional/specialty society officer;
- Appointment to granting agency review boards and study sections;
- Appointment as board examiner;
- Appointment as site visitor or committee membership for residency review committees; and
- Appointment to national accreditation committee for voluntary certification.

Procedure

1. Chair/medical director or designees will be responsible for monitoring and approving all educational travel. Deviations beyond the eighteen (18) away days must be based on a prospective annual travel plan reviewed and approved by the chair/medical director. Deviations for chair/medical director must be approved by the chair of the board of the governors.
2. The absence of the physician beyond the eighteen (18) days must not seriously impair professional care of patients or require the employment or replacement of personnel.

Appropriate Meetings and Guidelines (Participant/Nonparticipant Travel)

1. Professional, medical, and scientific meetings that provide a forum for the presentation and discussion of scientific information that will enhance the professional growth of the individual are considered appropriate meetings for either participant or nonparticipant travel. It is the responsibility of the department chair/medical director to decide as to the appropriateness of any given request, and it is the responsibility of the applicant to provide adequate documentation of the education/scientific merit of a requested meeting.
2. A trip for the purpose of taking a specialty board exam is considered appropriate time away for either nonparticipant travel or vacation benefit.
3. Panelists, moderators, or discussants listed in an official program of a society are also eligible for participant benefits. The case of an invited discussant of a scientific paper whose name has not been listed on the formal program shall be reimbursed at the chair/medical director's discretion. It is expected that the chair/medical director's action will be based on proof that the discussion has exceptional merit.
4. Eligibility for officership in a national professional society shall be limited to no more than three (3) major societies for each specialty and subspecialty and include the following offices: president, president-elect, immediate-past president, vice president, secretary, treasurer, board of directors, or board of trustees.
5. Scientific exhibits and movies shall be shown during a period not to exceed twelve (12) consecutive months at national and regional society meetings.

   To be eligible for meeting funds, each scientific commitment and official position must be listed in the official printed program of the society meetings or, in lieu of a printed program, be documented in an official letter of invitation.

Reimbursement Process for Professional Development Travel

1. A request for professional travel shall be submitted to the chair/medical director for approval as far in advance as possible (minimum of two (2) weeks prior to the event).
2. Original receipts shall be required for all expenditures and shall be submitted with an itemized record of expenses upon completion of travel.
3. Reimbursement of travel expenses by medical societies, grant funds, or other sources shall be considered the first source of payment for travel expenses incurred. Expenses covered by other sources are ineligible for reimbursement by the Practice.
4. Completed professional travel forms, original receipts, and itemized record of expenses should be submitted to the Practice administration within thirty (30) days after the approved trip.

Travel Costs and Expense Limits

Subject to the previously outlined conditions, travel costs for all categories of education/away time (including nonparticipant and PDA expense) shall be reimbursed based on receipts and itemized records in accordance with the following limitations and classifications:

1. Travelers should use the lowest possible airfare available, taking advantage of any and all discounts offered by the airlines. Airfare reimbursement shall not exceed coach-class rates;

2. Automobile mileage will be compensated at a rate established by the IRS not to exceed the cost of coach airfare to the destination;
3. Lodging will be reimbursed at corporate discounted rates. Reimbursement for lodging expenses substantially greater than discounted rates will be subject to HR committee approval;
4. Conference registration fees will be covered;
5. Transportation costs from destination hotels to airports shall be reimbursed, as shall airport parking fees where commercial transportation is not used. Mileage to or from the airport and to or from home is reimbursable;
6. A per diem stipend to be annually determined by the HR committee shall be provided for meals. The physician is not responsible for maintaining reimbursement records for transportation and other approved expenses for IRS purposes; and
7. Reimbursement for rental-car-related expenses must be approved in advance by the chair/medical director. Approval should be granted only when the accomplishment of the travel purpose would require frequent long-distance travel (greater than twenty (20) miles) on a nonscheduled basis.

Foreign Travel

1. Reimbursement for coach airfare shall be at the lowest available (discounted) round-trip rate to the city in which the meeting is being held regardless of actual travel arrangements. Any expense above the lowest available rate is the personal responsibility of the traveler.
2. Reimbursement for other expenses associated with the meeting shall be based on the same guidelines and limitations as for other participant travel.
3. Reimbursement for foreign travel shall be at the U.S. exchange rate. The U.S. exchange rate should be recorded on the professional travel form prior to submitting it to the Practice's travel office.

Professional Development Allowance

1. For each calendar year, the HR committee shall establish, with the operations council's approval, a Professional Development Allowance (PDA) for each staff category. Such allowance shall be prorated based on the physician's full-time equivalent (FTE) level as of January 1st of each year. Unused allotment of a PDA may be carried over to the subsequent year and cannot exceed more than one (1) year's accumulation.
2. Each eligible physician may request reimbursement in any year for the following types of expenses to his or her PDA:
   a. Nonparticipant travel costs;
   b. Professional society dues for societies or organizations relating to the physician's specialty, including the physician's balance for the American Medical Association county and state annual membership dues; and
   c. Books, periodicals, videotapes, seminar materials or tuition, and other similar materials relating to the continuing education or other professional development of the eligible physician in his or her professional specialty. Books, periodicals, videotapes, audiotapes, etc., shall become the property of the Practice. Upon termination/retirement of the physician, any materials retained may be subject to taxable income as defined by the IRS.

3. Reimbursable continuing education or professional development expenses are those that assist the eligible physician in maintaining or improving his or her professional skills or meet the requirements of (1) the Practice for continued employment, (2) a professional specialty or society for membership, or (3) any law or regulation governing the eligible physician's area of practice.
4. The requesting physician should submit a reimbursement request for nontravel expenses for continuing education or professional development materials to the Practice administration. Approval by the chair/medical director is not required if the item is on the approved eligibility list.

CHAPTER 3

Compensation

Compensation Philosophy

Compensation is central to collegiality in medical groups, but not necessarily in the way most people think. The level of earnings is important to physicians, but the level of earnings relative to all others in the group is even more important. Physician compensation policies are about fairness more than about pure compensation. They point to the values of the group in a very tangible way, sometimes serving as the glue that holds a group together, and at other times as the dynamite that threatens to blow it apart.

Basic Considerations

Physician compensation policies take many forms. They might appear as a clause in a physician employment contract, as a separate written policy, as minutes from a board meeting, or in a nonverbal spreadsheet with formulas for distributing revenues and expenses. The form is less important to organizational culture than the impact the policy has on individual physician performance and on the group's collegiality. Physician compensation policies lay the foundations for physician recruitment and retention. They need to reflect the market realities for the specialty, and they need to provide a framework for physicians to meet their needs and expectations for personal and corporate financial sustainability. Policies need to outline the connections between physician productivity and financial rewards. They need to reflect the values of the organization, respect the values of individual physicians, and discern the boundaries of acceptable performance that reduce the risk of either party taking advantage of the other. When those boundaries are breached, the policies should provide guidance about how the relationship can be rebalanced and restored.

Designing compensation policies that reflect the market should begin with understanding market benchmarks. MGMA Physician Compensation and Production Surveys offer industry-leading data to outline the correlation between work and reward. Policymakers should craft formulas and rules of engagement that correspond with the market data found in the surveys. Likewise, changing physician compensation policies should involve a heavy dose of market research and discernment about the dynamics within each specialty. Rarely does one formula fit all equally well. The market data points to the unique qualities of each specialty, but managers need to temper their findings with organizational qualities and strategic intentions in tailoring physician compensation policies to achieve the common good.

Organizational culture is shaped by physician compensation policies, and vice versa, perhaps more than any other type of policy. Most policies can be viewed on a continuum ranging from highly group-focused to highly individualized. A physician client once described the range as "from Marx to Machiavelli." When compensation is negotiated to be relatively equal among peers with minimal opportunity for productivity bonuses, the impact might be high on collegiality but low in profitability. The mantra might be reminiscent of the Three Musketeers: "One for all, all for one."

On the other end of the spectrum is the "eat what you kill" approach, prided by many in physician-owned medical group settings. This phrase seems grossly incongruent with the world of compassionate physicians. If a reference must be made to eating at all, something like "eat what you treat" might be the preferred choice, but the concept is clear. Physicians should be rewarded for their personal efforts, particularly in a fee-for-service reimbursement environment dominated by insurers who reimburse physicians based on the volume and intensity of services performed.

Physician compensation policies should reflect the reimbursement environment so individual performance within the organization is rewarded the same way the organization is rewarded by third-party payers. Groups with productivity-focused compensation policies that balance managed care contracts with indemnity insurance agreements sometimes face a schizophrenic dilemma. They need to reward physicians for volume and intensity with traditional fee-for-service patients, and reward them for opposing behaviors with patients covered by capitation plans. Organizations with a relatively equal balance of both reimbursement structures may find it easier to opt for a Three Musketeers plan rather than a highly productivity-driven compensation policy. If bundled payments emerge as a dominant form of physician reimbursement, more organizations may lean away from productivity-based compensation systems to simplify the schizophrenic dilemma that will come with it.

Purpose

Compensation policies have a few key functions. They need to correlate physician performance with physician compensation. They need to govern how revenues and expenses get distributed fairly while keeping the organization solvent, and they need to manage the differences that will inevitably arise between physicians in issues involving money.

Correlating physician performance with compensation has never been easy. Mathematical formulas are used to make it appear easy, but performance is shaped by several nonlinear qualities. For example, some physicians correlate the quality of care with the amount of time spent with each patient. They may argue that their productivity might be lower because their quality is superior. Of course, their colleagues who run fuller schedules will argue that quality has nothing to do with time and that the low producer should have fewer excuses and more patients.

In other settings, physicians with teaching or research responsibilities may make the case that they are contributing in intangible ways to the reputation of the group, drawing patients and professional accolades that attribute to the common good. Their detractors might argue that teaching and research don't pay like direct patient care, so the rewards should also be diminished accordingly. Physician compensation policies have the unenviable task of balancing such arguments while building and nurturing physician collegiality. When policymakers are successful, medical groups grow. When they are not, groups suffer, but in both cases, the policy-construction process shines valuable light on organizational culture and points the way toward solidarity and functionality.

Governing how revenues and expenses get distributed is implied in physician compensation policies even when the formula doesn't reference revenues and expenses directly. Some policies are very direct. Revenues are allocated on the basis of direct payments received for work performed individually. Overhead expenses might be allocated by the square footage used by each division within a large organization, by the percentage of visit volume or work relative value units (RVUs) of each physician, or some other formula, or a combination of methods. In my experience, the lower the trust level between physicians in a group, the greater the complexity of allocating revenues and expenses. Distrust builds high fences. In some groups, the fences are almost electrified. Ironically, after all the minute dissections of revenues and expenses are completed, the net result of the difference in compensation between partners is often relatively minor.

Physician compensation policies based more on group effort than individual effort still need to find a balance between revenues and expenses, even if the terms are not integrated into the language of the policy. Hospitals and integrated delivery systems might develop compensation structures based on the "enterprise value" of physician practices, subsidizing individual physicians indirectly for their referrals to ancillaries, acute care services, and post-acute services under the control of the larger system. The math that goes into the subsidization may be hidden from view, but it can still play a role in compensation decisions. The synergy may be difficult to quantify, but sustainable enterprises need to keep the actual cash revenues moving in properly balanced directions.

Physician compensation policies also need to offer ways to **manage differences that will inevitably arise between physicians**. The most effective policies are built with consensus. Modifications also require consensus. No physician compensation policy can last forever. These policies require changes to adapt to different reimbursement structures, corporate strategies, and sometimes also to the unique dynamics within a group. For example, a compensation structure that requires full-time engagement of all physicians might need alterations when one of the key members experiences a disability or goes on maternity leave. Many groups are developing policies to engage part-time physicians in environments that require full-time commitment to capital investments and infrastructure. Policies may be silent on every potential possibility, but a structure should be in place to address circumstances that fall outside the policies. In small physician-owned groups, a board meeting might need to be devoted to dealing with a particular variation to the policy. In larger groups and hospital-owned practices, a committee might be appointed to manage requests for policy changes or exceptions.

In any case, physician compensation policies should offer both rigidity to ensure fairness and flexibility to manage exceptions. Both qualities work together to foster a healthy organizational culture.

Components

Physician compensation policies will need to address the following issues at a minimum:

1. How base compensation is determined;
2. How productivity is measured, if it is used as an incentive;
3. How call coverage will be shared; and
4. Other expectations that come with being part of the group.

They may also address how to appeal for an exception to the compensation policy, scheduling expectations, or the mechanics of payroll processing and benefits-related policies, which are explored more thoroughly in Chapter 2: Benefits. Some groups use midlevel practitioners assigned directly to physicians. In those cases, the compensation policies may also address how the productivity, expenses, and compensation of the assigned midlevel practitioner impact the compensation of the physician.

Conclusion

Sound physician compensation policies are an integral part of a healthy medical practice. They are a key part of the glue that holds a group together. Physicians will align their personal behavior with the way they are rewarded. If the compensation policy rewards individual efforts more than citizenship in the group, the organization may function as a collection of silos rather than a collaborative group. If equality reigns supreme, personal productivity and the group's financial stability may pale. Between the two poles are an infinite number of possibilities, limited only by the imagination of policymakers and the managers who support them.

Policy 3.1

Compensation Policy[1]

The board shall be guided on matters of compensation by information provided in the bylaws and the Physician Employment Agreement and by the recommendations of the compensation committee.

The board shall develop a compensation formula to cover such factors as: income generated by physicians; payer contract reimbursement formulas; physician-related expenses and "overhead" expenses, including contingency expenses and reserve needs; and service hours, including on-call expectations. The physician's stipend (draw) will be negotiated annually with 70 percent fixed and 30 percent variable.

Variable incentives include several nonpatient care factors, such as marketing/public speaking, citizenship/community relations, publications, participation in task forces and on committees, special recognition, and on the results of a 360-degree performance evaluation based on feedback from diverse "customers" (e.g., self, department chair, medical director, administrator, peers, team, staff, patients). Patient care documentation deficiencies, tardiness for appointments, inappropriate employee overtime, over- or inappropriate utilization of resources, team dissatisfaction, and patient complaints will reflect negatively on compensation.

The board shall reserve the right to review and revise the compensation system on at least an annual basis to ensure that it meets the Practice's current needs.

Responsibility

The medical director and the compensation committee shall assume responsibility for ensuring that the compensation system is fair, equitable, and contemporary.

Goals of Physician Compensation

1. Attract and retain excellent physicians at the Practice in all specialties offered by the Practice.
2. Provide compensation that will be competitive with national trends in the respective specialty.
3. Determine a compensation calculation method that will promote and reward physician work that improves the financial and clinical success of the Practice.
4. Establish a compensation system that supports the transition to capitated managed care.
5. Promote physician cooperation within departments.
6. Ensure a total physician payroll cost that will allow the Practice to remain a financially successful and growing business to the benefit of its owners and employees.

1 Printed in *HR Policies and Procedures Manual for Medical Practices, 4th Edition,* by Courtney Price, PhD, and Alys Novak, MBA (Englewood, CO: Medical Group Management Association, 2007).

Pay Computation

The policy of the Practice is to provide equitable compensation for each physician based on the position description, individual performance, and the Practice's pay computation plan.

Procedure

1. The pay computation policy provides the basis for determining individual salary levels.
2. A pay computation plan ensures pay equity for physicians.
3. Pay grades and salary ranges that are affordable, comparable to, or better than similar jobs within the local healthcare region and the industry are established for each position.
4. Within each pay grade, minimum, midpoint, maximum, and intermediate steps are established.
5. A physician's salary rate is always set within the pay grade assigned to a position.
6. The department manager determines the initial hiring rate and step, with approval of the division manager, the human resources (HR) department, and the finance director.
7. A performance- and/or longevity-related spread is established for a physician's pay rate throughout the pay grade.
8. The Practice maintains open communication with physicians regarding its compensation policy and emphasizes how its compensation plan compares to industry-wide norms, using physician compensation surveys like those provided by MGMA.
9. The Practice is responsible for developing and maintaining compensation guidelines and pay commutation in conjunction with the Practice's administration. It is responsible for communicating the compensation policy to physicians through appropriate channels and explaining the pay computation plan.
10. Wage and salary surveys are used when considering salary adjustments. The compensation salary review committee reviews the medical Practice's salary structure at least annually.
11. Physicians are paid on the 15th day and the last day of each month. If the regular payday occurs on a Saturday, Sunday, or holiday, physicians are paid on the last working day immediately preceding the regular payday. Physicians are offered the option of having their pay deposited directly into their designated bank accounts.
12. On each payday, physicians receive a statement showing gross pay, deductions, and net pay after deductions. City, state, federal, and Social Security (FICA) taxes and physician contributions to the group's benefit plans, as well as any physician-incurred expenses, such as parking or cafeteria charges, or donations to a charitable organization, such as United Way, are automatically deducted and shown on the pay statement. Also shown is any additional compensation for expenses, such as mileage. The statement also shows the amount of leave time taken and remaining.

Sample: Physician Compensation Formula

1. The compensation pool for the Practice physicians will be equal to all collections for professional services minus all direct and indirect expenses.
2. Once the compensation pool is determined, it will be divided into a fixed component equal to 30 percent of the total compensation pool and a production component equal to 70 percent of the total compensation pool.
3. Each physician will receive a share of the fixed compensation pool based on the physician's work schedule. Each week will include ten (10) "work blocks." A work block is defined as one half day of scheduled Practice site-appointment time or operating-room time. A physician receives one (1) point for every scheduled work block per week and one point for being in the call rotation. The total number of points for each physician is divided by the total number of Practice points to arrive at the percentage of the fixed compensation pool that each physician receives. For example, if there are ten (10) physicians and each physician works ten (10) work blocks per week and participates in the call schedule, each physician will receive 10 percent of the total fixed compensation pool. (Eleven (11) individual points / 110 total points = 10 percent)
4. Each physician will receive a share of the production compensation pool based on the individual physician's percentage of gross collections. For example, if a physician's collections are equal to 12 percent of the total Practice collections, that physician will receive 12 percent of the production compensation pool.
5. Calculations of compensation by the previous formula will be performed on a monthly basis using collections for the most recent twelve- (12-) month period to determine each physician's percentage of collections.
6. The total compensation for a physician is the sum of his or her portion of the fixed compensation pool and production compensation pool. The costs of fringe benefits such as health, dental, and life insurance, and 401K match equal approximately 15 percent of a physician's compensation but are NOT included in the compensation calculation. Instead, it is assumed that the benefit costs are equal for all physicians; thus the costs of fringe benefits are included as direct expenses.

Productivity Bonus

For the fiscal year beginning [MONTH] [DAY], [YEAR], and each fiscal year thereafter, it is expected that the physician will achieve a minimum of __________ RVUs, and this figure is the "Threshold Level" of RVUs for a fiscal year. A "fiscal year" shall be a year commencing [MONTH] and ending the following [MONTH]. The "Target Level" of RVUs for each fiscal year will be __________. The physician will be eligible to earn a productivity bonus up to a maximum of $__________ based on the achievement of the following Target Level of RVUs for the fiscal year:

Total Annual RVUs	Amount of Productivity Bonus
Threshold Level = __________	$0
Target Level = __________	$__________ (maximum productivity bonus)

If the physician achieves the Target Level of RVUs for the fiscal year, the physician will be entitled to the maximum productivity bonus. If the physician does not achieve the Target Level of RVUs but exceeds the Threshold Level of RVUs, the maximum productivity bonus will be prorated based on the percentage achievement of the Target Level as compared to the Threshold Level, and the prorated amount will be the physician's productivity bonus for the fiscal year. Any productivity bonus earned will be paid quarterly on a tentative basis less a 20 percent withhold for annual year-end adjustment and reconciliation ("Annual Reconciliation"), and the Practice will use its best efforts to make the quarterly payments within thirty (30) days of the end of each quarter. The Annual Reconciliation will occur, and any additional payment due to the physician for the fiscal year will be paid, within ninety (90) days of the end of the fiscal year.

Sample: Physician Compensation Methodology Plan

Encounters and Satisfaction Survey Results

- The Plan is designed to reward and attract highly productive physicians.
- The Plan will strive to reward physicians with compensation that is market competitive.
- This Physician Compensation Methodology (PCM) incorporates a number of factors.
- The Plan is designed to reward physicians based on individual productivity, as measured by encounters.
- The Plan considers patient satisfaction and rewards physicians for achieving satisfaction scoring.
- The PCM is benchmarked against the national survey data as reported by MGMA. MGMA benchmarks are reported annually in the fall and will be adopted on the next fall following January 1 for the PCM.
- PCM factors follow these points:
  - Factor One — Base Compensation: The annually reported median compensation (adjusted for FTE) for physicians, by specialty, will be set as a "blended rate," which for the calendar year is set, as an example only, at $211,197— determined by adding the median reported compensation for three benchmarks (see the following). As an example, should physicians in a particular specialty have survey results reported nationally, which are divided by three (3) and multiplied by 33 percent:
    - National Benchmark $205,385
    - Western U.S. Benchmark $224,082
    - Hospital-Employed Benchmark $204,124
    - Total $633,591
    - Divide by three (3) $211,197
    - Multiply by 33 percent $69,695
  - Factor Two — Encounters: A dollar amount for each encounter will be set annually and multiplied by the total number of encounters by the physician.
    - For 2011, the amount for each encounter between 8 a.m. and 6 p.m. will be thirty-two dollars ($32).
    - For 2011, the amount for each encounter between 6 p.m. and 8 a.m. will be forty dollars ($40).
  - Factor Three — Patient Satisfaction: Satisfaction survey results will be categorized within four (4) percentile rank categories:
    - Percentile Rank 65–70
    - Percentile Rank 71–80
    - Percentile Rank 81–89
    - Percentile Rank 90+
    - The annual dollar amount payable to each physician (adjusted for FTE) within each of the previous percentile rankings will be:

65–70	$5,500
71–80	$8,000
81–89	$10,500
90+	$13,000

Sample continues next page

Sample: Physician Compensation Methodology Plan (continued)

Physicians scoring below 65 receive no satisfaction factor amount.

- Physicians will be entitled to a monthly "draw" against the actual PCM result of not less than $__________ — adjusted for FTE — and an annual minimum guaranteed salary of two hundred eleven thousand one hundred ninety-seven dollars ($211,197) — adjusted for FTE.
- If there is a positive result at the end of any calendar quarter, that amount will be paid equally over the next three (3) months as an increase in the "draw"; or the physician may elect to take all or a portion of the result as a lump-sum payment.
- The compensation for each physician will be periodically evaluated to verify that it is reasonable.

As an example, the following is provided:

Factor One — Base ($211,197 × 33 percent)	$69,695
Factor Two — 4,250 encounters (8 a.m.–6 p.m.) × $32	$136,000
250 encounters (6 p.m.–8 a.m.) × 40	$10,000
Factor Three — Satisfaction Percentile: 78	$8,000
Total Annual Compensation Result	$223,695
Base "Draw"	$212,000
Settlement Amount	$11,695
Estimated per Quarter	$3,898

Professional Collections

- The Plan is designed to reward and attract highly productive physicians.
- Physician compensation is composed of three (3) distinct categories:
  - Base salary;
  - Professional collections for personally performed services; and
  - Patient satisfaction.
- Base salary will be set on an annual basis considering the physician's total contributions to the organization and recognizing his or her historic work effort. This base salary will constitute approximately 60 percent of his or her maximum total attainable compensation.
- Approximately 40 percent of total attainable compensation will be calculated utilizing professional collections to the extent that they exceed the median professional collections for each specialty:
  - Base salary will be set by the organization annually.
  - For the Incentive Portion, physicians will be paid on set percentages of net professional collections when those collections exceed the nationally reported median, with a set conversion factor times the number of dollars collected between the median and the 75th percentile; a higher conversion factor for dollars collected between the 75th and 90th percentiles; and a higher conversion factor for collections above the 90th percentile; utilizing the national benchmarks for professional collections reported by specialty by MGMA.
  - Each collected dollar that exceeds the median will be multiplied by a dollar value conversion factor for each specialty.

Sample continues next page

Sample: Physician Compensation Methodology Plan (continued)

- Professional collections are defined as professional charges less write-offs for nonallowed charges, discounts, and uncollectible amounts resulting from charges for those services that are personally performed by the physician (i.e., those services that the physician personally performs). The CPT[2] code ranges for these services are typically in the 10000–69999 and 90000–99999 ranges.
- MGMA benchmarks are reported annually in the fall and will be adopted on the next following January 1 for the PCM.
- The conversion factors utilized at each quartile will be set annually, based on funds available for distribution from Practice operations.
- Physicians will be entitled to a monthly "draw" set at 80 percent of the previous year's annual result.
- This PCM will be calculated every six (6) months. If there is a positive result at the end of the six- (6-) month calculation, that amount will be paid equally over the next six (6) months as an increase in the "draw," or the physician may elect to take all or a portion of the result as a lump-sum payment.
- If there is a negative result (physician has "drawn" in excess of his or her result) at the end of any calendar quarter, that amount will be reflected as a decrease in his or her monthly draw for the next six (6) months.
- Any disallowed charges, including penalties and interest, will be charged against the individual physician's collections.
- Physicians will be eligible for an additional amount, not to exceed 10 percent of the physician's base salary, based on the results from patient satisfaction surveying.
- The compensation for each physician will be periodically evaluated to verify that it is reasonable.

Time Units

- The Plan is designed to reward and attract highly productive physicians.
- Physician compensation is composed of three distinct categories:
  - Base salary;
  - Time unit production; and
  - Patient satisfaction.
- Base salary will be set on an annual basis considering the physician's total contributions to the organization and recognizing his or her historic work effort. This base salary will constitute approximately 60 percent of his or her maximum total attainable compensation.
- Base salary will be set by the organization annually.
- Approximately 40 percent of total attainable compensation will be calculated utilizing TVUs (time value units). Each CPT code has been given a value of time measure equal to the amount of time it would take an efficient physician to complete the task. This creates an equal playing field for all subspecialties and equates an hour of work regardless of where that work takes place (e.g., Practice site, hospital units, diagnostic testing). Value is also given to time spent driving to outreach or satellite Practice sites. Value is also provided to physicians starting new practices in new locations. This allows the group to grow while not disadvantaging any individual. There may be some value given to "good citizenship" activities, such as marketing the group, although this has not been completely defined

Sample continues next page

2 CPT © 2011 American Medical Association. All rights reserved.

Sample: Physician Compensation Methodology Plan (continued)

at this time. The payment mechanism of the compensation model is a four-tiered model. An initial pool of $100,000 is set aside from the annual budgeted physician monies to be split equally by all physicians in the specialty/subspecialties of __________. This provides them with an additional amount above other subspecialties in keeping with the current national market. Otherwise, 75 percent of all monies are split equally. The second tier provides everyone greater than 75 percent of the mean an equal split of an additional 10 percent of the monies. The third tier rewards all above 85 percent of the mean with an additional 10 percent, and the final tier rewards those greater than 110 percent of the mean with an equal split of 5 percent. Thus, anyone over 85 percent of the mean of the total TVUs receives an equal amount of 95 percent of the compensation pool. The TVU committee will meet quarterly to adjudicate any issues brought regarding the productivity and compensation plan.

- The "per hour unit" will be calculated considering the physician's individual productivity, with a unit value set for each CPT code, intending that there is equal value for each hour of activity, regardless of the activity. For example, one (1) hour of interpretation of diagnostic studies will equate to one (1) hour of patient appointment encounters.
- The percentage utilized at each quartile will be set annually, based on funds available for distribution from Practice operations.
- Physicians will be entitled to a monthly "draw" set at 80 percent of the previous year's annual result.
- This time unit determination will be calculated at least every six (6) months.
- The patient satisfaction reward will be completed at least once a year.
- The base salary will be viewed as a "draw" against the actual total compensation methodology result.
- Additional incentives (time unit and patient satisfaction) will be payable within thirty (30) days of the calculation of these two (2) components (as outlined previously — time unit at least every six (6) months and patient satisfaction at least annually).
- Any disallowed charges for services (CPT codes and related time unit values), including penalties and interest, will be charged against the individual physician's total.
- Finally, patient satisfaction will offer the opportunity for a physician to receive an additional amount, up to 10 percent of the physician's base salary amount based on the results of patient satisfaction surveying.
- The compensation for each physician will be periodically evaluated to verify that it is reasonable.

Reconciliation in the Event of Physician Termination without Cause or Termination by Physician

In the event that the physician's employment is terminated as stated prior to __________ [MONTH] of any fiscal year, the Target Level of RVUs and the Threshold Level of RVUs set forth previously, which are required for the physician to earn a productivity bonus, will be prorated based on the percentage of the fiscal year during which he or she was employed. A prorated year-end reconciliation will be performed within thirty (30) days of the termination date, and the physician will be entitled to any monies due. In addition, the physician will be entitled to any distributions withheld during the previous quarters, such amount to be paid within ninety (90) days of the termination date.

Sample continues next page

Sample: Physician Compensation Methodology Plan (continued)

Reconciliation in the Event of Physician Termination for Cause

In the event that the physician's employment is terminated as stated previously, the physician must be employed on the last day of the quarter to be entitled to the productivity bonus earned that quarter. Furthermore, the physician will not be entitled to a year-end reconciliation and will not receive distribution of withheld monies earned during the previous quarters (including the 20-percent withhold described previously) in the event that the physician's employment is terminated prior to the last day of the fiscal year.

Prior to payment of any productivity bonus, the physician must achieve the following quality standards.

Quality of Care Standards

1. **Patient Satisfaction**
   Patient satisfaction will be measured based on completed patient surveys that reflect the patient's or family's perception of the physician's performance. Patient surveys will be reasonably designed, administered, and scored.
2. **Chart Review**
   Medical chart review will be conducted by the Practice to determine (a) the adequacy and completeness of the physician's clinical records, (b) compliance with accreditation criteria for documentation of patient care, and (c) whether the documentation in the medical records supports the level of patient examination according to Medicare guidelines.

The average of the physician's scores for patient satisfaction and medical chart review must be greater or equal to 85 percent for the physician to be eligible to receive ANY productivity bonus.

Policy 3.2

Licensure Policy

Licensure, certification, and registration become important "prerequisites for getting onto the playing field" not only at the time of medical school completion, but also at the time of recruitment and throughout a physician's career to verify his or her "right" to continue practicing. Relicensure and recertification are ongoing requirements. If a license expires, the Practice will designate that the physician stop practicing on the premises until the license is reinstated.

For current physicians, the Practice will pay licensure fees for medical, dental, psychiatry, psychology, and various other counseling or professional licenses. The Practice will reimburse newly accepted staff members on a prorated basis for the following licensure fees: [STATE] Medical License, [STATE] Board Controlled Substance License, and Drug Enforcement Administration (DEA) Certificate. Physicians must maintain licensure while on staff and meet the necessary continuing medical education (CME) requirements as they are outlined in the delineation of privileges for their respective specialties.

The Practice will not pay late charges. Each license has a due date stamped on the front of the application.

The Practice will reimburse all examination fees and travel expenses in accordance with the guidelines and up to the limits delineated under "participant" professional travel. A professional development allowance is available to cover examination fees for required licensure/certification.

Procedure

To pay for licensure fees:

1. Physicians should submit an annual relicensure statement to Practice administration after completing the appropriate areas;
2. Practice administration will request a check and will mail the check with the application to the appropriate agency;
3. If a physician elects to submit the application and write a personal check, proof of payment must be submitted to Practice administration for reimbursement (reimbursement will exclude any late fees);
4. If the application is submitted to Practice administration after the due date indicated, a personal check for the late fees must accompany the application;
5. Request for license renewal and/or reimbursement must be made during the calendar year the license is effective; and
6. Accreditation standards require that a copy of the physician's [STATE] Board Controlled Substance License be contained within the credentials file. Upon receipt of the license, the physician should forward a copy of the license to his or her chair/medical director and Practice administration.

To obtain reimbursement for licenses obtained prior to appointment to the Practice:

1. Physician should submit copies of licenses with proof of payment to Practice administration following date of hire;
2. Practice administration will request a check and will forward the reimbursement check directly to the physician; and
3. Reimbursement will be prorated based on the date of acceptance into the Practice and the time remaining on the unexpired license(s).

To obtain approval to use professional travel and a professional development allowance for examinations and other tests:

1. The physician must submit a formal request for professional travel to the chair/medical director at least (2) two weeks prior to the expected departure date;
2. Receipts and requests for reimbursable costs must be submitted on a professional travel expense report form for approval to the chair/medical director within two (2) weeks after returning; and
3. The approved reimbursable expenses, expense report, and receipts are sent to Practice administration for processing.

Absences for Examinations/Certifications

An absence from the Practice required for examination by a recognized primary specialty board and/or subspecialty board will constitute meeting time. Also, absences for self-assessment examinations and other tests required for relicensure and recertification may be charged to meeting time.

Procedure

To obtain approval to use professional travel time and a professional development allowance for examinations and other tests:

1. A request for professional travel form must be submitted to the chair/medical director at least two (2) weeks prior to the expected departure date. Appropriate documentation should be submitted with the request;
2. The chair/medical director will return the approved/disapproved request to the physician;
3. Upon completion of the event (e.g., self-assessment examination), the physician will complete the expense report and forward the report with receipts to the chair/medical director to secure reimbursement for the use of the professional development allowance; and
4. Copies of all licenses, certifications, and/or registrations should be submitted to both the chair/medical director and staff services.

Reinstatement of Expired Licenses

In the event that a physician allows his or her medical license to expire, the medical legal affairs office will be contacted, and the physician will be asked to refrain from practicing his or her profession on the premises until the license is reinstated. Reinstatement for medical license must be requested in person at the office of the board of medicine. After reinstatement, the physician must present proof of reinstatement to the chair/medical director and Practice administration.

Policy 3.3

Board Certification and Registration Policy

Proof of licensure or certification is required at the time of employment and continually thereafter.

Procedure

1. Prior to employment, licensure/certification is verified by phone or letter to the appropriate state board. The license must be active.
2. At the time of employment, copies of the professional licensure/certification are filed in the physician's personnel folder.

3. The Practice's HR department maintains license/certification number and expiration date for all applicable employees and notifies physicians of renewal dates.
4. If a license/certificate is not renewed in a timely manner, the physician may be suspended until the license is reinstated.
5. The Practice will pay licensure fees but not late charges. To receive reimbursement, the employee should use the appropriate forms available from HR.

Responsibility

The medical director, department chairs, and HR shall take necessary actions to ensure compliance with this policy.

Policy 3.4

Medical Directorship Policy

A key role in any medical practice is that of medical director. Whether this role is held by the president/CEO in a small practice, is rotated among physicians, or is a dedicated full-time position, there must be someone to assume constant and consistent responsibility for the clinical aspects and practice of medicine matters.

The board must identify through policy how it wants to handle the role of medical director and what that position implies. Input from physicians will be critical in the development of this policy and also over time.

Position Description: Medical Director

The medical director should be a practicing physician. He or she is appointed by the board of directors for a two- (2-) year term and reports directly to the executive director and the board of directors. He or she is compensated for performing these duties with a salary determined by the board of directors. The medical director will be responsible for overseeing the design, development, and implementation of a comprehensive medical management system supporting the Practice's entrance into capitated managed care as well as all other medical care issues.

Specific responsibilities of this position include, but are not limited to, the following.

Inside the Organization

The medical director serves as chairperson of the Practice's managed care committee, a small group of physicians who will meet on a regular basis to design, develop, and implement the Practice's managed care system, including:

1. Review the actuarial analysis and provide input on evaluation of proposed capitation arrangements;

2. Advise on proposed allocation of capitation/subcapitation funds, including recommending plans for distribution of surplus earnings (savings);
3. Utilize management (referral authorizations, including referrals to specialists, elective hospital admissions, and outpatient surgery, as well as major ancillary services);
4. Profile physician practice patterns (by diagnosis, service providers, etc.);
5. Review of the financial performance reporting (actual versus expected);
6. Develop and maintain the preferred drug formulary for managed care contracts;
7. Coordinate development of screening, diagnostic, and treatment guidelines (promoting the use of "best practices," epidemiological evidence supporting clinical guidelines, and individual medical decisions);
8. Implement population health assessment and focused case management;
9. Measure outcomes and other quality data, with ultimate convergence into quality report cards; and
10. Work with the Practice's executive director to develop and recommend to the joint policy board an annual budget for managed care operating expenses.

The medical director oversees the Practice's quality assurance/improvement program, including but not limited to:

1. Conducting quality of service assessments provided by each department;
2. Assisting each department in planning and implementing quality improvement initiatives;
3. Receiving and coordinating the responses to all complaints regarding professional services; and
4. Reviewing physician credentialing:
    - Monitoring all professional liability claims and recommending action when necessary;
    - Developing and implementing educational programs relevant to managed care, medical management, outcomes management, and quality improvement for physicians and support staff;
    - Monitoring standards for medical care practices;
    - Ensuring administrative policies for medical staff; and
    - Writing criteria for physician responsibilities.

    Quality Assurance

    - Ensuring credentials evaluation of new physicians; and
    - Ensuring competency evaluation of medical staff.

    Physician Management

    - Serving as a liaison for physicians;
    - Mediating conflict among physicians; and
    - Ensuring grievance procedures for physicians.

Outside the Organization

The medical director will:

1. Promote the Practice to the community;
2. Represent the organization to other medical healthcare organizations;
3. Serve as liaison between the Practice and other physicians in the community; and
4. Serve as one of the Practice's primary medical liaisons.

Qualifications

The medical director must be a physician licensed to practice medicine in the state and must meet all other standards of a physician employed by the Practice. Several years of private practice experience is required. Previous experience as a medical director or medical manager in primary care is preferred. Previous experience in quality assurance of a hospital and/or multispecialty group practice is also preferred.

The medical director should be literate in matters of healthcare financing and managed healthcare trends and should have a vision, appreciation, and acceptance of the future of healthcare delivery.

Outstanding communication/negotiation/persuasive skills are required. The medical director should be a good listener and should be able to interact effectively with a wide variety of individuals, including physicians, allied health professionals, administrators, and support staff.

A team player, the medical director should be able to effectively gain consensus among multiple constituencies.

Reporting Relationships

The medical director is hired and serves at the pleasure of the Practice's board of directors. He or she reports to the board of directors through the president of the Practice. The medical director is supported by and works in concert with the Practice's executive director and assigned support staff.

Policy 3.5 Loan Repayment/Education Debt Forgiveness Policy

As an additional benefit to the physician, the Practice shall pay on behalf of the physician amounts incurred by the physician during his or her education/training/residency/fellowship to a maximum of $__________, provided the physician remains an employee of the Practice for a minimum of __________ years.

Such payments of outstanding loan amounts will be paid at the rate of $__________ per calendar month, beginning __________ [DATE] and ending __________ [DATE], with payments to be made to __________.

Should the physician leave the employment of the Practice on or before __________ [DATE], such amounts shall be deemed as owing to the Practice and physician will enter into a Promissory Note for payment/reimbursement of paid amounts to the Practice.

It is recognized that the physician has incurred significant indebtedness while pursuing his or her doctor of medicine degree as well as continuing his or her training as a resident/fellow in the specialty of __________.

The Practice is agreeable to the payment of such indebtedness obligation in an amount not to exceed $__________ and provided the physician remains a member of the Practice for a period of at least sixty (60) months. Should the physician leave the employment of the Practice prior to the completion of sixty (60) months of employment, the physician will repay the Practice for amounts paid on the physician's behalf based on the following schedule:

Employment Term	Amount Due to the Practice
0–12 months	100%
13–24 months	80%
25–36 months	60%
37–48 months	40%
49–60 months	20%

As a condition of employment and continuing employment, the Practice will pay on behalf of the physician dollar amounts incurred by the physician for education and training still outstanding. Such outstanding loan amounts will be paid by the Practice, and the physician shall be obligated for reimbursement/payment to the Practice for all amounts paid on his or her behalf, except outlined as follows:

- Should the physician continue as an employee for sixty (60) months or longer, NO amount will be due. All loan payments will be forgiven.
- Should the physician leave the employment of the Practice, except in the case of death or permanent disability, the physician shall be obligated to pay amounts paid on his or her behalf as outlined in the following schedule. The physician agrees to execute a promissory note that documents his or her obligation.

Physician Leaves Employment	Amount Payable to the Practice
On/before __________ [DATE]	90%
On/before __________ [DATE]	80%
On/before __________ [DATE]	70%
On/before __________ [DATE]	60%
On/before __________ [DATE]	50%

Policy 3.6

Professional Development Policy

The Practice encourages and expects its physicians to attend scientific meetings, professional conventions, post-graduate courses and seminars, and other educational meetings in their field of medicine at least within the minimum requirements for state licensure. The cost of travel, meals, lodging, tuition, and registration for attending such activities shall be paid by the Practice; however, such costs incurred by the physician in connection with such activities shall be at the sole expense of the physician and deducted as direct expenses in determining the physician's salary.

The physician shall participate in continuing medical education (CME) programs as required to maintain his or her state license to practice medicine and to remain board certified in his or her specialty. (See also Policy 2.16: Professional Development/ Education.)

Sample: CME Discretionary Budget

In addition to time off for CME, the Practice pays for costs associated with CME. Amounts are determined by provider category:

Practice	Discretionary CME Budgets
Physicians	$5,000
Allied health professionals	$3,000
Practice executive/administrator	$5,000

The Practice shall provide to all full-time physicians an allowance for professional development. Such monies are available for the payment on behalf of the physician (or reimbursement upon submission of original receipts) for costs incurred/related to professional development.

Such costs include professional meeting expenses (registration, travel, lodging, meals), subscriptions to professional publications, dues to professional societies/academies/ associations, and educational materials that relate directly to the physician's practice.

Physicians shall accrue funds for such costs at the rate of $__________ per calendar month to a maximum of $__________.

Policy 3.7

Stipends Policy

Many practices utilize a stipend as a recruiting incentive to attract new residents and fellows to their practices, often at a much lower cost than a traditional search firm.

If the Practice agrees to provide a physician in fellowship or residency with a stipend as compensation, a total of $20,000 per year will be paid in equal monthly installments of $1,666.66 on or about the first day of each month beginning with the first month during which this Agreement is executed.

In the unlikely event that the new physician does not commence employment, or in the event that this physician's Employment Agreement is terminated for any reason during the first twelve (12) months of full-time employment, any stipend amounts paid shall be returned to the Practice in full within thirty (30) days of the happening of the earlier of such events. If payment in full is not made within thirty (30) days, the Practice reserves the right to reduce the physician's compensation by the full amount of the un-repaid balance or pursue additional collection remedies, including adding interest charges of 15 percent per annum on the un-repaid balance.

Policy 3.8 Governing Board Policy

The bylaws of the Practice specify that a board of directors shall govern the Practice. The bylaws also shall designate membership and term.

The responsibilities of a board director are to:

1. Develop and remain committed to the organization's mission, vision, and values;
2. Select a chief executive officer (CEO) and, on an ongoing basis, provide support, appropriate compensation, and periodic written evaluation of the CEO's performance;
3. Understand and support and respective roles and responsibilities of the board and the CEO;
4. Review and approve organizational policies pertaining to finance, investments, human resources, delivery of services, quality of care, clinical practice guidelines, business administration, and operational management of the organization;
5. Approve the scheduling and agenda for a strategic planning session at least once every fifteen (15) months. Review, approve, and monitor all strategic plans, including new projects and services;
6. Review and approve quality improvement/management (QI/M) plans and monitor indicators of the quality of care and quality of services, including the result of QI/M studies. Such studies shall include not only clinical studies, but also administrative and cost-of-care studies;
7. Exert external influence on behalf of the organization, serving as a "diplomat" in financial, medical, and community circles;
8. Ensure that the organization fulfills all legal requirements and obligations and is compliant with the rules/regulations/statutes governing the practice of medicine in [STATE]; and
9. Promote and ensure financial viability through budgeting, financial oversight, investment management, and fund development.

A member of the governing body (a director) carries out the powers of his or her office only when acting as a voting member during a duly constituted meeting of the board on one of its appointed bodies. A director respects the responsibilities delegated by the board to the CEO and management, avoiding interference with their duties, but insisting upon accountability and reporting mechanisms for assessing actual performance. A director is ultimately accountable to the Practice and seeks to represent its best interests as a whole and not the interests of a single constituency.

Performance Standards for a Director

1. The director attends all meetings, unless absence is approved in advance. A minimum attendance at 75 percent of meetings is required to continue as a director. Mandatory attendance is required for all planning sessions.
2. The director comes to meetings prepared, asks informed questions, makes a positive contribution to discussions, and respects the opinions of others.
3. The director actively contributes a specific skill, expertise, or external influence that is needed on the board (e.g., business management, finance, medicine, or health).
4. The director respects the confidentiality of the boardroom.
5. The director supports the decisions and policies of the board in discussions outside the boardroom, even if the director voiced other views during a board discussion.
6. The director discloses to the board any potential conflict of interest and removes himself or herself from discussions where a potential conflict of interest exists, annually signing a Conflict of Interest Statement.
7. The director recognizes the role of management in carrying out board directives and is careful not to interfere with the functions delegated to management.
8. The director takes advantage of opportunities to be educated and informed about the board and the healthcare field and brings important external views to the board.
9. The director engages in the self-evaluation of the board.
10. The director acts as any reasonably prudent person would behave.

Responsibility

The board and legal counsel shall take necessary actions to ensure compliance with this policy.

Sample Board of Directors Policies

1. **Number, Election, and Tenure.** The number of Practice directors shall be five (5). Except as provided in the case of a vacancy, the directors shall be elected at the annual meeting of shareholders. Those persons who receive the highest number of votes at a meeting at which a quorum is present shall be deemed elected.

   Each director shall hold office for the term elected and until the director's successor is elected and qualified.
2. **Term.** Directors shall be elected for a two- (2-) year term; with three (3) directors elected in the even years and two (2) in the odd years. Directors may be reelected for subsequent terms.

3. **Qualifications.** All directors must be shareholders of the Practice. No more than two (2) directors serving at the same time may be practicing regularly at the same Practice site. For the purposes of these bylaws, the term "practice site" means any one of the Practice's locations in which any physician regularly schedules patient appointments.
4. **Regular Meetings.** The directors shall meet no less often than monthly. The annual meeting of the directors shall be held without other notice than this bylaw immediately after, and at the same place as, the annual meeting of shareholders. The directors may provide, by resolution, the time and place for the holding of additional regular meetings without other notice than such resolution.
5. **Special Meetings.** Special meetings of the directors may be called by, or at the request of, the president or any two (2) directors. The person or persons authorized to call special meetings of the directors may fix the place for holding any special meeting.
6. **Notice.** Notice of any special meeting shall be given at least five (5) days previously thereto by written notice to each director at the director's business address. If mailed, such notice shall be deemed delivered when deposited in the U.S. mail so addressed with postage thereon prepaid. The attendance of a director at a meeting shall constitute a waiver of notice of such meeting, except where a director attends a meeting for the express purpose of objecting to the transaction of any business because the meeting is not lawfully called or convened.
7. **Quorum.** At any meeting of the directors, three (3) directors shall constitute a quorum for the transaction of business, but if less than said number is present at a meeting, a majority of the directors present may adjourn the meeting from time to time without further notice.
8. **Manner of Acting.** The act of the majority of the directors present at a meeting at which a quorum is present shall be the act of the directors, but in no event may the board act without the affirmative vote of three (3) directors.
9. **Newly Created Directorships and Vacancies.** Newly created directorships resulting from an increase in the number of directors and vacancies occurring in the board for any reason, except the removal of directors without cause, may be filled by a vote of a majority of the directors then in office, although less than a quorum exists. Vacancies occurring by reason of the removal of directors without cause shall be filled by the vote of the shareholders. A director elected to fill a vacancy caused by resignation, death, or removal shall be elected to hold office for the unexpired term of his or her predecessor.
10. **Removal of Directors.** Any or all directors may be removed for cause by vote of the shareholders or by action of the board. Directors may be removed without cause only by vote of the shareholders.
11. **Resignation.** A director may resign at any time by giving written notice to the board, president, or secretary of the Practice. Unless otherwise specified on the notice, the resignation shall take effect upon receipt thereof by the board or such officer, and the acceptance of the resignation shall not be necessary to make it effective.
12. **Compensation.** No compensation shall be paid to directors for their services; but by resolution of the board, a fixed sum for actual expenses incurred in the role of director may be paid. Nothing herein contained shall be construed to preclude any director from serving the Practice in any other capacity and receiving compensation.

13. **Presumption of Assent.** A director of the Practice who is present at a meeting of the directors at which any action on any Practice matter is taken shall be presumed to have assented to the action taken, unless the director's dissent shall be entered in the minutes of the meeting or unless the director shall file the directors' written dissent to such action with the person acting as the secretary of the meeting before the adjournment thereof or shall forward such dissent by registered mail to the secretary of the Practice immediately after adjournment of the meeting. Such right to dissent shall not apply to a director who voted in favor of such action.
14. **Executive and Other Committees.** The board, by resolution, may designate from among its members an executive committee and other committees, each consisting of a minimum of three (3) directors. The board may also, by resolution, designate advisory committees, each consisting of one (1) or more directors and one (1) or more shareholders. Such advisory committees shall have the authority granted by the board in the resolution creating the advisory committee. Advisory committees may be granted authority over such matters as office-site physician scheduling and call coverage and other matters designated by the board. All committees shall serve at the pleasure of the board.

Shareholder's Rights

It is our historical practice to grant broad rights to our physician owners. This includes:

1. The right to attend and listen at any meeting of the governance structure outlined previously;
2. The right to view any legal document, contract, minutes, or final worksheet used to document a decision of the governance structure previously described;
3. The right to request that an item be placed on the agenda of the appropriate body for discussion; and
4. The right to appeal any decision to the president, followed by the executive committee, and ultimately to the board.

Board Officers

Board officers shall function as designated in the bylaws, as follows:

1. The president shall be elected by the governing body for a term of one (1) year, with the option of serving an additional two (2) terms. The president shall call and preside over board meetings and shall also chair the executive committee. The president shall appoint all committees and shall represent the organization;
2. The vice president shall be elected by the governing body and shall serve in the president's absence and is designated as president-elect. The vice president shall assume any responsibilities delegated by the president;
3. The secretary shall be selected by the governing body and shall be responsible for the official records and other official organization documents and for the board minutes;
4. The treasurer shall be selected by the governing body and be responsible for the organization's official financial statements. The treasurer also shall be responsible for check-signing procedures;
5. The vice president, secretary, and treasurer shall also serve on the executive committee; and
6. At a meeting of the whole, the governing body will fill vacancies in these positions.

Responsibility

The board and legal counsel shall take actions necessary to ensure compliance with this policy.

Limited Liability Practice Governance — Board of Managers

1. The management of all affairs, property, and interests of the Practice shall be vested in the board of managers ("Managers"). In addition to the powers and authorities expressly conferred upon it by this Operating Agreement ("Agreement"), the board of managers may exercise all such powers of the Practice and do all such lawful acts as are not prohibited by statute or by this Agreement or as directed or required to be exercised or done by the members ("Members"). Members may, by a vote at any meeting of the Members, rescind or modify any action taken by the Managers.
2. No individual Manager shall have the authority to sign agreements and other instruments on behalf of the Practice without approval of the board as a group as provided in this article, except pursuant to resolution of the Members, or by contract with the Practice.
3. Without prejudice to the generality of this section, and subject to the same limitations, the Managers shall have the power, and shall not delegate this power, to:
   a. Select and remove all officers and agents of the Practice;
   b. Change the principal executive office or the principal business office in the state of [STATE] from one location to another; cause the Practice to do business in any other state, territory, dependency, or country; conduct business within or without the state of [STATE]; and designate any place within or without the state of [STATE] for the holding of any Member meetings, including annual meetings except that a Member meeting outside the state of [STATE] shall require Member approval;
   c. Borrow money and incur indebtedness on behalf of the Practice and cause to be executed and delivered for the Practice's purposes, in the Practice name, promissory notes, bonds, debentures, deeds of trust, mortgages, pledges, hypothecations, and other evidences of debt and securities, all of the foregoing within the dollar limits, if any, proposed by the Managers and approved by the Members; and
   d. Prescribe rules and regulations pertaining to the practice of medicine by physicians employed by, or associated with, the Practice, with the power to amend said regulations from time to time upon notice to the Members.
4. The Managers shall be elected by the affirmative vote of the majority of the Members at the annual meeting of the Members or at a special meeting of the Members called for that purpose. A Manager shall hold office for the term for which he or she is elected and until his or her successor has been elected and qualified.

   The Managers shall be obliged to devote as much of their time to the Practice's business as shall be reasonably required in light of the Practice's business and objectives. A Manager shall perform his or her duties as a Manager in good faith, in a manner he or she reasonably believes to be in the best interests of the Practice, and with such care as an ordinarily prudent person in a like position would use under similar circumstances. A person who so performs his or her duties shall not have any liability by reason of being or having been a Manager of the Practice.

5. A Manager shall discharge the duties of a Manager, including duties as a Member of a committee:
   a. In good faith;
   b. With the care an ordinary prudent person in a like position would exercise under similar circumstances; and
   c. In a manner the Manager reasonably believes to be in the best interests of the Practice.
6. The Managers shall consist of no fewer than seven (7) persons who shall be Members of the Practice. Managers shall be elected by the Members at each annual meeting to hold office for a period of three (3) years or until their respective successors are elected and qualified. Each Manager must be a Member of the Practice and must be duly licensed in the state of [STATE] as a physician. In the event that any incumbent Manager ceases to be so licensed or associated with the Practice, or in the event that a Manager has given written notice of intent to terminate his or her membership, that person shall immediately cease to be a Manager of the Practice.
7. The number of Managers may at any time be established, increased, or decreased by a vote of the majority of the Members at any annual, special, or regular meeting; however, there shall never be fewer than seven (7) Managers, provided that no decrease in the number of Managers shall have the effect of shortening the term of any incumbent Manager.
8. The Managers shall exercise the powers and authority of the Members between meetings of the Members.
9. The election and duties of the Managers shall be governed pursuant to the following:
   a. Each Member shall serve a three- (3-) year term, being elected to office as his or her predecessor's term expires. The exception to this will be during the elections when three (3) Members will be elected to a three- (3-) year term, expiring in [YEAR]; three (3) Members will be elected for a two- (2-) year term expiring in [YEAR]; and one (1) Member will be elected to a one- (1-) year term expiring in [YEAR]. If more than seven (7) Members are serving as Managers, then their terms shall be appropriately staggered so as to cause the terms of no more than one-third of the Managers to expire each year.
   b. At the annual meeting, one (1) Member will be elected to a three- (3-) year term.
   c. At the annual meeting in [YEAR], two (2) Members will be elected to a three- (3-) year term. Thereafter, Members will be elected to the same term as the Manager whose term is then expiring.
   d. Any Member is eligible for election. No later than October 30th of each year, the chairperson will appoint a nominating committee composed of current Members, of whom not more than two (2) shall be current Managers. The nominating committee will present to the Managers at their November meeting a slate of candidates to stand for election at the next annual meeting of the Practice. No later than thirty (30) days prior to the annual meeting of the Practice, the list of candidates will be posted.
   e. Each Member at the Members meeting may cast a vote for a number of candidates equal to the number of positions open. The candidates with the largest vote totals will be declared elected. An additional secret ballot may be required if ties occur for the last position or positions.

f. A Member who will be absent from a Members meeting when an election is scheduled may deliver his or her secret election ballot to the chairperson prior to the meeting, but such ballot shall be void should he or she attend. Any Manager not present for at least 70 percent of the Managers' meetings during a calendar year will have his or her Manager position considered to be vacated at the end of such year and will be automatically replaced by election for the remainder of his or her term at the next annual meeting according to the procedures set forth in this Agreement.

g. A qualified Member should not declare his or her candidacy unless he or she is quite willing to attend all meetings and give generously of his or her time and efforts to the deliberations and activities as a Manager.

h. Meetings of the Managers shall be held at times agreed to by a two-thirds majority of the Managers.

i. Subjects to be discussed shall be set forth in a written agenda and delivered to the Manager's office at the Practice at least forty-eight (48) hours prior to a meeting. All Managers present may place additional subjects on the agenda at the time of the meeting if there is unanimous consent.

j. Any Member may attend the Managers meetings and voice his or her opinions, but only Managers shall have a vote. All Members and employed physicians are welcome and encouraged to attend at least one Managers meeting a year.

k. Minutes will be prepared and approved by the Managers, and the original copy kept on file in the executive offices of the Practice. A copy of these minutes will be sent electronically to each Member for information (except Members who have given notice of intent to terminate, unless approved by the Managers).

l. A quorum shall consist of a majority of the Managers then serving.

m. Deliberations will be decided by a majority of all of the Managers present at a meeting. Robert's Rules of Order shall prevail, except where specified to the contrary in this Agreement.

n. The Managers shall transact the Practice business between Members' meetings, except matters of extreme importance that must be referred to a meeting of the Members. The Managers shall approve physician employment contracts.

o. Every Manager is an agent of the Practice for the purpose of its business, and the act of every Manager, including the execution in the Practice name of any instrument for apparently carrying on in the usual way the business of the Practice, binds the Practice, unless such act is in contravention of the Articles of Organization or this Agreement, or unless the Manager so acting otherwise lacks the authority to act for the Practice and the person with whom he or she is dealing has knowledge of the fact that he or she has no such authority.

Removal of Managers

1. Subject to the provisions of the act and subject to the satisfaction of the conditions specified in this section and obtaining the required vote of the Members pursuant to the Agreement, the Members may remove all or any lesser number of Managers with or without cause. The vacant position shall be filled by a vote of the Members at the next regular meeting of the Members.
2. Any removal of a Manager shall become effective on such date as may be specified by the Members voting in favor thereof and in a notice delivered to any remaining

Managers or the Manager elected to replace the removed Manager (except that it cannot be effective on a date earlier than the date such notice is delivered to the remaining or newly elected Manager). Such Member will continue to participate in the Practice as a Member and receive his or her share of the Practice's income, gains, losses, deductions, and credits pursuant to this Agreement.

Resignation of Manager

A Manager may resign from his or her position as a Manager at any time by notice to the Members. Such resignation shall become effective as set forth in such notice.

Vacancies

All vacancies in the board of managers, whether caused by resignation, death, an increase in the number of Managers, or otherwise, shall be filled by the affirmative vote of a majority of the remaining Managers in office though less than a quorum of the board. The Manager so elected shall fill the unexpired term until the next Member meeting at which Managers are elected and until his or her successor is elected and qualified. Any Manager position to be filled by reason of an increase in the number of Managers may be filled by the board for a term of office continuing only until the next election of Managers by the Members and until his or her successor is elected and qualified.

Regular Meetings

Regular meetings of the board or any committee may be held without notice at the principal place of business of the Practice or at such other place or places, either within or without the state of [STATE], as the board or such committee, as the case may be, may from time to time designate. The annual meeting of the board shall be held without notice immediately after adjournment of the annual meeting of Members.

Special Meetings

1. Special meetings of the board may be called at any time by the chairperson or by any Manager to be held at the principal place of business of the Practice or at such other reasonable place or places as the board or the person or persons calling such meeting may from time to time designate. Notice of all special meetings of the board, stating the date, time, and place thereof, shall be given no less than two (2) days prior to the date of the meeting. Such notice need not specify the business to be transacted at, or the purpose of, the meeting.
2. Special meetings of any committee of the board may be called at any time by such person or persons and with such notice as shall be specified for such committee by the board, or in the absence of such specification, in the manner and with the notice required for special meetings of the board.

Waiver of Notice

A Manager may waive any notice required by law, by this Agreement, before or after the time stated for the meeting, and such waiver shall be equivalent to the giving of such notice. Such waiver must be in writing, signed by the Manager entitled to such notice, and delivered to the Practice for inclusion in the minutes or filing with the Practice's records. A Manager's attendance at or participation in a meeting shall constitute a waiver of any required notice to the Manager of the meeting unless the Manager at the beginning of the meeting, or promptly upon the Manager's arrival, objects to holding the meeting or transacting business at the meeting and does not thereafter vote for or assent to action taken at the meeting.

Quorum

A majority of the full board of managers shall be necessary at all meetings to constitute a quorum for the transaction of business. If a quorum is present when a vote is taken, the affirmative vote of a majority of Managers present is the act of the board of managers.

Registering Dissent

A Manager who is present at a meeting of the board at which action on a Practice matter is taken is deemed to have assented to such action unless:

1. The Manager objects at the beginning of the meeting, or promptly upon the Manager's arrival, to the holding of, or transaction of business at, the meeting;
2. The Manager's dissent or abstention from the action is entered in the minutes of the meeting; or
3. The Manager delivers written notice of the Manager's dissent or abstention to the presiding officer of the meeting before its adjournment or to the Practice within a reasonable time after adjournment of the meeting. The right to dissent or abstain is not available to a Manager who voted in favor of the action taken.

Action by Managers without a Meeting

1. Any action required or permitted to be taken at a meeting of the board, or of a committee thereof, may be taken without a meeting if all members of the board take the action. The action must be evidenced by one or more written consents setting forth the action taken; signed by each and all of the Managers or by each and all of the members of the committee, as the case may be, either before or after the action taken; and delivered to the Practice for inclusion in the minutes or filing with the Practice's records.
2. Action taken under this section is effective when the last Manager signs the consent, unless the consent specifies a later effective date.

Participation by Means of Communications Equipment

Any or all Managers may participate in a regular or special meeting of the board of managers (or of a committee thereof) by, or may conduct the meeting through the use of, any means of communication by which all Managers participating can hear each other during the meeting.

Remuneration

No stated salary shall be paid to Managers, as such, for their service, but by resolution of the Members, a fixed sum and expenses of attendance, if any, may be allowed for attendance at each regular or special meeting of the board of managers or of a committee thereof, provided that nothing herein contained shall be construed to preclude any Manager from serving the Practice in any other capacity and receiving compensation therefore.

Committees

The board of managers may create one or more committees by resolution adopted by the affirmative vote of a majority of all Managers in office when the vote is taken. Each committee must have two (2) or more Members who serve at the pleasure of the board of managers. Each committee may exercise the authority specifically granted to it by the board of managers.

Officers

The officers of the Practice shall be a chairperson, a vice chairperson, a secretary-treasurer, and the executive administrator. The board of managers shall appoint all officers. All officers of the Practice, other than the executive administrator, must be duly licensed in the state of [STATE] to render the professional services of a physician. Any such officer who ceases to be so licensed or associated by the Practice shall immediately cease to be an officer of the Practice.

Election and Term of Office

The officers of the Practice shall be elected annually by the board of managers at the first meeting of the Managers held after each annual meeting of the Members, except that the chairperson shall hold office for two (2) years. The person elected vice-chairperson shall automatically succeed to the office of chairperson after the term of the chairperson's position has expired, unless the Managers shall specifically vote not to permit such automatic succession to take place. Each officer shall hold office until a successor shall have been elected and qualified, or until such officer's earlier death, resignation, or removal.

Powers and Duties

If the board elects persons to fill the following positions, such officers shall have the following powers and duties:

1. **Chairperson.** The chairperson of the Practice shall, subject to the direction and control of the Managers, have general control and management of the business affairs and policies of the Practice. The chairperson shall act as liaison from and as spokesman for the board of managers. The chairperson shall participate in long-range planning for the Practice and shall be available to the other officers of the Practice for consultation. The chairperson shall possess power to sign all certificates, contracts, and other instruments of the Practice. The chairperson shall preside at all meetings of the Members and of the board of managers. The chairperson shall perform all other duties as are incident to the office of chairperson or are properly required by the Managers.
2. **Vice-Chairperson.** The position of vice-chairperson shall be a Manager. During the absence or disability of the chairperson, the vice-chairperson shall exercise all the functions of the chairperson.
3. **Secretary-Treasurer.** The secretary-treasurer shall issue notices for all meetings — except for notices for special meetings of the Members and special meetings of the Managers that are called by the requisite percentage of Members or number of Managers — shall keep minutes of all meetings, and shall have charge of the seal and the Practice's books. The secretary-treasurer shall have the custody of all monies and securities of the Practice and shall keep regular books of account. The secretary-treasurer shall disburse the funds of the Practice in payment of the

just demands against the Practice or as may be ordered by the board of managers, taking proper vouchers or receipts for such disbursements, and shall render to the board of managers from time to time as may be required an account of all transactions as treasurer and of the financial condition of the Practice. The secretary-treasurer shall perform other duties incident to his or her office or that are properly required of him or her by the board of managers.

4. **Executive Administrator.** The executive administrator shall be the executive officer of the Practice and, subject to the direction and control of the board of managers and the chairperson, shall have responsibility for the operational management and business administration of the Practice. He or she shall report to the chairperson. The individual serving in this position shall only so serve as long as he or she is an employee of the Practice holding the employment title of executive administrator. The terms of employment will be set forth in a written Employment Agreement.

Standards of Conduct for Officer

An officer with discretionary authority shall discharge such officer's duties under that authority:

1. In good faith;
2. With the care an ordinary prudent person in a like position would exercise under similar circumstances; and
3. In a manner the officer reasonably believes to be in the best interests of the Practice.

Delegation

In the case of absence or the inability to act of any officer of the Practice and of any person herein authorized to act in such officer's place, the board of managers may from time to time delegate the powers or duties of such officer to any other officer or any Manager or other person whom it may in its sole discretion select.

Vacancies

Vacancies in any office arising from any cause may be filled by the Managers at any regular or special meeting of the board.

Other Officers

The board of managers, or a duly appointed officer to whom such authority has been delegated by board resolution, may appoint such other officers and agents as it shall deem necessary or expedient, who shall hold their offices for such terms and shall exercise such powers and perform such duties as shall be determined from time to time by the board of managers.

Resignation

An officer may resign at any time by delivering notice to the Practice. Such notice shall be effective when delivered unless the notice specifies a later effective date. Any such resignation shall not affect the Practice's contract rights, if any, with the officer.

Removal

Any officer elected or appointed by the board of managers may be removed at any time, with or without cause, by the affirmative vote of a majority of the whole board of managers, but such removal shall be without prejudice to the contract rights, if any, of the person so removed.

Salaries and Contract Rights

The salaries, if any, of the officers shall be fixed from time to time by the board of managers. The appointment of an officer shall not of itself create contract rights.

Compensation

Indemnification of officers, managers, employees, and agents.

1. **Definitions.** For purposes of this article:
   a. "Practice" includes any domestic or foreign predecessor entity of the Practice in a merger or other transaction in which the predecessor's existence ceased upon consummation of the transaction.
   b. "Manager" means an individual who is or was a Manager of the Practice or an individual who, while a Manager of the Practice, is or was serving at the Practice's request as a Manager, officer, partner, trustee, employee, or agent of another foreign or domestic Practice, partnership, joint venture, trust, employee benefit plan, or other enterprise. A Manager is considered to be serving an employee benefit plan at the Practice's request if the Manager's duties to the Practice also impose duties on, or otherwise involve services by, the Manager to the plan or to participants in or beneficiaries of the plan. "Manager" includes, unless the context requires otherwise, "the estate or personal representative of a Manager."
   c. "Expenses" include counsel fees.
   d. "Liability" means the obligation to pay a judgment; settlement; penalty; fine, including an excise tax assessed with respect to an employee benefit plan; or reasonable expenses incurred with respect to a proceeding.
   e. "Official capacity" means: (1) When used with respect to a Manager, the office of Manager in the Practice; and (2) when used with respect to an individual other than a Manager, the office in the Practice held by the officer, or the employment or agency relationship undertaken by the member, employee, or agent on behalf of the Practice. "Official capacity" does not include service for any other foreign or domestic Practice or any partnership, joint venture, trust, employee benefit plan, or other enterprise.
   f. "Party" includes any individual who was or is threatened to be named defendant or respondent in a proceeding.
   g. "Proceeding" means any threatened, pending, or completed action, suit, or proceeding, whether civil, criminal, administrative, or investigative, and whether formal or informal.
2. **Right to Indemnification.**
   a. The Practice shall indemnify any person who was or is a party to any proceeding, whether or not brought by or in the right of the Practice, by reason of the fact that such person is or was a Manager of the Practice, against

all reasonable expenses incurred by the Manager in connection with the proceeding.

b. Except as provided in subsection (2e) of this section, the Practice shall indemnify an individual made a party to a proceeding because the individual is or was a Manager against liability incurred in the proceeding if:
    (1) The individual acted in good faith;
    (2) The individual reasonably believed;
        (a) In the case of conduct in the individual's official capacity with the Practice, that the individual's conduct was in the Practice's best interests; and
        (b) In all other cases, that the individual's conduct was at least not opposed to the Practice's best interests;
    (3) In the case of any criminal proceeding, the individual had no reasonable cause to believe that the individual's conduct was unlawful.

c. A Manager's conduct with respect to an employee benefit plan for a purpose the Manager reasonably believed to be in the interests of the participants in and beneficiaries of the plan is conduct that satisfies the requirement of subsection 2b(2) of this section.

d. A proceeding by judgment, order, settlement, conviction, or a plea of nolo contendere or its equivalent is not, of itself, determinative that the person did not meet the standard of conduct described in this section for indemnification.

e. The Practice shall not indemnify a Manager under this section:
    (1) In connection with a proceeding by or in the right of the Practice in which the Manager was adjudged liable to the Practice; or
    (2) In connection with any other proceeding charging improper personal benefit to the Manager, whether or not involving action in the Manager's official capacity, in which the Manager was adjudged liable on the basis that personal benefit was improperly received by the Manager.

f. Indemnification under this section in connection with a proceeding by or in the right of the Practice is limited to reasonable expenses incurred in connection with the proceeding.

3. **Advance for Expenses.**

a. The Practice shall pay for or reimburse the reasonable expenses incurred by a Manager who is a party to a proceeding in advance of final disposition of the proceeding and in advance of any determination and authorization if:
    (1) The Manager furnishes the Practice a written affirmation of the Manager's good faith belief that the Manager has met the standard of conduct described in this section of this Agreement; and
    (2) The Manager furnishes the Practice a written undertaking, executed personally or on the Manager's behalf, to repay the advance if it is ultimately determined that the Manager did not meet the standard of conduct.

b. The undertaking must be an unlimited general obligation of the Manager but need not be secured and may be accepted without reference to financial ability to make repayment.

4. **Court-Ordered Indemnification.**

   A Manager of the Practice who is a party to a proceeding may apply for indemnification or advance of expenses to the court conducting the proceeding or to another court of competent jurisdiction. On receipt of an application, the court, after giving any notice the court considers necessary, may order indemnification or advance of expenses if it determines:

   a. The Manager is entitled to mandatory indemnification pursuant to revised code of the state of [STATE], in which case the court shall also order the Practice to pay the Manager's reasonable expenses incurred to obtain court-ordered indemnification;

   b. The Manager is fairly and reasonably entitled to indemnification in view of all the relevant circumstances, whether or not the Manager met the standard of conduct set forth herein or was adjudged liable as described in this Agreement, but if the Manager was adjudged so liable, the Manager's indemnification is limited to reasonable expenses incurred; or

   c. In the case of an advance of expenses, the Manager is entitled pursuant to any applicable resolution or contract to payment or reimbursement of the Manager's reasonable expenses incurred as a party to the proceeding in advance of final disposition of the proceeding.

5. **Determination and Authorization of Indemnification.**

   a. The Practice shall not indemnify a Manager under this article unless authorized in the specific case after a determination has been made that indemnification of the Manager is permissible in the circumstances because the Manager has met the standard of conduct set forth in this article.

   b. The determination shall be made:

      (1) By the board of managers by majority vote of a quorum consisting of Managers not at the time parties to the proceeding;

      (2) If a quorum cannot be obtained under (1) of this subsection, by majority vote of a committee duly designated by the board of managers, in which designation Managers who are parties may participate, consisting solely of two (2) or more Managers not at the time parties to the proceeding;

      (3) By legal counsel:

         (a) Selected by the board of managers or its committee in the manner prescribed in this subsection; or

         (b) If a quorum of the board of managers cannot be obtained under this subsection, and a committee cannot be designated under this subsection, selected by majority vote of the full board of managers, in which selection Managers who are parties may participate.

      (4) By the Members, but units owned by or voted under the control of Managers who are at the time parties to the proceeding may not be voted on the determination.

         (a) Authorization of indemnification and evaluation as to reasonableness of expenses shall be made in the same manner as the determination that indemnification is permissible, except that if the determination is made by special legal counsel, authorization of indemnification and evaluation as to reasonableness of expenses shall be made by those entitled under subsection 5b(3) of this section to select counsel.

6. **Indemnification of Officers.**
   a. An officer of the Practice who is not a Manager shall be indemnified pursuant to the state code and is entitled to apply for court-ordered indemnification in each case to the same extent as a Manager.
   b. The Practice shall indemnify and advance expenses to an officer who is not a Manager to the same extent as to a Manager under this article.
   c. The Practice may also indemnify and advance expenses to an officer who is not a Manager to the extent, consistent with the law, that may be provided by a general or specific action of its board of managers or contract.
7. **Indemnification of Employees and Agents.**
   a. The Practice may indemnify employees and agents of the Practice pursuant to the state code and may afford the right to such employees or agents to apply for court-ordered indemnification under Section 4 of this article in each case to the same extent as a Manager.
   b. The Practice may indemnify and advance expenses to an employee or agent of the Practice who is not a Manager to the same extent as to a Manager under this article.
   c. The Practice may also indemnify and advance expenses to an employee or agent who is not a Manager to the extent, consistent with law, that may be provided by a general or specific action of its board of managers or contract.
8. **Insurance.**

   The Practice may purchase and maintain insurance on behalf of an individual who is or was a manager, officer, member, employee, or agent of the Practice, or who, while a manager, officer, member, employee, or agent of the Practice, is or was serving at the request of the Practice as a manager, officer, member, partner, trustee, employee, or agent of another foreign or domestic practice, partnership, joint venture, trust, employee benefit plan, or other enterprise. This insurance would be for liability asserted against or incurred by the individual in that capacity or arising from the individual's status as a manager, officer, member, employee, or agent, whether or not the Practice would have the power to indemnify the individual against the same liability under this article.
9. **Indemnification as a Witness.**

   This article does not limit the Practice's power to pay or reimburse expenses incurred by a Manager in connection with the Manager's appearance as a witness in a proceeding at a time when the Manager has not been made a named defendant or respondent to the proceeding.
10. **Report to Members.**

    If the Practice indemnifies or advances expenses to a Manager pursuant to this article in connection with a proceeding by or in the right of the Practice, the Practice shall report the indemnification or advance in writing to the Members with or before the notice of the next Members' meeting.
11. **Member-Authorized Indemnification.**
    a. If authorized by a resolution adopted or ratified before or after the event by the Members of the Practice, the Practice shall have the power to indemnify or agree to indemnify a Manager made a party to a proceeding, or obligate itself to advance or reimburse expenses incurred in a proceeding, without regard to

the limitations contained in this article (other than this section), provided that no such indemnity shall indemnify any Manager from or on account of:

(1) Acts or omissions of the Manager finally adjudged to be intentional misconduct or a knowing violation of law;

(2) Conduct of the Manager finally adjudged to be an unlawful distribution under revised code of the state of [STATE]; or

(3) Any transaction with respect to which it was finally adjudged that such Manager personally received a benefit in money, property, or services to which the Manager was not legally entitled.

b. Unless a resolution adopted or ratified by the Members of the Practice provides otherwise, any determination as to any indemnity or advance of expenses under this section shall be made in accordance with Section 4 of this article.

12. **Validity of Indemnification.**

A provision addressing the Practice's indemnification of or advance for expenses to Managers that is contained in these bylaws, a resolution of its Members or board of managers in a contract or otherwise is valid only if and to the extent that the provision is consistent with revised code of the state of [STATE].

13. **Interpretation.**

The provisions contained in this article shall be interpreted and applied to provide indemnification to managers, officers, employees, and agents of the Practice to the fullest extent allowed by applicable law, as such law may be amended, interpreted, and applied from time to time.

14. **Savings Clause.**

If this article or any portion thereof shall be invalidated on any ground by any court of competent jurisdiction, the Practice shall nevertheless indemnify each Manager as to reasonable expenses and liabilities with respect to any proceeding, whether or not brought by or in the right of the Practice, to the full extent permitted by any applicable portion of this article that shall not have been invalidated, or by any other applicable law.

15. **Nonexclusivity of Rights.**

The right to indemnification under this article for managers, officers, members, employees, and agents shall not be exclusive of any other right that any person may have or may hereafter acquire under any statute, provision of this or any other agreement, vote of Members or disinterested Managers, insurance policy, principles of common law or equity, or otherwise.

Policy 3.9

Call Coverage Policy

Call Coverage Addendum to Physician Compensation Plan

A portion of the Practice's net income shall be distributed as "adjustment" income, with each physician receiving the following "adjustment": One thousand dollars ($1,000) for each night the physician provides weeknight on-call services for the Practice; one thousand five hundred dollars ($1,500) for each day the physician provides weekend on-call services for the Practice; one thousand dollars ($1,000) for each day the physician works at a satellite location; two thousand dollars ($2,000) for each day the physician works at the medical center in a hospitalist capacity.

Each physician shall also, as part of the income adjustment, be assessed a deduction adjustment in the amount of one thousand dollars ($1,000) per Monday through Friday weekday vacation taken. Each physician shall be assessed a deduction for a minimum of fifty (50) weekdays of vacation annually. The income adjustments noted will be divided by two (2) for each half-day assignment.

Sale of Call

The Practice will serve as a "broker" for the purchase and sale of call. There must be a willing seller and a willing buyer. The Practice will annually set a "price" for call; however, the parties to the transaction (seller and buyer) may determine their own price. For the current year, the established pricing is based on the most recent MGMA *Medical Directorship and On-Call Compensation Survey Report.*

Weeknight/Daily call	$[X]
Weekend call (per day)	$[Y]
Holiday call (per day)	$[Z]

Policy 3.10

Pay for Administrative Duties Policy

Position Description: Administrator

- **General Summary of Duties:** Provides leadership, direction, and administration for all aspects of the Practice activities to ensure accomplishment of its objectives.
- **Supervision Received:** Reports directly to the board of directors.
- **Supervision Exercised:** Supervises department heads and oversees the activities of all Practice staff and activities.
- **Typical Physical Demands:** Requires prolonged sitting, some bending, stooping, and stretching. Requires eye-hand coordination and manual dexterity sufficient to operate a keyboard, photocopier, telephone, calculator, and other office equipment. Requires normal range of hearing and eyesight to record, prepare, and communicate appropriate reports.
- **Typical Working Conditions:** Normal office environment. Occasional evening or weekend work.

Examples of Duties

(This list may not include all of the duties assigned.)

1. Participates with governing board in charting and implementing the Practice's mission in response to the changing needs of the community.
2. Recommends, develops, and updates strategic long-range plans to support the Practice's philosophy and goals.

3. Informs board about current trends, problems, and activities in the medical field to facilitate policy-making.
4. Recommends Practice policy positions regarding administrative and legislative matters.
5. Participates and coordinates selection and training of new board members.
6. Coordinates with the board, medical staff, and other Practice personnel in the monitoring of medical activities to ensure the fulfillment of the community's needs for quality healthcare.
7. Consults with relevant staff and departments prior to recommending and establishing new policies to ensure the availability of support and resources.
8. Coordinates efforts of medical staff, board, and administrative staff in the recruitment, development, evaluation, and retention of medical personnel.
9. Coordinates the long-range financial development and management of the organization.
10. Ensures the provision of affordable healthcare services by the acquisition, utilization, and organization of resources (human, financial, and physical). Develops improved management techniques and practices.
11. Ensures compliance with all regulatory agencies governing healthcare delivery and the rules of accrediting bodies. Continually monitors operations, programs, and physical properties. Initiates appropriate changes.
12. Encourages the integration of the Practice with the community through effective communication and public relations programs.
13. Represents the Practice in its relationships with other health organizations, government agencies, and third-party payers.
14. Directs and supervises all Practice activities through department heads and administrative support staff. Consults with and advises department heads on a regular basis.
15. Provides assistance to supervisory personnel in establishing department philosophy and objectives related to staffing and performance standards, policies and procedures, job classifications, and compliance with government regulations.
16. Serves as liaison and channel of communication between the board and its committees, and the medical and administrative staffs.
17. Resolves any medical-administrative problems and keeps lines of communication open with staff to ensure high physician morale and a professional, healthful Practice atmosphere.
18. Maintains professional affiliations and enhances professional growth and development to keep current with the latest trends in practice administration.
19. Maintains strictest confidentiality.
20. Performs related work as required.

Performance Requirements

Knowledge, skills, and abilities:

- Knowledge of the principles and practices of health planning and management sufficient to manage, direct, and coordinate the operation of a major healthcare organization;

- Knowledge of the purposes, organization, and policies of the community's health systems sufficient to interact with other healthcare providers;
- Knowledge of the policies and procedures of a practice sufficient to direct its operations and to provide effective patient care;
- Knowledge of the principles and practices of employee development sufficient to ensure organizational productivity;
- Knowledge of computer programs and applications;
- Skill in exercising a high degree of initiative, judgment, discretion, and decision-making to achieve organizational objectives;
- Skill in analyzing situations accurately and taking effective action;
- Skill in establishing and maintaining effective working relationships with employees, policy-making bodies, third-party payers, patients, and the public;
- Skill in organizing work, making assignments, and achieving goals and objectives;
- Skill in exercising judgment and discretion in developing, applying, interpreting, and coordinating departmental policies and procedures;
- Ability to assume responsibility and exercise authority over assigned work functions;
- Ability to establish and maintain quality control standards;
- Ability to organize and integrate organizational priorities and deadlines; and
- Ability to prepare comprehensive reports.

Education

- MHA, MBA, or MS in health administration.
- Professional development courses in healthcare management.

Experience

Seven (7) years of executive-level experience is required, including (5) years of experience in the administration of a major medical group practice.

Certificate/License

None required. Certification or fellowship in MGMA's American College of Medical Practice Executives (CMPE or FACMPE) is preferred.

Alternatives to Minimum Qualifications

Additional appropriate education may be substituted for four (4) years of executive-level experience.

Compensation

Administrator's compensation will be reviewed annually with the governing body using MGMA Management Compensation Surveys as a guide to establish the compensation ranges.

Compensation will be a combination of a base salary and a performance bonus. The performance bonus will be a maximum of 25 percent of the administrator's base salary and will consist of objective factors that the administrator manages, including staff turnover, days in accounts receivable, attainment of budget targets, completion of assigned initiatives, as well as a subjective "board factor."

Policy 3.11

Seniority Pay Policy[3]

This traditional system rewards length of service. Physicians are eligible for pay-range increases at set intervals. Increases tend to be the same for every physician with a satisfactory performance report. This system reduces conflicts between the supervisor and the physician and with the union. It does not reward physicians, however, for excellent performance. This system is being used less and less frequently these days.

If you do not monitor raises carefully, you may put physicians in jeopardy of becoming ineligible for a pay raise because they reach the maximum end of the pay range. This can happen if raises are given automatically. If a raise is given beyond the maximum, the salary is indicated as out of range and puts the physician and his or her supervisor in an awkward spot. Remind supervisors to stay out of this spot by helping them to work with physicians to get the training and assistance needed to move up to another pay grade before they reach the end of the range. Some physicians may not have the qualifications or desire to move up, and their salaries must remain capped.

3 Printed in *HR Policies and Procedures Manual for Medical Practices, 4th Edition,* by Courtney Price, PhD, and Alys Novak, MBA (Englewood, CO: Medical Group Management Association, 2007).

PART II

Clinical Practice

Clinical Practice Philosophy

Compensation and benefits policies fuel the foundation for trust between physicians and their employers. Clinical policies push in another direction. For some physicians, clinical policies carry a restrictive flavor. They inhibit rather than encourage. They smack of conformity, rules, and compliance more than of comfort. They intrude and trample on perceptions about professionalism. Clinical policies get in the way more than show the way.

It doesn't have to be like that. Clinical policies, like all other policies, offer opportunities for consistency, standardization of complex processes, and accountability among peers. Clinical policies can drive medical excellence. They can help to ensure that physician colleagues will support each other and serve each other as they strive for best practices in patient care. Clinical policies can become essential tools to maintain and improve a culture devoted to high quality of care.

Basic Considerations

Perhaps the first thing to be said about clinical policies is that they are not intended to replace professional judgment. They are intended to make sure that the best professional judgments are applied consistently. If clinical policies are construed as "cookbook medicine," they are doomed to fail. The medical profession is evolving rapidly. As new medical research unveils the mysteries of the human body and devises promising diagnostic and treatment tools, physicians are gaining power over disease and morbidity. When less was known, physicians had to be their own researchers. They had to look for patterns within their own patients and practice their healing craft, their profession, with the highest degree of professional discernment.

The remarkable strides of the medical profession in the last 100 years have produced a library — a massive library — of new knowledge, clinical protocols, and best practices that can guide physicians as they carry out their solemn oath. Modern medical research has revealed how former practices failed to protect patients and may have caused them harm. Fresh pharmacological research is now producing effective therapies for diseases that have plagued mankind for centuries, as well as for diseases that were unknown just a few decades ago.

As the body of knowledge grows, physicians need new tools to access that knowledge and to apply it where it can do the greatest good. That is the role of clinical policies. They can serve as annotated bibliographies for libraries of clinical research. They can condense the ever-changing news of effective therapies into standardized guidelines and protocols, and they can offer assurance that physician peers will act consistently in providing the best care for each patient.

The quest for effective clinical policies is growing, fueled in part by health reform efforts. As the healthcare industry redesigns itself for accountable care, clinical policies are likely to take center stage. Physicians will be held accountable to best practices built on sound research and articulated in clinical policies. They will be drawn together to form a consensus about clinical policies and apply them consistently to provide better outcomes at lower costs. Their paychecks may depend on it.

Purpose

Clinical policies are not new, although they may not have played the central role within organizations that they are likely to play in the future. Clinical policies have appeared in forms that might not have been thought of as policies. Each specialty has its professional standards that come out of obscurity and are placed under the microscope with every professional liability misadventure. Professional standards catalogued in clinical policies and adopted in advance may help to prevent medical misadventures.

Pay-for-performance contracts also set the stage for the effective use of clinical policies. Managed care contracts that offer bonuses for achieving clinical outcomes provide tangible rewards for complying with clinical policies. When physicians work together within a medical group to meet or exceed clinical targets for diabetic management, immunizations, and smoking cessation consultations, their agreed-upon clinical policies offer glue to hold the group together and tangible incentives for compliance. Beyond the tangible reward, physicians can find satisfaction in doing the right thing for patients and in achieving better quality at lower cost.

Clinical policies can also aid in reducing clinical variance among physicians within the group. They set the stage for peer reviews and mutual accountability. If a pattern of patient complaints or suboptimal outcomes emerges with a particular physician, his or her colleagues can draw attention to clinical policies as the standard for accountability. When those policies are based on sound clinical research, they become a guidebook for best practices built on informed consensus.

Components

Clinical policies can vary widely between medical groups, both in their number and scope. Some of the more common categories of clinical policies include the following:

- **Specialty-Specific Competency.** Each medical specialty has unique standards that go beyond basic medical competencies. In surgical specialties, competency policies might focus on indications for surgery or protocols for post-operative care. Pediatricians might focus on policies about immunization standards, and obstetricians may concentrate on prenatal care.

- **Pay for Performance.** Clinical policies may emerge from managed care contracts to align physician performance with reimbursement.
- **Bioethics.** Some medical groups may create clinical policies to address bioethical issues related to end-of-life care.
- **Coordination of Care.** Clinical policies can offer guidance, particularly with multispecialty groups, concerning the coordination of care. When patients present with comorbidities requiring multidisciplinary interventions, clinical policies can streamline the diagnostic and treatment process while simultaneously setting the stage for improving patient satisfaction.
- **Medical Records.** Electronic health record adoption may be reducing the variance of physicians' documentation habits, but there can still be a wide range of options for templates, data-gathering methods, and communications between referral sources. Clinical policies can close the gap to strengthen consistency between physicians within the group and solidify communications between groups.
- **Business Relationships.** Clinical policies can also offer guidance about how physicians should relate to pharmaceutical representatives, medical supplies and equipment resources, and insurance companies. In a similar manner, clinical policies can also address referral patterns to ensure compliance with Stark laws and coding patterns to stay clear of fraud and abuse issues.

Conclusion

Clinical policies may seem redundant and unnecessary to veteran physicians. Those who engage patients consistently without consulting any manuals may be irritated by requirements to comply with written clinical policies. But clinical policies may hold the key, particularly in the era of accountable care, to improving clinical outcomes while reducing costs for patients as well as for hospitals and medical groups. They are another tool for building a culture of compassion, consistency, and quality of care.

CHAPTER 4

Clinical Competency

Policy 4.1

Physician Training Policy

The Practice uses training opportunities to create an atmosphere that encourages active physician participation and ensures maximum use of physicians' skills and abilities. The types of training offered will focus on specific job skills, techniques, new medical knowledge, and computer and health information technology.

Training provides physicians with necessary technical training, promoting efficiency, competency, and economy. It often reduces learning-time errors and improves the quality of service and productivity.

The Practice will coordinate with the human resources (HR) department to provide any training related to clinical skills. The Practice will also devote training time and resources for efficient employee use of the Practice's computer systems and software tools.

Procedure

1. Management cooperates with employees in planning for further training and recommending additional training and development programs.

2. Management strives to provide training and education for employees displaced by changes in technology or Practice structure.
3. Physicians are required to participate in training and development programs when it is considered necessary for satisfactory job performance.
4. The Practice provides training opportunities for physicians wanting to transition to first-level supervisory or administrative/managerial positions.
5. The Practice recognizes the need for all levels of management to constantly upgrade their skills. It provides training and development programs whenever feasible, based on available resources.
6. The Practice offers safety and health programs to promote a safe and healthful working environment. If continuing education and in-service programs are required for licensing or certification, the Practice considers sponsoring and/or conducting such programs.
7. Physicians may volunteer for training and development opportunities, or management may recommend them. Regardless of the procedure, all employees must receive supervisory approval to attend such programs conducted during work hours.
8. All management-required training is provided without cost to the physician. Approval for payment fees for voluntary training and development programs is subject to the discretion of management.
9. Management encourages physicians to take advantage of training and development opportunities whenever possible. However, completing such programs does not guarantee advancement.
10. As a rule, only full-time, regular physicians are eligible for paid training and development programs. Management may, however, recommend other physicians for such programs, as appropriate.
11. All training and development programs sponsored or conducted by the Practice are evaluated on the quality of instruction, content, and effectiveness. Participants in such programs may be required to take tests to determine the extent of their learning.
12. The HR department is responsible for announcing clinic-sponsored or conducted development programs. Such opportunities are posted on the employee bulletin board.
13. Certificates of completion are awarded to all physicians who successfully complete any program sponsored or conducted by the Practice.
14. The HR department maintains records of training and development programs completed by each physician.

Policy 4.2 Physician Training and CME Reimbursement Policy

Continuing medical education (CME), professional dues, and license fees are reimbursed for contractual providers. It is the responsibility of the physician to submit CME registration/seminar information or continuing education forms to the executive director for approval prior to attending the session. A copy of the actual seminar description that the physician is requesting to attend must be attached.

Purpose

Physicians are allotted days off the regular work schedule and reimbursement for expenses per employment contract and reimbursement for license fees, professional dues, and continuing medical education as it pertains to maintaining licensure in the state and according to this policy. The purpose of this policy is to address the Practice's policy regarding attendance of continuing education seminars and professional dues and license. Reimbursement for CME and reimbursement for professional dues and license fees will be offered as per employment contract or the Practice policy and as approved according to this policy. The executive director will have final approval on reimbursement.

Physicians will be compensated for the number of days of attendance to a seminar. Additional days off will be considered vacation days. For example, each day of the conference will account for one (1) CME day, or eight (8) CME hours. Reimbursement for CME expenses will be granted for days of conference attendance only. CME time off will not be granted for independent study that occurs without actual attendance.

Guidelines

Upon approval of the seminar, the executive director will assist if necessary with registering the physician for the seminar and return the approved seminar request to the physician. The physician is responsible for securing hotel accommodations, airline, or travel arrangements. Reimbursement is based on approved expenses only and shall not exceed the physician's anniversary/contractual year allowance as indicated in the Employment Agreement. Money and CME days NOT used during the physician's anniversary year will NOT be carried over to any additional years and are based on the allowable amount as per contract.

Upon attendance and completion of the seminar, the physician will return original approved requests for reimbursement to the executive director and a copy of the certificate of attendance.

Reimbursement expenses (with accompanying receipts) related to seminar/CME will be limited to:

1. Registration fees;
2. Daily food allowance of $80.00/day;
3. Gratuities;
4. Parking/tolls;
5. Coach-class transportation via airplane, bus, or train;
6. Hotel/lodging accommodations limited to room, taxes, and gratuities for days in attendance at conference only;
7. Car rental; and
8. Mileage at current rate per mile if physician drives his or her vehicle.

All request-for-expense reimbursement as related to seminars, dues, and licenses must be accompanied by receipts showing actual payment.

Sample: Request for Coverage of Education or Credentialing Expenses

To: HR Coordinator
From: __________ [PHYSICIAN NAME]
Location: __________
DOH: __________

I request payment by the Practice for the following educational or credentialing activity. This activity/credentialing is appropriate to my responsibilities and will benefit both the Practice and me.

Educational or Credentialing Activity: __________ *(Attach relevant application material)*
Location: __________
Total cost: $ __________
Amount requested: $__________
Check payable to: __________

I understand and agree that should I cease to be employed by the Practice within one (1) year following completion of this activity/credentialing, I will be responsible for the prorated cost of this activity/credentialing. Should that occur, I authorize the Practice to deduct any such amounts due from my final paycheck. If this request is for a course for which I have not taken the test, I understand that I may return all materials in unused condition to the Practice and there will be no charge.

Date: __________
Associate's Signature: ____________________

PORTION BELOW TO BE COMPLETED BY MANAGEMENT

I recommend approval of the above request. I believe that this activity is consistent with this physician's responsibilities and will benefit the Practice.

__________ Charge to the physician's educational allowance if funds are available.
__________ Education activity required by the Practice *(Must specify on reverse why activity is being required by the Practice)*

Charge to (Location): __________
Date: __________
Supervisor's signature: ____________________

PORTION BELOW TO BE COMPLETED BY CORPORATE OFFICE
Educational allowance currently available for physician: $ ___________
Charge to Physician's educational allowance: $ __________
Department educational allowance/fund: $___________
Administrative approval: ____________________
Date: __________

Policy 4.3

Documentation of Patient Care Policy[1]

The clinical record can be an asset or a liability to the physician. If the physician ensures that each patient encounter is recorded quickly, accurately, and completely, this documentation will fulfill legal and payer requirements. One of the most efficient means to record the patient encounter is via the electronic health record (EHR). If the physician does not complete the record in the EHR or doesn't complete his or her charting in a paper-based system by the end of the day, the accuracy of the record could be compromised. Completeness is also imperative. Omissions in the clinical record fall upon the physician for proof. The payer requires correct documentation for reimbursement.

As in hospitals, every patient has a separate clinical record with the same standard data elements for each encounter. The physician must sign each patient encounter.

Clinical-record progress notes include current vital signs and are presented in the SOAP format:

- **S**ubjective — complaints of patient;
- **O**bjective — observations and examination by physician;
- **A**ssessment — diagnosis; and
- **P**lan — actions to be taken.

The need to document seems obvious, but it is not unusual to find a progress note without a patient name. Each progress note should have a patient name and birth date.

Procedure

1. Physicians at the Practice will fully and accurately document each patient encounter to facilitate communication among treating physicians and maintain patient safety.
2. Physicians will complete patient charts by the end of the patient encounter or before the end of each business day or shift.
3. Physicians at the Practice should remember the adage, "If treatment is not documented, it did not happen."

1 Printed in *Rx for Business Success: Joining a Practice for Physicians* by MGMA (Englewood, CO: Medical Group Management Association, 2005).

Policy 4.4 Electronic Signatures Policy[2]

A push toward greater administrative efficiencies and improved accuracy and retention of clinical records has led to the growing adoption of electronic signatures, or e-signatures. In addition, legislation has been passed that requires the protection of patient information and records.

To maintain the security of transmitted data and act in compliance with national standards and regulations, the Practice requires the following:

- Health data transactions include computer disks, magnetic tapes, and compact disks. Transmission mediums include dial-up lines, private networks, leased lines, the intranet, the Internet, and extranet;
- There are four categories of security standards: (1) administrative procedures, (2) physical safeguards, (3) technical security services, and (4) technical security mechanisms;
- Electronic signatures must be cryptographically based digital signatures;
- Electronic signature compliance requirements include user authentication, message integrity, and nonrepudiation; and
- Any vendor used to establish an electronic signature system must be compliant with the following:
  - Health Insurance Portability and Accountability Act (HIPAA): HIPAA calls for standardizing *electronic* data for improving efficiency and protecting the confidentiality and integrity of patients' health information; and
  - The Food and Drug Administration's (FDA's) 21 CFR Part 11: This enables the use of electronic records and signatures in all FDA-regulated companies and makes electronic records as valid as paper records.

Medicare Signature Requirements

For medical review purposes, Medicare requires that the author authenticate services provided/ordered. The method used shall be a handwritten or an electronic signature. Stamp signatures are not acceptable.

Handwritten Signature

A handwritten signature is a mark or sign by an individual on a document to signify knowledge, approval, acceptance, or obligation:

- If the signature is illegible, Medicare Administrative Contractors (MACs), Affiliated Contractors (ACs), Comprehensive Error Rate Testing (CERT) contractors, Program Safeguard Contractors (PSCs), and Zone Program Integrity Contractors (ZPICs) shall consider evidence in a signature log or attestation statement to determine the identity of the author of a clinical record entry;

2 Copyright 2010 CIGNA, www.cignagovernmentservices.com/jc/forms/pdf/JC_CMS_Signature_Req.pdf (accessed February3, 2011); E-Lock Solutions, "Digital Signatures for Health Care and Pharma Organizations," www.elock.com/healthcare.html (accessed July 5, 2011); MGMA, "HIPAA Background and Provisions," www.mgma.com/policy/default.aspx?id=5018 (accessed July 5, 2011).

- If the signature is missing from an order, ACs, MACs, PSCs, ZPICs, and CERT contractors shall disregard the order during the review of the claim; and
- If the signature is missing from any other clinical documentation, ACs, MACs, PSCs, ZPICs, and CERT contractors shall accept a signature attestation from the author of the clinical record entry.

Signature Log

A signature log lists the typed or printed name of the author associated with initials or an illegible signature. The signature log might be included on the actual page where the initials or illegible signature are used or might be a separate document. The physician should also list his or her credentials in the log.

Signature Attestation Statement

An attestation statement may be submitted to authenticate an illegible or missing signature on clinical documentation. In order to be considered valid for Medicare medical review purposes, an attestation statement must be signed and dated by the author of the clinical record entry and must contain sufficient information to identify the beneficiary.

Reviewers will consider all attestations that meet CMS requirements regardless of the date the attestation was created, except in those cases where the regulations or policy indicate that a signature must be in place prior to a given event or a given date.

The following sample contains an acceptable form that suppliers may use as an attestation statement. However, CMS is neither requiring nor instructing suppliers to use this form or format and it is provided as an example only.

Electronic Signatures

Due to the potential for misuse or abuse with alternate signature methods, physicians should use a system and software products that are protected against modification and should apply administrative procedures that are adequate and correspond to recognized standards and laws. The individual whose name is on the alternate signature method and the physician bear the responsibility for the authenticity of the information being attested to.

Please refer to the CMS Pub. 100-08, *Medicare Program Integrity Manual*, Chapter Three, Section 3.4.1.1, for additional information concerning signature requirements.

Sample: Clinical Record Signature Attestation Statement

<table><tr><td>
Note: This form provides a suggested format for a signature attestation statement. Submission of a signature attestation statement and use of this form is optional.

Name of Patient: __________
Medicare Number: __________

I, __________ [PHYSICIAN/PRACTITIONER'S FULL NAME] hereby attest that the clinical record entry for __________ [DATE OF SERVICE] accurately reflects signatures/notations that I made in my capacity as a(n) __________ [CREDENTIALS, e.g., MD] when I treated/diagnosed the above-listed Medicare beneficiary. I do hereby attest that this information is true, accurate, and complete to the best of my knowledge, and I understand that any falsification, omission, or concealment of material fact may subject me to administrative, civil, or criminal liability.

__________ [Signature of Author of the Clinical Record]
__________ [Date]

In order to be considered valid for Medicare medical review purposes, an attestation statement must be signed and dated by the author of the clinical record entry. Reviewers will not consider attestation statements where there is no associated clinical record entry or someone other than the author (even a colleague in the same group practice) of the clinical record entry in question signs this statement.
</td></tr></table>

Policy 4.5 E-Prescribing Policy[3]

The following e-prescribing principles will guide the ethical, technical, and financial aspects of this policy for the Practice. Stakeholders are encouraged to utilize these as strategic and tactical initiatives on electronic prescribing are developed.

Principle 1

We believe widespread adoption of e-prescribing can provide many benefits, including:

- Improved medication safety;
- Enhanced practice efficiency;
- Cost savings;
- More effective medication management;
- Increased patient adherence; and
- Improved integrity of the prescribing process.

3 eHealth Initiative, CIMM, AMA, AAFP, ACP, MGMA, "A Clinician's Guide to Electronic Prescribing," October 2008, 22–23; 37. www.rheumatology.org/practice/office/hit/e-Prescribing_Clinicians_Guide_Final.pdf (accessed February 3, 2011).

Principle 2

All healthcare stakeholders should collaborate to encourage widespread adoption and optimal use of standards-based e-prescribing through:

- Appropriately aligned incentives to support effective use of the technology in diverse practice settings;
- Collaborative development and delivery of innovative programs, education resources, training, and support;
- Efficiencies in workflow for the physician and pharmacist in diverse practice settings; and
- Connectivity and tools to facilitate medication reconciliation, formulary and medication history information, and transmission.

Principle 3

E-prescribing system design and/or the implementation of e-prescribing should:

- Enhance the patient–clinician relationship by providing more comprehensive clinical information at the point of care;
- Preserve the patient's choice of pharmacy;
- Facilitate the clinician's informed choice of medication; and
- Be part of an integrated plan toward full implementation of an EHR.

Principle 4

Both EHRs and stand-alone e-prescribing may be utilized to realize the functionality and benefits of e-prescribing. Overall quality of care can be enhanced by implementation of e-prescribing that is integrated within an EHR.

Principle 5

The Practice staff and physicians should help patients understand and experience the benefits of e-prescribing. Informed patients will play an important role in the encouragement for physicians and pharmacists to use e-prescribing.

Procedure

1. Set default routing to electronically send prescriptions to the pharmacy rather than faxing them. Systems that provide the option for prescribers to decide whether to fax, print, or electronically send prescriptions tend to result in underuse of electronic transmission. However, clinicians should always have the ability to print the prescription or a receipt of the prescription order for the patient.
2. Utilize electronic prescription renewal functionality as this increases efficiency and improves patient service when patients are able to get their prescriptions renewed more quickly. Electronic renewals can also encourage more staff involvement in the prescribing process and lead to stronger commitment to e-prescribing. Automating the process to authorize prescription renewals as part of e-prescribing is a key benefit for the practice and a key driver of utilization. Instructing patients to request refills through their pharmacy instead of calling the physician office can decrease phone calls to the office and increase the efficiency of handling the requests when they come electronically directly from the pharmacy.

3. Integrate patient demographic information from the practice management system in advance of e-prescribing implementation. Not having the Practice patient-demographic information loaded in the e-prescribing application system during a patient visit can be a major source of dissatisfaction for both prescribers and Practice staff. Also be sure that the system you plan to implement can regularly update new patients and changes in demographic information from your practice management system.
4. Designate a prescriber or staff person to retrieve and manage responses for renewal authorization requests that are sent electronically from pharmacies. This person can help to successfully implement the electronic renewal process by checking your prescribing system each day, or several times a day, for electronic requests. Consider distributing patient educational materials on e-prescribing that instruct them to contact their pharmacy first for refill requests or displaying signage in the office to remind patients of the best process.
5. Make sure you know how to select your patient's pharmacy of choice using your e-prescribing application. You should be familiar with how to select both the name and location of your patient's pharmacy of choice and how pharmacy information is displayed and updated in your prescribing application. Once you start using your application, make it a practice to ask your patients to select or confirm their pharmacy of choice when they check in for their visit. You or your staff can then add the pharmacies' names to the patients' electronic records and speed the process of preparing their prescriptions using your e-prescribing application. As an added step, you may wish to build a "favorites" list of pharmacies within your application, using your patients' favorite locations, for quick selection during the check-in process.
6. Respond to electronic renewal requests as soon as possible and always within twenty-four (24) hours on business days. If pharmacies do not see a response within that time frame, they may send duplicate renewal authorization requests. This may also happen if the patient is waiting in the pharmacy to pick up a renewed prescription that has not yet been authorized. It helps to designate someone to manage the electronic refill response process.
7. Avoid queuing or "batching" prescriptions before sending them to pharmacies electronically. Sending prescriptions to pharmacies as soon as possible after they are prepared ensures that the pharmacy has adequate time to receive the prescription before a patient arrives to pick it up. Otherwise, the practice may receive unnecessary calls from pharmacies asking where the prescription is, further delaying the patient's receipt of the medication.
8. Follow Drug Enforcement Administration regulations by refraining from electronic transmission of prescriptions for controlled substances until these regulations are changed to allow electronic transmission. Prescriptions for Schedule II drugs can never be sent electronically. Hand-signed hard copies of prescriptions for Schedule III through V drugs can be sent via fax. Neither

computer-generated faxes containing electronic signatures nor totally electronic prescriptions for controlled substances can be sent to pharmacies at this time.

9. Inform local pharmacies that the Practice is preparing to exchange prescription information electronically. When your e-prescribing application is set up at your Practice, your vendor should inform pharmacies in your area that you will be prescribing electronically. The ongoing use of the prescribing application will then reinforce this notice and will allow pharmacies to start sending refill requests to your prescribing application — if you are set up to manage these requests electronically.

   Independent pharmacies, especially, do appreciate hearing directly from practices and clinics that are planning to e-prescribe. This can also help encourage those who are not yet able to manage e-prescriptions to get connected.

10. Communicate with patients about e-prescribing and its benefits, and remind them to call the pharmacy rather than the practice when they need their prescriptions renewed.

Policy 4.6 Peer Review Policy

Professional peer review focuses on the performance of professionals, with a view to improving quality, upholding standards, or providing certification. Professional peer review activity is widespread in the field of healthcare, where it is best termed "clinical peer review" and is most commonly conducted in hospitals, but it may also occur in other practice settings, including surgical centers and large group practices.

The primary purpose of peer review is to improve the quality and safety of care. Secondarily, it serves to reduce the organization's vicarious malpractice liability and meet regulatory requirements. In the United States, these include accreditation, licensure, and Medicare participation.[4]

Peer review also supports the other processes that healthcare organizations have in place to ensure that physicians are competent and practice within the boundaries of professionally accepted norms.

See Appendix for Physician Peer Review Form.

4 S. Haines, "Hospital Peer Review Systems: An Overview." *Health Matrix*, V. 2, No. 4 (1984–1985): 30–32. www.en.wikipedia.org/wiki/Clinical_peer_review.

Sample: Peer Assessment Form

Peer Name: ______________________________
Date: __________

Assessment Key

5 = Exceeds requirements; consistently surpasses all requirements. Truly an outstanding performer.

4 = Consistently meets requirements; performance meets all requirements and may even exceed some of them. Strong performer.

3 = Satisfactory; performance meets most expectations of average.

2 = Often meets requirements; performance meets most requirements. Some deficiencies evident.

1 = Does not meet requirements; improvement plan is necessary. Unsatisfactory performance.

( ) = Not applicable

I. Clinical	
A. Patient relations	
• Communication timely, follow-up performed, compliments/complaints received	1 2 3 4 5 ( )
Comments:	
B. Clinical record-keeping	
• Punctual dictation	1 2 3 4 5 ( )
• Documentation	1 2 3 4 5 ( )
• Follows policies regarding records, charges, and appropriate coding	1 2 3 4 5 ( )
Comments:	
C. Technical skills	
• Appropriateness of testing, hospital admits, etc.	1 2 3 4 5 ( )
Comments:	
D. Productivity	
• Consistently builds practice by scheduling enough clinic hours	1 2 3 4 5 ( )
• Cost-effectiveness	1 2 3 4 5 ( )
• Willingness to adapt to changing conditions to maintain smooth clinic operations	1 2 3 4 5 ( )
Comments:	

Sample continues next page

Sample: Peer Assessment Form (continued)

E. Professional growth • Participation in quality CME to maintain best possible standards of medical care	 1 2 3 4 5 ( )
II. Nonclinical	
A. Understanding of the Practice's organization and policies including own role; placing group interest ahead of individual interest. Comments:	1 2 3 4 5 ( )
B. Group commitment • Attends committee, department, and staff meetings • Participates in professional, community service organizations, hospitals, etc., which adds prestige to the group Comments:	 1 2 3 4 5 ( ) 1 2 3 4 5 ( )
C. Dependability and reliability in consistently and accurately completing assignments in a timely fashion Comments:	1 2 3 4 5 ( )
D. Willingness to accept constructive criticism Comments:	1 2 3 4 5 ( )
E. Adaptability to changing work situations, demands, and outside pressures Comments:	1 2 3 4 5 ( )
F. Professional relationships • Relationships with peers • Relationships with employees • Relationships with hospital Comments:	 1 2 3 4 5 ( ) 1 2 3 4 5 ( ) 1 2 3 4 5 ( )
G. Contributes to a positive work environment • Attitude, sense of enthusiasm Comments:	 1 2 3 4 5 ( )
General Comments:	

Sample: Peer Physician Review

For: ____________________
Date: __________

Please evaluate on a scale of 1 to 3 (3 = outstanding; 2 = satisfactory; 1 = needs improvement). A note of explanation on the following page should accompany any score of 1.

Clinical Performance	Score
1. Maintains a current knowledge of appropriate areas of his or her specialty	
2. Makes an effort to expand present knowledge base	
3. Communicates knowledge effectively to referring physicians	
4. Skills are effective, safe, and time-efficient	
5. Thoroughness of patient examinations and dictation	
Work Habits	**Score**
1. Contributes willingly and appropriately to group needs	
2. Shows positive attitude toward workload and demands of practice	
3. Can be relied upon to complete assignments and responsibilities eagerly, doing them well and promptly	
4. Responds well to crises, unexpected needs, in groups, etc.	
5. Functions well under pressure and on-call schedules	
6. Keeps up with office/hospital charts and dictation	
7. Communicates with colleagues as needed when on call	
8. Communicates patient information/progress to referring physicians	
9. Initiates follow-up patient phone calls or responds to requests to do so in a timely manner	
10. Adapts flexibly to changing daily practice demands	
11. Establishes good rapport with patients and treats patients with respect	
12. Shows respect for supporting staff	
13. Maintains professional appearance in grooming and dress	
Nonclinical Aspects	**Score**
1. Teaches and empowers supporting staff (hospitals and office)	
2. Willingly gives lectures, speaks to civil groups, etc.	
3. Contributes to establishing and maintaining a good practice environment	
4. Accepts responsibility in group corporate/business matters	
5. Accepts responsibility in hospital matters	

Sample continues next page

Sample: Peer Physician Review (continued)

6. Supports professional society and related organizations	
7. Cultivates existing referral relations and makes an effort to develop new referral patterns	
8. Shows leadership in managing work environment and group matters	
9. Has appropriate concern about group finances	

Key Strengths (List Top 3)	Key Weaknesses (List Top 3)
1.	1.
2.	2.
3.	3.

Areas of needed improvement (any score of 1 under clinical performance, work habits, or nonclinical aspects): ______________________________

Rating performed by: ____________________ (Optional Signature)

Policy 4.7

Referrals Policy

In the absence of a patient discharge summary, the Practice physicians can send a letter to the referring physician. This method of communication is used most often when consulting and signing off on a patient. This summarizes the patient's clinical course from the specialist's viewpoint and serves as a mini-discharge summary to be utilized when the patient returns to the office in follow-up.

In addition, this letter generates goodwill and communication with the referring physician and other subspecialists attending to the patient during the hospitalization. Alternatively, if the Practice's physician is not the admitting physician during a hospitalization, a summary may be dictated by the Practice physician on the hospital dictation or EHR system and sent with a form letter to the referring physician. This alleviates additional transcription for office transcriptionists.

Sample: Referring Physician Survey

Instructions: As a valued referring physician to our group, you are invited to help us improve our service to you and to your patients. Your candid and honest response is appreciated. You may return the completed survey to us using the enclosed self-addressed envelope.

Sincerely,

__________, MD

1. Describe the factors that determine your decision and/or willingness to consult with and/or refer to our service?
   a. ______________________________
   b. ______________________________
   c. ______________________________
2. Rate your level of overall satisfaction with timeliness/access of our services?
   a. Totally satisfied
   b. Generally satisfied
   c. Marginally satisfied
   d. Dissatisfied
3. Rate your level of overall satisfaction with the medical care and advice we provide?
   a. Totally satisfied
   b. Generally satisfied
   c. Marginally satisfied
   d. Dissatisfied
4. Rate your level of overall satisfaction with the timeliness of our communications with you?
   a. Totally satisfied
   b. Generally satisfied
   c. Marginally satisfied
   d. Dissatisfied
5. What type of feedback have you received from your patients regarding access to our services and the care they received?
   - Totally satisfied __________%
   - Generally satisfied __________%
   - Marginally satisfied __________%
   - Dissatisfied __________%
6. Describe what we can do to improve.
   a. ______________________________
   b. ______________________________
   c. ______________________________
7. Comments:
   ____
   ____
   ____

__________ Respondent (Optional)

__________ Group (Optional)

Policy 4.8

Use of EHR System Policy

The Practice's providers must maintain a health record that properly documents care and services provided to its patients. In addition to their clinical purposes, health records must also be maintained for business and evidentiary purposes. Many electronic health record (EHR) systems have limitations that may affect their use for such purposes, regardless of whether the media used to create and store health records is electronic or paper based.

Because the EHR is a legal business record for the Practice, it must be maintained in a manner that complies with applicable regulations, accreditation standards, professional practice standards, and legal standards. These standards may vary based on care setting, legal jurisdiction, and locale. Therefore, the Practice must identify the content required for its own legal health record as well as the standards for maintaining the integrity of that content.

Procedure

1. Appropriate orientation to the EHR system will occur during the first two (2) weeks of physician orientation.
2. Physicians will be expected to become familiar with consult-note generation, progress-note generation, prescription entering, electronic signatures for chart notes, hospital admission orders, transfusion orders, and memos.
3. Physicians will also be expected to learn how to sign off on electronically submitted laboratory studies generated by in-house labs and from outside reference laboratories.
4. The physician is expected to "sign-off" electronically, in a timely manner, all notes and reports generated by that physician.
5. Additional policies and procedures can be found at www.mgma.com and www.ahima.org.

Policy 4.9

Clinical Guidelines Policy

Step I. Guideline Development Process

The healthcare program committee selects the guideline topic. The committee then examines the Practice's patient population health, encounter frequency, and cost data to determine:

1. Which health conditions are most common and/or costly in a population;
2. What potential impact guidelines could have on those conditions; and
3. The feasibility of developing and implementing guidelines on those conditions.

Based on their findings, the committee targets specific health conditions for improvement through guidelines.

Step II. Assemble Guideline Work Group

For each health condition, a cross-disciplinary work group of experts is assembled. Each work group includes a lead physician, facilitator, purchasing representative, and measurement advisor. Experts in the pertinent disciplines, including physicians, other healthcare physicians, and health educators, round out the team. Generally, work groups consist of eight (8) to twelve (12) members. The lead physician shares the responsibility of guiding the group process with the facilitator. The lead physician has the final responsibility for the content of the guideline and arbitrates medical differences of opinion between work group members. The facilitator assists the lead in managing the work group and providing staff support. Facilitators are nurses with group facilitation and continuous quality improvement experience who are employed by a member medical group. The measurement advisor leads the work group in identifying a limited number of potential process and short-term outcome measures and evaluating their feasibility.

Step III. Guideline Work Group: Draft Guideline

The work group generally meets for three (3) hours every other week over a four- (4-) month period for a total of eight (8) sessions. It conducts an intensive review of the current literature and national guidelines for the condition under study. After analyzing the various procedures and weighing the outcomes data, a guideline draft is written outlining the treatment method that yields the best, most consistent outcome. A companion document is also drafted providing the rationale and references for the guideline, the measurement specifications to monitor the guideline, and suggestions for its implementation.

Step IV. All Participants: Review Draft Guideline (Critical Review)

1. The guideline draft and companion document undergo thorough review. Written comments are solicited from clinical, measurement, and management experts from within the member medical groups during an eight- (8-) week period of "Critical Review." Each of the Practice's participating medical groups determines its own process for distributing the guideline and obtaining feedback. Clinicians are asked to suggest modifications based on their understanding of the scientific literature coupled with their clinical expertise. Representatives from all departments involved in implementation and measurement review the guideline to determine its operational impact.
2. Each medical group designates a person who coordinates their review and implementation activities. These representatives are assembled for an "Implementation Ideas Exchange," where they share their concerns and strategies with staff and each other.
3. An advisory team composed of quality-improvement measurement experts from the member medical groups reviews the measurement plan. They provide input to the work group about data collection feasibility, validity, and reliability.
4. The draft guideline is widely circulated to other interested participants, including purchasers, who review guideline components related to work-site interventions, members of the healthcare program committee, and department of the health plan that are likely to be affected.

Step V. Guideline Work Group: Revise Guideline

Following the completion of the Critical Review period, the guideline work group meets one (1) to two (2) times to review the feedback. The original guideline and companion documents are revised as necessary, and a written response is prepared to address each of the suggestions received from reviewers.

Step VI. Healthcare Program Committee: Review Revised Guideline and Approve for Use on Trial Basis

Two (2) members of the healthcare program committee carefully review the Critical Review input, the work group responses, and the revised draft of the guideline and companion document. They report their findings to the entire committee, which either approves the guideline for plot implementation as submitted or negotiates changes with the work group representative present at the meeting.

Step VII. Medical Groups: Implement Guideline on Trial Basis (Pilot Implementation)

Medical groups introduce the guideline at pilot sites, providing training to the clinical staff and incorporating it into the Practice's scheduling, computer, and other Practice systems. Evaluation and assessment occurs throughout the pilot-test phase, which usually lasts for three (3) months. Comments and suggestions are solicited in the same manner as used during the Critical Review phase.

Step VIII. Guideline Work Group: Revise Guideline

The guideline work group uses the post–Critical Review process defined in Step V. The work group reviews the pilot sites' experiences and makes the necessary revisions to the guideline.

Step IX. Healthcare Program Committee: Review Revised Guideline and Approve for Implementation

The healthcare program committee follows the same process defined in Step VIII.

Step X. All Medical Groups: Implement Guidelines at All Sites (Full Implementation)

Following approval for full implementation, medical groups extend their use of the guideline to all of their sites and regularly provide the data specified in the measurement plan. Practice representatives periodically attend Implementation Ideas Exchange meetings to discuss and share implementation strategies.

Step XI. Guideline Work Group: Reevaluate and Revise Guidelines Annually

Approximately every twelve (12) months, the work group is reassembled to reevaluate all aspects of the guideline. The scientific literature is surveyed, and data collected by the medical groups is analyzed. A revised guideline is prepared that incorporates the improvements needed to ensure the best quality of care possible.

Step XII. All Participants: Review Draft Guideline Revision

If significant changes have been made to the guideline, the process outlined in Steps IV and V is followed. Guidelines undergoing little or no change are submitted directly to the healthcare program committee for approval.

CHAPTER 5

Quality

Policy 5.1

Quality Improvement/Risk Management Policy

The Practice shall have a comprehensive quality improvement plan to ensure the highest possible level of care and patient satisfaction.

Quality improvement activities will include:

- Quality care team monitors;
- Risk management monitors;
- External chart review;
- Patient/client satisfaction surveys;
- Occurrence reports;
- Complaint resolution/analysis;
- Policy and procedure review;
- Utilization review;
- Report from human resources; and
- Report from education coordinator.

Procedure

1. A quality improvement plan will be established and evaluated at least annually.
2. The quality improvement plan may be revised as necessary by the quality improvement manager, the medical director, and department chairs.
3. The preferred process improvement models include a Plan-Do-Check-Act (PDCA) cycle and the quality improvement/management standards and elements of The Joint Commission (TJC), the Accreditation Association for Ambulatory Health Care (AAAHC), and the National Committee for Quality Assurance (NCQA).
4. The senior management team will monitor the implementation and effectiveness of the quality improvement plan and quality care teams.
5. The improvement and effectiveness of the clinical components of the quality improvement plan will be the responsibility of the medical director.
6. The chief executive officer and board of directors are ultimately responsible for the quality of care and services delivered.
7. The quality improvement manager is responsible for the overall supervision of the quality improvement plan.
8. The managers and staff will implement the quality improvement process for their department.
9. Quality improvement information shall be provided to all involved services for appropriate action and follow-through.
10. The quality improvement manager and medical director are responsible for providing quarterly and annual reports summarizing quality improvement activities to the board of directors.
11. Confidentiality shall be maintained throughout the quality improvement process, and reports will not contain any identifiable patient or physician information.

Sample: Performance Improvement Program

Contents

Sample continues next page

Sample: Performance Improvement Program (continued)

Total Quality Management Plan

Purpose and Mission

The purpose and mission of the performance improvement program at the Practice is to achieve high-quality patient care, optimal patient outcomes, and efficient use of resources. This is achieved by looking prospectively through performance improvement and retrospectively through quality assurance. The total quality management plan (TQMP) of the Practice is an ongoing program that strives to demonstrate measurable improvement in patient-health outcomes and to improve patient safety by the use of quality indicators/ performance measures associated with improved health outcomes/patient safety and by identifying and reducing medical errors.

Commitment to Performance

The governing body, administration, management, employees, and medical staff of the Practice are committed to improving the quality of services provided. It is believed that improvement in performance is possible and that, as an organization, we will strive to meet or exceed reasonable customer expectations at a cost that represents value to the customers. We believe we can improve overall performance by taking actions that result in measurable change in identified performance dimensions (efficacy, appropriateness, availability, timeliness, effectiveness, continuity, safety, efficiency, respect, and caring) by improving those governance, managerial, clinical, and support processes that most effect patient outcomes.

Performance improvement at the Practice stresses continual improvement of processes through design and redesign. The TQMP includes the following aspects.

Performance Improvement. Performance improvement is proactive in nature and seeks to build product and service quality into the treatment of patients. The Practice strives to continually improve the quality and performance of the care rendered to its patients. The goal is the elimination of variations or defects by removing the causes of variations. Priorities for performance improvement activities include:

- High-risk, high-volume, and problem-prone areas;
- Determination of the incidence, prevalence, and severity of high-risk, high-volume, and problem-prone areas; and
- Activities that affect health outcomes, patient safety, and quality of care.

Performance improvement activities must track adverse patient events, examine their causes, implement improvements, and ensure that improvements are sustained over time.

Annual performance improvement projects must reflect the scope and complexity of services and operations.

Quality Assurance. Quality assurance is retrospective in nature, reviewing/analyzing specific indicators to identify problem areas that might include the following:

- Objectively and systematically monitoring and evaluating the quality and appropriateness of patient care on an ongoing basis in order to establish that quality is improved or maintained. Identifying and pursuing opportunities to improve patient care;
- Systematically monitoring the nursing standards of practice, standards of care, performance, and consumer satisfaction;
- Documenting adverse patient events;

Sample continues next page

Sample: Performance Improvement Program (continued)

- Implementing infection control;
- Demonstrating effective actions that result in maintaining and/or improving quality nursing care;
- Showing evidence of problem resolution by way of tracking and follow-up;
- Promoting individual accountability among staff at the Practice;
- Identifying needs for specific educational training of personnel;
- Identifying environmental hazards and sources of potential infection;
- Identifying trends; and
- Identifying problems requiring action by the Practice and/or committees and referring such problems for further investigation and action.

Infection Control. A review of all infections identified with follow-up studies until resolution.

Risk Management. A review of all incident reports to include follow-up evaluation and communication with the governing body when necessary.

Utilization Review. The study of financial issues, such as cost per case as compared to reimbursement for that case.

Abuse Identification. Information to identify possible child and elderly abuse.

Strategic Plan

Strategic planning is the basis for performance improvement. Assessing our healthcare delivery system for opportunities to improve care and services is an ongoing process at the Practice. The leaders and physicians understand that planning is a dynamic process that demands the capacity for changing focus as needed. Although some aspects of care for performance improvement are planned, when opportunities arise, they are addressed through the notification report system.

Objectives

- To improve patient care quality by assessing and improving those governance, managerial, clinical, and support processes that most affect patient outcomes.
- To integrate and coordinate performance improvement activities throughout the organization.
- To enhance customer satisfaction (internal and external customers).
- To ensure participation of all aspects in the performance improvement process.
- To provide effective mechanisms to identify and resolve problems as they relate to the clinical aspects of patient care and services provided, as well as problems identified with any operational systems.
- To ensure communication and reporting pathways between the Practice, the medical staff, administration, and the governing body.
- To continuously expand our knowledge and use of appropriate management tools that will enable us to meet increasingly challenging standards and expectations.

Authority and Accountability

The leaders of the Practice, which include the RN nursing director (performance improvement coordinator), administrator, medical director, medical staff, and governing body, are responsible for:

Sample continues next page

Sample: Performance Improvement Program (continued)

- Setting expectations, developing plans, and implementing procedures to assess and improve the quality of governance, management, clinical, and support processes;
- Becoming educated regarding the approaches and methods of performance improvement;
- Setting priorities for organization-wide performance improvement activities that are designed to improve patient care quality;
- Allocating adequate resources for assessment and improvement of governance, managerial, clinical, and support processes;
- Ensuring that staff members are educated in assessing and improving the processes that contribute to improved patient care quality;
- Developing and participating, individually and jointly, in mechanisms that foster communication and coordination of departmental and organization-wide activities to include all contracted services; and
- Analyzing and evaluating the effectiveness of their contributions to improving quality.

In addition, the Practice leaders establish performance improvement responsibilities in the organization to include the following.

I. Governing Body

- Fosters the concepts of performance improvement in healthcare through their personal commitment to the success of the performance improvement program.
- Defines the organization's commitment to continually improving the quality of patient care and services in the facilities mission statement.
- Incorporates the findings from performance improvement assessment and improvement activities in strategic, program, and resource planning.
- Approves appropriate clinical privileges for each eligible individual for the credentials committee.
- Participates in education concerning the approach and methods of continuous performance improvement in the Practice.
- Commits to the provision of financial support for the performance improvement so that the administration and the medical staff have the necessary resources for education, services, equipment, information management, and personnel required to support performance improvement activities.
- Receives regular reports of the facility's information to ensure compliance with the intent of the program and to effect constructive change.
- Participates in a review of the effectiveness of the performance improvement program in achieving desired priorities and performance improvement goals.

II. Medical Director

- Ensures that performance improvement activities are ongoing.
- Appoints medical staff members to the various performance improvement committees and appropriate facility committees, encouraging their active participation.
- Receives and reviews performance improvement reports from medical staff and acts appropriately on their recommendations.
- Ensures that the governing body regularly receives reports on medical staff performance-improvement activities.

Sample continues next page

Sample: Performance Improvement Program (continued)

- Recommends to the governing body appropriate clinical privileges for each eligible individual for credentials.
- Ensures assessment and improvement in the use of surgical and other invasive procedures.
- Ensures assessment and improvement in the medical record function.
- Ensures assessment and improvement in the pharmacy and therapeutics function.
- Recommends to the governing body the performance improvement activities of the medical staff.

III. Administration

- Ensures that employees are educated concerning the approach and methods of performance improvement.
- Oversees the design of the organization's approach to improve performance, and ensures that this approach is carried out.
- Establishes priorities and defines at least one interdepartmental process to be focused on annually for improvement.
- Allocates resources for assessment and improvement of the facility's governance, managerial, clinical, and support processes.
- Ensures that the organization-wide performance improvement activities of infection control, utilization management, quality assurance, performance improvement, and risk management are performed.
- Reviews reports of clinical and nonclinical performance improvement activities.
- Reviews annually the performance improvement activities.
- Develops and participates in mechanisms to foster communication among individuals and departments, to coordinate internal activities, and to ensure ongoing recognition and celebration of achievements.
- Ensures that the governing body and medical staff are regularly informed regarding performance improvement activities.

IV. RN Nursing Director (Performance Improvement Coordinator)

- Ensures that employees are educated concerning the methods of performance improvement.
- Ensures that the facility's full range of care or service has been reviewed in order to identify important aspects of care and service.
- Ensures that those important aspects of care and service that affect large numbers of patients, are of high benefit or high risk for individual patients, and/or are suspected of producing problems for patients or employees are identified.
- Sets priorities for monitoring the specific aspects of care and service as well as other feedback that may indicate an opportunity to improve the quality of care or service, including customer satisfaction.
- Establishes indicators and realistic benchmarks.
- Evaluates results and takes appropriate action.
- Ensures that employees understand performance improvement and are actively involved in performance improvement activities.
- Establishes focus teams for the purpose of making department improvements (and interdepartmental improvements).

Sample continues next page

Sample: Performance Improvement Program (continued)

- Uses the results of performance improvement activities in the performance evaluation process.
- Uses the results from performance improvement activities to study and improve processes that affect patient care outcomes.
- Ensures communication of results to relevant individuals and groups. Reports results quarterly to medical advisory and governing bodies.
- Tracks the status of identified opportunities or problems to ensure improvement and resolution.
- Completes an annual summary of activities and improvements.

V. Physicians

- Participate in the identification of the full range of care/services, important aspects of care, indicators and benchmarks for evaluation of the care/service.
- Participate in the data collection, assessment, and improvement process as requested.
- Identify areas of concern related to customer care/service or departmental/organizational processes.
- Participate in the identification of causes of process/system failure and offer recommendations for improvement.
- Participate in reevaluating whether improvement has occurred, and take action to correct situations as they occur to achieve improved care/services.

VI. Performance Improvement (PI) Committee

- Coordinates the monitoring and evaluation activities for the Practice.
- Provides concurrent review of patient care activities to identify and facilitate opportunities to improve care/services.
- Provides information relative to medical staff practice to the credentials committee for physician appointment and reappointment.
- Provides technical assistance to the staff necessary to complete performance improvement activities.
- Assists the leaders in fulfilling the performance improvement process to include monitoring and ensuring plan/process development, reporting processes, implementation of actions related to identified opportunities, and annual appraisal.
- Provides the governing body, medical staff, and administration information necessary to monitor the assessment and improvement of care/services.
- Ensures that information from clinical risk review related to patient care and safety is accessible to the performance improvement function.
- Provides the governing body and the medical staff with annual review information for all Practice clinical and nonclinical functions for the purpose of evaluating process effectiveness.
- Assesses the quality and appropriateness of nursing care.
- Makes recommendations for action when problems or opportunities for improvement are identified.
- Identifies needs for specific educational training of personnel.
- Identifies and monitors environmental hazards and sources of potential infections.
- Establishes tracking mechanisms to identify adverse trends in patient care.

Sample continues next page

Sample: Performance Improvement Program (continued)

- Identifies and monitors opportunities to improve patient care and establishes resolutions to that end.
- Organizes structure of the PI committee:
  - Physician (at least one);
  - RN nursing director (coordinator);
  - Staff nurse (at least one);
  - Administrator; and
  - Others as assigned (focus groups such as RPh, lab, housekeeping, etc.).
- PI committee named at the Practice:

  ____

  ____

  (Performance Improvement coordinator)

  ____

  ____

Meetings. The PI committee meeting will occur, but will not be limited to, the following designated times: annual meetings for planning session; quarterly meetings within three (3) weeks before next scheduled medical advisory board and governing body meeting; and whenever deemed necessary.

Identification and Prioritization of Opportunities for Improvement

I. Organization-Wide

Annually or as needed, the leadership of the Practice conducts a review of assessment efforts related to organization-wide activities. As a result, at least one (1) area is prioritized for performance improvement efforts. Teams are established, which involve multiple departments and/or services. (For example, the Practice will evaluate patient scheduling problems related to time of call from office until the procedure is scheduled. This would involve working with the physician's office, the facility scheduler, the lab, etc. Thus, a multidisciplinary approach.)

II. Community

The healthcare needs of the county and surrounding county communities are assessed regularly to determine priorities related to service development.

III. Other

On an ongoing basis, through the use of a variety of assessment tools, the Practice personnel will identify opportunities to improve performance. These opportunities represent a range of involvement from single departments/services to those that involve several areas. Through the performance improvement reporting system, efforts are prioritized as they relate to the anticipated impact of improvement, particularly as related to patient care. Specific emphasis is placed on the expectation of the customer(s).

Scope of Performance

The performance improvement program applies to all areas of the Practice to include:

1. Scheduling/front desk;
2. Admitting;
3. Pre-op area;
4. Procedure rooms;

Sample continues next page

Sample: Performance Improvement Program (continued)

5. Post-op area;
6. Contract services; and
7. Billing services.

To meet the established nursing standards and goals and to properly monitor the quality of care provided in these areas, many data sources are reviewed.

Department-Wide Monitor. Indicators of quality care are monitored on a continual basis. These are reviewed and decided upon annually by the PI committee. Individual areas are involved in monitoring patient care specific to their important aspects of care.

Other data sources may include:

1. Infection control findings;
2. Medication variances;
3. Fall variances;
4. Procedural variance;
5. Patient/family/staff contact, which might include:
    - Direct family/patient contact;
    - Survey of interview;
    - Patient/staff complaints;
    - Staff concern expressed formally or informally;
    - Education and staff development findings;
    - Policy and procedure findings;
    - Discharge planning;
    - Identification of a patient care problem;
    - Medical staff findings;
6. Monitoring activity tools might include:
    - Patient medical record;
    - Monitoring activities of the medical and professional staff;
    - Notification forms;
    - Patient surveys;
    - Department logs;
    - Staff comments;
    - Direct observation of patients or staff;
    - Risk management data;
    - Infection control data;
    - Drug use/adverse reactions;
    - Utilization management; and
    - Medical staff departments: physicians performing procedures, allied health personnel.

Performance Improvement Quality Assurance Process

Methodology

Performance improvement will utilize a systematic approach to monitoring activities. The following areas are directed toward that goal.

Sample continues next page

Sample: Performance Improvement Program (continued)

Responsibility

The responsibility for the implementation of the performance improvement program has been outlined. The majority of the monitoring of activities will take place at the committee level. Responsibility will rest with the performance improvement coordinator.

Scope of Care

The Practice is dedicated to providing __________ [SPECIALTY] care/services and assessing and meeting individual care and educational needs throughout the patient event.

Important Aspects of Care

Each area will identify the important aspects of care related to the service provided. Clinical activities that involve a high volume of patients or entail a high degree of risk for patients, or those that tend to create problems for staff or patients, should be identified as most important for monitoring.

Indicators

An indicator is a defined, measurable dimension of quality or appropriateness of an important aspect of care or service. Indicators specify the patient care activities, events, occurrences, and outcomes that are to be monitored and evaluated in order to determine whether those aspects of care conform to current standards of quality. Activities are based on indicators that are agreed upon by the PI committee. Indicators are based on scope of care.

- **Generic indicators** are designated as generic by the PI committee and are common to most areas. Generic indicators include but are not limited to variances, infection, patient satisfaction, and procedural variance. Screening criteria, when present, are considered part of the indicator.
- **Thresholds** are pre-established levels of performance described for each indicator. The threshold is the point in the cumulative data that "triggers" intensive evaluation by the nursing professional. Thresholds will be set for each indicator.

Collection, Organization, and Evaluation of Data

Activities are accomplished by the routine collection and periodic evaluation of data. Data necessary to evaluate the degree of compliance with the indicator is collected according to times designated on the calendar and the performance improvement plan, or more frequently as appropriate. The data is tabulated and reported as a percentage of compliance or as a raw number, whichever is more appropriate. The data is evaluated and an assessment of findings documented on the performance improvement report. The assessment should include conclusions based on the findings. The performance improvement plan will designate who will be responsible for collecting data and the time frame for collecting data.

Taking Action to Improve Care

Activities result in appropriate actions to resolve identified problems. The evaluation of monitoring activities is followed by action taken to resolve identified problems. It is ultimately the performance improvement coordinator's responsibility to take action. The action taken is to be documented on the performance improvement report. The PI committee with the nursing staff, when appropriate, formulates a plan to resolve or reduce identified problems or opportunities to improve care of performance.

Sample continues next page

Sample: Performance Improvement Program (continued)

The performance improvement coordinator will tabulate the names of noncompliant personnel using established indicators for purposes of trending and performance review. The performance improvement coordinator is responsible for taking definitive action when trends or significant problems are identified. The coordinator may choose to develop classes or other training activities, provide reference sources, or restructure existing educational procedures when performance problems result from a lack of knowledge. The coordinator may choose to initiate changes in policy and procedures (redistribute staff, alter use of equipment and supplies, etc.) or correct problems in communication when performance results from defects in the system.

A plan of corrective action determines:

1. Who or what is expected to change;
2. Who is responsible for implementing action;
3. What action is appropriate in view of the cause, scope, and severity of the problem; and
4. When a change is expected to occur.

Recommendations made at the PI committee meeting are forwarded to the governing body that has the authority to act when required action exceeds the area's authority.

Follow-Up

Activities are continuous in an effort to ensure that improvements in care and performance are sustained. Monitoring and evaluation of activities continue after actions have been taken. When problems are identified, monitoring may take place either as planned or instantly, when appropriate, in order to show whether or not actions taken have been effective, to ensure that a high level of quality and uniform appropriateness are maintained, and to ensure that any need for further improvement is addressed.

"Pending follow-up" requires that a comment be entered and the date defined when the indicators will be reassessed to demonstrate the effects of action taken. The problem is reassessed, and ideally, new action taken with follow-up when the quality and appropriateness of care in an identified area does not improve. A focus review can be done whenever appropriate to study a problem in depth.

Communication of Performance Improvement

The communication of performance improvement effects occurs at multiple levels throughout the facility. The performance improvement coordinator (RN nursing director) is responsible for communicating performance improvement activities to the employees, medical staff, medical director, and governing body on a quarterly basis (at minimum) and always as needed. This is achieved in the following manner.

The coordinator will include performance improvement activities on the agenda of area staff meetings where identified problems are discussed, suggestions for actions are received, and instructions to staff are given.

The coordinator maintains a manual that includes:

1. Statement of scope of care, listing important aspects of care;
2. Performance improvement calendar for monitoring and evaluation activities;
3. Performance improvement plan;
4. Copy of performance improvement reports submitted monthly;

Sample continues next page

Sample: Performance Improvement Program (continued)

5. Copies of data retrieval sheets (these are filed and kept separate from the performance improvement manual);
6. Indicator trending report;
7. Staff noncompliance trending report; and
8. Standards of care and standards of practice.

Minutes

Performance improvement minutes are written by the chairperson or designated alternate. A copy is sent to the medical director, governing body, and all committee members prior to the next scheduled quarterly meeting.

Program Evaluation

The performance improvement program will be evaluated annually and as needed for effectiveness. The evaluation will be systemic and follow a predetermined outline. The area plans will be evaluated annually and as needed for effectiveness, and changes will be made accordingly.

Confidentiality

All records, data, and knowledge collected for performance improvement are confidential, and all committee members and other persons collecting such information shall preserve its confidentiality. All data and information acquired and prepared for the performance improvement program are not discoverable as put forth in state confidentiality statutes.

Quality Improvement Meeting Agenda

__________ [DATE]

1. Roll call
2. Review of last meeting's minutes
3. Nursing report:
   a. Log books
   b. Notification reports
   c. Pharmacy report
   d. Report from ad hoc meetings
   e. Plan of action from last meeting
4. Infection control
5. Medical record review
   a. Report and forms
   b. Status of medical records through __________
   c. Plan of action from last meeting
6. Patient satisfaction
7. Peer review
   a. Report and forms
   b. Plan of action from last meeting
8. Old business
9. New business
10. Adjournment

Sample continues next page

Sample: Performance Improvement Program (continued)

Quality Improvement Nursing Report

1. Log books
   a. Daily logs
      - Staffing log
      - Patient procedure log
      - Facility checklist, daily log
      - Code chart
   b. Weekly logs
      - Spore tests
      - Drug inventory
      - Janitorial cleaning
   c. Monthly logs
      - Backup power supply
   d. Quarterly logs
      - Fire alarm test
      - Equipment maintenance/biomed electrical check, power source
      - Fire drill
   e. Ongoing intermittent logs
      - Employee files and orientation
      - In-services
      - Facility enhancements, repairs
2. Notification reports

Performance Improvement Review

What is performance improvement? The last thirty (30) years have shown a progressive change in evaluating care given to the patient. Accreditation groups, such as AAAHC, are structuring their evaluation around the word "performance." They feel that an organization's commitment to providing high-quality care is not enough — it must prove that it is committed to an ongoing delivery of such care. While quality is the overriding theme to this process, the measurement of performance in all aspects of care and delivery is key.

Let's review your performance improvement program:

1. Describe the current efforts in assessing the performance of care provided by the Practice.
   a. Are these efforts organized into a formal program?
   b. Does the review include assessment of the following areas?
      - Patient care
      - Physical facilities
      - Practice systems
      - Patient satisfaction
      - Confidentiality of patient information
      - Other
   c. Does the Practice's performance assessment program relate to affiliated hospital programs or professional review organizations?

Sample continues next page

Sample: Performance Improvement Program (continued)

   d. How often is a review team in your Practice? Who is a member of the performance review team in your Practice?
      - How often does the team meet?
      - Are the governing body, medical director, and administrator involved in this process?
      - Are quality review teams trained in review techniques and procedures?
      - Could further education be offered to these individuals to assist them in the review process?
      - Who is the responsible party overseeing all performance review programs? How did he or she obtain this position?

   e. Are performance review programs an ongoing process in your Practice?

2. How do you monitor performance?
   a. Which of the following techniques does your Practice use to measure and ensure the highest level of performance in care? Why?
      - *Medical record audit* — random audit or audit of patients with specific conditions
      - *Physician peer review* — direct observation of work and examination of charts
      - *Clinical audit* — observation of clinic systems at work and clinical management
      - *Patient surveys or interviews* — collection of opinions about quality
      - *Baseline audit* — review of healthcare services at work and clinical management
      - *Criteria mapping* — comparison of care given by the "ideal" physician and care given by the physicians in your Practice
      - *Structure audit* — an explicit critique of facilities and staff against predetermined criteria
      - *Outcome statistics* — based on data from the Practice, such as mortality rates
      - Other (specify)

   b. Do you recognize any deficiencies or limitations in the methodologies you employ? Explain your response. Are there limitations in the amount and accuracy of data records used to judge healthcare?

3. What is the process or approach that your Practice utilizes to assess the overall performance of care? Does your overall assessment cover all aspects of care, including process, structure, and outcome?
   a. *Process of care* — specific activities that the physician performs when interacting with patients:
      - Physical exams, including blood pressure, weight, and height measurements
      - Personal medical history, and recording symptoms and complaints
      - Number of tests and types of laboratory testing (such as drawing blood or collecting urine samples)
      - Number and types of radiology tests
      - Physician/patient phone calls

   b. *Structure of care* — overall physical and organizational environment of the Practice:
      - Safety and adequacy of the physical facility
      - Design of the facility (oriented to the patient, comfortable, pleasing to the eye)
      - Organization of the Practice, including strategic planning and routine meetings of medical staff

Sample continues next page

Sample: Performance Improvement Program (continued)

- Operational management, including management information systems, medical records management, scheduling, and referrals following acceptable legal and medical standards

c. *Outcome of care* — measurable results of group medical care:

- Physician follow-up on care
- Type of recovery, length of wellness, and time from first appointment to treatment to wellness
- Presence or absence of symptoms
- Patient opinions on own health after treatment
- Procedure-specific and service-specific morbidity and mortality

4. Answer the following questions concerning the formal audit of the technical performance of care performed by your Practice:

a. Who determines specific audit procedures, criteria, and standards? Upon whose views are criteria measurements based — professional review organizations, outside consultants, national professional associations, or the Practice's own practitioners?

b. Who determines the topics of the audit? Who selects physicians, procedures, or diagnoses to analyze?

c. What is the role of the medical records department in the audit?

- Does it retrieve patient files, gain access to the records, and collect the data? Are there appropriate releases on file signed by patients?
- How important is confidentiality when examining patient records?

d. How efficient and accurate are current processes for data collection, identification of records, and presentation of data for interpretation?

- Do medical records staff members review all records on an adult topic, or is a random sample taken?
- Are computers used to collect data and review clinical records?
- What information is requested on audit forms? When was the last time these forms were updated and reviewed?
- Are results of the data search randomly checked for errors?

e. Who presents the final results of the audit?

f. In the past, what have the results of the audit indicated about problems with practitioners, as well as problems in these areas:

- Equipment
- Laboratory results
- Clinical records
- Facility limitations
- Other (specify)

g. How are the results of the audit used to improve the quality of care provided by the Practice?

Quality improvement studies will represent a mix of studies addressing:

- Clinical issues;
- Administrative issues; and
- Cost of care.

Policy 5.2

Electronic Health Records Policy

Under the guidance of an electronic health record (EHR) medical director and with the assistance of the administrator, a clinical records department will be established to develop and maintain patient information in a complete and confidential manner. See also Policy 4.8: Use of EHR System.

Procedure

1. The EHR and clinical records supervisors will work with the physicians to ensure timely, legible completion of records (within [X] days) using appropriate coding. If physicians fail to do so, their right to practice will be suspended following a verbal and written warning. If a physician should consistently fail to complete and return records, such failure may lead to termination.
2. Clinical records will be securely maintained in the records department and can only be made available to other departments via appropriate routing processes. Access to the records will be limited to authorized personnel, who will be fully informed of their confidential-information obligations.
3. Records will be saved, either on site or in a safeguarded external site, in accordance with federal and state statutes.

Responsibility

The EHR medical director, clinical records supervisor, and practice administrator shall take necessary actions to ensure compliance with this policy.

Policy 5.3

Nonphysician Provider Supervision Policy[1]

Practice administrators, billers, and coders may be confused when billing for services not personally performed by the Practice's physicians. Medicare's "incident-to" provisions allow your organization to bill for such qualified services as if the billing practitioner personally performed them.

Procedure

For a service to qualify as incident to a physician's care, it must be:

- An integral part of the physician's plan of care:
  - Under the normal course of treatment;

1 Laurie A. Desjardins, CPC, PCS, "Avoiding the Pitfalls of Medicare's 'Incident-to' Rules," *MGMA Connexion*, 23–24, November/December 2008.

   - Initial care personally provided by the physician, who writes orders for ongoing care; or
   - Requiring ongoing physician involvement;
- Directly supervised by the physician — someone, either the ordering physician or a physician member of the practice, must be in the office and immediately available if needed; and
- Normally provided at no charge or when costs are included with the physician's service. In this context, the term "physician" includes allied health professionals (physician assistants, nurse practitioners, clinical nurse specialists, nurse midwives, and clinical psychologists). The service must be billed under the ID number of the practitioner who provided the direct supervision.

Incident-To Billing for Allied Health Professionals, Ancillary Personnel

If an allied health professional (AHP) provides care following the aforementioned guidelines, Medicare will reimburse the practice at 100 percent of the Medicare fee schedule rather than the 85 percent it normally pays when these professionals render care under their own IDs. Incident-to services must be billed under the supervising physician's ID. But keep in mind that the services may not be for a new patient or new problem.

Nonincident-to services may be provided to any patient or for any problem, new or established, as long as the AHP acts within the scope of his or her license and the care provided is billed using the AHP's provider number. For example, a patient is seen for a follow-up appointment for diabetes per Dr. Smith's orders. The patient's care today is supervised by Dr. Jones. A SOAP (subjective, objective, assessment, and plan) note is documented, signed by the nurse practitioner, and cosigned by Dr. Jones.

Nurses, medical assistants, or other clinical trained personnel may also perform incident-to services, such as immunizations, injections, or brief evaluation and management (E&M) services (CPT[2] code 99211). A physician, physician assistant, nurse practitioner, clinical nurse specialist, nurse midwife, or clinical psychologist may provide direct supervision for ancillary personnel.

Documentation of Incident-To Services

In documenting incident-to care, include:

- The practitioner whose care plan is being followed;
- A brief SOAP note describing care provided; and
- The name of the supervising practitioner.

For example, an ancillary caregiver might enter the following chart note: "CC: patient in for recheck of elevated BP per Dr. Jones, who is also supervising today. Patient states BP at home ranging from 120/75 to 135/80. Has been following low-sodium diet. BP today 126/78. Patient to see Dr. Jones next week."

2 CPT © 2011 American Medical Association. All rights reserved.

Policy 5.4 Virtual Consultations/E-mailing Patients Policy

It is recommended that guidelines be developed for appropriate use and management of e-mail between Practice physicians and patients. These written policies and procedures must be maintained when using electronic mail (e-mail) for physician–patient communications. The following criteria must be adhered to when using e-mail:

- All e-mail messages used to communicate between physicians and patients must be in accordance with the Practice's Physician/Patient Communication Policy (Policy 6.3 on page 194) and this policy.
- E-mail communications will only be used with established patients.
- Patients who elect to use e-mail must be advised of the Practice's e-mail policy and sign an informed consent agreement for Practice/patient e-communications before corresponding with physicians or staff through e-mail.
- Access to the e-mail system is restricted to only those patients who have signed the agreement for Practice/patient e-communication. If the agreement allowing correspondence via e-mail has not been signed, the Practice personnel must have the patient sign an agreement before any further correspondence is initiated. To ensure compliance with the __________[STATE] Board of Medical Examiner rules on physician–patient Internet use, it is imperative that the Practice physicians obtain this agreement prior to initiating e-mail communications with patients.
- E-mail communications are restricted to conditions and situations that do not require immediate attention.
- A copy of the signed agreement for Practice/patient e-communications is given to the patient, and the original is filed in the patient's clinical record.
- Automatic replies to all incoming messages will state: "Your message has been received by [PRACTICE NAME]. We will attempt to process your request within [ONE] business day. If your matter cannot wait, please call the office at [PRACTICE PHONE NUMBER], or if you feel this matter is life threatening, dial 9-1-1 immediately."
- The Practice physicians should make every attempt to respond to patients' e-mails within [ONE] business day, unless the physician is on leave and not in the office or the clinic directs the patient to an alternate provider.
- If an action is taken based on a patient's e-mail, the physician must respond to the patient's e-mail notifying him or her of the action taken. (For example, if the patient requests via e-mail that he or she needs a prescription refilled, the physician must reply to the patient to let him or her know that the prescription has been refilled and that it has been called in to the pharmacy.)
- E-mail communications are a permanent part of the patient's medical record, as required by the Practice's Electronic Health Records Policy (Policy 5.2 on page 159). They should be retained in the paper record and/or electronically, consistent with the [STATE] medical records retention rules.

- If the patient did not include his or her name and unit history number in the e-mail and the physician responded, the physician or the physician's staff will be responsible for writing this information on the e-mail, if it has been printed, or adding this information in the e-mail electronically before forwarding the e-mail for filing in the patient's clinical record.
- E-mails containing protected health information (PHI) must be treated with the same degree of security, privacy, and confidentiality as the patient's clinical record. Confidentiality of patient information will be maintained at all times to protect the integrity of patient-identifiable information.
- Practice personnel may not send or forward any PHI outside the Practice network via e-mail unless the communication is with the patient and the patient has signed an agreement for the Practice regarding patient e-communications. In some rare instances, exceptions will be granted by the Practice's privacy officer or Practice administrator. The Practice may also provide an encryption or VPN technological solution, depending on the recipient.
- When using e-mail, the Practice personnel should limit the information transmitted to the minimum necessary to meet the requester's needs and use de-identified PHI whenever applicable. However, these two requirements do not apply if the physician and the patient have signed an agreement on Practice/patient e-communications.
- The Practice personnel shall not compile patient e-mail addresses for marketing or fundraising purposes or supply patient e-mail addresses to any third party for advertising, solicitations, or any other use.
- Each desktop workstation will have a password-protected screen saver.

Violation of this policy may result in disciplinary action up to and including termination of employment for physicians. Additionally, individuals may be subject to the loss of access to privileges as well as civil and/or criminal prosecution.

Record Management of E-mail Correspondence between Practice Personnel and Patients

E-mails between the physician and patient are to be stored in the clinical record, as required by the Practice's Electronic Health Records Policy (Policy 5.2 on page 159). In addition, all patient-related e-mails should be deleted from the physician's e-mail account as required by and in accordance with the Practice's records retentions schedule.

Topics of E-mail Communication

E-mail communication can be used to address administrative issues, relay follow-up information, and answer questions following a face-to-face evaluation and consultation. Initial evaluation and diagnosis and topics of a sensitive nature should not be communicated through e-mail. The healthcare provider should use "due care" in corresponding with any patient through e-mail.

The following topics are considered appropriate for e-mail communication:

- Prescription refills;
- General medical advice after an initial face-to-face visit;

- Lab test results;
- Appointment requests for nonurgent problems;
- Simple treatment instructions; and
- Patient education to improve health literacy.

Examples of *inappropriate* topics may include:

- Discussion of HIV status;
- Adverse lab results;
- Workers' Compensation claims; and
- Urgent matters.

Composition of E-mail to Patients

First and foremost, confidentiality of patient information will be maintained at all times to protect the integrity of patient-identifiable information.

E-mails should be considered the same as a formal letter to the patient. E-mail communication lends itself to a sense of informal conversation; thus, physicians need to be aware of the tendency to lean toward informality, which may be inappropriate. All e-mails between physicians and patients must include:

- In the subject line header, all outgoing messages will contain a discreet message stating, "This is a confidential medical communication"; and
- In the header or footer or at the end of the e-mail, "To my patients, please note that e-mail is not necessarily a confidential medium and should be used for routine, nonurgent matters only. Urgent or emergent issues should be handled by telephone. E-mails may not be read in a timely manner if I am out of the office. If you have not received a response within two (2) business days, please contact my office at [PRACTICE PHONE NUMBER]."

In addition, when sending patient information via e-mail, the sender is expected to double-check all "To" fields before transmitting. And as with any form of medical record documentation, unprofessional remarks or comments in e-mail communications are prohibited.

E-mail Correspondence between Physicians

The Practice physicians may e-mail other Practice physicians regarding patient matters if the e-mail is sent within the Practice system and the correspondence is an informal consultation. It is left up to the discretion of the physician initiating the informal consultation as to whether the e-mail containing the informal consultation should be placed in the patient's clinical record. However, formal consultations for a specific patient should be addressed using the Practice's electronic health record or the written consultation process. Lastly, Practice physicians cannot use e-mail for informal consultations with non-Practice physicians unless all patient identifiers have been removed and the information is de-identified. Again, as with any form of medical record documentation, unprofessional remarks or comments in e-mail communications are prohibited.

Responding to Unsolicited E-mails

If Practice personnel receive unsolicited e-mail from a patient or a prospective patient and either does not have an agreement for Practice/patient e-communication in place or does not wish to communicate with the patient over e-mail, the individual should respond to the patient with the following statement: "Please contact our office to schedule an appointment to discuss any and all issues regarding your health concerns, as we believe an office visit is the appropriate method to address your concerns. You may reach the office by contacting [PRACTICE PHONE NUMBER]."

References

- The Health Insurance Portability and Accountability Act of 1996, codified at 42 USC §1320d through d-8 (HIPAA)
- 45 CFR Part 164 (HIPAA Privacy Regulations)
- 45 CFR Part 142 (HIPAA Security Regulations)
- 22 TAC §§174.1–174.5 (the Texas State Board of Medical Examiners rules governing the use of the Internet in the practice of medicine)
- UTMB (University of Texas Medical Branch) *Institutional Handbook of Operating Procedures*, www.utmb.edu/Policies_And_Procedures/Clinical/PNP_005051 (accessed February 4, 2011).
- UTMB (University of Texas Medical Branch) *Institutional Handbook of Operating Procedures*, 2.19.6 Information Resources

See Appendix for Practice and Patient e-Communications Agreement. See also Policy 9.12: Internet Usage.

Sample: Internet and E-mail Use Policy

Employees with access to the Internet and e-mail will use these communication devices in a safe, professional, and appropriate manner.

Purpose

Provide guidelines for the appropriate use of electronic communication (Internet and e-mail).

Guidelines

1. Internet/E-mail access is to be used solely for the purpose of conducting Practice business.
2. No software/files may be downloaded or added to a computer without prior approval of the administrator.
3. The Practice's administrator(s) reserves the right to intercept, monitor, copy, review, and download any communications or files received or stored on Practice-owned PCs.
4. Exposure of information (e.g., patient, business-related information) is strictly prohibited and is subject to the organization's policies governing confidentiality.
5. All e-mail communication will be professional and courteous in nature. Examples of improper use includes but is not limited to the following:
   a. Harassing or anonymous messages;
   b. Chain letters;

Sample continues next page

Sample: Internet and E-mail Use Policy (continued)

   c. Solicitation; and
   d. Visits to sexual or discriminatory Websites.
6. Inappropriate use of electronic communications is subject to corrective action.

Statement

It is the policy of the Practice to provide information systems technology tools (i.e., electronically transmitted mail) to enhance the effectiveness and timeliness of communications both internally and externally. These tools shall be used professionally, ethically, and in a lawful manner.

Intent

This policy describes appropriate use and monitoring of e-mail.

Definition

User: Any person authorized to access the Practice's e-mail system, including physicians, members of the medical staff, independent contractors, consultants, temporary workers, students, and other individuals or entities who use or have access to the Practice e-mail system.

Practice

1. **User's Duty of Care**
   User shall use the same care in the tone and content of e-mail and other electronic documents as he or she would for any other written communication. User recognizes that sending e-mail over the Internet/intranet is instantaneous and generally irretrievable. User further recognizes that his or her e-mail address identifies the Practice and understands that any statements, even those containing a personal communications disclaimer, may be attributed to the organization. User shall endeavor to make all electronic communications truthful and accurate. User acknowledges that anything created or stored on the computer system may, and likely will, be reviewed by individuals other than the original addressee. User shall strive to use good grammar and correct punctuation. In the absence of explanation, User recognizes that e-mail messages may be ambiguous and convey an incorrect impression. To minimize the risk of misdirected messages, User shall be responsible for verifying the address of an e-mail account. User shall not knowingly violate the acceptable-use policies of any entity through which electronic communications are transmitted or received and agrees that all messages shall be in accordance with accepted professional and business practices.
2. **Ownership of Systems and Data**
   User understands that the Practice owns the e-mail system and other communications systems and networks and all messages stored on them or transmitted using them, and such communications systems may only be used for approved purposes as further defined herein.
3. **Permitted Use**
   a. User shall be permitted access to the Practice's e-mail system and other communications systems and networks to assist in the performance of the User's job functions. Occasional, limited, appropriate personal use of the e-mail system is permitted if usage does not:
      (1) Interfere with the User's work performance;
      (2) Interfere with any other User's work performance;

Sample continues next page

Sample: Internet and E-mail Use Policy (continued)

(3) Have undue impact on the operation of the organization's computer system; or

(4) Violate any other provision of this policy or any other Practice policy, guideline, or standard.

b. At all times, User is responsible for using the e-mail system in a professional, ethical, and lawful manner. User understands that incidental personal use of the e-mail system is a privilege that may be revoked at any time.

c. User further understands that no right exists to obtain the contents of e-mail communications once his or her employment is terminated.

4. **Prohibited Activities**

   a. Material that is indecent, obscene, offensive, profane, defamatory, or derogatory, including, without limitation, sexual comments or images, racial or ethnic slurs, off-color or discriminatory jokes or cartoons, or otherwise unlawful or inappropriate content may not be sent by e-mail or other form of electronic communication (e.g., bulletin board systems, newsgroups, and chat groups) or displayed or stored on the Practice's computer system. If User encounters or receives this kind of material, he or she immediately shall report the incident to his or her supervisor. Similarly, links to sites containing sexually explicit or other prohibited content as described in this section may not be transmitted by e-mail or other form of electronic communication.

   b. User understands that use of the e-mail system for harassment, stalking, violating the privacy of another, committing fraud, or otherwise disrupting the ability of another to communicate electronically is prohibited.

   c. User shall not gain or attempt to gain unauthorized access to e-mail belonging to any other user, except that authorized employees may gain access to e-mail belonging to other users for the purposes of monitoring adherence to established policies/procedures.

   d. User further understands that use of the e-mail system to conduct an outside business or to shop for personal items is prohibited.

   e. Without prior written permission from his or her supervisor, the Practice's e-mail system also may not be used for dissemination or storage of commercial or personal advertisements, solicitations, promotions, religious or political debate, or any other unauthorized use as may be specified by the organization from time to time.

5. **Communication of Propriety Information**
   Sending, transmitting, or otherwise disseminating proprietary data, trade secrets, or other confidential information of the Practice, except as authorized by Practice policy, contracts, or for business purposes, is prohibited. Infringing on the proprietary rights (including copyrights) of others is prohibited. User shall label proprietary data, trade secrets, or other confidential information appropriately in e-mail communications to ensure that such information is not treated in the same manner as ordinary business records. Prior to transmitting proprietary data, trade secrets, or other confidential information, User first shall determine whether another mode of transmission is warranted. User understands that unauthorized dissemination of this information may result in substantial civil liability or criminal penalties.

6. **Communication of Information Subject to the Physician–Patient, Psychotherapist–Patient, or Other Privilege, or Otherwise Protected from Discovery**

   a. User understands that information necessary to perform his or her job functions may include information subject to the physician–patient, psychotherapist–patient, and/or other privilege or statutory protection from discovery and that such information must be maintained in accordance with applicable statutory mandates for the privileged or statutorily protected status of such communications to be

Sample continues next page

Sample: Internet and E-mail Use Policy (continued)

preserved. User further understands that privileged or statutorily protected communications must be treated with appropriate confidentiality and security and that such communications must not be distributed to individuals outside the scope of the privilege or statutory protection. Whenever there is any question whether certain information is privileged or statutorily protected, User shall verify the nature of such communications with the appropriate person at the Practice (i.e., the general counsel or colleagues who are familiar with such privileged communications) prior to transmitting the information. User shall exercise due care when transmitting information subject to a privilege or statutory protection via e-mail, including observance of the following steps:

(1) Include the following or a similar caption at the top of each message: "PRIVILEGED AND CONFIDENTIAL." Such information should not, in most cases, be forwarded to others. Therefore, User may also add, "DO NOT FORWARD WITHOUT SENDER'S PERMISSION";

(2) If using group mailing or other distribution lists, ensure that all addressees are appropriate recipients of the privileged or statutorily protected information;

(3) Verify all header fields prior to sending messages to ensure that the information contained therein is correct;

(4) Do not forward privileged or statutorily protected communications or their contents to others inside or outside the organization without appropriate authorization; and

(5) Store printed incoming and outgoing messages in a manner consistent with their privileged or statutorily protected nature.

b. Additional Special Requirements: Information Subject to the Physician–Patient, Psychotherapist–Patient, Chemical Dependency, or Other Privilege

In addition to observing the transmission steps described in this section, User shall handle all communications containing information subject to the physician–patient, psychotherapist–patient, or other privilege in accordance with the following:

(1) In transmitting sensitive healthcare information including HIV test results and AIDS records, mental health and developmental disability records, alcohol and drug-abuse diagnosis and treatment records, and genetic information, User shall disclose the minimum information necessary consistent with the request for disclosure; and

(2) User shall ensure that patient information and records are disclosed only in accordance with applicable state and federal laws and regulations and Practice policies/procedures.

c. Additional Special Requirements: Attorney–Client Communications

In addition to observing the transmission steps described in this section, User shall handle all attorney–client communications in accordance with the following:

(1) Prior to transmitting any e-mail communications to in-house counsel or an attorney representing the Practice, User shall label the communication as "PRIVILEGED AND CONFIDENTIAL" or a similar heading.

d. Additional Special Requirements: Peer Review Information and Documents

In addition to observing the transmission steps described in this section, User shall handle all communications relating to credentialing, quality assurance, and peer review matters by labeling them as "PEER REVIEW: PRIVILEGED AND CONFIDENTIAL" or a similar heading.

Sample continues next page

Sample: Internet and E-mail Use Policy (continued)

7. **Use of Encrypted Software or Data**
The federal government has imposed restrictions on the export of programs or files containing encryption technology (such as e-mail programs that permit encryption of messages and electronic commerce software that encodes transactions). User shall not place software containing encryption technology on the Internet or transmit such software in any form outside the United States without prior authorization from the system administrator. User shall not install or use encryption software on any of the Practice's computers without first obtaining permission from the system administrator.
8. **Virus Detection**
User shall be responsible for ensuring that all incoming e-mail and attached files (including, without limitation, messages from newsgroups or other online services) are scanned for viruses, self-replicating code, or other destructive programs with virus-checking software approved/installed by the Practice. If User suspects that a virus has been introduced into the organization's computer network, he or she shall notify the system administrator immediately.
9. **Right to Monitor**
User acknowledges that the e-mail account provided by the Practice is to assist User in the performance of his or her job functions. User understands that log-on passwords are intended to control access to individual workstations, rather than to restrict access to the content of any communications originated by User, and User recognizes that personal e-mail communications should not be considered to be either private or secure and may be discoverable in compliance audits, litigation, external investigations by law enforcement personnel, and internal security investigations. User understands that the Practice has the right, but not the duty, to use human or automated means to monitor, without prior notice, both individual usage and the content of all material created, stored, sent, or received on its e-mail system and other communications systems and networks to ensure that the e-mail system is being used for legitimate business purposes and that any incidental personal use is in accordance with this policy. The Practice further reserves the right to disclose facts about system usage and the content of messages to law enforcement officials and any other third parties as appropriate. User expressly waives any right of privacy in anything he or she creates, stores, sends, or receives on the Practice's computer system or through the Internet or any other computer network, and consents to the Practice's access to and review of all materials created, stored, sent, or received by User.
10. **Document Retention and Record-Keeping**
    a. User shall discard or file in an archive of some kind inactive e-mail after no more than six (6) months. User agrees that incoming and outgoing e-mail communications shall be printed out or saved electronically for specified periods as necessary to meet applicable business, regulatory, and legal record-keeping requirements as enforced by his or her supervisor.
    b. The Practice shall suspend automatic deletion of e-mail and User shall take immediate steps to preserve such communications, both on the organization's e-mail system and individual computer hard disk drive, if such communications are identified as relevant to a threatened or pending litigation or other formal investigation upon notification from his or her supervisor.
11. **Illegal Copying**
User shall not illegally copy material protected under copyright law from the Internet, online services, or other sources and include it in e-mail communications to make it available to others for copying. User shall be further responsible for complying with copyright law and applicable licenses that apply to software, files, documents, messages, and other material that he or she wishes to download or copy and transmit via e-mail. If User becomes aware of any misuse of software or violation of copyright law, User shall report the incident to his or her supervisor immediately.

Sample continues next page

Sample: Internet and E-mail Use Policy (continued)

12. **Chain E-mail**
User shall not initiate or forward chain e-mail (i.e., a message sent to a number of people asking each recipient to send copies with the same request to a specified number of others).
13. **Sending Unsolicited E-mail ("Spamming")**
Without the express permission of his or her supervisor, User shall not send unsolicited e-mail to third parties with whom they do not have a prior relationship or for other than legitimate business purposes associated with the Practice.
14. **Altering Attribution Information ("Spoofing")**
User shall not alter the "From" line or other attribution-of-origin information in e-mail messages or postings. User understands that anonymous or pseudonymous electronic communications are prohibited. User further understands that the use of anonymous re-mailers (i.e., a mail server that receives incoming messages, removes the header information that identifies the original sender, and then sends the message to the intended recipient) is prohibited.
15. **Computer Security**
User shall be responsible for ensuring that his or her use of the Practice's e-mail system and other communications systems and networks (including accessing e-mail remotely) does not compromise the security of the Practice's computer network. User further shall be responsible for taking reasonable precautions to prevent intruders from accessing the organization's computer network without authorization and to prevent the introduction and spread of viruses. User shall not attempt to circumvent the Practice's data protection measures or uncover security loopholes or bugs. User shall avoid leaving open e-mail on his or her computer workstation and shall employ password-activated screen savers for his or her computer workstations located in both the Practice and in other approved remote-access locations.
16. **Duty Not to Waste Computer Resources**
User shall not deliberately perform acts that waste computer resources or unfairly monopolize such resources to the exclusion of others. These acts include, but are not limited to, sending mass e-mailings or chain letters, subscribing to nonbusiness-related list servers and mailing lists, engaging in online "chat groups," or otherwise creating unnecessary network traffic. Audio, video, picture, or other attached e-mail files that require significant storage space may not be downloaded to the Practice's computer system unless such files are business related.
17. **Compliance with Other Policies and Agreements**
User agrees to abide by all other Practice administrative policies that apply to electronic communications, including:
    a. Computer information access and confidentiality;
    b. Any policy the Practice may develop related to the Internet/Web communications;
    c. Organizational and/or departmental record-keeping/record-retention policies; and
    d. Physician, medical staff, or other required confidentiality agreements.
18. **Compliance with Applicable Laws**
User agrees to comply with all applicable federal and state laws and regulations in the use of the Practice's e-mail system and other communications systems and networks.
19. **Sanctions for Violating Policy**
User understands that sanctions for violating the Practice's e-mail policy may include revocation of User's e-mail privileges and disciplinary action up to and including termination of employment.

Reference

American Health Lawyers Association

Sample: User Consent to Use Practice Internet

By signing this document, I am aware and will abide by all that follows.

1. I understand that the Internet supplied to me by my place of employment is for my use to benefit my place of employment. I understand that, at any time as deemed necessary by a practice administrator, my productivity in the workplace can be monitored for private misuse of the Practice's Internet services.
2. I understand that the Internet supplied to me by my place of employment is not to be used in any way that interferes with my productivity at work, as observed by my employer.
3. I understand that the Internet is not to be used for personal matters, which include but are not limited to personal e-mail accounts, accessing Websites for nonwork-related matters, or game playing.
4. I understand that, if at any time my Internet usage must be monitored for the previously stated reasons, the content of my Internet usage will not be reviewed for any reason other than to determine if the usage is considered private or business related.
5. I understand that my productivity in my place of employment is of the utmost importance and will be monitored for this reason.
6. I understand that by violating this contract, as determined by the administrator, I am subject to disciplinary action as deemed necessary by the administrator, which may include termination of my employment with this Practice.
7. I understand that this document is to be signed by all Practice exchange server users (username@practicename.com users) and Internet resource users for the use of monitoring productivity in the workplace and misuse of system resources for private exhibition.
8. I understand that by not signing this document, I forfeit all rights to the use of the Internet and may, if deemed necessary by the Practice's administrator, have restrictions to the Internet placed on my workstation.

By signing this document, I agree to abide with the previously stated.

___________ [EMPLOYEE SIGNATURE]
___________ [DATE]

Policy 5.5 Communicating Test Results Policy

Too often, abnormal test results are not acted upon, delaying care and sometimes harming patients. Clear procedures on handling and communicating test results can help address the problem.

Developing a Policy on Communicating Test Results[3]

1. Policies should be introduced with clear definitions of key terms.
2. Policies should clearly outline provider responsibilities.
3. Policies should specify procedures for fail-safe communication of abnormal test results.
4. Policies must define verbal and/or electronic reporting procedures for both critical and significantly abnormal laboratory, imaging, and other test values.
5. Policies should specify "critical tests" and acceptable length of time between their ordering and reporting.
6. Policies should define time lines between the availability of test results and patient notification, and institutions should specify preferred mechanisms for patient notification.
7. Policies must be of "real world" value and written with feedback from key stakeholders.
8. Policies should establish responsibilities for monitoring and evaluating communication procedures.

Procedure[4]

1. Route test results to ordering physicians, and make them responsible for following up or ensuring that the patient's primary care doctor takes action on the findings.
2. Decide which test results are urgent enough to merit immediate notification. Use the read-back method to make sure that the physician or other healthcare professional receiving the results understands them.
3. Have a plan for what to do when the ordering physician cannot be reached.
4. To alleviate patients' anxieties, physicians should report clinical test results to patients within a reasonable time frame. Since many variables contribute to the urgency of a particular situation, physicians should use their best professional judgment when determining what length of time is reasonable for the particular situation at hand. Anticipated delays should be explained to patients at the time of testing.[5]

---

3 Hardeep Singh, MD, MPH, and Meena S. Vij, MD, "Eight Recommendations for Policies for Communicating Abnormal Test Results," *The Joint Commission Journal on Quality and Patient Safety*, www.ingentaconnect.com/content/jcaho/jcjqs/2010/00000036/00000005/art00006 (accessed January 31, 2011).

4 Kevin B. O'Reilly, "Flood of Test Results Prompts New Attention on How to Manage Flow," May 24, 2010, www.ama-assn.org/amednews/2010/05/24/prl10524.htm (accessed January 31, 2011).

5 American Medical Association, "CEJA Report 12 — A-98: Reporting Clinical Test Results: General Guidelines," 1998, www.ama-assn.org/ama1/pub/upload/mm/369/ceja_12a98.pdf (accessed January 31, 2011).

5. Physicians should adopt a consistent reporting policy that accommodates the demands of their practice while at the same time being considerate of patients' anxieties. The reporting policy should be disclosed to patients during the clinical encounter when tests are administered so patients know what to expect. Reporting policies should take into consideration the circumstances in which test results are reported to the patient and who will communicate with the patient. Any anticipated inconsistencies should be disclosed to patients as soon as they are discovered.
6. Physicians should provide test results in language understandable to the patient and in the manner deemed most appropriate by the physician. Any information gathered from test results that would be necessary for patients to make intelligent medical decisions and give informed consent on future medical treatments must be disclosed to them.
7. Physicians should take all appropriate precautions to ensure the confidentiality of test results. Such precautions may include, but are not limited to, not leaving test results on an answering machine, on voice mail, or with a third party unless previously given permission to do so by the patient; not delivering test results via electronic mail; and not sending test results through the mail in any form other than a sealed envelope.

Considerations for Reporting Clinical Test Results[6]

Patients' Anxieties. When a physician recommends that a patient undergo clinical tests, the patient's emotions are understandably heightened. The role of the physician as a reassuring presence and a good communicator is important.

Prompt Reporting. The urgent nature of the test result and the seriousness of the condition should be considered when calculating a reasonable time frame for reporting test results. Physicians should use their best professional judgment when determining what length of time is reasonable for the particular situation at hand. If the physician anticipates delays in receiving test results, this should be explained to patients at the time of testing (e.g., if a test must be sent away to a distant laboratory, patients should be informed that the test results will take longer to return).

Consistency. Physicians should adopt a consistent reporting policy that accommodates the demands of their practice while at the same time being considerate of patients' anxieties. For instance, an appropriate reporting policy may consist of the primary care physician calling the patient only if the test result is positive and otherwise sending the test results via the mail in a sealed envelope. Alternatively, primary care physicians may adopt a test-result reporting policy that consists of always calling the patient to inform him or her of their test results regardless of the status of the results. Further consideration should be given to which steps will be taken if the test results are life threatening. In all cases, the policy should be consistent and should be disclosed to patients during the clinical encounter so they know what to expect.

When formulating reporting policies, physicians should consider under what circumstances and by whom tests are appropriately reported to the patient. For example, it is common for physicians to seek additional consultation to conduct clinical tests that are essential for accurate diagnosis and treatment. Communication among the

6 American Medical Association, "CEJA Report 12 — A-98: Reporting Clinical Test Results: General Guidelines."

care team regarding expectations, such as how to expect test results to be reported, is essential so that the patient can receive consistent care. Any anticipated inconsistencies should be disclosed to patients as soon as they are discovered.

Patient Information and Informed Consent. Physicians should provide test results in language understandable to the patient and in the manner deemed most appropriate by the physician. Patients have the right to receive information from physicians that is necessary to discuss benefits, risks, and costs of appropriate medical treatment. Patients can effectively exercise their right to self-decision and informed consent only if they possess enough information to enable an intelligent choice.

Disclosure of significant information gathered from clinical tests is necessary in order for the patient to fully explore treatment options.

Confidentiality. Clinical records are confidential documents. The information included in the clinical record should not be shared with third parties without the patient's prior written consent. Test results fall under this confidentiality protection because they will ultimately become part of the information contained in the patient's clinical record. When physicians report test results, they should be mindful of methods that might make the test results accessible to third parties. All appropriate precautions should be taken to ensure the confidentiality of test results when reporting them to the patient. Such precautions may include, but are not limited to, not leaving test results on an answering machine, on voice mail, or with a third party unless previously given permission to do so by the patient; not delivering test results via electronic mail; and not sending test results through the mail in any form other than a sealed envelope.

Policy 5.6 Coordination of Care Policy

Care coordination can be defined as "the deliberate integration of patient care activities between two or more participants involved in a patient's care to facilitate the appropriate delivery of healthcare services."[7]

Care coordination involves developing structured relationships with individuals and facilities outside of the primary care setting that are necessary to provide comprehensive care. A need for care beyond the scope of the primary care office occurs frequently, and it is important to include this care in the overall management of the patient.

Care coordination expands the definition of *team* to include *all* providers, locations, and resources necessary to meet the patient's healthcare needs. This extended care team can include specialists, hospital facilities, home health facilities, long-term care facilities, durable medical equipment vendors, public health entities, pharmacists, social workers, psychologists, physical therapists, and any other healthcare entity that affects the patient's healthcare. Effective care coordination provides for an understanding of each

7 K.M. McDonald, V. Sundaram, D.M. Bravata, et al., "Closing the Quality Gap: A Critical Analysis of Quality Improvement Strategies," V. 7: Care Coordination, Report No. 4 (2007): 0051-7 (Rockville, MD: Agency for Healthcare Research and Quality).

team member's role and responsibility at the time of the patient interaction and a clearly defined information flow between team members. Each team member has accurate, current information for *every* patient at *each* encounter.

Care coordination becomes increasingly complex as the patient's needs become more complex. Primary care has commonly been seen as the point where this coordination should take place. Unfortunately, as patient care has become more complex and demands on primary care providers have become more intense, care coordination has been given little recognition or financial support. Patients often take it upon themselves to coordinate and manage their own care by self-referring or choosing to be noncompliant. Processes and systems have become fragmented and broken, resulting in repeated and unnecessary care, medication and treatment errors, an increase of patient noncompliance, an overall increase in healthcare costs, and a decrease in healthcare quality. Therefore, care coordination provides a significant improvement in healthcare efficiency and quality by effectively creating a united healthcare team. Primary care physicians can find early wins in care coordination efforts and use these wins as the opportunity to advocate for payment reform. As care coordination improves efficiency and quality, there is increasing evidence validating the importance of primary care in a high-quality, efficient healthcare system.

There is acknowledged overlap with care coordination and care management activities in the primary care practice. Both activities improve coordination and management of preventive, acute, and chronic care. To simplify, activities involving care provided outside of the primary care setting will be referred to as *care coordination* and care provided in the primary care setting will be presented as *care management* activities.

Policy 5.7

Charge Capture Policy[8]

Manual Professional Service Record

It is the policy of the Practice to ensure that professional service records are user-friendly and routinely updated.

Procedure

1. Professional service records, which are also known as encounter forms and superbills, are very effective in saving time and ensuring correct communication of services to be billed to the billing office. While most medical practices rely on paper professional service records, EHR systems have allowed practices to automate the professional service record. Whether manual or electronic, for best results, the professional service record should be customized to the Practice, including current procedure and diagnosis codes that are frequently used by the Practice.

8 Deborah Walker Keegan, PhD, FACMPE, Elizabeth W. Woodcock, MBA, FACMPE, CPC, and Sara M. Larch, MSHA, FACMPE, *The Physician Billing Process: 12 Potholes to Avoid in the Road to Getting Paid, 2nd Edition,* Chapter 5 (Englewood, CO: Medical Group Management Association, 2009).

2. Physicians are responsible for the selection of the procedure and diagnosis codes relevant to the service that was rendered and documented. To ensure appropriate reimbursement, it is imperative to design a professional service record with a layout that facilitates appropriate code selection with ease and accuracy.
3. The professional service record is an internal document to communicate the codes for the services rendered between the physician(s) and the billing office. It is not a substitute for the documentation of the encounter. Patient care documentation to substantiate the level of service provided, coded, and billed is crucial. Some examples of necessary documentation in the patient chart include the level of history taken, a description of the extent of the examination, the complexity of the decision made, counseling, and the time spent with the patient.
4. Professional service records can also be used as receipts for patients, tracking documents for patient flow and/or orders, as well as a communication vehicle regarding the recommended follow-up appointments for patients. The form can also be used to capture patients' signatures to verify their presence in the practice and/or as their agreement to assign their benefits to the practice. If the form is used to capture signatures, a signature line should be added for patients. The Practice should take into account these alternative uses when developing the professional service record; accuracy and ease-of-use considerations should be made as well.
5. To ensure billing of all services, utilize an automated professional service record-tracking system provided by your practice management system or sequentially number all forms to provide an audit trail for daily reconciliation.

Layout

1. The top of the professional service record should include all the information required for charge entry. It should include information about the Practice (Practice name, physicians, address, and telephone number) and other data fields, including location of service. The formatting of this information should flow in the order of your charge entry screen.
2. Query the practice management system vendor for a layout that is compatible with your system. The specifications provided by the practice management system vendor for the patient's name, date of service, payer, and other relevant information that is printed by the practice management system should be accommodated. It is preferable that this information print together at the top or the bottom of the form, allowing the Practice to use the remainder of the space to efficiently format coding choices.
3. The layout of the information regarding procedure and diagnosis codes on the encounter form should be set up in a logical order to facilitate ease of selection and immediate recognition of code selection by the physician. The subject areas should be in the same logical order as in the procedure coding books:
   - Office visits;
   - Consultations;
   - Preventive medicine services;
   - Surgical procedures;
   - Pathology/laboratory;
   - Injections/immunizations;
   - Medical supplies; and
   - Diagnosis codes.

4. After the code, brief descriptions (e.g., "level-1 office visit") should be provided. For procedure codes, after the description, the fee — or a blank space for the fee — should be included. (If the practice uses the professional service record as a receipt for the patient, it is recommended that fees not be preprinted on the form.) The procedure codes should be listed in the order of level where appropriate (e.g., 99211 followed by 99212, and so on). For the E&M codes, include all code levels in the series (e.g., 99211, 99212, 99213, 99214, and 99215). If only the higher-level codes are preprinted, this raises the suspicion of upcoding if a payer performs an audit.
5. Include on the form the most frequently used diagnosis codes (with appropriate level of specificity). Leave room for writing in seldom-used procedure codes and modifiers, as well as diagnosis codes. Use shading to highlight and/or delineate sections. Do not crowd the information. If there is too little space on the form for the Practice to include all of the codes that need to be referenced, print some of the information on the back of the form, or maintain a listing of the codes in each exam room on a laminated form.
6. If the Practice has multiple specialties, develop and customize a professional service record for each specialty (and, if appropriate, subspecialty). The layout should be consistent for all specialties to facilitate efficient processing in the billing office.
7. The Practice should review and update the professional service record when new codes and changes to existing codes are announced. If the practice offers a new service, immediately update the encounter form to reflect the codes associated with the service.

Off-site Professional Service Records

1. Use separate professional service records, with the same design format, for services provided out of the office (e.g., hospital, ambulatory surgery center, nursing home, and all other places of service). If the physician is responsible for collecting demographic and insurance information at the off-site facility, allow ample room for the information to be stamped, recorded, or attached to the professional service record. Since off-site forms may contain information for multiple dates of service, make sure that the format allows for recording multiple dates, as well as hospital discharge and admission dates.
2. When the billing office receives an off-site professional service record, the patient's demographic and insurance information should be promptly reviewed. If no information can be located in the Practice's registration system (e.g., the patient has never been seen in the office or by the Practice before), seek assistance from the registration department of the facility at which the patient was seen. Registration information should be confirmed within 24 hours of receipt by the billing office.
3. For off-site professional service records, record the proper procedure and diagnosis codes (based on the physician's level of service and diagnosis). The physician who rendered the services or a designated coder may code these services. Batch the professional service records and route to charge entry personnel for keying. These charges should be posted within forty-eight (48) hours of receipt.
4. These procedures ensure correct and complete charge capture and provide a convenient record-keeping method with accurate communication to the billing office.

Professional Service Record Accuracy and Completeness

It is the policy of the Practice that professional service records will be accurate and complete at the time of service.

Procedure

1. The physician will document all services rendered to the patient.
2. The physician will complete paper or electronic charge documents at the time the service is rendered.
3. Diagnosis "rule outs" are not permitted. A diagnosis must be made and coded based on the information available and the symptoms presented.
4. Physicians will match procedure codes to the appropriate diagnosis codes using a numeric method and/or via the methodology provided by the practice management system for linking multiple procedures and diagnoses.
5. Illegible, unscannable, incorrect, or incomplete professional service records will be returned to the physician for correction within 24 hours so that timely charge entry can be performed.

Charge and Office Visit Reconciliation

Charges for office and outpatient visits will be collected and entered throughout the day. Charges should be reconciled with the appointment schedule and sign-in sheet (if used) to ensure that all services are billed. A missing charge report will be generated to confirm that all charges have been entered for each patient that received medical services.

Procedure

1. Staff will generate a professional service record for all scheduled appointments. If a patient cancels or does not present for his or her visit, staff will mark this fact on the professional service record and record the information regarding the cancellation or no-show in the practice management system. If a patient walks in without a scheduled appointment, staff will generate the appointment and a professional service record at that time.
2. At the end of the day, the billing office will generate a missing charge report that will confirm all patients and charges for the day are included.
3. Staff will generate an appointment reconciliation report to compare the scheduled patients who kept their appointments to those patients with charges on their accounts.
4. All professional service records will be sequentially numbered to provide an additional mechanism for monitoring missing tickets.
5. In the event that a missing professional service record cannot be found, a supervisor must be notified. The supervisor will conduct a review of the search process and will notify the physician immediately if the form cannot be located. The physician will be asked to generate a professional service record to document the services that were rendered and select the appropriate procedure and diagnosis code(s).

Charge and Service Reconciliation (Nonoffice Services)

It is the policy of the Practice that a closed-loop process will be used to ensure that all charges are captured for billing purposes.

Procedure

1. Formal logs will be developed to record all charges that are submitted to the billing office. In this fashion, missing dates of service and missing practice site data will be identified.
2. Logs will be developed for each key service in the Practice. These logs will involve a comparison of source documents to the charges that have been submitted to ensure that all charges are captured. Source documents include hospital census reports, labor and delivery logs, operating room logs, ECG logs, and other similar documentation.
3. A service analysis report will be developed for each key service in the Practice. The service analysis will be compared to projected service volumes to assist in identifying variation from expected productivity levels, which could signify missing charges.
4. In the event that missing charges are identified, the staff will first check with the coding unit to determine if the charge has been pended. If the coding unit does not have the charge document, the staff will send an internal electronic communication to the physician(s) listed as performing the service, with a copy to the billing manager. Charges must be submitted within 48 hours of this notification. Before the charge is entered, documentation must be obtained and reviewed to ensure that the service was rendered, coded, and charged correctly.

Policy 5.8

Physician Quality Reporting System Policy[9]

Eligible Professionals

Under the Physician Quality Reporting System (PQRS), covered professional services are those paid under or based on the Medicare Physician Fee Schedule (PFS). To the extent that eligible professionals are providing services that get paid under or based on the PFS, those services are eligible for the PQRS.

Eligible and Able to Participate

The following professionals are eligible to participate in PQRS:

1. Medicare physicians
    - Doctor of Medicine (MD)
    - Doctor of Osteopathy (DO)

9 Centers for Medicare and Medicaid Services, "Overview: Physician Quality Reporting System Formerly Known as the Physician Quality Reporting Initiative," www.cms.gov/PQRS; CMS, "Eligible Professionals" PDF download from www.cms.gov/PQRS/Downloads/EligibleProfessionals.pdf (accessed February 4, 2011).

- Doctor of Podiatric Medicine (DPM)
- Doctor of Optometry (OD)
- Doctor of Oral Surgery (MD and/or DDS/DDM)
- Doctor of Dental Medicine (DDM)
- Doctor of Dental Science (DDS)
- Doctor of Chiropractic (DC)

2. Practitioners
   - Physician Assistant (PA)
   - Nurse Practitioner (NP, APNP, FNP)
   - Clinical Nurse Specialist (CNS)
   - Certified Registered Nurse Anesthetist (CRNA)
   - Anesthesiology Assistant (AA)
   - Certified Nurse Midwife (NMW)
   - Clinical Social Worker (MSW)
   - Clinical Psychologist (PhD)
   - Registered Dietician (RD)
   - Nutrition Professional
   - Audiologist
3. Therapists
   - Physical Therapist (PT)
   - Occupational Therapist (OT)
   - Vocational Therapist (VT)
   - Qualified Speech-Language Therapist

Eligible But Not Able to Participate

The following professionals are eligible to participate but are not able to participate for one or more reasons:

1. Providers paid under the Medicare PFS billing Medicare fiscal intermediaries fiscal intermediaries/Medicare Administrative Contractors (FI/MACs). The FI/MAC claims processing systems currently cannot accommodate billing at the individual physician or practitioner level:
   - Critical access hospital (CAH), method II payment, where the physician or practitioner has reassigned his or her benefits to the CAH. In this situation, the CAH bills the regular FI for the professional services provided by the physician or practitioner.
   - All institutional providers that bill for outpatient therapy provided by physical and occupational therapists and speech-language pathologists (e.g., hospital, skilled nursing facility Part B, home health agency, comprehensive outpatient rehabilitation facility, or outpatient rehabilitation facility). This does not apply to skilled nursing facilities under Part A.
2. Providers not defined as eligible professionals in the Tax Relief and Health Care Act of 2006 or the Medicare Improvements for Patients and Providers Act of 2008 are not eligible to participate in PQRS and do not qualify for an incentive. Services payable under fee schedules or methodologies other than the PFS are not included

in PQRS (e.g., services provided in federally qualified health centers, independent diagnostic testing facilities, portable X-ray suppliers, independent laboratories, hospitals [including critical access], rural health clinics, ambulance providers, and ambulatory surgery center facilities). In addition, suppliers of durable medical equipment (DME) are not eligible for PQRS since DME is not paid under the PFS.

Eligible professionals participating in the PQRS should familiarize themselves and their office staff with the PQRS measures that appear to apply to their patients for the relevant program year.

Maintenance of Certification Program Incentive

Beginning in 2011, physicians now have the opportunity to earn an additional incentive of 0.5 percent by working with a Maintenance of Certification entity and by completing the following:

- Satisfactorily submitting data, without regard to method, on quality measures under Physician Quality Reporting, for a twelve- (12-) month reporting period either as an individual physician or as a member of a selected group practice;

AND

- More frequently than is required to qualify for or maintain board certification:
  - Participate in a Maintenance of Certification Program, and
  - Successfully complete a qualified Maintenance of Certification Program practice assessment.

CHAPTER 6

Patient Relations

Patient Relations Philosophy

Very few industries treat their customers like they do in the healthcare industry. On one hand, the intimacy of physician–patient relationships is unrivaled. Mutual respect and trust are part of the therapeutic formula for best outcomes. On the other hand, the healthcare industry has been notoriously physician centric. Although the era of "doctor knows best" may be fading, many segments of the healthcare industry still seem to be set up to serve physicians more than patients. One indication of delayed development is the reluctance to consistently measure patient satisfaction. By some estimates, less than a quarter of medical practices regularly ask their patients for feedback.

That may be about to change. Health reform dynamics point to increasing accountability of doctors to patients for both clinical outcomes and basic respect in clinical encounters. Healthy organizations make it a point to satisfy or even exceed the expectations of their customers. It is only appropriate that intimate physician–patient relationships adopt a similar goal.

Basic Considerations

Policies about patient satisfaction begin with a simple commitment to superior service. If physicians ignore patients or discount their opinions, the staff at the medical practice will pick up on the disrespect and repeat it in their interactions. Perhaps the single most important person for creating a culture of service in the medical practice is the receptionist, the person who answers the phone or greets patients upon their arrival. If patients obtain a first impression of respect, they are more likely to feel respected behind the closed door of the exam room. If physicians are not committed to staying on schedule, for example, they transmit a disrespectful message to patients and staff. The staff can become flustered and impatient with demanding patients, affirming the culture of disrespect and compromising the therapeutic benefits of the physician–patient relationship. So patient relations must begin with a commitment to satisfy — and even delight — every patient.

Those committed to building a culture of satisfying patients have been on the cutting edge. Their motives may have been born of competitive pressures, trying to distinguish their services from others in the community. Those who consistently measure patient satisfaction and use the findings to improve their services often enjoy stronger patient loyalty, and with it, greater profitability and fewer conflicts.

After committing to improving patient satisfaction, the next step is to measure it. In the past several years, information technology has simplified methods for gathering and interpreting patient feedback. Medical group managers who remember the labor-intensive process of gathering paper questionnaires and tabulating and summarizing the results, only to be met with resistance when reporting them to physicians, may be reluctant to measure patient satisfaction again. But new technologies should reopen the doors to cost-effective tools for building patient loyalty.

Purpose

Patient satisfaction data can provide a meaningful foundation for operational improvements. Ratings and comments can identify opportunities for improving both clinical care and patient flow. The data can serve as a motivating force to unite physicians and support staff. We all want to be admired and proud of our work. We want people to like us. Patient satisfaction data can tell the truth about their opinions.

Policies and systems for gauging patient satisfaction can also be a risk management tool. The act of asking for feedback demonstrates respect. When practices act on that feedback in ways that patients can see, it increases their engagement with the practice and decreases their discontent. When they have a less-than-satisfactory experience, they are more likely to bring it to the attention of the manager or physician, expecting a satisfactory resolution. Patient satisfaction systems raise the opportunity for discovering dissatisfaction in the early stages and doing something about it before it becomes a lawsuit.

When medical groups adopt policies to please patients, they are in effect acknowledging that patients are part of the therapeutic team. The policies outline a philosophy about physician–patient relationships that places them in mutual dependence with each other. When the policy, the philosophy, and the practice flow together, physicians listen to patients without interrupting them. Patients are less likely to feel rushed and are more likely to hear what their physicians need them to hear. Policies and philosophies about satisfying patients fortify good patient care.

Patient satisfaction policies can become a simple form of peer review. Patients may not be physicians' professional peers, but they are human peers. Their emotional makeup is quite similar. Patients and physicians alike have ambitions, goals, curiosity, a need for admiration, and a desire for respect. Patients may be less able to measure medical quality than human respect, but they will use the human respect they feel as a surrogate measure of the medical quality that they cannot see. To put it more simply, patients measure quality by how well they are treated as people by the physicians, nurses, and especially the receptionists.

Components

Patient satisfaction survey instruments do not need to be extensive questionnaires to provide helpful information. In some respects, simpler is better. What is important is that patient satisfaction be measured, not simply by the absence of complaints, but also by the solicitation of feedback and the sincere invitation to communicate concerns.

Components found in patient satisfaction policies and surveys typically include the following:

- **Patient-Flow Processes.** How easy was it to get a timely appointment? Once the appointment was made, did it begin and end consistent with patients' expectations?
- **Respect.** Did the patients feel respected by each staff member? Did they feel they were listened to? Were their opinions discounted or valued?
- **Communications.** How effective were communications between patients and staff? Were there areas of miscommunication? Was body language consistent with verbal messages?

Some organizations fully committed to excellent patient service may also adopt policies that go beyond traditional patient satisfaction surveys. They may empower frontline staff to resolve service problems according to established protocols. When a staff member at the front desk or checkout station identifies a need for further communication between the patient and the physician or nurse, he or she may be encouraged to go the extra step to get the answer or reconnect the patient with the nurse to the patient's satisfaction. Early intervention and complete resolution can be keys to superior patient service.

Conclusion

Policies for patient satisfaction are no longer an option for medical practices. They are quickly becoming an imperative in competitive environments and an integral part of accountable care. A commitment to improving patient satisfaction increases patient loyalty, strengthens the therapeutic value of physician–patient relationships, and feeds the foundations of trust and respect essential for every healthy organization.

Policy 6.1

Patient Relations Policy

The Practice is committed to fulfilling its mission of quality patient care through both a high level of clinical competence and a high level of patient satisfaction. As part of its continuous quality improvement efforts, the Practice will consistently seek to meet the expectations of patients.

Procedure

1. The Practice will regularly conduct patient satisfaction surveys as a means of learning about areas of improvement.
2. The Practice will collaborate, as appropriate, with payers on such surveys; for example, the Practice will include customized questions and will share results with payers.
3. During orientation, each new physician and staff member will be introduced to the Practice's patient relations expectations.
4. Ongoing training on particular aspects of patient relations will be offered regularly.
5. Performance expectations related to patient relations will be included in the performance plans for physicians and staff, and results will be reflected in performance evaluations.
6. The quality improvement manager will coordinate patient relations activities, including staff education, patient satisfaction surveys, and patient complaints and will develop and implement corrective actions as appropriate.

Responsibility

The quality improvement manager shall take actions necessary to implement this policy.

Guidelines

All physicians will abide by the following Guest Relations guidelines:

1. **Confidentiality.** Do not discuss information relative to physicians, operations, vendors, volunteers, or coworkers on or off the job unless necessary to fulfill your/their job responsibilities. Always carefully guard any patient information.
2. **Positive Impression.** Look and act professional at all times; use appropriate language and gestures; follow all organization policies and procedures; wear your identification badge; introduce yourself to our guests by name and department; call our guests by their formal name, unless directed otherwise.
3. **Teamwork.** Support and assist your coworkers in work and deed; demonstrate your pride in our staff and services; don't "pass the buck" — take responsibility for our guests' problems, complaints, or requests for help; get the assistance you need to resolve the matter in a positive way.
4. **Courtesy.** Whether over the telephone or in person, be courteous to every guest, regardless of his or her problem, attitude, or request. Do your best to ensure that our guest is comfortable with you and the Practice.

5. **Respect.** Show respect for all guests. Age, physical or mental condition, and economic or social status should not change the way you deal with our guests.
6. **Communication.** Listen carefully. Speak clearly. Make sure you and our guest fully understand each other; be conscious of nonverbal communication.
7. **Mission.** Live the mission of the Practice, and demonstrate your appreciation of the mission statement in your thoughts, words, and deeds.

Physician/Patient Public Relations Protocol

All correspondence received by the Practice with reference to physician/patient public relations of a laudatory nature should be handled as follows.

Copies of all correspondence of this nature will be submitted to the executive director, the physician, department head physician, and the quality assurance committee. The original letter will be placed in the physician's file.

All correspondence of a nonlaudatory nature will be handled as follows:

1. Patients with complaints directed to anyone in the Practice regarding a physician's care or treatment will be asked to submit the complaint in writing to the executive director and medical director.
2. The physician against whom the complaint was directed should write a reply letter to the patient within seven (7) working days and submit it to the executive director, who will then send copies of the reply to each reviewer.
3. The medical director will assign two (2) members of the quality assurance committee on a rotating basis to review the reply to each complaint letter. No more than one (1) of the reviewers will be from the same department as the physician against whom the complaint is directed.
4. The reviewers should meet together as soon as possible and discuss the reply letter, making any amendments that they deem necessary.
5. The approved or revised reply will be handled or typed by the executive secretary. He or she must confirm with each reviewer that they have, indeed, participated in the approval or amending of the reply.

Sample: Top 10 Patient Service Standards of Excellence

1. Treat everyone with courtesy, compassion, and respect — the way you would like your family treated.
2. Ensure privacy, confidentiality, and safety. Keep patient-care areas neat, clean, safe, and quiet.
3. Be a gracious host to all patients. If they need assistance, personally escort them to their destination.
4. When someone needs help, get involved. Own the problem until it is resolved.
5. When patients talk, stop, make eye contact, and smile. Try to understand patients' needs first and then respond.
6. When the phone rings, answer it promptly. When patients approach you, acknowledge them promptly with a smile.
7. Resolve patients' needs during their first phone call.
8. Patients may not always be right, but they are always allowed to be wrong with dignity.
9. When patients are running late, listen to reason before deciding to reschedule.
10. Standard of care requires us to have all clinical records present for the patient's visit and completed within twenty-four (24) hours.

Sample: Customer Service Code of Conduct

As a physician of the Practice, I agree to abide by the following code of conduct:

Like Hippocrates, I will always remember that we are in the "healing" business. Many of our patients come to us not feeling well, and they have a right to expect us to do everything in our power to help them. We may not be able to fix their problem, but we must make doubly sure that we are always compassionate and gracious to them.

Professional behavior is demonstrated by the following actions:

- I will always take responsibility for my own actions. I will not blame others or make excuses. If I have a bad day at home, that is no excuse for me to come to work and take it out on others. *The true test of a person's character is not how they act when everything is going great, but how they act when nothing is going great.*
- I will use "please" and "thank you" as much as possible when asking a patient or staff member to do something. For example, "Please sign in," "Please step on the scale for me," and "Thank you for coming today." If I am running more than 15 minutes late, I will apologize to the patient for the delay. For example, "Ms. Smith, thank you for your patience. I apologize for the delay in seeing you."
- I will address a patient formally by their first and last name or last name when greeting them. I will wear my nametag and smile and introduce myself to each patient. (For example, "Good morning, Ms. Smith. My name is Dr. Jones.") I will look a patient in the eye when speaking with him or her.
- I will not shout at a patient or staff member, whether to call him or her to the front desk or announce their name in the waiting room. I will not shout through the hallways looking for my nurse or PA. I will keep my voice at a conversational level when talking with patients or other staff. I will not engage in loud conversation, laughing, or virtual communication with anyone in the presence of patients. I will not use my cell phone (verbally or by texting) during work hours.
- I will always do my job to the best of my ability. If I am aware of a problem or issue, I will take ownership and address the matter until resolved or until management reassigns responsibility. I will not say, "I can't help you." I may not be personally able to solve a problem, but I will seek out someone who can. I will not waste Practice time but will take care of my own responsibilities efficiently and effectively, and if I am not busy, I will inform management or I will volunteer to assist others.
- I will dress appropriately and be well groomed. I acknowledge that my speech and appearance make an impression on patients, and I want the impression to be positive.
- I will always treat patients, staff, and fellow physicians, regardless of circumstance, the way I would like to be treated.

I agree to abide by the Practice's Customer Service Code of Conduct.

Physician Signature: ____________________
Date: __________

Customer/Patient Service Expectations

It is imperative that the Practice and its designees (physicians and staff alike) see patients as patients, not as "customers." Therefore, we have substituted the words "Customer Service" for "Patient Service."

Exceptional patient service is the cornerstone of the Practice's mission, values, and service performance standards. Exceptional patient service is an expectation of all employees regardless of ownership status or pay grade. Service excellence will be recognized and rewarded. Conversely, patient service violations will result in corrective action, and major patient service violations will result in termination.

Definitions

The Practice's patient service strategy includes standard behavior expectations for all employees.

Patient Service Violations: Patient service violations are situations that signify unacceptable behavior. No list of patient service violations that may result in corrective action can be exhaustive. Examples in this policy do not replace sound judgment, common courtesy, or common-sense behavior.

Minor Patient Service Violations: Minor patient service violations include behavior/performance of such a nature that the first offense might warrant a written warning but may not warrant termination. Examples of minor rule violations are provided as follows. This list is not intended to be all-inclusive.

- Failing to provide assistance to a patient or family member who requests such
- Not using an appropriate tone of voice and manner when addressing anyone with whom you interact at the Practice
- Being rude or discourteous to coworkers, patients, physicians, or anyone else at the Practice
- Ignoring a patient who is waiting to be served
- Failing to follow established scripts and protocols

Major Patient Service Violations: Depending on the circumstances or seriousness of the violation and facts, one or more levels of warning in the physician corrective action process may be omitted. For example, a first offense may indicate that continued employment of the physician may not be in the best interest of the Practice. In this case, the physician may be terminated. Examples of major patient service violations are provided as follows. This list is not intended to be all-inclusive.

- Conducting inappropriate confidential conversation in a public setting
- Striking a patient
- Threatening a patient and/or family member
- Using obscene language
- Being verbally abusive

Potential Information Sources: Knowledge of a physician's patient service rule violations can be gained from a number of sources. Each must be considered in the context of the physician's past performance and validity of information. Sources may include:

- Personal observation;
- Patient or family member letter of complaint;
- Patient, family, or coworker verbal complaint; and
- Peer concerns shared with manager.

Development Plan: When giving any level of written warning, a development plan must be established that outlines the activities required for improvement. Development plans for customer service violations are to be reviewed within two (2) weeks in order to assess progress. If slow or no attempts have been made to demonstrate improvement, further corrective action or termination may result.

Provisional Period: Defined as the first six (6) months of employment. Any of the described violations, without improvement upon notice, will result in termination within the provisional period.

Procedure

1. Every patient service violation is significant, and consequently, any patient service violation may lead to corrective action. Movement from one level to the next occurs if sufficient progress is not made within the two- (2-) week time period following the development plan. Major service violations or a failure to improve service levels at an acceptable rate (as defined by the development plan) will result in termination.
2. Contact human resources to assist you through this process as you would with any physician corrective action issue.

Sample: If Disney Managed Your Practice

Managing employees at Disney is 10 times easier than being a hospital manager, as people are happy, not sick or scared. The following gives cues to the best experience for the customer/patient and the culture that will provide it.

1. **Redefine Your Competition and Focus on What Can't Be Measured**
    a. Competition is anyone your customer compares you to. Patients compare how they are treated and their impression of the practice in general. Clinical quality is where loyalty is won/lost — patients judge overall experience.
    b. Competition requires different skills — perception is the engine for growth, and impressions are won and lost in the parking lot, the elevator, the waiting room, the hallways, and the exam room.
        - Rudeness is not the enemy of courtesy — lack of cheer, friendliness, or caring is.
        - Avoidance = missed opportunity. Stop looking for mistakes and look for opportunities.
    c. Culture drives opportunity and must support behavior.
    d. Complaints miss what is important. People complain within the realm of expectations and don't complain about what will drive loyalty.
        - Focus on actively soliciting needs, expressing concern for privacy, briefing patients, and conveying empathy.

Sample continues next page

Sample: If Disney Managed Your Practice (continued)

2. **Make Courtesy More Important Than Efficiency**
   a. Disney priorities (in order): safety, courtesy, show, and efficiency. Hospitals rarely put patient courtesy second.
      - Disney uses a Ladder model instead of Pillars to reflect priority/guidance.

   b. Often suboptimize efficiency — move work somewhere else, true gains.
   c. Accountabilities drive structure; structure drives culture. By putting courtesy first, you eliminate false efficiencies and problems with communication and teamwork.
3. **Regard Patient Satisfaction as Fool's Gold**
   a. The only meaningful measure of satisfaction is Very Good/Very Satisfied. A satisfied customer is *not* a loyal customer. A satisfied customer is six times more likely to defect than a Very Satisfied customer. Very Satisfied = Loyal. Loyalty is the only protection against competition and therefore security.
   b. Satisfaction — if you can't remember anything, you are satisfied. It takes something memorable to be Very Satisfied. "If we don't do something special, our guests won't remember us, and if they don't remember us, why would they back?"
   c. Meeting standards creates satisfaction — but zero loyalty.
      - Law of the Memorable Event — one brief experience creates loyalty (or dissatisfaction). It just takes one person being personally involved.
      - Stories — satisfaction has no stories. Both loyalty and dissatisfaction do.

   d. Loyalty must be earned — focus on the person, not the episode.
   e. Courtesy/competence yields satisfaction. Compassion/commitment yields loyalty.
4. **Measure to Improve, Not to Impress**
   a. Manipulation of scores is not seeking loyalty.
   b. Need to dig into experience — "Was there anything frustrating/disappointing?" "What would make it better?"
   c. People do not know what it takes to be beyond expectations — surprise yields loyalty. It is nothing patients will ever be able to tell you; they can only tell you what they expect, which is the ordinary.
5. **Decentralize the Authority to Say YES**
   a. Staff is always right when satisfying a guest.
      - Service recovery (power to say YES) is passed to the front line. By the time an issue gets to leadership, no one wins.

   b. "A foolish consistency is the hobgoblin of little minds." "With consistency a great soul has simply nothing to do." — Ralph Waldo Emerson
   c. Centralization creep is pervasive and drives culture. Limits speed/responsiveness. Key to a service culture is spontaneity — the power of staff to meet/exceed customer needs.
   d. "First-rate managers hire first-rate people and turn them loose. Second-rate managers hire third-rate people who have to be told what to do and how to do it." — Dave Buker
      - A leader's success is not measured by what he or she can do but by what their people can do without them.

   e. Middle management must implement the top leadership's vision and expectations.
      - "What decisions do I retain that limit you from solving a problem?"

Sample continues next page

Sample: If Disney Managed Your Practice (continued)

f. In healthcare, write-offs only help the third-party payer. The Practice needs to find things that are meaningful to the patient. Actions are triggered by anything that results in customer frustration. Actions must be automatic, not be delayed until requested.

g. Huddle — daily brief, share information, ask for help, shorten decisions.

6. **Change the Concept from Service to Theater**
   a. Not service, but an experience of healing and wellness. Shift the focus from physician to *patient*. Experiences are memorable.
      - The objective is not excellent service, but a *memorable experience.*
      - This requires attention to the entire environment and how people interact.
      - Be alert to personal clues and react to them.
      - No rote dialogue — spontaneous, intentional interactions, not verbiage.

   b. Consider the flow of the patient experience: cheerful greeting, comment on anything individual, ask if there is anything that needs to be explained, and empathize.
      - Brainstorm: what we do; what guests need to know/feel.

   c. Hire based on one's ability to engage; the primary role is to engage patients in a memorable experience; make them feel welcome, cared about, and reassured.
7. **Harness the Motivating Power of Imagination**
   a. Motivation: imagination creates empathy and emotion, which are strong motivators. Empathy is an emotional response to an imagined event.
      - Healthcare requires both courtesy and compassion.
      - Not a moment of truth, but a moment of imagination.

   b. Use imagination as a coaching tool to create a more powerful response.

   c. Do frontline work on a regular basis to increase imagination.
8. **Create a Climate of Dissatisfaction**
   a. Dissatisfaction produces improvement. Good is the enemy of great; complacency is the adversary of excellence.

   b. Can't avoid hard work — there is no easy way. Vision alone is not enough.

   c. Measurement fuels dissatisfaction; analysis provides the information for improvement. Focus on the Very Good — not percentile/comparative data.

   d. The organization does not exist to satisfy staff; employees exist to satisfy customers.
      - There is no tolerance for staff members who deviate from cultural norms.
      - There is no causal relationship between employee and patient satisfaction. Satisfied patients and results may drive employee satisfaction, but employee satisfaction is not the final determinant of patient satisfaction.
9. **Cease Using Competitive Monetary Rewards**
   a. Competition results in lower attention to compassion and empathy.

   b. Separate recognition from competition — appreciation produces rewards.
      - Caught-in-the-act recognition programming — reviewed by administration and commented on before sending to individuals.

   c. Rewards become entitlements — extrinsic rewards create a culture of compliance and weak motivation.

   d. "A player who makes a team great is more valuable than a great player." — John Wooden

Sample continues next page

Sample: If Disney Managed Your Practice (continued)

10. **Close the Gap Between Knowing and Doing**
    a. Execution separates the Practice from other organizations.
    b. Identify traps:
       - Expecting training and committees to change culture — no authority
       - Hire coordinator — lack authority
       - Seek more knowledge — learn by doing
       - Substitute assessment for action
       - Stall with "How" — people typically know how but are unwilling to break old habits. The key is determining what matters most.
11. **Conclusion**
    a. "Nothing happens unless first a dream." — Carl Sandburg
    b. Develop statements reflecting the ideal state.
    c. Change focus: experience — citizenship — ownership — responsibility.

Policy 6.2

Patient Satisfaction Survey Policy

A patient satisfaction survey will be conducted annually or as needed.

Procedure

1. The Practice manager will coordinate the patient satisfaction survey.
2. The patient satisfaction surveys utilized by the Practice are included (see page 193 and Appendix).
3. Practice personnel will distribute the survey to each patient for a one- (1-) to four- (4-) week period to allow for an adequate response to the survey.
4. Practice personnel will instruct the patient to complete the survey and drop it into a sealed container before leaving the practice. Practice personnel will provide patients unable to complete the survey before leaving with a self-addressed envelope to return the completed survey.
5. The Practice manager will tabulate the surveys.
6. The Practice manager will prepare a report summarizing the results.
7. The survey results will be distributed to the director, medical director, physicians, Practice office staff, and managed care contractors.[1]

1 Kevin Sullivan and Meryl Luallin, *Star-Studded Service: 6 Steps to Winning Patient Satisfaction* (Englewood, CO: Medical Group Management Association, 2007).

Sample: Patient Satisfaction Survey

Please rank your satisfaction with our services in the following areas: A rating of "1" means you were **extremely dissatisfied**. A rating of "5" means you were **extremely satisfied**.

Length of time it took to get an appointment	1	2	3	4	5
Length of time spent in office waiting to be seen	1	2	3	4	5
Physical environment of office	1	2	3	4	5
Friendliness and helpfulness of staff	1	2	3	4	5
Friendliness and helpfulness of physician/practitioner	1	2	3	4	5
Medical knowledge of physician/practitioner	1	2	3	4	5
Explanation of diagnosis	1	2	3	4	5
Explanation of prescribed medications	1	2	3	4	5
Assistance with billing procedures and completion of insurance forms	1	2	3	4	5
Overall satisfaction with the practice	1	2	3	4	5

1. Would you recommend this practice to family or friends? ☐ Yes ☐ No
2. Was this your first visit to this office? ☐ Yes ☐ No
3. Which doctor did you see today?

   ____

4. What is your age? __________ years
5. How did you hear about our practice?
   - ☐ Referred by another physician
   - ☐ Friend or family member
   - ☐ Phone directory
   - ☐ Other (list) ______________________________
6. Were there any staff members who were especially helpful that you would like to mention?

   ____

7. What suggestions do you have for how we can improve our services?

   ____

   ____

   ____

8. If you would like someone to contact you, please answer the following questions:
9. Scheduling my appointment was
   - ☐ Quick and easy
   - ☐ Frustrating and time consuming
10. When you arrived, were you greeted with a smile?
    - ☐ Yes
    - ☐ No
11. How many minutes did you wait before being called in?
    - ☐ 0–10
    - ☐ 11–20
    - ☐ 20+
12. Did the doctor answer all of your questions?
    - ☐ Yes
    - ☐ No

Sample continues next page

Sample: Patient Satisfaction Survey (continued)

13. The billing department made things:
    - ☐ Quick and easy
    - ☐ Frustrating and time consuming
14. Overall, how would you rate the service you received?
    - ☐ Outstanding
    - ☐ Average
    - ☐ Below average
15. Who in particular impressed you? ____________________
16. Which provider is treating you? ____________________
17. How was your visit enjoyable/unpleasant?
    ____
    ____
    ____

Name: ____________________________
Date: ____________________________
Phone Number: ____________________

Thank you for taking the time to assist us with improving our services.

Policy 6.3

Physician–Patient Communication Policy

Physician–patient communication encompasses the verbal and nonverbal interactions that form the basis for the physician–patient relationship. A growing body of research and guidelines development acknowledges that physicians do not have to be born with excellent communication skills but rather can learn them as they practice the other aspects of medicine. Improvement in physician–patient communication can result in better patient care and help patients adapt to illness and treatment.

In addition, knowledge of communication strategies may decrease stress on physicians because delivering bad news, dealing with patients' emotions, and sharing decision-making, particularly around issues of informed consent or when medical information is extremely complex, have been recognized by physicians as communication challenges.[2]

This policy will provide expectations for establishing, maintaining, and improving patient outcomes through better physician–patient communication and discuss guidelines and practical suggestions immediately applicable to clinical practice.

Communicating Bad News

Communicating bad news is a fundamental physician skill. Physicians should be aware that their own sense of what constitutes a good encounter may differ from that of many patients, especially when cultural backgrounds differ. These conversations, when

2 Stephanie J. Lee, Anthony L. Back, Susan D. Block and Susan K. Stewart, "Enhancing Physician-Patient Communication," *Hematology 2002*, American Society of Hematology. http://asheducationbook.hematologylibrary.org/cgi/content/full/2002/1/464.

handled well, can help patients feel informed and hopeful and physicians feel affirmed in their commitment to care for patients. Physicians are best reminded that honesty — and humility — is the best policy.

Communicating with Angry, Anxious, and/or Depressed Patients

When patients are confronted with serious illness or injury, they can exhibit fear, anger, or anxiety. Physicians should remember that:

- Strong emotional responses are normal in the setting of life-threatening illness;
- Understanding the spectrum of responses to serious illness and injury allows the physician to support the patient and make appropriate referrals for specialty and psychosocial support;
- All communication problems are *relationship* problems. When communication is difficult, the physician should reflect on his or her possible contributions to the difficulties;
- Talking about fears, worries, and the impact of the illness or injury on the patient's life is almost always therapeutic;
- Persistent, unremitting anxiety or depression may represent psychiatric illness; such patients should be referred to a psychosocial clinician for counseling, and medication should be considered;
- Patients who are angry are usually helped by nondefensive listening, which communicates caring, concern, and understanding;
- Denial is an extreme response to anxiety and should be considered as a risk factor for depression; and
- When usual strategies of helping patients deal with emotions (listening, exploration of concerns) don't work, the clinician should consider the possibility of unrecognized substance abuse or personality disorder. A team approach is often helpful in dealing with such patients.

Responding to Patient Concerns (Variance Reports)

Patient concerns or complaints may be received by a variety of the Practice physicians during their daily routine. Common avenues for patients to voice concerns are in the business office; through direct communication to administrative staff; via e-mails, letters, and voice mails to physicians; or by speaking with physicians or physician staff outside the practice setting. Physicians are asked to complete a variance report or call the quality management coordinator directly about any significant concerns reported to them. A significant concern is one that is judged by the physician to reflect a potential injury to the patient, risk of litigation, or a risk to the reputation of the organization. The intensity of a patient's concern alone should prompt a variance report and an intervention plan. The variance report lists the categories of concerns that are most frequently voiced by patients. These may range from concerns about physician behavior to complaints about billing procedures or the physical facility.

The quality management coordinator or administrative staff will call each patient to discuss his or her concerns and attempt to resolve the problem. Patient complaints will be taken seriously and investigated thoroughly. Physicians receiving an inordinate number of patient concern reports about the services they provide will be brought to the attention of the medical director and the board president. The physician may be asked to meet to discuss these concerns with members of either the administrative or patient outcomes committee. Persistent patterns of behavior leading to frequent patient complaints or those judged by the medical director or board president to constitute a potential danger to patients or a financial risk to the organization will be brought to the attention of the board of directors for consideration and action.

In general, physicians are advised to refrain from writing e-mails or letters directly to patients in response to complaints without reviewing the letter with the medical director or quality management coordinator. Further, no individual negotiations with an unhappy patient should occur if it involves potential medical litigation or significant financial commitment on the part of the physician or the Practice.

Questions regarding management of the unhappy or concerned patient should be directed to the medical director or quality management coordinator. Their experience and resources should help to resolve conflicts with patients in a timely manner.

Responsibility

The Practice executive or quality improvement manager will take actions necessary to implement this policy.

See also Policy 5.4: Virtual Consultations/E-mailing Patients.

Policy 6.4 Patient Discharge and Practice Restriction Policy

Occasionally, the Practice may encounter patients who no longer want to be treated at the organization or we no longer wish to treat. Reasons for the Practice to terminate the physician-patient relationship may include chronic noncompliance, rudeness to office staff, or nonpayment of bills. While these patient behaviors can affect the interactive care-giving process, they may also identify patients with a propensity for possible litigation. To help reduce the risk of a future claim, a physician may terminate or discharge a patient from the practice.

Patient Discharge/Transfer from Service

1. Criteria for discharging a patient:
   a. The patient dies.
   b. The patient moves out of the area.
   c. A change in the patient's condition requires care or services other than those the Practice can provide.
   d. The patient or family/support is unwilling to comply with the physician's plan of care.
   e. The patient refuses to accept services and/or wishes to transfer to another provider.

Procedure

1. Notify the patient/family verbally and in writing of the reason for discharge from service. Complete the patient discharge letter (see page 199).
2. Work with the patient/family in making alternative plans and or transfer to another physician within or outside the Practice.
3. Notify all services involved in the case.
4. Document each step in the medical record.

It is requested that the following process be followed if you wish to discharge a patient from your practice:

1. Discuss the issue with the department chairperson (or a senior member of the department if you are the department chairperson). If this is "just" a personality conflict, it may be appropriate at this time to offer someone else in the department to take over the case. Continuity of care is most important. If there is a more wide-spread problem, this should go to the medical director;
2. Send the patient a certified letter outlining why you feel you must do this, and include alternatives for continued care by another provider; and
3. Send a copy to the office of the medical director and medical records.

There are, however, certain exceptions that apply to terminating a patient:

- You may not terminate your professional relationship for any discriminatory purpose or violate any laws or rules prohibiting discrimination such as the Americans with Disabilities Act; and
- You also are not permitted to terminate a patient where you know, or reasonably should know, that no other healthcare provider is currently able to provide the patient the type of care or services that you are providing to the patient.

Responsibility

The medical director has ultimate responsibility for ensuring that any patient discharge is handled with the highest level of professional standards and courtesy.

See page 199 for a Sample Patient Discharge Letter and the Appendix for an additional sample Discharge Letter.

Reduce the Risk of Abandonment for the Patient

Abandonment occurs when a physician suddenly terminates a patient relationship without giving the patient sufficient time to locate another practitioner.

- To reduce the risk of allegations of abandonment, it is recommended that you discuss with the patient in person the difficulties in the physician–patient relationship and your intention to discharge the patient from the practice.
- Be sure to document the discussion fully in the patient's medical record, also noting the presence of any witnesses such as a patient's family member or a member of your office staff.
- Write a formal discharge letter to the patient (a sample letter follows and another sample is also provided in the Appendix).

You are required by law to notify the patient in writing of the termination. The letter must state that you will no longer provide care to the patient as of a certain date. The date must be at least thirty (30) days from the date of the letter. You must also state in the letter that you will be available to provide emergency care or services, including provision of necessary prescriptions, during the thirty- (30-) day notice period.

The discharge letter should also include:

- A description of any urgent medical problems the patient may have;
- An offer to forward copies of the patient's medical records to the subsequent treating physician; and
- The name and phone number of a local physician referral service or the local/state medical society to assist the patient in locating a physician who is accepting new patients.

A patient, however, may withdraw from a physician's care at any time without notifying the physician.

The care of a patient is a mutual agreement and is in many ways a team effort between the provider and the patient, but when that relationship is strained and the physician no longer feels that he or she is able to provide quality care to the patient, it is time to end that patient–provider interaction. Make sure the physician has attempted all he or she can do to help, and when the provider realizes there is no more to do, discharging the patient may be the only course of action.

Discharge of a "Problem" Patient

Physicians who are confronted with a chronic "problem patient" may elect to initiate a formal process of termination of care. Documentation and procedural adherence must be followed. The patient should first have an opportunity to establish a relationship with an alternate Practice physician to be certain the problem does not represent a unique personality conflict between the patient and the physician(s). If similar behavior is displayed with the second physician, termination procedures may be warranted.

A "problem patient" may be recognized by the following behaviors:

1. Refuses to undergo recommended treatments;
2. Fails to follow a prescribed diet or self-care regimen;
3. Departs from the hospital against medical advice;
4. Fails to return for follow-up appointments or treatments;
5. Refuses to cooperate with staff or colleagues;
6. Insists on "being his or her own doctor" and disputes physician judgment;
7. Threatens lawsuits;
8. Repeatedly disputes fees that appear just and normal;
9. Displays a threatening, hostile attitude; or
10. Abuses prescription drugs or controlled substances.

The physician and organization have the legal right to withdraw medical services in such circumstances. However, in order to prevent liability due to "abandonment," the following procedures must be followed:

1. Notify the quality management coordinator (QMC) to terminate care;
2. The QMC will discuss the proposal with each physician involved in the patient's management and proceed accordingly;
3. A letter notifying the patient of the decision will be drafted and sent by registered mail by the QMC;
4. The patient will have thirty (30) days to find a new physician or transfer care to another organization, and a specific date of termination will be indicated;
5. Care will be continued during the transition phase of thirty (30) days; and
6. The letter to the patient will list other options for care and will include a form to allow for transfer of the medical record.

Sample: Patient Discharge Letter

[DATE]

Dear __________:

Because of the breakdown in the doctor–patient relationship, I regret to inform you that we will be unable to render any further medical care to you, effective 30 days from the date of this letter.

We will be available to see you on an emergency basis only for the period of 30 days from the receipt of this letter to give you time to find another doctor. After that, we will no longer provide you with medical services. Of course, we will cooperate by forwarding information from your medical record to your new care provider if and when you so authorize.

We will forward your medical records to the physician of your choice upon completion of the enclosed "Release of Records" form.

Please refer to your individual insurance plan, the [STATE] Medical Society, or the Yellow Pages for a list from which to choose your new physician.

Sincerely,

__________(Date)

Practice Restriction

This policy outlines the process by which any requests for Practice restrictions will be evaluated. Any questions about current Practice restrictions will be evaluated by these methods also. The board of directors will resolve any disputes.

1. **Medical**

   There are a variety of medical/physician–practice style issues that cause practices to have restrictions placed upon them. Some of these include:

   a. The Practice is filled;
   b. The Practice accepts physician referrals only;
   c. The new patient has a particular medical problem that a physician or department does not wish to see; and

d. The physician feels that the category of patients is more likely to be involved in litigation or requires additional burdens that don't seem necessary. Examples include legal second opinions, disability evaluations, etc.

It is appropriate that the medical director be responsible for reviewing restrictions and be notified of those restrictions by departments or physicians.

2. **Financial**

There may be a number of financial issues where a physician or department does not wish to be involved in taking care of new patients under certain financial circumstances. Some of these kinds of patients would include:

a. Medicaid patients;
b. Managed care patients; and
c. Workers' Compensation patients.

It is recommended that the administrative committee be notified and have the opportunity to review financial restrictions that are desired by a physician or department, particularly since the Practice may have a contractual requirement to provide certain services.

3. **Discharge of a Patient from the Practice**

Under certain specific circumstances, patients can be discharged from the Practice. There is an existing process and procedure through the office of the medical director that needs to be followed for patients with risk management issues. Requests to terminate care because of financial issues are forwarded to the executive committee for its action.

Policy 6.5 Patient Rights/Responsibilities Policy

The Practice has adopted the following policies in regard to patients' rights and responsibilities:

You have the right to:

1. Receive care in a respectful and courteous manner. To not be discriminated against and to receive care in a safe setting, free from abuse or harassment;
2. Receive privacy concerning your medical care. Discussions and consultations of your care as well as examinations, treatments, and records are confidential and should be conducted in a discreet manner;
3. Know the names of the physicians and the medical staff members that treat you;
4. Be fully informed about a treatment or procedure and the expected outcome before it is performed. Refuse treatment as permitted by law;
5. Know the provisions the Practice has arranged for handling emergency care and after-hours care;
6. Have all reasonable requests responded to promptly and adequately within the capacity of the Practice;

7. Be informed by a medical staff member of your continuing healthcare requirements after discharge from the Practice. You may have a designee assigned to receive this information;
8. Review your bill and receive a detailed explanation of all fees for specific services, regardless of the payment source;
9. Have your rights apply to any person with the legal responsibility to make medical care decisions for you;
10. An interpreter or use of alternative communication techniques/aids as needed;
11. Know that the Practice is privately owned and managed by a group of physicians who have been credentialed to work here; and
12. Know what responsibilities you have as a patient.

You have the responsibility to:

1. Observe the rules and regulations of the Practice for your stay and treatment. Be considerate of other patients and facility personnel;
2. Read and understand all consents you sign. Report to the staff if you do not understand the planned course of your treatment and what is expected of you;
3. Follow up on your physician's instructions, take medications when prescribed, and ask any questions you might have concerning your healthcare;
4. Inform providers of your current health status and all medication you take, including over-the-counter products and supplements;
5. Act responsibly in your treatment plan, and comply with treatment recommendations. Failure to do so can adversely impact the desired clinical results;
6. Indicate if you feel your privacy and/or safety is being violated;
7. When appropriate for your procedures, provide a responsible adult to transport you home. Have a responsible adult be accountable for you at home for the first twenty-four (24) hours after your procedures;
8. Pay financial obligations stated in our financial policy;
9. Respect Practice property and equipment; and
10. File a grievance within thirty (30) days of the occurrence if you feel your rights have been violated. The Office of Medicare Beneficiary Ombudsman is listed below, as well as the state agency to which you can report complaints.

Practice Contact ____________________
State Contact ____________________
Office of Medicare Beneficiary Ombudsman
www.medicare.gov/Ombudsman/activities.asp
#1-800-MEDICARE (1-800-633-4227)
TTY #1-877-486-2048
Centers for Medicare & Medicaid Services
7500 Security Boulevard
Baltimore, MD 21244-1850

PART III

Professionalism

Professionalism Philosophy

Few words strike an emotional chord like the word "professionalism." Depending on the context, the term might evoke pride and honor or shame and embarrassment. It implies a standard of behavior that escapes definition but carries weighty expectations. It hints of boundaries without spelling out where they are. We may have difficulty articulating what professionalism is, but we recognize it when we see it, and its absence can be glaring.

We have come to expect professionals to be self-regulating, but alas, professionals — including physicians — are still human. They are still capable of exhibiting lapses in judgment, episodes of irresponsibility, and momentary dereliction of duties. Policies about compensation, benefits, clinical practices, and patient satisfaction can all point in a proper direction, but they are insufficient to hold physicians accountable to the highest standards of their profession. Medical groups still benefit from policies that spell out the boundaries of acceptable professional behavior for physicians, with residual benefits that spill over to the rest of the staff. When physicians behave professionally, they set the tone for the rest of the team. Their exemplary leadership shapes the culture of the whole organization.

Basic Considerations

Professionalism should be easy to recognize in a medical practice because physicians are often regarded as iconic professionals. They embody the oft-cited marks of a profession:

1. Competence in a specialized body of knowledge and skill;
2. Acknowledgment of specific duties and responsibilities toward the individuals served and toward society;
3. The right to train, admit, discipline, and dismiss the profession's members for failure to sustain competence or observe their duties and responsibilities.

There is tension in the marks of a profession. On one hand, they hint of individualism, earned by perseverance and commitment to advanced study. Their specialization can make them almost one-of-a-kind, which carries privileges of allowing them to set their own terms of engagement.

On the other hand, the marks of a profession hint of community responsibility. Professionals should be equally committed to using their skills to advance the interests of others as they are to advancing their own interests. Professional privilege comes with accountability. Professionalism implies that a balance must be struck, and maintained, between what's good for the individual and what's good for the group. The glue that maintains a healthy balance is organizational culture.

Professionalism also sets the tone for the quality of care that is to be delivered, or at least the *perception of quality*. Patients are more likely to have confidence in the medical judgment of a white-coated, confident figure than in a sloppily clad, unsure presence. Patients may have no way of knowing whether the quality of medical decision-making is state of the art, but they substitute things they do understand, like appearance, for things they don't. An untidy waiting room can create a first impression that undermines the patient's confidence in a clinical encounter with the most qualified physician. An unpleasant receptionist or rude nurse can undo a patient's good opinion of the most compassionate doctor. The smell of popcorn wafting down the hall of an oncology office might seem to belie the seriousness of the disease the team is there to treat. People often discern the qualities of others by emotional clues more than by rationality. In an ideal world, professionals should be competent and have the appearance of competence, supported by a team that consistently reflects and affirms that competence.

Purpose

Physician policies for professionalism provide opportunities to articulate standards of behavior precisely and comprehensively. Professionalism, like common sense, is sometimes uncommon. Policies can spell out expectations and standards for physician behavior and set the tone for how the staff should relate to each other and to patients. They can provide a foundation for governing behavior and clarifying what is appropriate and what is inappropriate.

Individualistic professionals sometimes find it difficult to adhere to group decisions, so policies on professionalism can also be useful for managing circumstances when consensus is elusive. A single noncompliant physician can undermine the unity of a group and divide and confuse the staff. Policies on professionalism can spell out the expectation to present a unified front, recognizing that each member represents all the others with his or her behavior and attitudes as well as his or her words. When physicians criticize a colleague with a patient or staff member, the relational damage can have serious long-term consequences. Policies can prevent certain kinds of damage and help to manage breaches when they do occur.

Professionalism policies can also provide useful tools for managing potential conflicts of interest. For example, the option to moonlight might be seen as an individual professional choice, but if a prominent physician moonlights with a competitor, he or she might damage, or at least confuse, the reputation of his or her main group. Likewise, if business or family interests complicate referral patterns, policies can govern the risk of potentially damaging conflicts.

Components

In this section, you will find examples of professionalism policies covering three dimensions:

- Behavior and Performance — What are the expectations for working together with regard to ethical standards, resolving conflicts, and maintaining confidentiality and professional appearance?
- Citizenship — How do we hold each other equitable and accountable within the group? How do we ensure that each member is represented in major decisions?
- External Relations — What policies will govern our relationships with vendors, hospitals, referrals, and patients? When do external opportunities become conflicts of interest, and how should we manage them? How do we maintain a unified front despite internal unresolved differences?

Conclusion

Professionalism and organizational culture are intimately intertwined. Together they set the tone for a therapeutic environment that attracts and retains physicians, patients, and staff. Policies that define and refine professional expectations can serve as the backbone for a healthy organization, the kind of healthcare delivery system where professionals are proud to work and patients can be confident of the care they receive.

Important disclaimer: Several of the policies and procedures discussed in Part III will only apply to larger groups with significant personnel and related resources, and formal medical staff structures. While the principles and rationale stated may be instructive to various medical groups, the need for scalability and a tailored approach must be emphasized.

CHAPTER 7

Behavior and Performance

Policy 7.1 Position Descriptions Policy

Sample: Job Description Form for Clinic Physician

PRACTICE NAME: POSITION DESCRIPTION:	
Position Title: Clinic Physician **Job Code:**	**Policy Group:** **Review Date:**
Entity/Department Name:	**Approved by:**
Position Summary (This information may be used for posting or advertising the position.) The clinic physician is a member of the healthcare team who works in collaboration with other staff to provide comprehensive healthcare services to patients. The scope of practice of each physician is defined through the Practice's credentialing and privileging committee. The role of a clinic physician is to assess, maintain, and improve the individual and collective health status of individuals in the communities served. **Asterisked items indicate essential functions requiring physical or mental skills and abilities fundamental to the position.*	
Core Competencies	**Knowledge, Skills, and Abilities Needed**
1. Systematically assesses patients' health status, arrives at appropriate diagnosis(es), and implements care plan for effective clinical outcomes • Considers thorough range of treatment/preventive options and arrives at a recommended course of action that is age appropriate, culturally appropriate, realistic, and attainable • Appropriately manages patient care and health status following initiation of treatment/preventive plan, and monitors and adjusts as warranted • Communicates effectively with patients and family so that they understand their diagnosis, treatment plans, and need for follow-up care • Educates and encourages patients to become active participants in their own healthcare-related behavior and provides patient education materials for use in encouraging wellness	• Knowledge of developmental stages and age-appropriate outcomes and interventions • Knowledge of cultural differences and culturally appropriate outcomes and interventions • Has excellent communication and interpersonal skills • Has delegation skills • Understands and complies with Infection Control principles and practices • Knowledge of emergency and other relevant policies and procedures • Knowledge of electronic health records • Knowledge of quality improvement techniques

Sample continues next page

Sample: Job Description Form for Clinic Physician (continued)

<table>
<tr><th>Core Competencies</th><th>Knowledge, Skills, and Abilities Needed</th></tr>
<tr><td><ul><li>Seeks consultation and advises by providing adequate information to consulting physicians. Communicates requests effectively, or responds to such requests from the referral source in a courteous, professional, and timely manner</li><li>Documents according to established guidelines to facilitate ongoing quality of care in a timely manner</li><li>Performs the appropriate medical procedures within the scope of the Practice as defined by the Practice's credentialing and privileging processes</li><li>Delegates direct and indirect patient care activities to appropriate personnel</li><li>Responds appropriately to emergent situations</li><li>Maintains and improves skill level through participation in continuing medical education</li><li>Actively participates in clinical quality improvement initiatives</li><li>Reviews and follows up on complaints and concerns about medical care</li><li>Takes actions to ensure continuity of care for patients</li></ul></td><td></td></tr>
<tr><td>2. Contributes to effective and efficient practice management policies and practices that support patient access to medical care<ul><li>Participates in access planning for the Practice site, ensuring appropriate amount of same-day patient access</li><li>Meets number of Practice patient contact hours as outlined in the contract agreement</li><li>Collaborates in establishing personal numbers of relative value units to be budgeted and achieves targeted goal</li><li>Fulfills commitments for call assignments with clear communication and follows through on work initiated</li></ul></td><td><ul><li>Knowledge of practice management system, scheduling templates</li><li>Knowledge of coding and documentation</li><li>Knowledge of Practice policies and procedures</li></ul></td></tr>
</table>

Sample continues next page

Sample: Job Description Form for Clinic Physician (continued)

Core Competencies	Knowledge, Skills, and Abilities Needed
• Supports appropriate billing for professional services through timely documentation and maintaining adequate knowledge of the Practice's billing policies and procedures • Adheres to all relevant policies, procedures, and practice guidelines • Assists with the preparation for regulatory surveys • Responds to telephone calls in a timely fashion	
3. Manages patient care through appropriate use of available resources • Appropriately prescribes and orders ancillary services • Utilizes Practice referral network appropriately • Promotes the appropriate length of stay for patients • Manages chronic health/disease conditions	• Knowledge of referral networks • Knowledge of Institute for Clinical Systems Improvement (ICSI) guidelines
4. Provides leadership for Practice and community relations • Serves as a resource to colleagues and support staff, enhancing quality of care • Participates in the training, orientation, and evaluation of Practice support staff • Regularly attends and actively participates in Practice staff meetings or physician/staff meetings • Participates in short- and long-term planning for the site or care system, providing input to the annual operational and capital budget • Participates in appropriate committee structure • Participates in community education and other professional activities to promote Practice services and the site	• Knowledge of coaching and mentoring skills • Knowledge of Practice systems and services

Sample continues next page

Sample: Job Description Form for Clinic Physician (continued)

Universal Competencies	Knowledge, Skills, and Abilities Needed
*Demonstrates commitment to customers • Is aware of different customer needs/desires • Takes action to meet customer needs/desires with respect to customer diversity • Helps improve processes to meet customer needs • Suggests and acts on ideas to improve overall customer service • Respects confidentiality and shares information with only those who need to know	• Knowledge of different cultural groups' needs and desires • Customer service knowledge and skills • Process improvement skills • Knowledge of confidentiality policy
*Demonstrates commitment to fellow employees • Seeks to understand and value differences between employees • Treats other employees with dignity and respect • Demonstrates open, honest communication and behavior • Resolves conflict in a positive manner • Contributes to the productivity of the work group	• Communication skills • Conflict management skills • Time management skills
*Demonstrates commitment to the Practice • Lives the values of dignity, integrity, service, and compassion • Supports the Practice's mission/vision • Speaks positively about the Practice • Chooses to make the Practice a better place	• Knowledge of Practice values • Knowledge of Practice mission and vision
Organizational Expectations • Completes all initial and annual required learning relevant to the role • Complies with all relevant laws, regulations, and policies • Contributes to a safe working environment	
Note: This description is intended to provide only basic guidelines for meeting job requirements. Responsibilities, knowledge, skills, abilities, and working conditions may change as needs evolve.	

Sample continues next page

Sample: Job Description Form for Clinic Physician (continued)

Minimum Requirements to Fulfill Position Responsibilities		
Education: Identify below the level of education needed to perform this job.		
	Required	**Preferred**
Less than high school/no formal education required		
High school diploma/GED		
Vocational/technical training or associate's degree		
Bachelor's degree List:		
Advanced degree List:	X	
Other: License/certification/registration List: Medical license in appropriate state	X	
Experience: Identify below the level of experience needed to perform this job.		
	Required	**Preferred**
0 to 1 year	X	
1 to 3 years		
3 to 5 years		
5 to 10 years		
At least 10 years		

Additional Requirements: List position requirements not described above (e.g., computer hardware/software, other office equipment, laboratory equipment, prior supervisory experience, etc.).

- Meets applicable credentialing and privileging standards for specialty
- Board certification or board eligible with board certification obtained within four (4) years of employment, unless waived by the credentials committee
- Demonstrated leadership, teaching, evaluation, and communication skills
- Ability to influence/motivate others at all professional and administrative levels

Special Considerations (unique elements of this position, if any)

Due to differences in scope of care, practice, or service across settings, the specific experience required for this position may vary.

Job title to which this position reports: Site or regional medical director

Job titles that directly or indirectly report to this position: N/A

Number of FTEs: 0
Number of Employees: 0

Physical and Mental Demands: The Americans with Disabilities Act requires employers to make reasonable accommodations for a person with a disability. This information is needed to assist the Practice in meeting these obligations.

Sample continues next page

Sample: Job Description Form for Clinic Physician (continued)

Physical Demands			
Physical Demand (frequency based on an 8-hour shift)	**Occasionally (1–2.5 hours)**	**Frequently (2.5–6 hours)**	**Continuously (6–8 hours)**
Standing		X	
Walking		X	
Sitting			X
Reaching above shoulders	X		
Reaching waist level	X		
Reaching below knee	X		
Climbing			
Lifting above shoulder ______ max. # lb.			
Lifting waist level ______ max. # lb.			
Lifting below knee ______ max. # lb.			
Carrying above shoulder			
Carrying waist level			
Carrying below knee			
Writing		X	
Pushing			X
Hearing			
Squatting/kneeling			
Repetitive actions	X		
Keyboarding	X		
Driving			
Speaking			X
Seeing/visual			X

Physical Environment					
X	Noise		Fumes/gases	X	Chemicals
	Heat/cold	X	Human tissue/fluids	X	Biohazard materials
X	Infections/disease		Animal tissue/fluids		Dirt
	Moving machinery		Radiation		Lasers
	Vibration		Wet/humid environment	X	Work inside
	Work outside	X	Telephone usage		

Sample continues next page

Sample: Job Description Form for Clinic Physician (continued)

Mental Demands					
X	Reading — English	X	Frequent interruptions	X	Multiple concurrent tasks
X	Writing — English	X	Detailed work	X	Frequent deadlines
X	Irregular work schedule	X	Math aptitude	X	Organizational skills
X	Supervisory skills	X	Decision-making skills	X	Ability to work with others
X	Frequent contact with people	X	Concentration required	X	Ability to work independently

Policy 7.2

Code of Conduct Policy

To provide the best possible service for our patients and referring physicians as well as the medical community at large, all physicians must adhere to a strict code of conduct that is mutually agreed upon.

As members of a professional group, each of our individual actions and behaviors reflect on every member of the group. Our activities as professionals have a profound impact on the reputation of the group and the economic success of the business.

General

1. To establish the highest quality of medical care, all physicians must participate in regularly scheduled Practice meetings to develop Practice guidelines for the physicians. Ultimately, these guidelines are what we will share when communicating with our referring physicians. These guidelines will reflect the standards of care for the Practice. Physicians are required to attend 50 percent of the meetings per year.
2. To provide a unified front when working with systems, physicians, or other entities outside the Practice, individual Practice physicians (or small groups) must discuss any issues that potentially affect the Practice with the managing colleague, executive committee, or the entire board *prior* to discussing or acting on these issues.
3. Infringement of the guidelines set forth in this code of conduct will be referred to the executive committee.
4. To ensure the integrity and respect of the individual physician members, each physician should be treated with equal respect, irrespective of whether they are a Practice colleague or physician. This must extend beyond the walls of the Practice sites. Willful disrespect or disharmony outside the Practice (or in front of the Practice staff) cannot be condoned or accepted. Disagreements must remain within the circle of the Practice physicians and executive director/chief executive officer (CEO).

5. Issues will be referred the executive committee, which has the authority to require counseling.
6. To protect the interests of the Practice, all members are expected to comply with all laws and regulations that pertain to maintaining the privacy and confidentiality of medical, financial, proprietary, and any other sensitive information or records in our possession.
7. To ensure that all the contractual obligations and business strategies of the Practice are supported, each physician is expected to support the activities that the Practice has agreed upon, even if that physician is in disagreement with the decision. At no time does the Practice support any activities that are in violation of any laws or ethical standards.

Workplace

1. Treat all people with courtesy, respect, and fairness no matter how intense the pressure of the job. All physician, system, or service problems are directed to the executive director for review.
2. Avoid any form of discrimination or harassment and actively support all efforts to ensure that everyone is afforded the protections and rights provided by the law and by the policy stated in the employee manual.

Patient Care

1. Cooperate with all parties whose activities relate to patient treatment.
2. Avoid conduct that is disruptive to patient safety or patient care.
3. Provide excellent patient care and service, always putting our patients first.
4. Support the expertise of the Practice physicians by utilizing internal referral unless patient health plan or patient care issues dictate otherwise.
5. Treat all patients according to the Practice standards regardless of a patient's payment status.

Billing

1. Follow the Practice billing policies and procedures designed to ensure the accuracy and proper documentation of billing.
   a. Hospital billing must be completed and turned in within five (5) workdays.
   b. Office billing must be completed and turned in within one (1) workday.
2. Only bill for services that are actually rendered and properly documented in the medical record. Avoid knowingly submitting false, fraudulent, or fictitious claims for payment or reimbursement of any kind.
3. Support the activities of the group to ensure compliance with Medicare and other billing requirements.
   a. Attend seminars related to payer contracting rules that are required by the Practice at least once every two (2) years.
   b. Respond promptly to correct coding and documentation errors identified by compliance programs.

Responsibilities

The president and/or executive committee is responsible for meeting with and structuring improvement programs for offending physicians. The executive director/CEO is responsible for meeting with and appropriately disciplining nonphysician employees.

The executive committee may take appropriate actions not limited to:

- Requiring counseling;
- Requiring proctoring;
- Requiring a specific plan of action;
- Requesting resignation; or
- As provided in the physician contract, initiating termination of the physician.

See also Policy 5.7: Charge Capture.

Patient/Customer Service

Physicians will demonstrate courtesy and respect toward internal and external customers. A positive attitude will be presented during all encounters. The physician will:

1. Make it a top priority to see his or her patients in a timely manner;
2. Maintain reasonable access and hours for patients;
3. Make every attempt to adhere to the patient schedule. Physicians will strive to see patients within fifteen (15) minutes of their scheduled appointment time. If this is not possible, the patient will be informed of his or her status and alternatives. If the physician is consistently unable to adhere to the schedule, an adjustment to the schedule may be necessary;
4. Support and participate in efforts to improve patient satisfaction; and
5. Take measures to ensure that patients are not rescheduled unnecessarily, including submitting elective schedule changes by the 15th of each month for the following month (elective changes include vacation, personal time, continuing medical education time, etc.).

Work Ethic

The physician will demonstrate dedication and commitment to patients and the practice of medicine. The physician will strive to exceed work standards and excellence of practice. The physician will:

1. Be in compliance with departmental work standards regarding patient contact hours, participation in call coverage, hospital rounds, and other activities;
2. Maintain hospital affiliations in good standing;
3. Show dedication and commitment to the Practice's mission and vision;
4. Provide timely documentation of patient care, preferably on the date of service (see also Policy 5.2: Electronic Health Records);
5. Submit charges in a timely manner (e.g., professional service records, charge slips, fee tickets, etc.) (see also Policy 5.7: Charge Capture); and

6. Complete all forms related to patient care and the care plan for the patient in a timely manner (e.g., return to work, post-procedure instructions, care plan, follow-up appointment calendar, etc.).

See also Policy 6.1: Patient Relations

Policy 7.3 Code of Ethics Policy

- Care for all who are sick/injured, no matter what their race, religion, ethnic origin, financial status, or illness/injury.
- Demonstrate mutual respect and acknowledge interdependence with colleagues and employees (including clinical and administrative support staff) in caring for the patient.
- Conduct personal and professional activities with honesty, integrity, respect, and fairness.
- Use talents, resources, and time wisely in a sense of stewardship.
- Be truthful in communication and avoid any information that is false or misleading.
- Keep confidential anything learned about a patient, customer, colleague, or employee (including clinical and administrative support staff) while carrying out professional responsibilities.
- Inform individuals of their rights, responsibilities, and risks regarding healthcare services.
- Never knowingly harm any person.
- Never knowingly use a professional position for personal gain or to put another person at a disadvantage.
- Maintain competence and excellence in one's profession through personal evaluation and ongoing education.
- Comply with state and federal laws governing the practice of medicine and work responsibility, whether this be direct or indirect patient care.

See Sample: Customer Service Code of Conduct in Chapter 6.

Policy 7.4 Mission, Vision, Values, and Expectations Policy

The Practice is a [SPECIALTY] group practice providing comprehensive, quality healthcare in all aspects of medical/surgical care, with a full range of diagnostic and treatment alternatives provided by fellowship-trained physicians.

Mission Statement

The physicians and staff of the Practice are committed to enhancing and preserving quality of life for individuals with medical and surgical conditions.

Vision

To be the preeminent medical/surgical services provider in the United States.

Values

Committed to achieving the highest level of patient care through clinical excellence and compassion for all we serve:

- Our physicians are the source of our strength. They form the foundation of our corporate intelligence and corporate diversity;
- Our employees are the source of our support. They are our ambassadors of quality patient care. We will treat them with respect and will encourage their active participation in the care of our patients;
- We will be honest and fair in our relationships with others;
- We believe that patient and community education are vital to the successful treatment and prevention of disease and illness. The training and development of skilled, compassionate healthcare professionals are important to the future care of our patients. As the medical/surgical faculty for the medical school, we actively participate in the training of medical students, residents, fellows, and practicing physicians;
- We will be appropriately available to our patients and to other healthcare professionals;
- We will actively participate in clinical research activities that advance the field of medical/surgical care; and
- The education and training of skilled, compassionate healthcare professionals are important to the future care of our patients.

Performance Expectations

To be a successful physician-led specialty group practice, it is of utmost importance that all physician members of the Practice have a clear understanding of expectations for which they will be held accountable. As a member of the Practice,

- **I am committed to patient satisfaction.** I will treat patients in a manner that is friendly, courteous, and compassionate. I will be attentive and responsive to patient needs and encourage patients to be actively involved in their healthcare. At all times, I will maintain patient confidentiality and dignity;
- **I am committed to communicating both honestly and openly.** I will share information and knowledge in a clear and supportive manner. I will support our policies both internally and externally. When I disagree, I will do so in the appropriate forum;
- **I am committed to an active role in our organization.** I will participate in continuous improvement of our processes. I will take responsibility for problem-solving. As a member of a healthcare team, I am responsible for providing well-coordinated services. I will keep myself informed about policies and procedures; and

- **I am committed to personal achievement from my coworkers and myself.** I will treat all staff with respect, friendliness, courtesy, and compassion. I will take responsibility for my actions. I will maintain my appearance and conduct myself in a manner that represents the Practice well. I will continually strive to improve.

Specific Performance Expectations

Each member of the Practice professional staff is expected to adhere to the general standards of performance outlined as follows:

1. **Professional Activities** — Maintaining appropriate state licensure, hospital privileges, health plan, and other pertinent credentials; adhering to the Practice's compliance program; continuing professional development and medical education activities; obtaining board certification or recertification as required by the physician's particular specialty.
2. **Quality of Care** — Attaining and improving the quality-of-care expectations and guidelines, both formal and informal, that exist in the Practice. This area includes appropriate participation in the Practice's peer review and risk management programs. The Practice will provide high-quality healthcare to individuals.
3. **Practice Management** — The Practice expects clinicians and staff to work cooperatively to maintain high patient satisfaction, good access, and timely and appropriate documentation of patient care.
4. **Resource Allocation** — The Practice clinicians consider clinical quality and cost effectiveness as integral to their work. The Practice has made a commitment to a team approach to delivering care that we believe can reduce costs and improve quality. Cooperation both by participation in and efforts at continuous improvement is critical.
5. **Team Relations** — Good healthcare, whether delivered by an individual physician or several physicians, is a team effort, and mutually supportive team relationships are critical to our success. Therefore, participation in group meetings is expected.
6. **Contribution to the Community** — Our focus dictates that group members will be actively involved in working with other organizations that share our mission, values, and vision. We strongly encourage these efforts and will work with individuals to further their participation.
7. **Referring Physician Relationships** — I will treat referring physicians and members of the healthcare team with respect and courtesy.

Practice Goals

- To promote communication, cohesiveness, teamwork, and collaboration among employees and physicians.
- To enhance patient satisfaction by obtaining the highest level of customer service.
- To treat each other with respect.
- To optimize trust in our organization.
- To make the Practice a great place to work.
- To enhance our image and reputation.
- To strive for continuous performance improvement.
- To be the best medical/surgical services provider in the United States.

Policy 7.5

Call Schedule Policy

It is the goal of an organization to assign a fair distribution of call coverage. However, a fair distribution of call is often open to debate inside healthcare organizations. There are processes that can be adopted to lessen the strain attributed to call coverage assignment.

1. Begin with these principles of call coverage:
    - Never lose sight of the mission to provide quality care;
    - Understand that our Practice operates 24 hours a day, 365 days a year;
    - Understand that taking call is the most demanding responsibility our physicians have;
    - Never deviate from the call guidelines or rules established by the physicians; and
    - Remain unbiased.
2. Determine who will create the call coverage schedule.
    - The medical director or senior physician is the best position for this task.

Procedure for Call Coverage

1. Determine the length of time the schedule will cover. A one- (calendar) year call schedule is a standard length for call schedule.
2. Distribute a "request for time off" packet to the physicians consisting of a memo with a deadline for requests, a list of upcoming conferences, and an attendance/vacation record showing used and remaining time off.
3. Compile requests for time off and no call.
4. Discuss conflicts individually or in a Practice meeting.
5. Communicate elements of the schedule to physicians.

Be sure to consider these elements when determining call:

- Holiday call;
- Weekend call;
- Hospital rotations;
- Catheterization lab rotation;
- Electrophysiology lab rotation;
- Office rotations;
- Noninvasive reading assignments for offices;
- Weeknight call; and
- Invasive backup call.

Requests for Call Coverage Schedule Changes

A temporary or permanent call schedule request will be submitted in writing to medical director, senior physician, or board for approval.

Sample: Anesthesiology Call Coverage Policy

Notification of Arrival for Call Duty

When a backup physician is called in, he or she should notify the in-house physician of his or her arrival. If no notification is received, the in-house physician should assume that the backup has not yet arrived. It would then be appropriate to call or page the backup to clarify his or her location.

Weekdays

Note: Times noted here are examples only and not intended to be used verbatim.

Day call [SPECIALTY] is in house 0730 until relieved by the night call person. Night call is scheduled in the pecking order position just above the call physician from the previous day. Example: If post-[SPECIALTY] is number 10, then prenight call would be number 9. Night call is in house 1900 to 0730. After completion of the daily schedule, the number-one position is a second backup position (i.e., third call position) until the next day. The day [SPECIALTY] works in regular OR at 1600 if the ward is quiet but should call the [SPECIALTY] charge nurse before coming to the OR. If [SPECIALTY] coverage is still necessary, day call relieves the highest-numbered person (the one closest to going home) when coming into the OR. An anesthesiologist working in the OR may decline to cover [SPECIALTY], in which case relief should be offered to the next person in the order. Whenever possible, and with input from the point person, day call entering the OR should try to take over cases with the longest anticipated duration in order to eliminate multiple reliefs.

Other responsibilities of the day call include rounding on post-op pain epidurals, providing lunch breaks, coffee breaks, helping out in the regular OR, doing anesthesia consults, cardiac pre-ops, cardioversions, and assisting with the placement of lines. All-day call tasks are subject to availability of the anesthesiologist. It is appropriate for the point person to delegate such tasks to others, if the day call anesthesiologist is not available.

[SPECIALTY] Pre-ops: At 1900, the day call and night call should discuss any pending pre-op anesthesia consultations required on [SPECIALTY] patients scheduled for the next day to ensure that the pre-operative evaluation is done that evening.

Night Call: Does not work on the post-call day (after completion of shift) except in emergency situations while awaiting relief.

A physician working in a backup call position resulting in severe sleep deprivation would work the shortest column of the next day and would be finished after completion of that column, or sooner if relief was available. No add-on cases would be added to that column. The determination of severe sleep deprivation would be made by the point person after discussion with the post-call anesthesiologist.

Sleep deprivation is subject to many different interpretations. Common sense should apply. This policy also applies to the second backup call person in the event that more than one (1) physician was required after regular hours. In that case, this individual would work the second shortest room and have no add-on cases in his or her column thereafter.

Sample continues next page

Sample: Anesthesiology Call Coverage Policy (continued)

Weekend

- Position 1: In house Saturday 0730 to 1900, second backup at night, first backup Sunday during the day, in house 1900 to 0730.
- Position 2: In house Saturday 1900 to Sunday 0730, then second backup until 1900, then first backup Sunday night.
- Position 3: Second backup Saturday until 1900, then first backup until 0730 Sunday, then in house until Sunday 1900. The first backup call person on Sunday and holiday nights that are followed by a weekday will have priority over the next day's night call person for a shorter schedule by appearing lower in the pecking order on the post-call day. Example: Dr. A is on backup call Sunday night. Dr. B is the night call person Monday night. Dr. A would be off before Dr. B the following day.

Nonweekend Holiday Call Schedule

The call day will be split into three shifts:

1. No. 1 in house first shift, 0730 to 1430;
2. No. 2 in house second shift, 1430 to 2100; and
3. No. 3 in house third shift, 2100 to 0730.

The anesthesiologist working either of the first two in-house shifts becomes the second backup position for the next shift. No. 3 is off the following day. No. 1 assumes the "post-[SPECIALTY]" pecking order position the next day.

- 1st shift
- (0730–1430) 2nd shift
- (1430–2100) 3rd shift
- (2100–0730) Next day
- Position in house, 2nd backup, 1st backup post-[SPECIALTY]*
- Position 2, 1st backup, in house, 2nd backup post #1†
- Position 3, 2nd backup, 1st backup in house off

* Position 1 gets the lowest pecking order slot the following day, equivalent to post-[SPECIALTY].

† Position 2 gets equivalent of post #1 next day (just above next day's night call person).

Holiday call is assigned on a points-per-holiday basis in an attempt to achieve an equal distribution of holiday calls over the course of several schedules.

Relief Protocol

With few possible exceptions, the lowest (highest-numbered) remaining person in the pecking order should have his or her choice of cases where issues of relief are concerned. If the in-house anesthesiologist calls in a backup anesthesiologist, the backup would have first choice of assignment, unless the situation required immediate attention (e.g., crash C-section, trauma) of the backup anesthesiologist. Example: Night [SPECIALTY] is involved in ankle fracture and backup is called in because of a ruptured AAA. The backup could choose to finish the ankle fracture while the in-house person starts the AAA.

Policy 7.6 Performance Appraisal/Evaluation Policy

Note: This policy is illustrative but subordinate to any other provisions in the physician's employment contract; in the event of conflict between this policy and an employment contract, the latter provisions will control.

During the probationary period and throughout the year, performance will be evaluated on an ongoing basis by the physician's supervisor, at which time his or her rate of progress will be discussed. From time to time, however, it is important for the physician to talk to his or her supervisor on a more informal basis about responsibilities and improvement, or lack thereof, to determine what steps need to be taken to improve performance or potential, if any.

The Practice's policy is that supervisors will evaluate new physicians upon completion of the three- (3-) month probationary period. It is the responsibility of the new physician to schedule this evaluation with his or her supervisor. New physicians who are having difficulty adjusting to their new position may be evaluated more frequently or terminated before the three- (3-) month probation is up. Physicians shall receive a formal written performance review at least two (2) weeks prior to the three- (3-) month anniversary of their hire date and yearly thereafter, at least two (2) weeks prior to their anniversary date. Written evaluations of the physician's progress will be made, and the physician will receive a copy if he or she so desires. Physicians also have an opportunity to discuss questions regarding any aspect of their employment.

Evaluations will be performed for both full- and part-time physicians. The evaluation will assist physicians in attaining maximum development of their individual talents and abilities. No merit-pay increases can be given without a formal written evaluation. It is the physician's responsibility to schedule the evaluation so that it takes place at least two (2) weeks prior to the actual anniversary of his or her hire date, both at the end of probation and on his or her anniversary.

Should a merit-pay increase be indicated, it cannot be retroactive regardless of the circumstance involved in the evaluation process.

See Appendix for Performance Appraisal Form.

Policy 7.7 Problem Resolution/Grievance Process Policy

Procedure

1. A physician or other supervisor identifies unsatisfactory performance on the part of a physician on his or her team and discusses specific areas needing improvement

with the physician. Examples include waste of materials or supplies; patient complaints; failure to follow established practices regarding communication, dress, or hygiene; excessive absenteeism; or not meeting performance goals.

In the case of a specific infraction of a Practice rule, such as conduct endangering the person or property of a patient, physician, or company; sexual harassment or verbal abuse of a patient, staff member, or colleague; possession of weapons; breach of patient confidentiality; violation of stated policies of patient care; or illegal activity, such as falsification of medical records, the physician can be terminated immediately.

2. If improvement does not occur within a specified period of time, the physician will be scheduled for counseling with the human resources (HR) specialist.
3. If teamwork does not improve following counseling, the physician may request that he or she be transferred to another department. Every effort will be made to provide an equitable transfer; however, this cannot be guaranteed because of position openings.
4. If the performance does not improve and a transfer is not available, the physician may request a suspension of the physician for a specific period of time, from one to four weeks. At the end of that period, the physician may be terminated if no other options are available. Such suspension or termination must be approved by the department chair, the HR office, and the administrator.

Responsibility

The administrator shall be responsible through the HR office for ensuring that any actions related to physician suspension or termination are properly handled in accordance with employment laws and practices.

I. Physician-Shareholder Rights: Problem Resolution for Larger Practices

- **Board.** Seven (7) physician-shareholders are elected at the annual meeting by shareholders. The first order of business each year is to elect a chair. Ultimately responsible for the operations of the Practice, the board meets the first and third Wednesdays of the month from 7:30 a.m. to 10:00 a.m.
- **Physician Practice Council.** Consists of nine (9) physicians representing sections chaired by the medical director. Responsible for medical practice aspects of the operations of the Practice. Meets the second and fourth Mondays of the month from 5:30 p.m. to 8:00 p.m.
- **Executive Committee.** Chaired by the chair of the board, members include the president, medical director, and administrator. Responsible for reviewing and ensuring that board matters are ready for presentation. Also acts as an ad-hoc committee of the board for resolving problems of urgency or within board-designated authority. This committee also functions as the clearinghouse or traffic cop to assign corporate problems to the appropriate committee or individual and then ensure that the problem is addressed in a timely fashion. Meets every Friday from 7:30 a.m. to 10:00 a.m. or as needed.
- **Administrative Committee.** Chaired by the president, members include the administrator, three (3) associate administrators, and other individuals as needed. Responsible for day-to-day operational decisions within the authority designated by the board. Meets every Monday from 8:00 a.m. to 10:30 a.m. and more frequently during budget time.

- **Committee Structure.** Other standing committees and task forces/work groups are appointed as needed by the board. An example of a task force would be one appointed to study hospital alignment/integration. The standing committees are established by and responsible to the board. Yearly membership is appointed by the president. Current standing committees are benefits, capital equipment, pharmacy, quality improvement/management, patient education, and practice promotion.

II. Employee Grievance Policy for Use by Physicians

NOTE: Disposition of all grievances is subject to terms of the physician's employment contract. In case of conflict with this policy, the contract provisions shall control.

Informal Resolution

Wherever possible, complaints or grievances should be handled through informal means with your immediate supervisor. If you are a staff physician, discuss your area of concern with the division chief; if a division chief, discuss your area of concern with the department chair.

Formal Resolution

Step 1: If the issue remains unresolved after discussions at the informal level, obtain an official grievance form from human relations.

The physician must initiate a grievance within ten (10) working days after the issue or complaint arose or he or she should have reasonably known of it. In cases involving termination or suspension, a grievance must be filed within three (3) working days of the termination or suspension.

The written grievance is submitted to the department chair. A meeting between the chair and the physician will be scheduled for at least one (1) hour within five (5) working days of the grievance submission. A member of the HR staff will attend the meeting and serve as facilitator. The typical Step 1 session will be conducted as follows:

Step 1 Agenda	Time
Physician presents information	15 min.
Chair presents information and seeks clarification	15 min.
Physician presents rebuttal and seeks clarification	15 min.
Chair summarizes and seeks final clarification	15 min.
Chair adjourns meeting	

The department chair will respond in writing within five (5) working days of the meeting.

Step 2: If not satisfied with the response in Step 1, the physician may appeal the decision by submitting to the Practice president copies of the written grievance and the chair's written response to that grievance. In a cover letter, the physician will declare whether he or she chooses to present his or her appeal to a three- (3-) member review panel or to the president. The physician will also declare his or her understanding that the decision of either alternative is binding and not eligible for further appeal.

The president will notify the executive director that a grievance has been filed and advise the avenue of resolution the physician has chosen.

The executive director will notify the senior vice president of HR that a grievance has been filed and the avenue of resolution the physician has chosen.

Note: Should the president also be the department chair involved in the grievance, the physician will submit his or her appeal to the vice president of the Practice.

Step 3: Within ten (10) working days of receiving the appeal, the review panel or the president/vice president will review the facts and meet with the physician.

The aggrieving physician may invite witnesses who can provide factual data relevant to the complaint. Should the physician wish to have such witnesses present, he or she will notify in advance the party reviewing the grievance. The reviewing party retains the right to ask questions of the aggrieving physician's witnesses.

The party reviewing the grievance may invite the division chief, the department chair, the executive director, or other appropriate individuals to attend the meeting. Should the presence of these or additional attendees be requested, the aggrieving physician will be notified in advance. The aggrieving physician retains the right to ask questions of the reviewing party's invited attendees. A member of the HR staff will attend the meeting and serve as facilitator.

A typical Step 3 grievance will be conducted as follows:

Step 3 Agenda	Time
Facilitator introduces all parties and reviews agenda for meeting	5 min.
Chair presents rationale for decision	15 min.
Physician presents information	15 min.
Decision-maker(s) seeks clarification	15 min.
Chair makes final statement	5 min.
Physician makes final statement	5 min.
Decision-maker(s) asks if any other information should be considered	
Physician, chair, and other participants are asked to leave	
Decision-maker(s) reviews record and discusses issues	30 min.

The physician will receive a written summary of the final decision within five (5) days after the appeals meeting. Copies of the decision will be forwarded to the department chair, the executive director, and the senior vice president for HR.

Administration

In the instance of serious issues — for example, termination of employment — the review panel and the Practice president reserve the right to tape-record the appeals process. To ensure that all statements are accurately documented, the aggrieving physician, upon written request, will be provided a transcript of the tape.

The ad hoc review panel will be made up of three (3) members:

1. From the current board of directors, the aggrieving physician selects one nonchair panelist.
2. From the current board of directors, the chair of the aggrieving physician's department selects one nonchair panelist.
3. By mutual agreement, the chair and the aggrieving physician select the third panel member. This third panelist may be any nonchair member of the Practice. If the chair and the aggrieving physician cannot agree on the third panelist, the Practice president will select the third panelist.
4. The senior vice president for HR or his or her designee will serve as a nonvoting facilitator for the appeals hearing.

Conflict of Interest

At no time may a physician who is in the same department as the aggrieving physician be a member of the review panel. In addition, panelists are expected to disqualify themselves if they feel they will be unable to render an impartial decision.

Policy 7.8

Substance Abuse/Impairment Policy

The American Medical Association Council on Mental Health refers to physician impairment as "The inability to practice medicine with reasonable skill and safety to patients by reason of physical or mental illness, including alcoholism or drug dependence."[1] The Americans with Disabilities Act (ADA) enacted by Congress in 1990 classifies a person with a history or reputation of drug abuse, but who is not now using drugs, as a "person with a disability." Provisions of the ADA cover employed physicians who are impaired or regarded as having an impairment.

Procedure

1. A mentally, physically, or emotionally impaired physician may be referred or self-referred to the medical director.
2. The medical director may implement one of the following responses:
    a. Advise the council of department chairs and CEO; if deemed urgent, action can be taken to intervene immediately, pending due process. The Practice's primary commitment is to the safety of its patients. It must safeguard that responsibility; or

1 American Medical Association, Council on Mental Health, "The Sick Physician: Impairment by Psychiatric Disorder, Including Alcoholism and Drug Dependence," *JAMA* 233 (1973): 684–687.

   b. Convene the medical affairs and credentialing committee for review. Call a subcommittee meeting of the medical affairs committee specifically for the purpose of responding to the nature of the issue.

3. The committee should serve as an advocate for the impaired provider by serving to identify the nature of impairment and assist in obtaining intervention and/or treatment. The committee should be a multidisciplinary group including at least three (3) providers of whom one (1) is a psychiatrist or psychologist from the Practice. The group seeks to play a nondisciplinary role and to assist in treatment that will return the practitioner to the fullest extent of practice capability possible.

   Responsibilities of the committee should include, but are not limited to:

   a. Confidentially investigate allegations of impairment and inquiries and reports from as broad a group as possible, including providers, nurses, patients, family members, and others that suggest:
      - Impairment of the physician's ability to practice;
      - Serious mental, emotional, or physical problems;
      - Alcohol or other drug abuse; and
      - Behavioral problems (including unethical conduct).
   b. The work of the committee is considered part of the medical staff's peer review system and can thus receive the legal protection afforded such activities.
   c. Be aware of treatment options and be ready to make referrals.
   d. Serve as the liaison with treatment professionals to supervise interventions.
   e. Participate in interventions as advocates rather than adversaries.
   f. Assist in monitoring the recovery of the physician.
   g. Provide ongoing support to the physician.
   h. Educate the medical staff about impaired-physician issues.

4. After completing a thorough investigation, the committee will determine whether or not there is validity to the question of impairment. If impairment is thought to be present, one of three (3) actions may be undertaken:

   a. If a referral was made to the committee and the committee feels that impairment does not exist, this finding should be communicated to the person originally reporting a concern. That person should be asked to contact the committee, then if any new instances or problems do occur, the committee should follow up with the reporting person within six (6) months to make sure that there have not been any further instances suggesting a problem;
   b. If after review the committee feels that a problem exists but that problem is not clinically oriented within the scope of the committee, the reporting person will be encouraged to take the matter to the appropriate person or committee (either the full medical affairs and credentialing committee or another medical associates committee). If the matter is clearly disciplinary in nature, the committee may offer expertise and advice on how to handle the situation. If the problem falls within the role of the committee, delegated members will meet with the physician to discuss the problem informally; or
   c. In the case that a physician's behavior constitutes an imminent danger to a patient or staff member, many members will act prudently to involve appropriate individuals — the medical director, CEO, department head, and employee assistance coordinator — as the situation warrants to intervene at that time.

5. The committee should attempt to obtain agreement from the physician that:
   a. A problem exists and the nature of the problem;
   b. Establishes diagnosis with the assistance of a consultant; and
   c. Identifies treatment options.
6. If agreement about the nature of the problem and/or agreement about participation in a treatment or rehabilitation program cannot be reached with that physician, the committee has the following options:
   a. If the problem is not severe and/or the physician is not seen as impaired, the committee can continue to offer its help, support, and services to the physician on an informal basis; or
   b. If the physician is considered to be impaired to the point that behavior jeopardizes a patient or the Practice, the medical director may intervene directly and immediately.
7. If the physician agrees to participate in a rehabilitation program, a formal program would be proposed by the committee with the participation of the impaired physician. The treatment plan would be developed and signed by the physician.
8. A monitoring plan/monitoring agreement should be drawn up, and it should serve as the basis of a monitoring agreement between the committee and the provider. The following elements should be addressed as the plan is designed:
   a. **Treatment:** The committee should satisfy itself that the physician receives appropriate treatment sufficient to ensure that the problem is being addressed effectively. The committee should satisfy itself that the physician's current physical and mental health are sufficient to allow him or her to practice safely. The monitoring plan should incorporate the elements of an aftercare plan and recovery plan.
   b. **Release of Information:** The committee should require that the recovering physician authorize the treatment provider/facility to communicate information to the committee, including initial treatment as well as aftercare and/or ongoing care. Information should include timely reports, as required by the committee, and immediate notification should a relapse occur.
   c. **Recovery Plan:** The physician should have a specific, ongoing recovery plan. The monitoring plan should be designed to accumulate the information, which will document the physician's participation in this recovery program.
   d. **Monitoring the Recovering Provider:** Information about the health status of the provider in recovery and about his or her performance should be gathered and reviewed. The committee should meet with the recovering provider as needed to discuss progress and review the reports received.
   e. **Record-Keeping:** The record should include a copy of the signed monitoring agreement between the physician and the committee. The committee must have adequate information to assess the physician's status in recovery and compliance with the elements in the agreement. This information must be kept in strict confidence. This information should be kept as long as the physician is employed by the Practice, plus five (5) years. Disclosure outside of the committee can be made only with the written authorization of the impaired provider.
   f. **Response to Relapse:** The monitoring plan should take into consideration that relapse is not an uncommon phenomenon. The response to any relapse should be the same as the response to the initial diagnosis. The customary response

should be to review the initial treatment plan and consider possible alternative treatment approaches. Consideration should be given to the provider's health and to patient and staff safety in reaching a decision about whether a leave from patient care is appropriate.

Responsibility

The administrator and medical director, with the assistance of the HR office, shall take responsibility for implementing this policy.

Policy 7.9 Workplace Harassment Policy

Harassment is anything that constitutes a hostile work environment. Sexual harassment is a form of gender-based discrimination prohibited by Title VII of the Civil Rights Act of 1964. The U.S. Equal Employment Opportunity Commission defines sexual harassment as

> *Unwelcome sexual advances, requests for sexual favors, and other verbal or physical conduct of a sexual nature when submission to the conduct enters into employment decisions and/or the conduct unreasonably interferes with an individual's work performance and creates an intimidating, hostile, or offensive working environment.*[2]

The two most common forms of sexual harassment are "quid pro quo" and "hostile work environment." Quid pro quo harassment forces a physician to choose between the job and the sexual demands. Most people think of quid pro quo as meaning something for something. On the other hand, hostile-work-environment harassment is deemed to occur when there is a repeated pattern of verbally abusive, threatening, crude, and/or impolite behavior or various other types of unprofessional conduct that impair a physician's ability to perform his or her duties.

It is the policy of the Practice that it will not tolerate verbal or physical conduct by any physician, administrator, or staff member that harasses, disrupts, or interferes with another's work performance or that creates an intimidating, offensive, or hostile environment.

While all forms of harassment are prohibited, sexual harassment is specifically prohibited. Each supervisor has a responsibility to maintain a workplace free of any form of sexual harassment. No supervisor is to threaten or insinuate, either explicitly or implicitly, that a physician's refusal to submit to sexual advances will adversely affect

2 U.S. Equal Employment Opportunity Commission, "Facts about Sexual Harassment," EEOC Website, www.eeoc.gov/eeoc/publications/fs-sex.cfm (accessed July 9, 2011).

the physician's employment, evaluation, wages, advancement, assigned duties, shifts, or any other condition of employment or career development. In addition, no supervisor is to favor in any way any applicant or physician because that person has performed or shown a willingness to perform sexual favors for the supervisor.

Other sexually harassing or offensive conduct in the workplace, whether committed by supervisors or nonsupervisory personnel, is also prohibited. Such conduct includes:

- Sexual flirtations, touching, advances, or propositions;
- Verbal abuse of a sexual nature;
- Graphic or suggestive comments about an individual's dress or body;
- Sexually degrading words to describe an individual; and/or
- The display in the workplace of sexually suggestive objects or pictures, including nude photographs.

Any physician who believes that the actions or words of a supervisor or fellow physician constitute unwelcome harassment has a responsibility to report it through the physician grievance process or to complain immediately to the appropriate supervisor, or to the administrator/executive director if the complaint involves the supervisor.

Every complaint of sexual harassment will be taken seriously and investigated immediately in as impartial and confidential a manner as possible by the supervisor or administrator/executive director. Any individual involved in a sexual harassment complaint will have the opportunity to give a full account of his or her recollection of the incident(s). If a physician is not satisfied with the handling of a complaint or the action taken by the supervisor, the physician should bring the complaint to the attention of the administrator/executive director. In all cases, the physician is to be advised of the supervisor's, or administrator/executive director's, findings and conclusions.

Any physician, supervisor, or manager who is found, after appropriate investigation, to have engaged in harassment of another physician will be subject to progressive disciplinary action, depending on the circumstances, up to and including termination.

Policy 7.10 Personal Appearance and Dress Code Policy[3]

The board is committed to representing quality of service in every aspect of its relations with patients. Appearance and identification are representative of quality. The board expects all staff to dress professionally, appearing well-groomed, appropriate, and safe for the job being performed.

3 Printed in *HR Policies and Procedures Manual for Medical Practices, 4th Edition,* by Courtney Price, PhD, and Alys Novak, MBA (Englewood, CO: Medical Group Management Association, 2007).

Procedure

1. The medical director and administrator shall annually clarify appearance/identification expectations, including:
   a. The wearing of a nametag/badge with photo ID provided by the HR office at the time of hiring;
   b. Presenting a uniform look by those providing medical services (e.g., wearing a lab coat/jacket in the specific Practice colors); and
   c. Refraining from wearing blue jeans; thong-type sandals; low-cut shirts/blouses, tank tops, or spaghetti-strap tops, unless covered by a sweater/blazer; sweatsuits, running shorts, or other recreational attire; excessive perfume/cologne; or appearing for work barefoot. Office staff may wear walking shorts or skorts that fall just above the knee.
2. Each physician is responsible for appropriate personal appearance and hygiene standards, including dress, hairstyle, cleanliness, and makeup.
3. Any jewelry worn must be appropriate for our business atmosphere. Nursing pins, service award pins, and other pins directly related to the Practice and/or the management services organization are acceptable. Pins that advertise anything else are strictly prohibited. Jewelry or other items that may pose any form of safety hazard, or that may be offensive to patients or others, are forbidden. Nose rings and other piercings not on the ear lobe as well as excessively large items are not acceptable and may not be worn by any physician while on duty.
4. Hygiene: Fingernails are to be clean. Hair is to be neat, clean, groomed, and of appropriate length. Extremes in hairstyles and colors will not be tolerated. Facial hair is acceptable, provided it is neatly trimmed close to the skin. Common sense and moderation should be employed in the application of fragrances, cosmetics, etc. Body and breath odor are to be addressed by the physician's supervisor.
5. Physicians presenting at the workplace inappropriately attired will be sent home to change and will not be paid for the period of absence.

Dress Code

1. Physicians required to wear a uniform must be in uniform at all times while on duty. The physician is responsible for keeping it clean and pressed. Physicians whose jobs require street clothing should be well groomed and use good judgment in choosing apparel. They should dress in a neat and businesslike manner. Management may authorize casual dress days on occasion. Personal cleanliness and clean apparel are expected at all times.
2. Each physician shall be responsible for wearing appropriate professional attire and maintaining a neatly groomed appearance at all times. Examples of appropriate attire include business and business casual attire and clinical attire (uniforms, scrubs, lab coats). The Practice manager shall be responsible for determining what is appropriate and what is not.
3. Uniforms may be required in any Practice at physician expense.
4. Unacceptable attire includes but is not limited to:

- Any attire deemed to be extreme by the Practice manager;
- Denim slacks of any color;
- Shorts;
- T-shirts (with or without advertising);
- Sweat pants and shirts, coveralls, halter tops, and sheer clothing;
- Clothing that exposes bare shoulders/midriffs;
- Hats that are not part of a uniform;
- Sunglasses (unless the physician is outside or there is a medical reason to wear); and
- Any clothing that advertises or has lettering (logo polo shirts, etc.).

5. Footwear must be of professional style and color, and heel height must be appropriate to the type of work performed. Dress sandals are acceptable with appropriate hosiery. Flip-flops and similar footwear are not to be worn. Certain physician classification may be required to adhere to Occupational Safety and Health Administration regulations relative to footwear.

Policy 7.11 Satisfaction Surveys Policy

The Practice will conduct satisfaction surveys for every [X] number of referrals received. Results will be reviewed every [X] number of months, and actions steps will be taken to improve performance.

See Appendix for the Physician Satisfaction Survey Form.

Policy 7.12 Unions Policy

Employee Organization and Representation

The policy of the Practice is to acknowledge and respect the rights of its physicians to join or not join a union, participate in legal organizing activity, and be represented by an individual of their choosing. However, the Practice does not believe that physicians need collective bargaining units because it has a strong commitment to its physicians to provide competitive compensation, good working conditions, and opportunities for growth and development. The Practice treats its physicians fairly and honestly, provides job security, and refrains from staff reductions whenever possible.

Policy 7.13

Probation/Termination Policy

Note: This policy is explicitly subordinate to any other rights or procedures provided in a physician's employment contract; the latter provisions shall control in the event of conflict.

Probation

A physician not performing up to the expectations of the medical director, the board of directors, and the shareholders may be terminated with appropriate notice. For some physicians, a probationary period may be offered to allow correction of performance concerns. The medical director, with the agreement of a majority of the members of the board of directors, may place a physician on probation based on performance concerns.

Physicians on probation without a written contract remain employed at will and may be terminated by the Practice, at any time, with or without cost to the Practice in its discretion. The progressive disciplinary list that follows is simply the procedure the board may elect to enforce and does not constitute a contract.

The medical director and/or board president at the direction of the board of directors will deliver a probation notice to the physician and answer questions related to the notification. The probation notice will include:

1. Reasons for probation;
2. Time interval (start/stop) of probation;
3. Expectations of the physician during probation; and
4. Date of performance reevaluation by the board of directors.

The board of directors may:

1. Withdraw probation and restore full employment status;
2. Continue probation with or without financial penalties; or
3. Initiate employment termination (recommendation to shareholders).

New hires shall read the shareholder agreement and attachments, and their signature on a contract shall be acknowledgment that they have read and understood the compliance aspects of those documents. Compliance policies and procedures shall be furnished to each new hire and individually reviewed with the Practice administrator.

New hires shall be formally evaluated at least once before their first anniversary with the Practice, using the Performance Appraisal Form (see Appendix and Policy 7.6), which includes a review of compliance performance. At least two (2) colleagues in the physician's specialty shall perform such evaluations.

Withdrawing Colleague or Contractor

All withdrawing colleagues or contractors shall have a an exit interview, either formal or informal, with the Practice's administrator, managing member, or other designated member of the compliance committee, and will be given an opportunity to address any concerns or observations about compliance issues.

Sample: Termination Policy

Termination

1. **Involuntary Termination (for Cause).** This agreement shall be deemed terminated and the employment relationship severed between the parties upon occurrence of the following:
    a. The suspension, revocation, or cancellation of the physician's right to practice medicine in the state of [STATE];
    b. Any restrictions or limitations to physician's hospital privileges to such an extent that he or she cannot provide an adequate level of medical service to the Practice's patients;
    c. Any restrictions or limitations by any governmental authority having jurisdiction over the physician to such an extent that he or she cannot engage in the practice of medicine;
    d. The physician's failure to perform the usual and customary duties of the practice of medicine or comply with reasonable policies and standards of Practice;
    e. The physician conducts himself or herself in an unprofessional, unethical, or fraudulent manner or is found guilty of such conduct by an institution or professional society so that it discredits or is detrimental to the reputation of the Practice; or
    f. The full disability or death of the physician.
2. **Tail Insurance Coverage.** Immediately after termination of this agreement, the physician shall be required to purchase tail insurance coverage or provide proof of prior-acts coverage (mature policy) with retroactive dates inclusive of the time employed by the Practice in the same amounts as the Practice provided during the term of employment. The physician hereby authorizes the Practice to provide such coverage at the physician's expense by deducting the cost of such coverage from any amounts due to the physician upon termination of employment. If there are no amounts owing, the physician shall pay the Practice the cost of tail coverage within ten (10) days of the Practice obtaining a quote for such coverage.
3. **Conditions for Termination.** This agreement shall be terminated upon the occurrence of any of the following events:
    a. Whenever the physician shall cease to be a licensed physician in the state;
    b. Whenever the Practice and the physician shall mutually agree to the termination in writing;
    c. The death of the physician;
    d. Whenever the physician fails or refuses to perform faithfully and diligently the duties of employment and comply with the provisions of this agreement;
    e. Whenever the physician fails or refuses to comply with the reasonable policies, standards, and regulations of the Practice; or
    f. Notwithstanding any of the provisions of subparagraphs 3a through 3e, upon thirty (30) days' prior written notice by either the Practice or the physician to the other.
4. **Compensation Payable on Termination.** Upon termination of this agreement, the physician shall be entitled to receive only the compensation accrued as collected based on the physician's accounts receivable and deduction of both direct and indirect expenses (for a period of two (2) months) and a deduction of 5 percent of collections for the administrative expenses of collecting the accounts receivable.

Sample continues next page

Sample: Termination Policy (continued)

Termination Checklist

The following list can help to ensure the Practice's firm legal standing when terminating a physician:

1. Keep a written record of all oral warnings;
2. Follow Practice policies and procedures for disciplining physicians;
3. Provide the physician with a written plan for improvements to correct problems that may lead to termination; and
4. Give the physician guidance and support to improve performance.

Making the Decision to Terminate

1. Review your policies and procedures to ensure that they are up-to-date and legally sound.
2. Review your staff handbook to ensure that it is current. Make revisions as necessary.
3. Review your procedures for discipline, reprimand, and termination.
4. Review all documentation, including oral and written reprimands, and plans for improvement.
5. Identify whether the physician could be demoted, reassigned to a lateral position, or encouraged to resign.

Preparing for the Termination Meeting

1. Review your reasoning and what you plan to say at the termination meeting with the Practice's attorney.
2. Anticipate how you will handle the exit interview.
3. Arrange for the return of keys and supplies.
4. Consider the issue of giving references for the terminated physician.
5. Pick a discreet time and location for the termination.
6. Prepare the physician's final paycheck, including any vacation and other eligible benefits.
7. Give the paycheck to the physician during the termination meeting.

Policy 7.14 Disruptive Physician Policy

Inappropriate Behavior

The Practice discourages inappropriate behavior by medical staff members. Persistent inappropriate behavior can become a form of harassment and thereby become disruptive, and is subject to treatment as "disruptive behavior." Examples of inappropriate behavior include, but are not limited to, the following:

- Belittling or berating statements;
- Name calling;
- Use of profanity;
- Inappropriate comments written in a patient's medical record;
- Blatant failure to respond to patient care needs or staff requests;
- Deliberate lack of cooperation without good cause;
- Deliberate refusal to return phone calls, pages, or other messages concerning patient care or safety; and
- Intentionally degrading or demeaning comments regarding patients and their families, nurses, physicians, hospital or Practice personnel, and/or the Practice name.

Disruptive Behavior

Disruptive behavior by physicians is prohibited and will not be tolerated. Examples of disruptive behavior include, but are not limited to, the following:

- Physical or verbal intimidation or challenge, including disseminating threats or pushing, grabbing, or striking another person involved in the Practice;
- Physically threatening language directed at anyone in the Practice including other physicians, nurses, other medical staff members, administrators, members of the board of directors, and patients;
- Physical contact with another individual that is threatening or intimidating;
- Throwing instruments, charts, or other items;
- Threats of violence or retribution; and
- Sexual or other forms of harassment, including but not limited to persistent inappropriate behavior and repeated threats of litigation.

Interventions

Interventions should initially be nonadversarial in nature, if possible, with the focus on restoring trust, placing accountability on and rehabilitating the offending medical staff member, and protecting patient care and safety. The medical staff supports tiered, nonconfrontational intervention strategies, starting with informal discussion of the matter with the appropriate section chief or department chairperson. Further interventions can include an apology directly addressing the problem, a letter of admonition, a final written warning, or corrective action pursuant to the medical staff bylaws, if the behavior is or becomes disruptive.

The use of summary suspension should be considered only where the physician's disruptive behavior presents an imminent danger to the health of any individual. At any time, rehabilitation may be recommended. If there is reason to believe inappropriate or disruptive behavior is due to illness or impairment, the matter may be evaluated and managed confidentially according to the established procedures of the medical staff's health and well-being committee (or equivalent committee). (See also Policy 7.8: Substance Abuse/Impairment.)

Procedure

NOTE: This procedure is suggested for larger practices with "formal" medical staff structures attached to or part of a hospital. Smaller or less diversified groups may not choose to apply such a procedure.

Complaints about a physician regarding allegedly inappropriate or disruptive behavior should be in writing, signed and directed to the president of the medical staff, or if the President of the medical staff is the subject of the complaint, to the vice president of the medical staff, and should include to the extent feasible:

1. The date(s), time(s), and location of the inappropriate or disruptive behavior;
2. A factual description of the inappropriate or disruptive behavior;
3. The circumstances that precipitated the incident;
4. The name and medical record number of any patient or patient's family member who was involved in or witnessed the incident;
5. The names of other witnesses to the incident;
6. The consequences, if any, of the inappropriate or disruptive behavior as it relates to patient care or safety, or Practice personnel or operations; and
7. Any action taken to intervene in, or remedy, the incident, including the names of those intervening.

At the discretion of the Practice president (or vice president if the president is the subject of the complaint), the duties here assigned to the president can, from time to time, be delegated to another elected member of the medical staff ("designee").

The complainant will be provided a written acknowledgment of the complaint.

In all cases, the physician subject of the complaint shall be provided a copy of the Practice's Code of Conduct and the Code of Ethics (see Policies 7.2 and 7.3) and a copy of the complaint in a timely fashion, as determined by the organized medical staff, but in no case more than thirty (30) days from receipt of the complaint by the president or vice president of the medical staff. The physician will be notified that attempts to confront, intimidate, or otherwise retaliate against the complainant is a violation of this Code of Conduct and/or the Code of Ethics that may result in corrective action against the physician. An ad hoc committee (none of the members of which may be economic competitors of the physician) consisting of the president or vice president of the Practice, or designee, and at least two (2) additional elected members of the medical executive committee, one of whom shall be the physician's department chairperson, provided the chairperson is not the subject of the complaint, shall make such investigation as appropriate into the circumstances, which may include seeking to interview the complainant, any witnesses, and the subject of the complaint. The physician subject shall be provided an opportunity to respond in writing to the complaint.

The ad hoc committee will determine the authenticity and severity of the complaint. The ad hoc committee shall dismiss any unfounded complaint — and may dismiss any complaint if it is not possible to confirm its authenticity or severity — and will notify both the complainant and the subject of the complaint of the decision reached.

If the ad hoc committee determines the complaint is well founded, the complainant and the subject of the complaint will be informed of the decision, and the complaint will be addressed as follows:

1. If this is the first incident of inappropriate behavior, the appropriate section chief or chairperson of the offending physician's assigned department shall discuss the matter with the offending physician and emphasize that the behavior is inappropriate and must cease. The offending physician may be asked to apologize to the complainant. The approach during this initial intervention should be collegial and helpful.
2. Further isolated incidents that do not constitute persistent, repeated inappropriate behavior will be handled by providing the offending physician with notification of each incident, and a reminder of the expectation that the individual comply with the Practice's Code of Conduct and/or Code of Ethics.
3. If the ad hoc committee determines that the offending physician has demonstrated persistent, repeated inappropriate behavior constituting harassment (a form of disruptive behavior) or has engaged in disruptive behavior on the first offense, a letter of admonition will be sent to the offending physician, and, as appropriate, a rehabilitation action plan developed by the ad hoc committee with the advice and counsel of the medical executive committee.
4. If, in spite of this admonition and intervention, disruptive behavior recurs, the ad hoc committee shall meet with and advise the offending physician that such behavior must immediately cease or corrective action will be initiated. This "final warning" shall be sent to the offending physician in writing.
5. If after the "final warning" the disruptive behavior recurs, corrective action (including suspension or termination of privileges) shall be initiated pursuant to the medical staff bylaws of which the Code of Conduct and Code of Ethics are a part, and the offending physician shall have all of the due process rights set forth in the medical staff bylaws.
6. If a single incident of disruptive behavior or repeated incidents of disruptive behavior constitute an imminent danger to the health of an individual or individuals, the offending physician may be summarily suspended as provided in the medical staff bylaws. The physician shall have all of the due process rights set forth in the medical staff bylaws.
7. If no corrective action is taken pursuant to the medical staff bylaws, a confidential memorandum summarizing the disposition of the complaint, along with copies of any written warnings, letters of apology, and written responses from the offending physician, shall be retained in the physician's credentials file for two (2) years, and then must be expunged if no related action is taken or pending. Informal rehabilitation, a written apology, issuance of a warning, or referral to the health and well-being committee (or equivalent committee) will not constitute corrective action.
8. At any time during this procedure, the physician has a right to personally retain and be represented by legal counsel.

Inappropriate or Disruptive Behavior against a Medical Staff Member

Inappropriate or disruptive behavior that is directed against the organized medical staff or directed against a medical staff member by a physician, administrator, board member, contractor, or other member of the community shall be reported by the medical staff member to the Practice pursuant to policy or code of conduct, or directly to the Practice's governing board, the state or federal government, or relevant accrediting body, as appropriate.

Abuse of Process

Threats or actions directed against the complainant by the subject of the complaint will not be tolerated under any circumstance. Retaliation or attempted retaliation by physicians against complainants will give rise to corrective action pursuant to the medical staff bylaws. Individuals who falsely submit a complaint shall be subject to corrective action under the medical staff bylaws or Practice employment policies, whichever applies to the individual.

Promoting Awareness of the Code of Conduct

The medical staff shall, in cooperation with the Practice and affiliated hospitals, promote continuing awareness of the Practice's Code of Conduct among the medical staff and the medical community by:

1. Sponsoring or supporting educational programs on disruptive behavior to be offered to physicians;
2. Disseminating the Code of Conduct to all current physicians upon its adoption and to all new applicants for membership to the medical staff;
3. Encouraging the health and well-being committee (or equivalent committee) to assist members of the medical staff exhibiting inappropriate or disruptive behavior to obtain education, behavior modification, or other treatment to prevent further infractions; and
4. Informing the members and the Practice staff of the procedures put in place for effective communication to administration of any medical staff member's concerns, complaints, and suggestions regarding personnel, equipment, and systems.[4]

Policy 7.15 Disruptive Behavior Reporting Policy

It is the policy of the Practice that all individuals within its facilities be treated with courtesy, respect, and dignity. To that end, the executive committee requires that all individuals, including physicians and allied health professionals, conduct themselves in a professional and cooperative manner.

If an individual fails to conduct himself or herself appropriately, the matter shall be addressed in accordance with this policy. It is the intention of the Practice that this policy be enforced in a firm, fair, and equitable manner.

Disruptive behavior by employees and independent contractors will be referred to the medical director and/or the executive administrator. As the review process determines, the matter may be referred to the executive committee. A single egregious incident, such

4 Copyright 2004, American Medical Association. All Rights Reserved. May 24, www.ama-assn.org/ama1/pub/upload/mm/21/ama-medical-staff-code-of-conduct.pdf (accessed February 4, 2011).

as physical or sexual harassment, assault, a felony conviction, a fraudulent act, stealing or damaging property, or inappropriate physical behavior, may result in immediate suspension or termination.

Objective

The objective of this policy is to ensure optimum patient care by promoting a safe, cooperative, and professional healthcare environment and to prevent or eliminate, to the extent possible, conduct that:

- Disrupts the operation of the Practice,
- Affects the ability of others to do their jobs;
- Creates a "hostile work environment" for the Practice's employees or other medical staff members;
- Interferes with an individual's ability to practice competently; or
- Adversely affects or impacts the community's confidence in the Practice's ability to provide quality patient care.

Unacceptable disruptive conduct may include, but is not limited to, behavior such as:

1. Attacks — verbal or physical — leveled at other members of the medical staff, employees of the Practice, patients, or visitors that are personal, irrelevant, or beyond the bounds of fair professional conduct;
2. Impertinent and inappropriate comments (or illustrations) made in patient or employee records or other official documents impugning the quality of care in the Practice, or casting aspersions against individuals or the Practice's policies; and
3. Nonconstructive criticism that is addressed to its recipient in such a way as to intimidate, undermine confidence, belittle, or imply ignorance, stupidity, or incompetence.

Documentation of disruptive conduct is critical because it is ordinarily not one incident that leads to disciplinary action, but rather a pattern of inappropriate conduct. Such documentation shall include:

- The date and time of the questionable behavior;
- A statement of whether the behavior affected or involved a patient in any way, and if so, the patient record;
- The circumstances that precipitated the situation;
- A description of the questionable behavior that is limited to factual, objective language;
- The consequences, if any, of the disruptive behavior as it relates to patient care or organization operations; and
- A record of any action taken to remedy the situation, including the date, time, place, action, and name(s) of those intervening.

Any individual (physician, allied health professional, employee, patient, contractor, or visitor) may report potentially disruptive conduct. The report shall be submitted in writing. It will be forwarded to the vice president for medical affairs and the executive administrator. The department chair may be included in the review. The following options could be considered:

1. A single confirmed incident warrants a discussion with the offending individual; the vice president for medical affairs (or his or her designee) and the executive administrator (or his or her designee) shall initiate such a discussion and emphasize that such conduct is inappropriate and must cease. The initial approach should be collegial and helpful to the individual and the organization. This will be documented as a "verbal warning."
2. If it appears that a pattern of disruptive behavior is developing, the matter will be discussed with the individual, outlined as follows. This will be documented as a "written warning."
    - Emphasize that if such repeated behavior continues, more formal action, including suspension or termination, may result.
    - All meetings shall be documented and secured in administration, in the individual's file.
    - A follow-up letter to the individual shall state the nature of the problem and inform the individual that he or she is required to behave professionally and cooperatively within the Practice.

The involved individual may submit a rebuttal to the charge. Such rebuttal will be maintained as a permanent part of the record.

If such behavior continues, the executive committee shall meet with and advise the individual that such conduct is intolerable and must stop. This meeting is not a discussion, but rather constitutes the individual's final warning. It shall be followed with a letter reiterating the warning, which may result in suspension or termination.

Progressive Disciplinary Action Pathway/Protocol

- Step One: Verbal warning, meeting with the vice president for medical affairs and the executive administrator (and department chair and human resources, when indicated)
- Step Two: Written warning, meeting with the executive committee
- Step Three: Suspension or termination

It is everyone's business to prevent disruptive behavior in the workplace. You can help by reporting anything you see in the workplace that could indicate that a coworker is in trouble. You are in a better position than management to know what is happening with those you work with.

You are encouraged to report any incident that may involve a violation of any of the Practice's policies that are designed to provide a comfortable workplace environment. Concerns may be presented to your supervisor, Practice coordinator, or the business manager.

Responsibility

The medical director, president, Practice coordinator, and administrator shall take actions to ensure that this policy is implemented.

See Appendix for the following forms:

- Disruptive Physician: Common Behaviors
- Disruptive Physician: Verbal Warning Report Form
- Disruptive Physician: Written Warning Report Form
- Disruptive Physician: Incident Report Form.

Policy 7.16 Privacy Policy[5]

The Practice's human resources department, or its designee, maintains a confidential physician file. The file contains only physician-related information, including the physician's application, new-hire forms, wage and salary history, performance reviews, counseling and disciplinary reports, and other records regarding job-related events that occur during employment. The Practice does not provide confidential physician information concerning a current physician to outside parties without the prior written approval of the physician except as required by law. The Practice does not release physician medical information without the physician's written approval, except pursuant to the provider's benefit program. The Practice maintains health information in a separate file. When employment has been terminated, the Practice provides work references only if the physician gives written approval.

Procedure

1. Physicians have the right to review their physician file two (2) times per year, at reasonable intervals.
2. Physicians cannot review letters of reference, confidential information concerning other individuals, and management planning information.
3. Physicians have the right to submit a written statement to be included in their physician file regarding any information to which they object or believe to be incomplete or inaccurate.
4. Physicians may make copies of the documents in their files and are required to pay for copying costs.
5. The Practice limits access to physician files to those physicians who have a business need for such information.
6. The Practice supplies tax and payroll information to government agencies as required.
7. The Practice releases to collective bargaining representatives information that includes data necessary for administering or negotiating a collective bargaining agreement, such as seniority data, job classification, wage rate, hours of employment, and benefit information.

5 Printed in *HR Policies and Procedures Manual for Medical Practices, 4th Edition,* by Courtney Price, PhD, and Alys Novak, MBA (Englewood, CO: Medical Group Management Association, 2007).

Responsibility

The HR department is responsible for ensuring compliance with this policy.

Policy 7.17

Confidentiality Policy

The Practice seeks to act responsibly toward its physicians and patients, upholding a high ethical standard. Policy 7.3 (Code of Ethics) includes confidentiality.

The confidential relationship between a healthcare provider and each patient is a fundamental principle of medicine. Moreover, confidentiality extends beyond patient care to other aspects of the business of the Practice.

Each physician should respect and maintain the confidentiality regarding the transactions and affairs (financial and operational) of the Practice, including information concerning our patients' health status. Special care must be taken to ensure that personal information never be used carelessly or maliciously. Physicians should maintain the confidentiality of the software programs, documentation, and restricted business information to which they have access and should not disclose such programs, documentation, or information to others. In short, each physician is responsible for safeguarding information entrusted to him or her.

Procedure

Maintaining the confidentiality of patients' medical records and health status is critical to upholding the reputation of any healthcare practice.

1. The confidentiality of medical records is to be maintained by supervised access to files.
2. Files are to be pulled and reviewed for care or necessary business purposes only. When not in use, the records should remain properly filed. Records must not be removed from the premises.
3. Treatments, medications, symptoms, etc., are to be discussed only in terms of patient care.
4. Formal authorization should be obtained before relaying any information to anyone when the situation involved falls outside the physician's area of responsibility.
5. Violation of patient confidentiality is cause for dismissal.
6. All physicians must sign the Practice's Confidential Information Statement upon employment with the Practice.

See Appendix for Confidential Information Statement.

Policy 7.18

Burnout Avoidance Policy[6]

It is sometimes difficult to let go of some tasks or to stop standing over someone's shoulder as he or she does the task. But your time as a physician is much too valuable to be spent micromanaging staff.

In an effort to avoid physician burnout and retain its physicians, the Practice encourages and supports physicians and physician leaders in delegating responsibilities as needed.

Procedure

1. Allowing physicians to learn and grow by doing tasks on their own will help them gain confidence. It also will give them clear evidence via performance yardsticks that they are an important, trusted, and valuable part of the Practice's team.
2. Of course, you as the physician leader are ultimately responsible for the outcome of the assignment. The task to be accomplished or the goal to be attained must be documented so it is clear to all. Establish interim goals and a specific timeline so that progress can be easily measured.
3. Feedback is important. Just as you must know that the task is progressing, the physicians must know they are moving in the right direction. A leader must never leave a physician on his or her own without access to adequate guidance.
4. Delegating a task or goal should always be a learning experience, not a blaming experience. Delegating does not mean giving away a task or goal to someone else but simply identifying someone else to represent you in getting it done. If the staff member fails, you have failed also. If staff members succeed, they deserve any credit that is due.

See also Policy 5.6: Coordination of Care.

6 Bhagwan Satiani, MD, MBA, *The Smarter Physician: Demystifying the Business of Medicine in Your Practice, Vol. 1* (Englewood, CO: Medical Group Management Association, 2007).

CHAPTER 8

Citizenship

Policy 8.1

Shareholder/Ownership Track Policy

When a physician is first hired at the Practice, he or she is regarded as serving an initial employment period (trial period) as a physician until an offer of ownership is made to the physician.

During the "trial" years, a physician's salary is fixed at the offered level and protected from downward adjustments. For the purposes of subsequent salary computation, the first-year salary is considered to be an annualized salary figure.

As a basis for subsequent salary progression, any increase will be in the written contract. The salary percentage is calculated as the annual salary, divided by the base salary, which is defined as the calendar year-to-date base salary of physicians who have been employed for at least [X] years (full owners).

Procedure

1. Upon completion of the trial years, if the board decides to offer the physician shareholder status, the physician's salary will be adjusted so that his or her percentage of base salary increases each year in one of even percentage steps, moving from the first year percentage up to 100 percent.

2. Each step increase in salary percentage will be given on the anniversary of the date employment started. Any salary adjustments applied to the base salary will be similarly applied to all physicians who have completed their trial years, prorated by each physician's percentage of base salary. Each physician's salary will remain, on a monthly basis, at the assigned percentage of base salary.
3. In addition to base salary, each physician who has attained certain productivity objectives may share in the Practice's monthly residual revenue distributions.

Policy 8.2

Buy-In and Buy-Out Agreement Policy[1]

The buy/sell agreement is not an isolated event; it is an integral part of the group's strategic fabric. New buy/sell agreements, or a revision of an existing agreement that is vague or unworkable, seek an agreement that will support the following criteria:

- The values and mission of the group — If these are not articulated formally, do so before proceeding;
- The goals and objectives of the group — Similarly, these form an important reference point;
- The business plan or direction of the group —This need not be elaborate, and many successful groups operate without a formal plan, but most successful practices have a clear, collective sense of direction;
- The buy/sell agreement will not inhibit the practice's ability to recruit new physicians either for expansion and/or succession;
- The group will have reasonable sensitivity to the marketplace, recognizing that young physicians completing their training are generally averse to large buy-ins;
- The group will be objective of the awareness of its attractiveness as a long-term professional home for new physicians; and
- The buy/sell agreement or agreements (there may be more than one) will be structured to reflect the asset base of the group. For example, some groups have a single buy/sell agreement for a single entity; others have multiple agreements for multiple separate but related entities, such as real estate, other interests/investments, or practice assets that may be considered personal by each physician.

Because every practice has unique options to buy-in, this section offers 13 examples.

Example: Group One

New physicians are eligible for consideration for shareholder status at their 25th month of employment, following a 24-month "salary guarantee" period. Ownership is for the practice entity only and does not include related entities.

Share purchase price is set at $20,000, payable at the 25th month, by cashier's check, with no financing.

1 Medical Group Management Association, "Buy/Sell Agreements," Special *MGMA Connexion* Article Reprint for MGMA Health Care Consulting Group Clients, www.mgma.com/WorkArea/DownloadAsset.aspx?id=16348.

In addition, the new physician-shareholder purchases a pro-rata share of the current, valued accounts receivable (A/R), with such purchase payable over ten (10) years.

At termination/retirement/death/disability/resignation, the "buy out" includes the $20,000 payment immediately, and 85 percent of the pro-rata share of the accounts receivable as collected, but lasting no longer than eighteen (18) months.

Sale (buy-out) for ownership in related entities ownership is over sixty (60) months.

Example: Group Two

A share of Practice ownership is based on hard assets of the Practice. Valuation of these assets is set at 50 percent of their actual purchase price (and still recorded on the books of the Practice).

Example: Group Three

Shareholder purchase is set at $100,000, and each physician is eligible for consideration at his or her 25th month of employment, provided that he or she is board certified.

During the physician's initial employment period (twenty-four (24) months), he or she does NOT receive any margin from the Practice's ancillary revenue margins (which is intended as a "carrot" for the physician to become a shareholder). Compensation is determined by the physician's actual billed collections, less a flat 40-percent cost of practice allocation. Building partnership is a separate entity.

Example: Group Four

Ownership shares are currently $150,000, following two (2) years of association, during which time the new physician is paid a guaranteed salary with NO consideration for ancillary revenue margins.

Shareholders are responsible for Practice costs directly related to each individual (nurse, PA, education, professional liability insurance, fringe benefits) and an equal share of the general cost of practice (indirect costs).

The Practice's building partnership and the Practice are separate entities, and all shareholders are eligible to purchase shares at the current valuations.

Example: Group Five

The Practice considers a new associate an asset. Thus, the Practice welcomes producers that wish to work and contribute to the Practice's growth. If a new physician can meet the threshold level of production necessary to reach before being allowed to buy in, he or she is allowed to become a shareholder.

- Our components are also segregated. The Practice is separate as is one building's value.
- A/R is purchased at the collectible value; this is the physician's specific net collection percentage.
- No goodwill is factored in, although at some point, if ancillary revenue margins/ income reaches higher levels, this may change.
- Net asset value, after depreciation, is also figured in, and, as things stand right now, it is a low five-number figure.

Example: Group Six

The Practice's buy-in for shareholder ownership is as follows:

1. Each shareholder owns 200 shares;
2. New physicians can buy in after two (2) years of employment;
3. Buy-in costs $40,000 over three (3) years as a reduction in compensation; and
4. The $40,000 is only paid back if the shareholder dies, becomes disabled, or retires after the age of 55.

Example: Group Seven

New physicians buy in at net hard asset value — a low five-figure amount. At departure, "buy out" is a net hard asset value, payable over three (3) years.

Example: Group Eight

The Practice has a stock purchase and an A/R buy-in. The A/R buy-in is calculated using the gross collection rate multiplied against that physician's outstanding A/R at the end of the 24th month. This A/R buy-in is spread over twenty-four (24) months interest free.

Example: Group Nine

1. When gross collection rate is used for buy-in calculations, ensure that it is current. The rate declines over time, so if the rate is simply transferred from Buy-In Agreement to Buy-In Agreement, it can result in significant overpricing to the new shareholder.
2. When valuing buildings for buy-in, use an average of two (2) to three (3) commercial appraisals, informing them that this is to determine actual resell value, not loan basis.

Example: Group Ten

For a full share buy-in to the Practice, the rate has been between $100,000 and $150,000.

Individual collections for all physicians, overhead, and ancillaries are distributed monthly, so there is transparency on these issues.

The Practice's buy-in is a very simple process. The employment agreement stipulates when physicians are "eligible" to become directors/shareholders. Once the board votes to approve them, they pay half of a year's ancillary income share, and they are then a director/shareholder. Payment may be made by lump sum for 50 percent of an ancillary share for last year or take six (6) months of foregoing ancillary share. In either case, the income is distributed as equal income to the existing directors/shareholders.

The Practice owns the A/R, and when a physician departs, there is no buy-out of a director/shareholder, nor is there any payment for accrued A/R. It is a clean separation with no valuation or asset calculations.

Example: Group Eleven

Upon hire, the new physician has a base salary plus bonus until shareholder status, which has historically been offered at the 19th month of employment.

Share purchase is at the market rate for properties and depreciated value of assets for practice, plus a pro-rata share of ancillary A/R. Purchased (cash) at buy-in — no financing.

At departure, shares are purchased back by the Practice at the current valuation, payable over thirty-six (36) months in equal installments without interest.

Example: Group Twelve

All physicians have equal ownership in the practice, following two (2) years of employment. Buy-in is comprised of two (2) components:

1. **Accounts Receivable** — A/R is valued (70 percent of A/R on the books) as of the date the physician becomes an employee of the Practice. Valued A/R is divided by the number of physicians (including new associate/employee) as of the physician's date of employment. This determines his or her A/R buy-in component.
2. **Hard Assets** — The Practice's hard assets (book value on the books) are valued (as of the 25th month) and discounted by 15 percent and divided by the number of physicians (shareholders and employees on shareholder track) at the 25th month.

When the physician-shareholder leaves the Practice, the value (same methodology as above) of A/R and hard assets at his or her date of resignation, termination, retirement, death, or disability is divided by the number of physicians (including the departing physician), and that is the buy-out value, payable in equal installments over forty-eight (48) months.

Example: Group Thirteen

All physicians at their 36th month of employment are considered for shareholder status. All shareholders are equal owners. Share value is $2,500, which is returned to the physician at departure (i.e., resignation, retirement, death, disability, or termination).

Compensation methodology is "stair-step" over eight (8) years to attain parity on the compensation plan, although a physician can vote on all corporate matters, beginning with share purchase payment (37th month).

Sample: Buy-In and Buy-Out Agreement[2]

This Buy/Sell Agreement made and entered into this, the [DAY] day of [MONTH], [YEAR], by and between the Practice, a [STATE] corporation, acting by and through its president, __________, and its secretary, __________, and pursuant to a resolution passed by the board of directors of said Practice, party of the first part, hereinafter referred to as "PRACTICE," and __________, MD, party of the second part, hereinafter referred to as "PHYSICIAN/STOCKHOLDER."

WITNESSETH

WHEREAS, PRACTICE is a [CORPORATION, LLC, etc.] duly organized and existing under the laws of the state of [STATE] and in good standing with the state of [STATE]; and

Sample continues next page

2 Printed in *Rx for Business Success: Joining a Practice for Physicians* by MGMA (Englewood, CO: Medical Group Management Association, 2005).

Sample: Buy-In and Buy-Out Agreement (continued)

WHEREAS, PRACTICE has authorized to be issued [NUMER OF SHARES] shares of common stock without par value and with there being [NUMER OF SHARES] shares of common stock outstanding at this time; and

WHEREAS, the PRACTICE desires to sell [NUMER OF SHARES] shares of its common stock to the PHYSICIAN/STOCKHOLDER named above; and,

WHEREAS, the PRACTICE and PHYSICIAN/STOCKHOLDER desire to enter into an agreement providing for the purchase of [NUMER OF SHARES]) shares of stock by the PHYSICIAN/STOCKHOLDER and for a repurchase of this stock by the PRACTICE upon the happening of certain events; and

WHEREAS, the parties hereto have agreed to all terms and conditions to be contained in this Buy/Sell Agreement.

NOW, THEREFORE, for and in consideration of the mutual promises and covenants herein contained, said parties hereby agree as follows:

1. **PURPOSE OF AGREEMENT**

   The purpose of this agreement is to provide for the orderly continuation of the affairs of the PRACTICE in the event a PHYSICIAN/STOCKHOLDER leaves the employment of the PRACTICE or in the event of death, incapacity, or disqualification of the PHYSICIAN/STOCKHOLDER, or the occurrence of other events specified herein, if any. Such purpose shall be accomplished by the purchase by the PRACTICE of the shares of stock held by the PHYSICIAN/STOCKHOLDER at that time.

2. **PURCHASE OF STOCK — TERM OF PURCHASE**

   The PHYSICIAN/STOCKHOLDER agrees to purchase [NUMER OF SHARES] shares of common stock in the PRACTICE for the purchase price of $__________, with said amount to be paid by the PHYSICIAN/STOCKHOLDER to the PRACTICE in 120 equal monthly installments of $__________ each, with the first installment of $__________ to become due and payable on the 15th day of [MONTH], [YEAR], and a like installment of $__________ to be due and payable on the 15th day of each and every month thereafter until the 15th day of [MONTH], [YEAR], when the final installment shall become due and payable. The unpaid principal balance of the note shall bear no interest.

   The PHYSICIAN/STOCKHOLDER may prepay this note at any time.

3. **REPURCHASE BY PRACTICE — PURCHASE AND SALE**

   PRACTICE agrees to purchase and the PHYSICIAN/STOCKHOLDER agrees to sell and transfer to the PRACTICE his or her shares of stock in the PRACTICE at the time of the happening of one of the events contemplated herein for the consideration and in the manner set forth in this agreement.

4. **EVENTS REQUIRING SALE**

   Upon the happening of any of the following events, the PHYSICIAN/STOCKHOLDER, or his or her Estate, shall sell and transfer to the PRACTICE, and the PRACTICE shall purchase all of the shares of stock in the PRACTICE held by such PHYSICIAN/STOCKHOLDER at a price computed in accordance with the provisions of Article 5 of this agreement:

Sample continues next page

Sample: Buy-In and Buy-Out Agreement (continued)

a. The death of the PHYSICIAN/STOCKHOLDER.

b. The disqualification of the PHYSICIAN/STOCKHOLDER as defined in his or her Employment Agreement;

c. The permanent disability or incapacity of the PHYSICIAN/STOCKHOLDER rendering him or her unable to practice the profession for which he or she is licensed.

d. The call to military service of the PHYSICIAN/STOCKHOLDER while he or she is an employee of the PRACTICE, if such service continues for sixty (60) days or longer, unless PRACTICE shall otherwise elect to treat such military service as a leave of absence;

e. The voluntary retirement of the PHYSICIAN/STOCKHOLDER from medical practice; or

f. The termination of employment of the PHYSICIAN/STOCKHOLDER with the PRACTICE for any reason whatsoever.

There is an exception from these provisions of this section of the Stock Purchase Agreement, which is the loss of malpractice insurance by the PHYSICIAN/STOCKHOLDER. This Stock Purchase Agreement will not be implemented if the PHYSICIAN/STOCKHOLDER is able to obtain malpractice insurance within six (6) months from the date that his or her original policy was canceled, if the original policy was canceled. If the PHYSICIAN/STOCKHOLDER is unable to obtain additional malpractice insurance with the six- (6-) month period, then this Stock Purchase Agreement is to be implemented in accordance with the terms hereof.

5. **PURCHASE PRICE OF STOCK**

a. The value of the stock in the PRACTICE, for purposes of this agreement, shall be the balance of the PHYSICIAN/STOCKHOLDER'S equity as indicated on the year-end financial statements (for the year preceding the event requiring sale) prepared by the accountant for the PRACTICE, adjusted as follows;

(1) Subtraction from PHYSICIAN/STOCKHOLDER equity:

i. Accounts receivable, less allowance for doubtful accounts;

ii. Other receivables and prepaid expenses that affect operating income; and

iii. Cash value of life insurance.

(2) Additions to PHYSICIAN/STOCKHOLDER'S equity:

i. Accounts payable and accrued expenses that affect operating income.

(3) Adjustments to PHYSICIAN/STOCKHOLDER'S equity:

i. All equipment of the PRACTICE shall be adjusted to book value.

ii. All lands and buildings of the PRACTICE shall be adjusted to book value [alternatively, insert $__________ market value].

(4) Once the value of the stock in the PRACTICE is determined as set forth previously in Article 5a, such totals so computed shall then be divided by the number of issued and outstanding shares of the PRACTICE by the number of shares outstanding at the end of the year (preceding the event requiring sale).

i. It is specifically agreed and understood that no value shall be attributable to any goodwill of the PRACTICE in arriving at the purchase price.

ii. It is further specifically agreed that once the determination of the value of the stock is determined as set forth previously in Article 5a, it shall be binding upon the parties hereto, their heirs, and assigns.

Sample continues next page

Sample: Buy-In and Buy-Out Agreement (continued)

iii. It is further specifically understood and agreed that at any time a PHYSICIAN/STOCKHOLDER resells his or her stock to the corporation as set forth herein, he or she shall be entitled to receive as a minimum a full refund of the original purchase price of his or her stock, if at that time the value of the stock is less than the original purchase price paid. However, if at the time of resale to the PRACTICE under this agreement, the value of the stock is greater than the original purchase price paid by the PHYSICIAN/STOCKHOLDER, the PHYSICIAN/STOCKHOLDER shall be entitled to receive compensation for his or her shares according to one of the following methods that is applicable to the PHYSICIAN/STOCKHOLDER'S situation:

(1) If the PHYSICIAN/STOCKHOLDER has owned his or her stock for a period of less than three (3) years, the PHYSICIAN/STOCKHOLDER shall not be entitled to receive any gains in the value of the stock and shall be entitled only to receive the original purchase price; or

(2) If the PHYSICIAN/STOCKHOLDER has owned his or her stock for a period of three (3) years or longer, the PHYSICIAN/STOCKHOLDER shall be entitled to the full value of the stock, including any and all gains in the stock, as determined previously in Article 5a.

6. **METHOD OF PAYMENT**

a. In the event of repurchase by the PRACTICE of the PHYSICIAN/STOCKHOLDER'S stock in cash within thirty (30) days following the date upon which the event requiring purchase of the shares occurs, or at the option of the PRACTICE, and upon the notice given by the PHYSICIAN/STOCKHOLDER or his or her estate, the PRACTICE may repurchase the stock by executing a promissory note to the PHYSICIAN/STOCKHOLDER or his or her estate bearing no interest with the note to be paid in equal monthly payments over a period of ten (10) years, but with the right being given to the PRACTICE to prepay the note at any time without premium, fee, or penalty being charged.

b. In the event the PRACTICE elects to repurchase said stock by executing a promissory note, the note shall be secured by an appropriate security instrument retaining a lien on the stock in favor of the PHYSICIAN/STOCKHOLDER or his or her estate.

c. In the event the PRACTICE shall own certain insurance contract(s) on the previously named PHYSICIAN/STOCKHOLDER'S life, which was obtained for the purpose of providing funds for the purchase of the shares of the previously named PHYSICIAN/STOCKHOLDER, the proceeds of such insurance shall be immediately applied to the payment of the purchase price as set forth herein.

7. **RESTRICTION ON ENCUMBERING STOCK**

The PHYSICIAN/STOCKHOLDER shall not transfer, assign, hypothecate, or in any way alienate any of his or her shares or any right or interest therein, except as provided herein or in conformity with the provisions of the bylaws of the PRACTICE. The purchase price for shares of stock purchased by the PRACTICE or PHYSICIAN/STOCKHOLDER pursuant to said bylaws shall be paid for in the same manner as it is provided in Article 6 hereof.

Sample continues next page

Sample: Buy-In and Buy-Out Agreement (continued)

8. **ENDORSEMENT OF STOCK CERTIFICATES**

   The shares of the PRACTICE shall bear the following legend:

   "Ownership, issuance, and transfer of these shares are restricted by and subject to the provisions of the bylaws and/or minutes of this PRACTICE; a copy thereof is available for inspection at the principal offices of the PRACTICE."

9. **TERMINATION OF AGREEMENT**

   This agreement shall terminate:

   a. Upon the written agreement of all parties; or
   b. Upon dissolution or bankruptcy of the PRACTICE.

10. **MISCELLANEOUS**

    a. This agreement shall be binding upon the parties, their successors, assigns, personal representatives, heirs, and legatees.
    b. Each party agrees to perform any further acts and to execute and deliver any documents that may be reasonably necessary to carry out the provisions of the agreement.
    c. This agreement may be amended at any time by the written agreement of the PRACTICE and the PHYSICIAN/STOCKHOLDER.
    d. The PHYSICIAN/STOCKHOLDER agrees to insert in his or her will or to execute a codicil thereto directing and authorizing his or her executor to fulfill and comply with the provisions hereof and to sell and transfer his or her shares in accordance wherewith.
    e. Any notice required or permitted hereunder shall be deemed served if personally delivered or mailed by registered or certified mail, postage prepaid, and properly addressed to the respective party to whom such notice relates at the last known address of the party, or at such different address as shall be specified by notice given in the manner herein provided.
    f. If any section of this agreement is declared void and unenforceable, said decision shall not affect the legality of the rest of the Stock Purchase Agreement.
    g. By entering into this agreement, the PHYSICIAN/STOCKHOLDER is also agreeing to enter into all financial indebtedness that affects the value of the stock and has been voted on and approved by the board of directors of the PRACTICE. This is to include but is not limited to liabilities that are current and future obligations.

11. **ASSISTANCE IN INTERPRETATION**

    For purposes of assistance in interpretation of this agreement, an example of calculation is attached hereto, collectively as Exhibit A.

IN WITNESS WHEREOF, the parties have hereunto set their hands on this the [DAY] day of [MONTH], [YEAR].

____________________ (PRACTICE NAME)

____________________, President
____________________, Physician/Stockholder
____________________, Secretary
State of [STATE]
County of [COUNTY]

Sample continues next page

Sample: Buy-In and Buy-Out Agreement (continued)

Subscribed, sworn to, acknowledged and verified before me by[PRACTICE NAME] by and through its President, ________, MD, and its Secretary, ________, MD, to be the PRACTICE'S free act and deed, and their free act and deed as said Officers, on this the [DAY] day of [MONTH], [YEAR].

____

Notary Public, State-at-Large

My Commission Expires: __________

Policy 8.3 Physician Compacts Policy

The rate of change in healthcare is unprecedented, and the Practice's success is dependent on its ability to adapt quickly to these changes. This adaptability requires that the needs of the whole outweigh the needs of a single individual. We have reached a point in time where a new medical staff "compact" listing our expectations requires universal support; a time when a medical staff member's continued association with the Practice and his or her compensation are dependent upon this support.

What Does It Mean to Be a Member of the Practice's Staff?

1. **Patient/Customer Service**

   (See also Policy 7.2: Code of Conduct.)

   The physician will demonstrate courtesy and respect toward internal and external customers. A positive attitude will be presented during all encounters. The physician will:

   a. Make it a top priority to see his or her patients in a timely manner;

   b. Maintain reasonable access and hours for patients;

   c. Make every attempt to adhere to the patient schedule. Physicians will strive to see patients within fifteen (15) minutes of their scheduled appointment time. If this is not possible, the patient will be informed of his or her status and alternatives. If the physician is consistently unable to adhere to the schedule, an adjustment to the schedule may be necessary;

   d. Support and participate in efforts to improve patient satisfaction; and

   e. Take measures to ensure that patients are not rescheduled unnecessarily, including submitting elective schedule changes by the 15th of each month for the following month (elective changes include vacation, personal time, continuing medical education (CME) time, etc.).

2. **Work Ethic**

   The physician will demonstrate dedication and commitment to patients and the practice of medicine. The physician will strive to exceed work standards and excellence of practice. The physician will:

a. Be in compliance with departmental work standards regarding patient contact hours, participation in call coverage, hospital rounds, and other activities;
b. Maintain hospital affiliations in good standing;
c. Show dedication and commitment to the Practice's mission and vision;
d. Provide timely documentation of patient care, preferably on the date of service;
e. Submit charges in a timely manner (e.g., professional service records, charge slips, fee tickets); and
f. Complete all forms related to patient care and the care plan for the patient in a timely manner (e.g., return to work, post-procedure instructions, care plan, follow-up appointment calendar).

3. **Reliability**

The physician will perform tasks in a timely manner to ensure patient satisfaction. The physician will:

a. Answer phone messages in a timely manner. Urgent messages will be returned the same day. Nonurgent messages and medication refills should be completed within forty-eight (48) hours;
b. Arrive and be ready to begin work on time;
c. Be prompt in attending meetings; and
d. Interact with his or her staff on a daily basis to ensure flexibility and teamwork.

4. **Adaptability**

The physician will demonstrate acceptance to change and a willingness to learn. The physician will:

a. Accept and integrate changes within the department or the organization in a positive, enthusiastic manner;
b. Whenever possible, take an active role in the implementation of change;
c. Make efforts to improve Practice patterns based on the results of periodic performance evaluations and patient satisfaction surveys; and
d. Accept corrective feedback in a courteous manner.

5. **Teamwork**

The physician will show that he or she is a team player through helpful, cooperative interactions with coworkers. Relationships will be honest, nonjudgmental, respectful, and supportive of others. The physician will:

a. Recognize that everyone's job is important to the success of the organization;
b. Take the initiative to offer help to coworkers in overload situations and will willingly fill in for vacations, unexpected absences, and illnesses;
c. Avoid criticizing other members or departments of the clinic in front of patients or other physicians;
d. Avoid all unprofessional criticism;
e. Respond to requests from other providers and clinic staff in a timely, positive, and friendly manner; and
f. Strive to maintain all appropriate medical services within the medical group.

6. **Accountability**

The physician will be accountable for all of the following tasks and take responsibility that all necessary work is completed. The physician will:

a. Ensure that all charting/dictation is completed within twenty-four (24) hours of the patient visit;
b. Ensure that all paper-based chart entries are legible;
c. Submit all route slips within twenty-four (24) hours of the patient visit unless awaiting a pathologic diagnosis;
d. Strive to return all charts to medical records as quickly as possible;
e. Not keep charts longer than two (2) days without being returned to medical records;
f. Not remove charts from the clinic;
g. Allow all staff to access charts in physician offices without restriction;
h. Cooperate with periodic performance evaluations and other quality improvement initiatives;
i. Consistently arrange and communicate appropriate coverage; and
j. Actively participate in committee, departmental, and physician group meetings.

7. **Communication**

   The physician will demonstrate clear communication and active listening skills. The physician will:

   a. Recognize that excellence in patient care is dependent on active communication between all individuals caring for a patient;
   b. Dictate all initial consultations; and
   c. Communicate with patients regarding diagnoses, treatment plans, and status of care.

8. **Ability to Handle Stress**

   The physician will maintain a professional, cooperative attitude and a pleasant, even-tempered demeanor.

9. **Problem-Solving**

   The physician will demonstrate good problem-solving skills by investigating all aspects of a problem, identifying alternatives, and choosing the best solutions. The physician will:

   a. Look for appropriate, cost-effective care;
   b. Strive for optimal patient management and overall group success by appropriate resource management of referrals, guidelines, ancillary services, and hospital care;
   c. Use clinic pathways or disease management tools whenever appropriate; and
   d. Pay close attention to proper utilization in addition to quality of care.

10. **Sensitivity**

    The physician will demonstrate compassion, understanding, and respect for both internal and external customers. Dignity and a high regard for others will be exhibited at all times. The physician will:

    a. First and foremost be an advocate for the patient; and
    b. Be sensitive to the needs and concerns of clinic staff.

11. **Professionalism**

    The physician will present a professional image in dress and conduct. The physician will:

    a. Maintain patient confidentiality at all times;
    b. Limit personal phone calls and avoid loud voices and inappropriate discussions and/or behaviors;
    c. Abide by clinic policy regarding behavior and harassment;
    d. Maintain Basic Life Support (BLS) certification;
    e. Obtain and maintain board certification;
    f. Maintain CME credits and other requirements to maintain state licensure in good standing;
    g. Show respect for clinic property (including charts). Practice property will not be removed from the clinic, defaced, or mistreated in any way; and
    h. Ensure that appropriate credentialing criteria are maintained to allow for full participation in all contractual arrangements.

12. **Financial Standards**

    The physician will actively participate in the management of his or her Practice in order to maximize revenue and minimize costs while providing a compliant and professional encounter with his or her patient. The physician will:

    a. Submit completed route slips within twenty-four (24) hours of patient visit;
    b. Support guidelines established by the board of directors as they relate to collection policies;
    c. Follow purchasing guidelines and policies as to the acquisition of equipment and supplies;
    d. Submit all elective schedule changes by the 15th of each month for the following month. Elective changes are defined as vacation, personal time, CME, etc.;
    e. Provide documentation that will support compliant coding;
    f. Submit expenses along with supporting documentation and receipts within fifteen (15) days of incurred expense;
    g. Submit check request for CME registration to A/R no later than thirty (30) days prior to the application due date;
    h. Be financially responsible and fiscally prudent to the organization;
    i. Work cooperatively with the quality management and utilization management departments; and
    j. Document patient encounters to support compliant coding.

Sample: Physician Compact

<table>
<tr><td colspan="2">The Practice's Physician Compact is an explicit statement of the mutual obligations and responsibilities of Practice physicians and Practice leadership staff. This Compact reflects our shared mission, vision, and values, and provides the foundational support for all that we do.</td></tr>
<tr><th>The Practice's Pledge to Physicians</th><th>Physician's Pledge to the Practice</th></tr>
<tr><th colspan="2">Foster Excellence</th></tr>
<tr><td>• Recruit and retain superior physicians, allied health professionals, and support staff.
• Practice "state of the art" evidence-based management.
• Foster career development and professional satisfaction.
• Acknowledge provider contributions to patient care and the Practice.
• Promote a culture of collaboration, innovation, integrity, fiscal responsibility, and mutual respect.
• Develop and implement strategies to strengthen organization/provider alignment.
• Create and maintain a customer-centered service culture.</td><td>• Put patients first in all that we do.
• Practice "state of the art" evidence-based medicine.
• Involve patients and families in care decisions.
• Achieve and maintain optimal access to care.
• Insist on seamless and timely patient access to Practice-based ancillary services.
• Continuously improve quality, safety, service excellence, and compliance.</td></tr>
<tr><th colspan="2">Partnership</th></tr>
<tr><td>• Openly share information regarding goals, objectives, organizational priorities, and business strategies.
• Encourage involvement in Practice governance.
• Actively address and resolve patient, provider, and staff-related issues.
• Offer opportunities for constructive dialogue.
• Encourage and support the balance between work life and life outside of work.</td><td>• Communicate clinical information to patients and referring physicians in a timely manner.
• Provide and accept feedback from consultants and referring physicians.
• Clarify expectations of the Practice's team.
• Actively address and resolve clinical and operational issues.
• Resolve conflict with openness, fairness, and empathy.</td></tr>
<tr><th>Educate</th><th>Collaborate on Care Delivery</th></tr>
<tr><td>• Facilitate and fund participation in professional development for clinical staff, and promote training opportunities for support staff.
• Provide data and analysis needed to improve practice efficiency that enhances quality, satisfies patients, and improves productivity.
• Review financial performance continuously.</td><td>• Include staff, providers, and management in care delivery.
• Demonstrate the highest levels of ethical and professional conduct.
• Behave in a manner consistent with professional conduct, ethics, and organizational goals.
• Participate in community-wide healthcare initiatives.
• Understand the needs and expectations of stakeholders.</td></tr>
<tr><td colspan="2" align="right">Sample continues next page</td></tr>
</table>

Sample: Physician Compact (continued)

Educate	Collaborate on Care Delivery
• Perform ongoing coding, documentation, and compliance reviews. • Support resources needed to achieve and maintain accreditation.	
Reward	**Take Ownership**
• Design incentive-based compensation that is aligned with organizational goals. • Create an environment that supports collaboration as well as individual performance. • Develop programs for all staff to encourage practice efficiency and cost-effective operations. • Manage to accurate and industry-leading benchmarks.	• Exceed expectations for performance, productivity, and budget. • Support group and organizational decisions with active and ongoing participation. • Implement best practices in delivery of medical care. • Document patient care, including accurate coding for services, ensuring sign-off of the electronic record on the date of service.
Leadership	
• Lead with integrity and accountability. • Create alignment with clear goals, objectives, and strategies. • Ensure a safe and healthy environment for patients and staff. • Offer opportunities for constructive two-way dialogue. • Promote innovation and continuous improvement. • Manage accountability for behaviors and expectations.	• Embrace innovation and continuous improvement. • Participate actively in mutually agreed-upon organizational changes. • Welcome and adopt advances in technology and practice management. • Demonstrate accountability for behaviors and expectations. • Be involved in the organization and the community.

See Appendix for Physician Compact: Basic Performance Expectations and Customer Service.

Policy 8.4

Board Meeting Schedule Policy

The Practice shall establish and follow a meetings/communications protocol designed to improve the effectiveness of board efforts.

The board chair and the administrator shall arrange for appropriate communications training for each new board and committee member. The board chair shall, as needed, use outside consultants for such training and for facilitation and mediation/conflict resolution as needed.

The board chair shall establish performance expectations for board and committee members related to communications behavior in meetings and shall discipline members, if necessary, for inappropriate behavior.

Responsibility

The board chair and administrator are responsible for ensuring compliance with this policy.

Policy 8.5

Effective Meetings Policy

Successful meetings are structured. They:

- Are prepared in terms of determining purpose, choosing and contacting participants, choosing date/time/place, and ensuring that the physical environment is appropriate;
- Have an agenda that specifies objectives, roles, timing, results, and next steps;
- Make use of a facilitator who guides the process, keeps it on target, and records results;
- Are linked to a larger specific goal with milestones that measure progress and achievement;
- Have goals for each meeting to focus the session;
- Report progress against goals at each meeting and in its reports;
- Encourage the use of communication skills, including listening, sharing, positive confrontation, conflict resolution, and brainstorming;
- Celebrate creativity and innovation as well as productivity;
- Recognize that meetings must be customer-focused — that is, determining "whose meeting is this anyway?" in terms of who is the customer who must be satisfied by the results; and
- Make an equal commitment to following up on promises made in the meeting and to disseminating information to those who need to know what occurred and what was decided.

Sample: Meeting Agenda Template

Agenda [DATE]

- Call to Order
- Minutes of Last Meeting
- Financial Report

  ____

  ____
- Executive Report

  ____

  ____
- Decision Items

  ____

  ____
- Discussion Items

  ____

  ____
- Information Items

  ____

  ____
- Adjournment

Policy 8.6 Committee Participation Policy

The board, by resolution, may designate from among its members an executive committee and other committees, each consisting of three (3) or more directors. The board may also, by resolution, designate advisory committees, each consisting of one (1) or more directors and one (1) or more shareholders.

Such advisory committees shall have the authority granted by the board in the resolution creating the advisory committee. Advisory committees may be granted authority over such matters as off-site physician scheduling and call coverage and other matters designated by the board. All committees shall serve at the pleasure of the board.

In the case of advisory or ad hoc committees, the board shall establish the name of the committee, its purpose, its membership and time frame, and expected results.

The board chair is an ex-officio member of all committees established by the board and may attend all committee meetings.

Committee members shall be selected to reflect the skills and interests needed to satisfy the requirements of the committee, for example, technical knowledge, representation of the constituency, and knowledge of the Practice's goals.

Committee members shall commit to regular attendance, accepting and completing assignments, active and responsible decision-making, respect for conflicting opinions, and an objective approach to reaching consensus and results.

The chair shall schedule meetings for the greatest possible convenience of the members.

The administrator shall provide staff resources to the committees as designated by the committee chair, including input from staff persons with specific knowledge, and secretarial assistance.

Committee chairs shall report to the board on a schedule determined by the board chair.

Responsibility

The Practice board of directors is responsible for ensuring compliance with this policy.

Finance Committee

The Finance Committee shall carry out the long-term financial planning process consistent with the strategic plan and provide leadership and direction to the Practice administration and the controller for capital planning, annual budgeting, and investment policies of the organization.

Duties and Responsibilities

- Reviews and recommends the annual budget.
- Evaluates and reports the impact of nonbudgeted purchases.
- Monitors and controls the Practice's financial performance.
- Monitors and reviews the financial controls.

Reports to

Board of directors

Authorized to

Recommend annual budget and financial plans and policies, as defined in the decision-making authorization matrix.

Committee Member Qualifications

Demonstrated understanding of and interest in the Practice's financial reporting, budgeting process, and capital planning

Term

One (1) year, renewable for two (2) terms

Appointment

Appointed by the board of directors with counsel from the administrator

Member Compensation

To be determined by the board chair

Size

Three (3) to six (6) physicians, administrator, assistant administrator, and/or controller

Composition

Appropriate representation of senior/new physicians and primary care/specialty physicians

Minimum Meeting Times

Once a month

Board Committees

- The board shall, by resolution, establish one (1) or more committees of the board (herein termed "board committees"), except as otherwise specified in these bylaws.
- Such committees shall be distinguished from nonboard committees to which nonmembers and members who are not directors, as well as directors, may be appointed. Nonboard committees may not exercise any of the authority of the board.
- Each board committee shall consist of two (2) or more directors.
- To the extent provided in the resolution establishing any board committee, and these bylaws, the authority of the board may be delegated to such committee.
- The establishment of any such board committee and any delegation thereto of authority shall not operate to relieve the board or any director of any responsibility imposed on the board or individual director by law, by these bylaws, or by any applicable policy, rule, regulation, resolution, or any departmental rule. Further, no such committee shall have the authority of the board of directors in reference to amending, altering, or repealing the bylaws; electing, appointing, or removing any member of any such committee or any director or officer of the Practice; amending the Articles of Incorporation; adopting a plan of consolidation with another corporation; authorizing the sale, lease, exchange, or mortgage of any or all of the property and assets of the foundation; authorizing the voluntary dissolution of the foundation or revoking proceedings thereof; adopting a plan for the distribution of the assets of the foundation; or amending, altering, or repealing any resolution of the board of directors which, by its terms, provides that it shall not be amended, altered, or repealed by such committee.

Policy 8.7 Executive Committee Policy

There shall be an executive committee of the Practice, which shall be a board committee. The Practice's executive committee shall consist of the Practice president, vice president, the immediate-past president, ex officio, and four (4) other members of the board.

One (1) member of the committee shall be a departmental director, elected by and from the board of directors; one (1) member of the committee shall be a director, appointed by the Practice, and one (1) member shall be an at-large director, elected by and from the board of directors. The executive director shall serve on the executive committee, ex officio, without vote. The immediate-past president of the Practice will serve as a voting member of the executive committee until replaced by the next immediate-past president. Non-Practice committee members shall serve for a term of three (3) years and may be elected for two (2), but not more than two (2) successive terms. The preceding notwithstanding, officers who are members of the executive committee by virtue of the office shall serve on the committee for the full term of their office, and the Practice-designated member of the executive committee shall have a three- (3-) year term of office but may be reappointed indefinitely. For the purposes of this paragraph, a fractional term constitutes a "full" term in the calculation of consecutive terms.

A majority of voting members of the executive committee shall be a quorum of the committee.

Chair of the Executive Committee

The board of directors shall elect the president of the Practice from among the members of the full board. The Practice president shall serve ex officio as chair of the board and as chair of the executive committee. He or she shall serve at the pleasure of the board of directors for a term not to exceed one (1) year corresponding to such person's service as president of the Practice and may not serve more than two (2) consecutive terms. The vice president provided for in these bylaws shall serve as acting chair of the executive committee in the absence of the chair. In the absence of both the president and the vice president, the members of the executive committee shall elect an acting chair from among their members.

Role and Function of the Executive Committee

On behalf of the Practice and the board, the executive committee shall function as follows:

1. **Accountability.** The executive committee shall be directly accountable to the board of directors.
2. **Policy.** Subject to the established policies of the Practice and in consonance with Practice policies, the power to resolve all major policy questions relating to the affairs of the Practice shall reside in the board, unless delegated in writing to a board committee.

   To provide for efficiency and flexibility in Practice management while reserving to the board the power of decision with respect to major policy issues, the executive committee shall, subject to the reporting requirements set forth as follows, have discretion in applying the general policies of the Practice to specific situations pertinent to the operation and management of the Practice and its affairs. Further, the executive committee may assist the executive director in the interpretation of Practice policy as promulgated by the board and applied by the executive committee.

   The executive committee shall, from time to time, recommend to the board such changes in policy as the committee deems necessary or desirable.
3. **Practice Charges for Services.** The executive committee shall, within general board of directors and Practice guidelines, and in consultation with the

departmental directors concerned, ensure that all Practice charges to be made for services provided under the auspices of the Practice are reasonable.

4. **Reporting.** The executive committee shall prepare and provide the following to the board of directors:
    a. General Reports: Report on its activities with such recommendations as the committee deems appropriate, including reports on significant applications of Practice general policy to particular affairs of the Practice.
    b. Regular Fiscal Reports: Ensure the preparation and distribution of a regular monthly fiscal report.
    c. Management Reports: Ensure the preparation and distribution of regular reports describing the degree to which the management objectives established for the Practice by the board are being met.
    d. Minutes: Distribute its minutes of meetings to the members of the board.
    e. Special Reports and Recommendations: When requested by the board of directors, report on and make recommendations concerning any other matter.
5. **Other Functions.** In addition to the functions previously specified, the executive committee shall be required to:
    a. Review and approve the executive director's budget for the costs of Practice operation, including the amount of the deduction rate or rates to be applied against Practice funds to defray the costs of operation;
    b. Review and approve the components of departmental fund budgets related to shared Practice expenses and other shared costs of operation;
    c. Make recommendations concerning revision of the Practice bylaws to the board of directors;
    d. Review and recommend to the board of directors changes in the Practice flow-of-funds distribution system provided for in these bylaws; and
    e. Perform such actions as are necessary for the efficient operation of the Practice.

Nonboard Committees

Nonboard committees shall be distinguished from board committees. Nonboard committees may not exercise any of the authority of the board. Members and nonmembers may be appointed or elected to a nonboard committee.

Benefits Committee

There shall be a benefits committee of the Practice that shall be a nonboard committee serving in an advisory capacity to the executive committee. The chair of the committee shall be a department member and shall be elected by the committee. The chair of the benefit committee will provide periodic reports on the activities of the committee. Committee minutes will be submitted to the executive committee and board. It shall be the function and responsibility of the benefits committee to:

1. Provide input on the opinion of the membership concerning benefits;
2. Make recommendations on benefits consistent with prudent management of resources; and
3. Assist human resources in the education of Practice members on issues related to Practice benefit plans.

CHAPTER 9

External Relations

Policy 9.1

Professional Courtesy Policy

The policy of the Practice and all of its physicians is that professional courtesy shall NOT be offered to any physician, his or her family, or staff under any condition except financial hardship. All physicians, their families,[1] or staff will be charged the Practice's usual and customary fees, their insurance billed, and any remaining balance will be the responsibility of the individual or his or her responsible party.

In today's regulatory environment, professional courtesy or "insurance only" treatment (which is, in fact, a waiving of the copayment) represents a significant threat to both the

1 Family member includes husband or wife; birth or adoptive parent, child, or sibling; stepparent, stepchild, stepbrother, or stepsister; father-in-law, mother-in-law, son-in-law, daughter-in-law, brother-in-law, or sister-in-law; grandparent or grandchild; and spouse of a grandparent or grandchild.

physician granting the professional courtesy and the individual, or his or her family, receiving it since it calls into question the applicability of the federal anti-kickback laws.

The purpose of this policy is to establish the procedure for providing discounts to services in order to remain compliant with industry standards and government regulations.

Definitions

Copayment: An amount deemed by the payer as a "shared" payment due from the patient for approved medical services, also referred to as "coinsurance" by some payers.

Deductible: The portion of a charge a payer has deemed due from the patient.

Related Forms

Waiver of copayments and deductibles.

A provider (physician or allied health professional) may request a discount, but the discount must be applied uniformly to the entire bill.

For instance, a provider (physician or allied health professional) may not discount the copayment and not discount the amount billed to a third-party payer.

Procedure

1. Should a provider wish to grant a discount, the copayment, deductible, and the amount billed to the third-party payer must be reduced by the same percentage. For example, if the provider wishes to give a patient a 25-percent discount, that same amount must be discounted from the charge as well.
2. Discounting a charge after submission to an insurance carrier will not be permitted.
3. Professional courtesy or "insurance only" discounts will not be extended to any patients of the Practice, including other physicians, coworkers, or family members of physicians.

Historically, federal statutory restrictions regarding waiver of copayments/deductibles applied only to Medicare and Medicaid. However, the Health Insurance and Portability and Accountability Act of 1996 (HIPAA), also known as the Kennedy–Kassebaum bill, expanded federal fraud and abuse provisions to all federal health plans, such as the Civilian Health and Medical Program of the Uniformed Services (CHAMPUS) and the Federal Employees Health Benefits (FEHB) Program, not just Medicare and Medicaid, and now makes it a federal crime to defraud private insurance companies. Violations of the contracts with private insurers may be criminal fraud under HIPAA and could result in fines and criminal prosecution.

Waivers of copayments and deductibles arguably constitute federal healthcare fraud if the physician knowingly and willfully attempted to defraud a healthcare plan or obtain money or property by making false or fraudulent representation to the insurance company. Therefore, if the physician knows he or she was required to collect a copayment or deductible but only billed the insurance company, the physician has committed healthcare fraud. Furthermore, by representing the charge to be one amount but only holding the patient accountable for a lower amount (the fee minus the copay or deductible), the physician is making a false statement regarding the charge or fee of the service. In addition to fines, false statements under HIPAA may be punished by imprisonment. HIPAA also created penalties for healthcare fraud, including sizeable fines and prison terms.

Even though it is understood that in most situations private insurers and the federal government ban waiving the copay, Medicare has some provisions allowing the copay to be waived for documented indigence. It is also permissible to discount the entire bill.

The independent boards of directors of the Practice and the physician collectively agree that every effort should be made to be in total compliance with all federal statutes. Therefore, the physicians of the Practice shall not offer or provide a discount to any individual except to those who can document financial need.

Policy 9.2

Gifts Policy

The Practice is committed to a business that conducts itself with a high level of integrity at all times. To this end, the following guidelines are provided related to gifts and to personal gain:

1. No physician is to accept donations, gratuities, goods, or services from a patient for services rendered. Gifts/gratuities should be graciously declined. If the patient chooses to make a donation, it is to be submitted to the administrator on the patient's behalf, and a receipt is to be issued to the patient. No physician is to accept gifts from a vendor or from a referral source that have a significant monetary value. Token gifts of minor value (e.g., homemade cookies, garden fruits and vegetables, etc.) may be accepted but are not to be encouraged.
2. The acceptance or solicitation of gifts and gratuities is considered unprofessional conduct and will result in physician counseling.
3. Gifts/gratuities may be donated to the various units, departments, and Practice sites but not to any specific physician.
4. No physician is to become responsible for any patient's finances. Any such request should be referred to a supervisor. The supervisor must then advise the appropriate member of management and seek alternatives (e.g., notify family or the county Social Services Department).
5. No physician is to encourage a patient to hire the physician on a private basis.
6. No physician is to use his or her business relationship with the Practice for personal gain.

Policy 9.3

Noncompete Policy

Medical practices invest significant resources of time and effort in recruitment, orientation, and training, and of monetary value (e.g., equipment, space, salary, benefits, staff) when a physician joins the Practice. There is an expectation of a return on that investment over time as the physician becomes fully productive. Thus, it is a major loss when a physician decides to leave the Practice — particularly if he or she chooses to compete by setting up as a solo practitioner or joining another practice in the same marketplace. Because of this situation, medical practices, like many other businesses, incorporate a noncompete section in their physician employment agreements. It is also useful to present this statement as a policy in the governing policies manual.

The board declares that unless the Practice and the physician otherwise agree in writing, the physician shall agree that he or she shall not, during the term of the employment agreement and for a period of eighteen (18) months following any termination or expiration of such agreement, engage directly or indirectly as a proprietor, partner, shareholder, director, officer, physician, agent, consultant, or in any other capacity or manner whatsoever, in any medical practice within the boundaries of its marketplace (i.e., the county in which it is located).

The Practice and the physician acknowledge and agree that the Practice has an investment in the physician's development, the patients, and the development of the Practice and that the Practice would suffer economic injury if the physician were to terminate his or her employment with the Practice and compete with the Practice. As a result, the physician agrees that in the event that he or she terminates employment with the Practice — either voluntarily or involuntarily, as a result of retirement or permanent disability, or is terminated — and directly or indirectly engages in any medical practice, either as a proprietor, partner, shareholder, director, officer, agent, consultant, physician, or in any other similar capacity or manner, within a period of eighteen (18) months from termination and within the county without the prior consent of the Practice, the physician shall be liable to the Practice for damages suffered for such competition and loss of investment in startup, training, and development. The physician agrees to pay to the Practice as liquidated damages for the violation of such restriction $[X] per month based on gross billings for each month during which the breach occurs. The physician acknowledges and agrees that the foregoing measure of damages is reasonably related to the injury suffered by the Practice from such competition and the loss of the investment in training and development of the physician.

Responsibility

The medical director and administrator shall take actions necessary to inform physicians of this policy and to enforce its intent.

Covenant Not to Compete

Reliance and Consideration. It is further understood and agreed that in carrying out the terms of employment, the physician will become closely associated and involved with clients and patients of the Practice. In rendering personal services to these clients and patients, the physician occupies a unique position that exposes him or her to confidential information. As such, the physician is invested with the goodwill of the Practice. It is also understood and agreed that the Practice has made (and will continue to make) substantial investments in equipment, personnel, and other commitments in consideration of employing the physician. The Practice has also made (and will continue to make) substantial investments in the physician's recruitment, orientation, and training, and has further refrained from attempting to recruit or employ another physician with similar skills and interests. Therefore, the physician and the Practice agree, in consideration of the issues previously noted and the mutual promises contained within this agreement, to the Covenant Not to Compete and Remedies set forth in Sections 1 and 2 as follows.

1. **Covenant Not to Compete.** In the event of termination of employment with the Practice, the physician agrees not to engage, directly or indirectly, in the practice of medicine or surgery (whether as an individual, shareholder, partner, or physician, or in any other business form) anywhere within the geographically described and recognized boundaries of the Practice for a period of two (2) years after the date of such termination, without the express written consent of the Practice.
2. **Remedies.** In the event of a violation or breach of the Covenant Not to Compete, the parties recognize that the damage incurred and financial prejudice involved will be great and irreparable. The parties also recognize that the amount of such damage and prejudice is extremely difficult to determine with accuracy or certainty. Therefore, upon violation or breach of this covenant, the parties agree that the following liquidated damages represent as fair an estimation as is possible.
    a. **Violation within First Year after Termination.** In the event of a violation or breach of the Covenant Not to Compete within the first twelve (12) months following termination of employment, the physician agrees to pay as liquidated damages, an amount determined as follows: (1) a calculation is made of all gross billings produced by the physician during the twelve (12) months prior to termination, or for the entire period of employment if such employment does not exceed twelve (12) months, and (2) the physician will pay an amount equal to one-twelfth ($\frac{1}{12}$) of 25 percent of the value of such gross billings for each month or part thereof during the first year following termination in which the physician is in violation or breach of the Covenant Not to Compete. Such payment shall be made monthly on the last day of each relevant month during the violation of the Covenant Not to Compete.
    b. **Violation during the Second Year after Termination.** In the event of a violation or breach of the Covenant Not to Compete during the second year following termination of employment, the physician agrees to pay, as liquidated damages, an amount determined as follows: (1) a calculation is made of all gross billings produced during the twelve (12) months prior to termination, or for the entire period if employment does not exceed twelve (12) months, and (2) the physician will pay an amount equal to one-twelfth ($\frac{1}{12}$) of 10 percent of the value of such gross billings for each month or part thereof during the second year following termination in which the physician is in violation or breach of the Covenant Not to Compete. Such payment shall be made monthly on the last day of each relevant month during the violation of the Covenant Not to Compete.
    c. "Gross Billings" as used in Sections 2a and 2b include all amounts billed for the physician's professional medical services, including lab and X-ray, and

amounts received for other activities of the physician, as well as the recovered amount of institutional billings (e.g., Medicaid) and other government or privately supported medical programs.

d. **Interest.** Any payment required for violation of the Covenant Not to Compete shall bear interest at the rate of 2 percent over the prime interest rate per annum until fully paid. Interest shall commence on the date each payment is due to be paid under Sections 2a and 2b.

e. **Offset.** In the event that the Practice owes any amounts to the physician, including but not limited to accrued and unpaid salary, deferred compensation, and payments under any repurchase agreement, the Practice shall be entitled to deduct from such amounts any amount owed by the physician to the Practice under the Covenant Not to Compete.

f. **Nonexclusivity of Remedies.** In the event of violation of the Covenant Not to Compete, the Practice shall be further entitled to equitable relief in addition to those liquidated damages provided for previously, which remedies are considered cumulative, not exclusive. Any election by the Practice to pursue less than all remedies provided shall not bar subsequent enforcement of any other remedies. It is further recognized and agreed that the provisions with respect to liquidated damages shall in no event disentitle the Practice to injunctive relief. Furthermore, the parties understand and agree that the provisions of this covenant are severable, and if one or more provisions may be determined to be unenforceable, in whole or in part, the remaining provisions shall nonetheless be binding and enforceable.

g. The Covenant Not to Compete as described in Section 1 and the Remedies described in Sections 2, 2a, and 2b will become null and void after completing two (2) full years of services from the date of becoming a shareholder.

Policy 9.4

Outside Activities Policy

Physicians employed on a full-time basis by the Practice shall devote their full time to the tasks described in their employment agreement. However, during time off, physicians may engage in outside activities, such as consulting for legal cases, teaching/lecturing, speaking, and writing.

- The physician may retain any fees received by such activities.
- Physicians engaged in outside activities shall be held to the same performance standards and policies as all other physicians.
- Physicians and other staff may not engage in outside activities with entities in direct competition with or conflicting interests of the Practice.
- If the outside activity involves assignments that interfere with the physician's regular schedule and require time off, the physician must file a request with the department chair/medical director and seek approval at least two (2) weeks in advance.
- During the performance of outside activities, the physician shall carefully clarify the differentiation from his or her other service so there is no misinterpretation.

Procedure

1. Physicians must alert management about their interest in outside employment using an outside employment form (see Appendix for Outside Employment Form). The physician's immediate supervisor reviews this form and determines its appropriateness after a discussion with the physician. The supervisor sends the form to the human resources department, where it is placed in the physician's file.
2. Physicians are responsible for notifying their supervisor of any changes in their outside employment status. Physicians document the changes on a new form and submit it to the immediate supervisor.
3. Membership in the Armed Forces is not considered employment at another organization. The Practice will comply with all applicable laws relative to the scheduling of physicians who participate in any branch of the United States Armed Forces.
4. Physicians may not conduct any business related to other employment while on duty at any Practice facility or property, nor may any property, equipment, utilities, or materials of the Practice be utilized to carry out or complete any duties or business related to any entity other than the Practice.
5. The liability insurance provided as a benefit to physicians is not extended to cover them in their employment at other organizations. Professional liability insurance coverage is limited to care provided to Practice patients.
6. Management and supervisory personnel may not simultaneously maintain employment at the Practice and any entity in direct competition with the Practice, where there may be either an actual or perceived conflict of interest.
7. Failure to comply with the guidelines of this policy may result in immediate termination of employment.
8. Physicians who accept outside employment are not eligible for paid absences when the absence is the result of injury on the second job.

Responsibility

The medical director, department chairs, and administrator shall take actions to ensure that this policy is implemented.

Policy 9.5 Patents and Royalties Policy

The board shall approve of any research efforts conducted at the Practice that could result in the development of intellectual property. It shall monitor all such research and determine the feasibility of patenting the discovery. It shall recognize the right of the inventor to financial benefits from the invention or discovery.

Ownership

- The Practice shall be assigned all rights, title, and interest in improvements, discoveries, ideas, or inventions arising out of any staff activities related to physician duties and involving the use of Practice facilities/equipment. It has the discretion to waive such interests. It has no ownership interest in inventions developed outside of the Practice on nonorganization time.
- If the invention is deemed patentable, the Practice's legal counsel will handle these efforts and will keep the inventor informed.
- Any royalties will be divided among the Practice as a corporation, the department of the staff member, and the inventor(s) using a proportional formula that increases the inventor's portion over a five- (5-) year period.
- In cases where the Practice has ownership interest in an invention and either does not file a patent application within one (1) year or fails to make a determination regarding pursuit of a patent within a period of six (6) months from date of disclosure or decides not to pursue a patent, it will offer assignment to the inventor for 40 percent gross royalties, with the cost of filing to be at the inventor's expense. At its sole discretion, the Practice may waive such a share.
- Inventions or discoveries made by individuals employed by the Practice on their personal time and not involving the use of Practice facilities, not related to their medical staff duties, and not utilizing substantial know-how resulting from the physician's interaction with others at the Practice are the property of the inventor. Staff members and physicians must be able to demonstrate that such inventions were indeed invented during personal time. All inventions made on personal time should be disclosed to the Practice.

Eligibility

This policy applies to all classifications assigned to the Practice to include all professional staff members, residents, fellows, physicians, and trainees.

Procedure

1. The Practice must be notified in writing as soon as an inventor has reason to believe that his or her invention or discovery may be patentable or of commercial value.
2. The Practice will make a determination if it wants to patent the invention or discovery. It will notify the inventor of its decisions within six (6) months. If it decides to pursue the patent, the inventor will be kept current of the status of the patent application.
3. The Practice will negotiate the licensing arrangements. The inventor will be kept informed of the progress and results of the negotiations.
4. The inventor will receive his or her share of the royalty within thirty (30) days of the date the Practice receives payment.

Distribution of Royalties

This policy does not include royalties as prescribed by law or a research sponsor. According to federal law, the inventor must share in royalties arising from federally sponsored research.

Net royalty income shall be distributed as follows. The inventor will receive 25 percent. If more than one inventor is identified, they shall equally share the 25 percent. The inventor's research program or department will receive 50 percent. The Practice will keep all remaining royalties. Collaborators are not entitled to share in the royalties.

Net royalty income means gross royalties received by the Practice from the licensing of patentable and nonpatentable inventions or discoveries less costs incurred for patenting, licensing, and managing.

The Practice will continue to pay the inventor his or her share of the royalty even if the inventor terminates his or her employment with the Practice. Royalties assigned to his or her research project may be reassigned to the general fund.

Responsibility

The medical director, administrator, and legal counsel are responsible for ensuring compliance with this policy.

Policy 9.6 Risk Management Policy[2]

Medical malpractice is professional negligence committed by a physician or other healthcare provider resulting in an injured patient. A verdict of malpractice requires a finding of negligence and conduct that causes a negative outcome to the patient. If no injury occurs, there is no cause for a lawsuit.

Common causes of medical malpractice are:

- Medical errors — diagnosis and treatment failures;
- Prescription/medication errors;
- Inadequate physician/staff training (working beyond the scope of training);
- Physician misconduct;
- Physician impairment;
- Equipment malfunction; and
- Inadequate documentation.

Understanding these causes helps medical groups develop administrative systems for better medical care to prevent malpractice occurrences. It also is essential for physicians to remain personally ever-vigilant.

2 *Rx for Business Success: Joining a Practice for Physicians* by MGMA (Englewood, CO: Medical Group Management Association, 2005).

Medical Errors

Common medical errors are:

- Failure to diagnose or a delay in diagnosis — the number-one malpractice allegation;
- Negligent maternity care;
- Negligent fracture or trauma care;
- Failure to consult an expert in a timely manner;
- Negligent drug treatment;
- Negligent procedures;
- Failure to obtain informed consent;
- Failure to obtain and/or act on laboratory results; and
- Failure of administrative systems, such as misfiled laboratory reports.

Prescription/Medication Errors

Contraindicated medications, wrong dosages, and allergic reactions are the most common prescription errors.

Prescription mistakes often result from illegible or hasty handwriting or because a rushed and distracted physician may make errors in drug dosages and neglect to ask about drug allergies. It is the policy of the Practice that all prescriptions be submitted electronically to the pharmacies.

Medication lists are one easy way to reduce prescription errors. Clinical support staff puts one in each chart to record all of a patient's current prescriptions. The nurse/physician assistant/nurse practitioner should review the list with the patient prior to the physician's visit.

Advantages of a medication list include:

- Efficient charting;
- Safer refills;
- Better communication among physicians;
- Allergy documentation; and
- Documentation of over-the-counter medications, supplements, herbal therapies, and vitamins. These are often overlooked.

Working beyond the Scope of Training

A physician who performs a procedure that he or she is not adequately trained for puts the patient at risk. Physicians may do this out of a desire for additional income or from overconfidence. Performing procedures when you are tired or distracted, which can be viewed as a temporary impairment, can also cause an adverse outcome.

Always remember that all patient care is ultimately under the direct supervision of the physician. It is important that physician supervisors assign tasks for each physician at his or her appropriate skill level.

Procedure

1. All physicians will follow credentialing protocol.
2. Availability/accessibility of physicians to patients: Patients with urgent conditions will be seen within twenty-four (24) hours, with emergency conditions seen immediately and routine visits within four (4) to six (6) weeks.
3. Documentation in medical records will be in a complete and legible format and signed.
4. Pre-operative evaluations should be documented in all cases, and the evaluation should include notification of the primary physician in the event that his or her active participation in the pre- and post-operative care of the patient is required. This would make it necessary to notify the primary care physician before the patient is admitted to the hospital for any surgical procedure. This would improve the personal nature of the relationship and help in communication.
5. All informed consents will be initiated verbally with the patient and the next of kin when possible. The extent of the verbal communication will be documented in the progress note. The informed consent form will be completed and filed in the chart.
6. The transfer of patient care responsibilities between physicians should be clearly documented in the chart and also communicated to the family and to nursing staff to minimize confusion as to whom is responsible for the daily management of the patient.
7. All office procedures should have documented informed consent, and the patient should be informed of any potential risk or potential side effects before the procedure is initiated. Specific instruction sheets given to patients should be documented in the medical record.
8. All medications that the patient is currently receiving should be documented in the chart, along with any refills so as to enhance the management of the patient and to minimize the potential for interactions. Patient allergies should be clearly marked.
9. It is recommended that the attending physician or his or her "on call" associate round daily on all hospitalized patients.

Other Ethical Issues Encountered in Medical Practice

Fee Splitting. Payments to other medical professionals (fee splitting or kickbacks) for referrals are ethically and legally improper. The practice is fairly common in other countries where the referring primary care physician receives a percentage of the fees generated by the specialist, who is often the highest bidder. The Practice strictly prohibits fee splitting.

Rewarding Patients with Financial Incentives for Referrals. For certain specialties, referrals from satisfied patients represent a major source of new patients. Most offices verbally thank established patients or mail a thank-you card as an expression of gratitude. However, financial or other gifts of value may encourage unnecessary referrals and are strongly discouraged by the Council on Ethical and Judicial Affairs of the American Medical Association (AMA).[3] In addition, the Practice may run afoul of

3 Michael S. Goldrich, "Report of the Council on Ethical and Judicial Affairs: Financial Incentives to Patients for Referrals." Copyright 2004 by American Medical Association, www.ama-assn.org/resources/doc/code-medical-ethics/6021a.pdf (accessed July 10, 2011).

federal regulations when treating Medicare patients and, therefore, rewarding patients with financial incentives for referrals and is strictly prohibited by the Practice.

Office of the Inspector General's Compliance Program Guidance for Pharmaceutical Manufacturers

Any item of tangible value provided to a physician who has an opportunity to prescribe the manufacturer's product can elicit a concern about either inducing or rewarding referrals and, therefore, is covered under the anti-kickback statutes.[4] If the gifts, goods, or services to the physician eliminate an expense that would have been incurred by the physician, purposeful inducement of business may be illegal, even if there is another legitimate purpose (education) or a fair market value payment.

Interactions with Pharmaceutical Industry Representatives

Pharmaceutical manufacturers come under two voluntary but powerful guidance documents meant to establish the ground rules for interactions between drug producers and representatives and healthcare professionals. These documents include the 2003 Department of Health and Human Services Office of the Inspector General's (DHHS OIG) Compliance Program Guidance for Pharmaceutical Manufacturers and the 2002 Pharmaceutical Research and Manufacturers of America's (PhRMA) PhRMA Code on Interactions with Healthcare Professionals. The HIPAA privacy regulations are also implicated by physician relationships with pharmaceutical representatives.

While the OIG's guidance approaches this subject from the perspective of the manufacturer's potential liabilities, a physician would be wise to steer clear of risky scenarios. Remunerative relationships between the manufacturer and physician, or others who are in a position to generate federal healthcare business for the manufacturer, could be problematic. If the purpose of the remuneration may be to induce or reward the referral of business payable by a federal healthcare program, the anti-kickback statute is implicated.

Physicians should beware of gifts or other incentives offered by manufacturers or their representatives if the underlying intent is to create business billable to the federal government (e.g., TriCare, Medicare, Medicaid). Even where the gift or service is for a legitimate purpose (e.g., physical education) or is provided at fair market value, any illegal intent will make the whole gift suspect. Potential legal issues will be abated with certainty only if the incentive arrangement fits squarely into a safe harbor.

The guidance document discusses the most common potentially illegal arrangements, including:

1. "Switching" arrangements (in which the physician is encouraged to switch patients to the manufacturer's drug from a competing drug);
2. Consulting and advisory payments (e.g., where the physician's "consulting" or "advising" is passive or involves marketing activities);
3. Payments for detailing (e.g., where the physician is paid for completing minimal paperwork following time spent reviewing or listening to marketing communications);

4 *Federal Register*, V. 68, No. 86, May 5, 2003. Notices, http://edocket.access.gpo.gov/2003/pdf/03-10949.pdf (accessed July 10, 2011).

4. Business courtesies and other gratuities; and
5. Educational and research activities (e.g., where physicians are paid above market rates or for unnecessary research).

When an arrangement between a provider and manufacturer cannot be made to fit exactly into a safe harbor, a number of factors will be taken into consideration to determine the propriety of the arrangement. Factors include:

1. The nature of the relationship between the parties (e.g., physician's influence on generation of business for manufacturing);
2. How remuneration is determined;
3. The value of the remuneration;
4. The potential impact of the remuneration on federal programs; and
5. Potential conflicts of interest (e.g., effects on professional objectivity).

Since these factors must be balanced in order to determine if an arrangement is appropriate, there is a good deal of uncertainty involved. Legal counsel should be consulted to assess risk.

PhRMA Code on Interactions with Healthcare Professionals

The PhRMA Code establishes voluntary guidelines for pharmaceutical manufacturers as related to marketing interactions with healthcare professionals, and specifically the gifts and gratuities given to healthcare professionals. The OIG guidance reminds that compliance with the Code does not constitute a safe harbor. The OIG does state, however, that compliance "will substantially reduce the risk of fraud and abuse and help demonstrate a good faith effort to comply [with applicable federal laws]."

The Code attempts to ensure that "all interactions [between manufacturers and healthcare professionals are] focused on informing healthcare professionals about products, providing scientific and educational information, and supporting medical research and education," according to PhRMA.

The Code suggests that manufacturer gifts and services to physicians must primarily benefit patients or be for the education of the physician, not be of substantial value (under $100), and only offered occasionally.

Certain sales traditions of the past are no longer allowable under the HIPAA privacy regulations. Drug representatives may not have free access to exam rooms or patient records. While the regulations do not require a drug representative to sign a Business Associate Agreement or a more general confidentiality agreement, the Practice's physicians should take basic precautions to protect patient confidentiality. Records must never be left in plain view, nor should representatives have free access to the office. Of course, if a physician would feel more comfortable to have a confidentiality agreement in place, the regulations do not prohibit such measures.

Any activity that would give a sales representative access to protected health information (PHI), such as sitting in the exam room or viewing an patient's file for general data, first requires that the patient sign an authorization allowing the PHI to be shared.

To learn more about appropriate disclosures under HIPAA, see the OIG's Website.

Sample: Pharmaceutical Rep Interaction

Relationships between physicians and the pharmaceutical industry are common. The constant drumbeat in the medical literature and media has led to a critical reevaluation of existing guidelines and their implications for research and education. Full and open disclosure may serve to preserve the benefits of a relationship while avoiding ethical pitfalls.

The American Medical Association (AMA) has had a code of ethics since 1847, and the AMA's Council on Ethical and Judicial Affairs continuously updates its policies.[5] In addition, the Pharmaceutical Research and Manufacturers of America (PhRMA) published guidelines and a voluntary code of ethics for physicians and the industry, adopted July 1, 2002, and they are listed on its Website[6] (also described above). Although the code is specifically written for healthcare professionals, the assumption is that it applies to managerial and office staff as well. These guidelines can be summarized as follows:

- All interactions should ultimately benefit patients;
- Pharmaceutical industry employees and agents should be viewed as professional sales representatives who provide product information, scientific information to educate physicians and staff, and supporting medical education or research;
- Funding of continuing medical education (CME) activities should occur through the institution sponsoring the educational offering in the form of an educational grant and not directly through payments to the medical professional;
- The content of the CME offering should not be controlled or sponsored by any pharmaceutical representative or organization;
- Financial support for spouses or guests of medical professionals is improper and likely illegal;
- Independence of prescribing should be of great concern, and prescribing in return for industry support is unethical and illegal under federal anti-kickback laws;
- Any compensation for speaking at an industry-sponsored conference should be reasonable; and
- Gifts to physicians or office staff should not be valued over $10.

A number of medical practices have now adopted a policy that pharmaceutical sales representatives may not provide meals to physicians or staff. Further, some medical practices will no longer accept or dispense pharmaceutical samples, while others, eliminating the presence of samples in medical group practice areas, will provide the patient with a "sample prescription" to be filled at a cooperating pharmacy (one that will accept and dispense samples). Another approach has been for medical practices to establish a "sample room" where all samples are maintained, under lock and key, and managed by a registered nurse who, upon orders from the physician, may provide the patient with a sample medication.

See Appendix for Letter to Pharmaceutical Representatives.

5 American Medical Association, "Principles of Medical Ethics," June 17, 2001, www.ama-assn.org/ama/pub/category/2512.html (accessed May 6, 2006).
6 Pharmaceutical Research and Manufacturers of America, www.phrma.org (accessed July 10, 2011).

Legality of Patient Assistance Programs Sponsored by Pharmaceutical Companies

Major pharmaceutical companies have always provided assistance in fulfilling physician-requested assistance to patients, particularly seniors, on the basis of financial need. The DHHS has previously warned that such programs may carry "a high risk of fraud and abuse," and as a result, several large companies were reluctant to assist those in financial need. The primary reason for the stance was the concern that the companies would use this program to boost sales of their brand-name drugs in lieu of generic drugs and, therefore, increase the cost to Medicare. With the advent of Medicare prescription coverage (Part D), the DHHS Inspector General issued an opinion allowing assistance to those in need provided:[7]

- The program is operated outside the Medicare drug benefit program;
- The companies inform the government of benefits provided so that Medicare drug plans can be informed of the availability of the drugs;
- The availability should be based only on financial need;
- The benefit is independent of the type of drug program in which the intended recipients are enrolled; and
- The value of the drugs does not count toward the Medicare Part D program's $4,550 out-of-pocket threshold in 2011 for catastrophic coverage.[8]

Check Internal Policies

Medical practices from the smallest to the largest should have policies in place regarding how their clinicians and staff may interact with pharmaceutical industry representatives and what gifts they may not accept. Institutional policies vary widely. For example, the University of Michigan (U-M) and Henry Ford Health Systems restrict pharmaceutical representatives and equipment vendors from calling on physicians within the hospital without an appointment and checking in.[9] The *Detroit Free Press* reported that, "While the program kept about $2.5 million worth of free pizza, chicken kabobs, and pita sandwiches from reaching U-M doctors' and residents' stomachs, U-M credits the program with boosting generic drug use..." A number of hospitals now ban the acceptance of free drug samples. The Hospital of the University of Pennsylvania has announced that its Center for Evidence-Based Practice will be the clearinghouse for pharmaceutical industry representatives to schedule information sessions about new drugs.[10]

Responsibility

The quality improvement manager, medical director, and board of directors are responsible for ensuring compliance with this policy.

---

7 The Advisory Board Company, www.advisoryboardcompany.com (accessed April 19, 2006).

8 Q1Medicare.com, "What Is the Outlook for Medicare Part D 2011?" www.q1medicare.com/PartD-The-2011-Medicare-Part-D-Outlook.php.

9 K. Merx, "Drug Marketing: Freebies for Doctors Curbed," *Detroit Free Press*, http://freep.com/cgi-bin/forms (accessed July 12, 2005).

10 The Advisory Board Company, www.advisoryboardcompany.com (accessed May 3, 2006).

Policy 9.7

Business Ethics Policy

The Practice is committed to continuing its business with the highest ethical standards. To that end, it shall establish a code of ethics and reinforce its intent through specific procedures.

Procedure

1. A code of ethics shall be developed by the executive committee and approved by the board. It shall be communicated to all physicians and staff at orientation and throughout their service with the Practice, including through training.
2. An annual ethics audit will be conducted by an external resource and the results used to make any necessary corrective actions.
3. Any physician or staff member who identifies a potential business ethics issue (e.g., conflict of interest, gifts, fraud, and abuse) should refer the concern to a department chair. If resolution does not result, the information should be taken to the administrator. For purposes of confidentiality, a "Help Line" also has been established in case the person wishes to remain anonymous. Any such referral will be investigated immediately and thoroughly, and corrective action, including termination, taken.
4. Behavior related to ethical issues will be measured and reviewed during performance reviews.

I. Conflict of Interest

Purpose: To ensure that no conflict of interest arises between board members, officers, and the organization.

All new board members and officers will complete a Conflict of Interest Statement upon joining the board and annually thereafter.

In the event of a contract or transaction between the medical practice and a director or officer, or between the corporation and any other entity in which a director or officer has a financial interest, the following conditions must be met:

1. The material facts as to the director's or officer's relationship or interest are disclosed to the board or are known by the board, and the interested director or officer abstains from voting; and
2. The contract or transaction is fair as to the medical practice at the time it is approved by the board.

See Appendix for Conflict of Interest Statement.

Sample: Code of Ethics for Professional Staff

- Care for all who are sick/injured, no matter what their race, religion, ethnic origin, financial status, or illness/injury.
- Demonstrate mutual respect and acknowledge interdependence with colleagues and employees (including clinical and administrative support staff) in caring for the patient.
- Conduct personal and professional activities with honesty, integrity, respect, and fairness.
- Use talents, resources, and time wisely in a sense of stewardship.
- Be truthful in communication and avoid any information that is false or misleading.
- Keep confidential anything learned about a patient, customer, colleague, or employee (including clinical and administrative support staff) while carrying out professional responsibilities.
- Inform individuals of their rights, responsibilities, and risks regarding healthcare services.
- Never knowingly harm any person.
- Never knowingly use a professional position for personal gain or to put another person at a disadvantage.
- Maintain competence and excellence in one's profession through personal evaluation and ongoing education.
- Comply with state and federal laws governing the practice of medicine and work responsibility, whether this is direct or indirect patient care.

Also see Policy 7.3 on page 217.

II. Confidentiality

The physician recognizes and agrees that the meetings of the Practice and its committees are conducted in strictest confidence and matters are discussed which are sensitive in nature and therefore confidential and of a proprietary nature within the Practice. Accordingly, the physician agrees in connection with any and all participation at meetings of the Practice or its committees, task forces, work groups, or related entities, to maintain all information relating to the Practice and its business operations, strategic plans, initiatives, and any such data pertaining to such and any other information specifically identified as confidential and proprietary in strictest confidence, absent specific authorization to release or disclose information to third parties by the board.

See Appendix for Confidential Information Statement.

III. Fraud and Abuse

Purpose: To clearly specify the philosophy of the Practice to completely and absolutely adhere to the highest of business ethical standards and human morals.

It is the policy of the Practice to operate all of its programs and services fully within the boundaries of all applicable federal and state laws and regulations and to ensure that its physicians are informed of and comply with these laws and regulations. As a result, the Practice will not tolerate any activity involving fraud or abuse in any aspect of any physician's service, nor in any aspect of its programs and administration. Physicians are expected to perform their job duties free of fraud and abuse and to report any instances of fraud and abuse anywhere within the Practice to the chief executive office.

In complying with this policy, no physician will be disciplined, harassed, or retaliated against in any aspect of employment for any good faith disclosure related to actual or perceived fraud or abuse. Failure to comply with this policy will lead to disciplinary action up to and including termination.

Procedure

As part of their orientation to the Practice, all physicians shall receive physician handbooks that detail both the Practice's policies designed to comply with laws and regulations and expectations of physicians in achieving this compliance. All physicians will be required upon hiring to sign a statement that they understand that fraud and abuse in any form will not be tolerated and that any fraud or abuse committed or known but not disclosed by them will be cause for termination. Physicians will be required to sign similar statements annually.

See Appendix for Physician Statement on Fraud and Abuse.

IV. Media Relations

Providing medical advice to television shows or displaying procedures in the media may be permissible. The underlying theme remains that the patient's interest should be paramount. Guidelines issued by the AMA's Council on Ethical and Judicial Affairs suggest a proper consent with respect to patient confidentiality, accuracy of the information, and realistic expectations:[11]

- All media requests are to be submitted to the human resources department for review and recommendation for participation to the executive director; and
- NO public comment is to be made to the media without the expressed *written* approval of the executive director.

Practical Ways to Steer Clear of Perceptions of Impropriety

1. **Read the AMA and PhRMA guidelines.** While the entire code of ethics of the AMA and PhRMA is worth reading, the sections dealing with common day-to-day realities are particularly useful. They can provide some guidance when confronted with awkward situations.
2. **Use your moral compass.** The common refrain, "If you would feel uncomfortable reading about your relationship with a vendor in the newspaper . . ." is applicable. Have the courage to graciously decline anything that is out of line or donate it to a charitable entity.
3. **Abide by the rules.** Follow or exceed the existing general guidelines regarding the dollar limits acceptable within a relationship.
4. **Seek advice.** If a physician is employed by a large organization (academic institution or healthcare organization), advice from the ethics/compliance officer or attorney is entirely appropriate. In smaller practices, advice may be sought externally from legal representatives with deep health law experience.

11 Priscilla Ray, MD, "Report of the Council on Ethical and Judicial Affairs: Ethics of Physician Participation in Reality Television for Entertainment (Resolution 607, I-04)." Copyright 2005 by American Medical Association, www.ama-assn .org/resources/doc/code-medical-ethics/5045b.pdf (accessed July 10, 2011).

Policy 9.8

Expert Witness Policy[12]

Most states in the United States require an "expert witness" to review and agree to testify on behalf of a plaintiff in a medical malpractice action against any physician. When there is an overwhelming difference in compensation between practicing medicine and being "on call" for plaintiff attorneys, the supply of physician "expert witnesses" for the plaintiff will rise. Until recently, tort reform proposals generally have not focused enough on the critical issue of defining the qualifications and expertise of the expert or the rules governing the scientific evidence that may be used in medical malpractice cases. This discussion is not intended to be complete, nor is it meant to be a substitute for expert legal opinion.

Law and Medicine

The difficulty in balancing the right of a plaintiff to bring an expert witness that could be important to their case versus disallowing "pseudoscience" in the courtroom is problematic. This difficulty stems partially because the "truth" in law and the "truth" in medicine are indeed different. The truth in medicine is almost always arrived at by empirical testing and by stepwise confirmation of a working hypothesis and logical work supported by statistical analysis. Contrariwise, legal truth allows the court to consider a plaintiff's claim and all the relevant evidence, and if a plaintiff can prove his or her claim by "preponderance of the evidence" (more than 50 percent certainty), damages may be awarded even in the absence of scientific certainty. Because medicine is both a science and an art with constantly evolving knowledge, theories held by a minority of the medical scientists may not necessarily be "junk science" and instead could be budding scientific consensus. Courts have to allow for this sort of testimony, which may not meet the formerly applied "general acceptance" test (Frye test).

The limitation of the *Daubert* decision is that state law governs most tort or criminal cases that use scientific evidence, and the Supreme Court's interpretation of Federal Rules of Evidence (with its cases decided under the U.S. Constitution) does not bind state courts or legislatures.

Finally, a comprehensive study found that court-appointed experts were infrequently used in the federal courts, based in part on the judges' concerns that it may be more productive in the short term for members of our society to direct their efforts toward developing and testing materials useful for helping judges and juries distinguish science from pseudoscience.

12 Printed in Bhagwan Satiani, MD, MBA, *The Smarter Physician: Demystifying the Business of Medicine in Your Practice, Vol. 1* (Englewood, CO: Medical Group Management Association, 2007). Reprinted by permission of Sage Publications from Bhagwan Satiani, MD, MBA, "Expert Witness Testimony: Rules of Engagement," *Vascular and Endovascular Surgery* V. 40, No. 3: 223–27. Copyright 2006 by Westminster Publications, Inc.

Policy 9.9

Consulting and Speaker Roles Policy

The pharmaceutical industry and its critics differ on whether consulting and speaker roles for physicians are appropriate as a means of educating prescribers about new therapies. Although the debate continues, currently published guidelines follow.

- There is a legitimate role for payment for bona fide consulting or lecturing at industry-sponsored events, including reimbursement for lodging, travel, meals, and a reasonable honorarium depending on the time and distance traveled. The arrangements should be agreed upon prior to the event, be in writing, be focused on education, and be handled through a CME provider not directly by a pharmaceutical company.
- It is also reasonable for physicians to be paid for participating in speakers' bureaus in a consulting role or as training for new procedures for industry. The company should arrange proper training in an educational environment rather than a purely social gathering.
- It is not considered ethical — and may be illegal — for physicians to receive payment for travel, meals, lodging, and an honorarium simply for attending a seminar.
- Serving as an advisor for industry — a controversial role for physicians or other professionals — is permissible so long as payment is consistent with the participant's status and level of participation and in line with similar payments to other professional consultants brought in by the company. An advisor typically spends one (1) or two (2) days a year participating in reviewing scientific data, giving advice on business decisions, and recommending further areas of research for a product. The company generally does not pay expenses for spouses.
- Training physicians and other healthcare professionals to learn about a product and how to speak to audiences about it, and to acquire information on regulatory restrictions so they can disseminate the information to other audiences may be permissible. However, the Advisory Board Company reports that "the physician speakers earn an average of $750 per session, but in most cases, drug makers say they nearly 'double the return' on investment."[13] It also reports on a study by Merck showing that physician-to-physician events had almost doubled the return on initial investment compared to sales-representative-to-physician contacts.

13 The Advisory Board Company, "Drug Manufacturers Employ Physician Speakers to Promote Products," www.advisoryboardcompany.com (accessed July 15, 2005).

Sample: Educational Presentation Policy

Outside Income from Administrative and Nonpatient Care Professional Services

From time to time, physician-shareholders provide nonpatient care professional services. The success of the Practice can be enhanced by physician-shareholder participation in leadership roles outside the Practice. All outside income generated by a physician-shareholder will be turned over to the Practice and redistributed to the physician-shareholder as a part of his or her professional services revenue according to the following percentages:

1. Educational presentations made from 8 a.m. through 5:30 p.m. any weekday excluding holidays — 75 percent; and
2. Educational presentation made after 5:30 p.m. on any weekday or anytime on a Saturday, Sunday, or holiday — 100 percent.

Research and Education

Funding of education and research by pharmaceutical companies and industry has been of significant mutual benefit, particularly in the academic environment. Nevertheless, the general consensus is that acceptance of research monies should come with some caveats:

- Allow funding of educational grants to encourage resident and student participation in conferences or meetings. The selection of the participants must be left to the students' or residents' institutions.
- Private grants from industry must be in the form of unrestricted grants to the institution or foundation rather than directly linked to the researcher.

Physician Independence

The AMA and PhRMA guidelines also address the important issue of the independence of medical professionals in recommending medications, procedures, and treatment options. These should never be negotiable. That is, there should be no link or tie-in to research funding, consulting contracts, or payment to healthcare professionals. Payment to physicians and others should not be linked to the purchase of equipment, devices, and drugs by hospitals. This may be a particular problem if the physician receiving the monies is on a committee involved in the selection of the product. The conflicted physician should recuse himself or herself from a decision in such a forum and disclose the conflict of interest.

Disclosures of conflicts of interest are now required by institutions, journals, professional organizations, and hospital committees to counter any appearance of impropriety. Disclosure of financial conflict of interest to patients is insufficient to protect patients because the disclosure may be incomplete, unverified, and too complex for patients to comprehend.[14] It is suggested that eliminating the conflict of interest is preferable instead of trying to "sanitize" the problem with a disclosure.

14 Brennan et al., "Health Industry Practices That Create Conflicts of Interest: A Policy Proposal for Academic Medical Centers," *JAMA*, V. 295, No. 4, January 25, 2006. Copyright 2006 American Medical Association.

Policy 9.10

Samples to Patients Policy[15]

In March 2006, the Department of Health and Human Services (DHHS) and the Food and Drug Administration issued revised guidelines to limit the regulatory burden on free clinics dispensing free samples to patients. Partnership for Prescription Assistance, a program launched by pharmaceutical research companies, is designed to assist patients in need of medications that they cannot afford. As mentioned, several institutions are disallowing free samples for patients, and instead recommend providing vouchers, so patients can obtain medications directly from the pharmacy.[16]

See also Sample: Pharmaceutical Rep Interaction in Policy 9.6: Risk Management.

Policy 9.11

Whistleblower Policy

Qui Tam Provision

The Practice will uphold the qui tam provisions set forth by the United States government.

Physician Response to Qui Tam Procedure

1. **Voluntary Disclosure.** If the physician has uncovered improper billing practices, one option is to voluntarily disclose the findings to the DHHS, the Office of the Inspector General (OIG), as a means of mitigating liability. The argument is that, because of future aggressive government enforcement efforts or *qui tam* action, such behavior will eventually be discovered. Under federal sentencing guidelines, voluntary disclosure of improper billing practices allows some leniency from a judicial standpoint. However, one has to remember that if a Practice conducts an audit after discovering, as an example, a single improper billing incident and finds further evidence of illegal actions, voluntary disclosure can be the basis for criminal, civil, and/or administrative liability. Most legal authorities advise that, as a general rule, a physician or the professional corporation (a) is not legally required to report to the government knowledge of its own unlawful activities and (b) should not voluntary disclose any evidence of such conduct. On the other hand, the Social Security Act, which governs the Medicare and Medicaid programs, requires self-disclosure of the discovery of improper claims submissions to the Medicare or Medicaid programs whenever a party has knowledge of the occurrence of any events affecting initial or the continued right to any such benefit or payments (from Medicare or Medicaid) and conceals or fails to disclose such activities with an intent to fraudulently secure such benefit or payment. It is unclear when and how

15 Printed in Bhagwan Satiani, MD, MBA, *The Smarter Physician: Demystifying the Business of Medicine in Your Practice, Vol. 1* (Englewood, CO: Medical Group Management Association, 2007).
16 U.S. Food and Drug Administration, "Guidance for Industry Prescription Drug Marketing Act — Donation of Prescription Drug Samples to Free Clinics," March 2006, www.fda.gov/cder/guidance/5519fnl.htm (accessed May 13, 2006).

this statute applies to individual cases. In practice, only a handful of medical practices have voluntarily disclosed such improper actions, for fear of being extensively audited and singled out for public flagellation.

2. **Voluntary Disclosure to the Local U.S. Attorney's Office Rather Than the OIG.** The advantage of this slightly different option is that reporting to the latter does not offer any advantage in terms of lessening any chance of prosecution. The U.S. attorney's office may be able to resolve any culpability more expeditiously and to resolve any civil penalties at the same time.
3. **Return of Improper Payments.** The more common action taken by medical groups upon discovery of improper receipts is to return the payments, possibly with interest and an explanation to the insurance intermediary (an agent of the government, in this case). If the intermediary then deems the matter egregious, they may forward it to the government, which in turn may elect to prosecute the matter as a criminal act or for failure to disclose the illegal act and may ask for triple damages and civil penalties.

Avoiding Governmental Intervention

Because most physician practices are organized as professional corporations, a well-written and executed corporate compliance program is essential to reduce the chance of governmental legal action against individual physicians and officers of the corporation. As such, the Practice will establish a compliance program (including regular billing audits), utilize voluntary disclosure, and act as a "good" corporate citizen by adhering to the following guidelines:[17]

1. Developing and distributing written standards of conduct and written policies, procedures, and protocols;
2. Designating a compliance officer and establishing of a reporting mechanism to a board or governing body;
3. Developing and implementing a regular, effective education program for the affected physician;
4. Creating and maintaining a mechanism whereby there is an open, anonymous, and protected method of communication between physicians and the compliance officer;
5. Monitoring and ensuring compliance with written standards through audits, risk evaluation, and identification of problem areas;
6. Ensuring that no discretionary authority is vested in individuals who are known (or should be known) to have engaged in criminal conduct or violated corporate and/or other rules/statutes; and
7. Responding appropriately and consistently to any detected violations, taking corrective action, and preventing recurrences.

17 United States Sentencing Commission Guidelines, "Sentencing for Organizations," *Federal Register* V. 227, No. 62, May 1991.

Policy 9.12 Internet Usage Policy

The Practice is dedicated to providing its physicians with the most technologically advanced tools to perform their job functions. Along with this goal comes the need for restrictions for appropriate usage of the technology. Every physician must follow the procedures below regarding appropriate usage of the Internet and e-mail applications.

Procedure

1. Physicians surfing the Internet for personal reasons must do so before or after working hours or during the lunch break. Physicians may always access Practice-related and other appropriate sites.
2. The Practice prohibits physicians from downloading programs from the Internet (including but not limited to Instant Messenger) unless a manager in the IT department provides express written permission to do so. All staff must exercise caution when downloading files attached to e-mails and should avoid opening any suspicious e-mail that could contain a virus.
3. The Practice strictly prohibits accessing Websites or e-mail messages that contain explicit images including cartoons, ethnic slurs, racial epithets, or anything of a sexual nature. Other physicians, patients, and visitors could construe such activity as harassment or discrimination.
4. The Practice reserves the right to monitor computer activity, including but not limited to monitoring Internet surfing and examining e-mail at any time without notice. The Practice views Internet access and e-mail as necessary tools to conducting business activities, but these tools are owned and maintained by the Practice. If a physician violates this policy, management takes corrective action in accordance with the policy.
5. Physicians may use e-mail for business purposes. Management allows a minimum of personal e-mail. Physicians may not send e-mail messages that contain sexually explicit material, racial slurs, or racial epithets, nor any other material that anyone could reasonably view as harassment or discriminatory. The Practice has the right to determine when a physician is sending too many e-mail messages or ones that are improper.
6. Access to the Practice's intranet and e-mail system is exclusively for physicians and other specific individuals. The IT department manager authorizes those individuals who are granted access and issues a username and password for those individuals. It is the responsibility of the physician to protect the security and confidentiality of logins and passwords. For privacy reasons, physicians may not attempt to gain access to another physician's computer or e-mail without the owner's expressed permission.

Responsibility

All staff members are responsible for ensuring compliance with this policy.

Sample: Internet Security Policy

This Internet security policy defines roles, responsibilities, and policies for Practice physicians, agents, and contractors using the Practice's communications equipment and facilities to access third-party electronic media and services, such as the Internet. Such individuals will be referred to as "the user."

Security is everyone's responsibility. Every user must be aware of his or her responsibility in the protection of the Practice's electronic information assets. This policy is provided to enhance the security awareness of users and to protect confidential patient and sensitive Practice information stored on the computer resources.

Medical staff may have access to various forms of electronic media and services, including computers, e-mail, telephones, voice mail, fax machines, external electronic bulletin boards, wire services, online services, and the Internet. The Practice encourages the use of these media and associated services for daily work because information technology is a critical part of the service provided to patients and, in many cases, is required to efficiently conduct research or transactions with outside entities that support patient care. However, Practice-provided access mechanisms to electronic media and services are the Practice's property, and their purpose is to facilitate medical care to patients.

Due to the rapidly changing nature of electronic media, this Internet policy cannot cover every possible situation. Instead, this policy expresses the Practice's philosophy and sets general guidelines for the use of electronic media and services. This policy applies to all Practice physicians, agents, and contractors using electronic media and services that are accessed on or from Practice premises; accessed using Practice computer equipment; accessed via Practice-paid access methods; and/or used in a manner that identifies the individual with the Practice collectively and individually.

Procedure

1. Users are accountable and responsible for helping to protect electronic information assets. They should be used in an efficient and economical manner and not in a way that is likely to cause network congestion or significantly hamper the ability of other people to access and use the Practice's computer system.
2. Any software that is designed to destroy data, provide unauthorized access to computer systems, or disrupt computing processes is prohibited.
3. Access to electronic assets will be provided on a need-to-know and appropriate basis.
4. Users will be uniquely identified and authenticated before accessing sensitive electronic-information assets.
5. Users will access only what they have been authorized to access.
6. Users will not act in a manner that will defeat the effectiveness of security measures.
7. Users will direct all data files to their designated folders on the server to ensure consistent and current backup of all data. Clinical data is not to be stored on local hard drives.
8. Users will not install any software on their computers without permission of the system administrator. This includes software downloaded from the Internet or personally brought into the Practice.
9. All software installed on the server and local computers will be fully licensed.
10. All users will be assigned a username and password and will be required to use them upon logging in to the system.

Sample continues next page

Sample: Internet Security Policy (continued)

11. Data will be transmitted securely between networks as per the security standards and based on a need-to-know and appropriate basis.
12. Contracts/agreements will be fully executed to ensure security and confidentiality of data in order to electronically provide information to business partners.
13. Virus-checking software will be loaded on all workstations and updated automatically to ensure the detection of viruses. If at any time a virus is detected on a computer, the department manager must be notified immediately.
14. Users will notify the department manager of any security-related incidents or potential security weaknesses.
15. Users will use computer resources in compliance with the Practice's compliance policy on confidentiality of information.
16. All users must sign an Information Security and Confidentiality Agreement to gain access to computer systems.
17. The Practice Website will be used to provide educational material to patients and interested parties visiting the site. It will not be used to provide diagnosis or clinical advice.
18. Periodic audits will be run on users' computers to monitor software installation.
19. Use of Practice-provided access to the Internet is intended primarily for the Practice's business-related purposes. Internet access is monitored, and actual Website connections are recorded. Excessive use of Practice-provided access to the Internet for nonbusiness-related purposes may result in loss of access privileges and/or disciplinary action, up to and including termination of employment.
20. Access to selected Internet hosts or networks that the Practice designates as inappropriate may be denied.
21. The Practice may apply filters as appropriate to block certain news groups. Disclosing any information related to the business or information that violates the Practice's confidentiality policy is prohibited.
22. Users should always portray the Practice as a reputable company and maintain its reputation and goodwill through appropriate Internet use.

Sample: Information Security and Confidentiality Agreement

I, the undersigned, have been provided access to certain computer systems in order to efficiently provide medical services to patients of this Practice. Confidential patient and sensitive business information is this Practice's most valuable asset residing on computer systems within the Practice. The privacy of the Practice's confidential patient and sensitive business information depends on the protection of this information against theft, destruction, or unauthorized disclosure to outside interests.

In order to be granted access, I understand and agree to be bound by the information security policies in effect for the Practice.

Therefore, in consideration of being allowed access to one or more of the Practice's software systems and patient records, I, the undersigned, hereby agree to the following provisions:

- I will only access software systems to review patient records when I have a need to know and it is appropriate to support patient medical care.
- I will not transmit or transfer any confidential information regarding patients or employees without proper authorization and authority.
- I will abide by the policies and procedures set forth by the Practice regarding the use of all electronic media and transmission of data.
- I will maintain assigned passwords or access methods that allow access to computer systems and equipment in strictest confidence and not disclose a password or access method to anyone, at any time, for any reason, as I acknowledge this increases the possibility of accidental disclosure.
- I will contact the Practice director or department manager immediately and request a new password if mine is accidentally revealed.
- I will not disclose any portion of the Practice's computerized system to any unauthorized individual.
- I will not disclose any portion of a patient's medical record except to a recipient authorized by the patient to receive that information.
- I will report activity that is contrary to the provisions of this agreement to the Practice director or department manager.

I understand that failure to comply with the terms of this agreement and the authorization to access information/software systems and the previously referenced policies may result in formal disciplinary action up to and possibly including termination.

Physician Signature: ____________________________________
Printed Name: ____
Date: __________

Appendix

Confidential Information Statement
Conflict of Interest Statement
Discharge Letter
Disruptive Physician: Common Behaviors
Disruptive Physician: Incident Report Form
Disruptive Physician: Verbal Warning Report Form
Disruptive Physician: Written Warning Report Form
Employment Contract for Part-Time or Partially Retired Physicians
Letter to Pharmaceutical Representatives
Outside Employment Form
Patient Satisfaction Survey Form
Performance Appraisal Form
Physician Compact: Basic Performance Expectations and Customer Service
Physician Peer Review Form
Physician Satisfaction Survey Form
Physician Statement on Fraud and Abuse
Practice and Patient E-Communications Agreement

Confidential Information Statement

The undersigned recognizes and agrees that the meetings of the Practice and its committees are conducted in strictest confidence, and matters are discussed that are sensitive in nature and, therefore, confidential and of a proprietary nature within the Practice. Accordingly, the undersigned agrees in connection with any and all participation at meetings of the Practice or its committees, task forces, work groups, or related entities, to maintain all information relating to the Practice and its business operations, strategic plans, initiatives, and any such data pertaining to such and any other information specifically identified as confidential and proprietary in strictest confidence, absent specific authorization to release or disclose information to third parties by the board.

I have read the Practice's Confidentiality Policy and understand that I must adhere to the aforementioned policy, and any violation of the policy is cause for immediate dismissal.

Physician signature: ____________________ Date: __________
Practice representative signature: ____________________ Date: __________

Conflict of Interest Statement

Conflict of Interest and Declaration:

____

____

The [NAME OF PRACTICE] ("the Practice") regularly enters into agreements with third parties for the purchase of goods or services. Where the Practice physician or member of the medical staff has a financial interest in or with a third party that contracts with the Practice, the potential exists for an appearance of impropriety as a result of that financial interest, and even for the abuse of the physician or medical staff member's position for their personal gain. The creation of this Conflict of Interest and Declaration Policy is designed to provide for the disclosure of the physician's interest in third-party transactions with the Practice and the independent review and approval of such transactions.

It is the policy of the Practice to require administration and members of the medical staff, and others as deemed necessary, to declare in writing a list of all business or other organizations of which he or she or any of his or her immediate family member(s) is an officer, 5 percent or more owner, employee, or contractor, with which the Practice or any affiliated organization of the Practice has, or might reasonably in the future, enter into a financial relationship. Further, it is necessary to declare any and all professional or business relationships with organizations or parties whereby the administration and members of the medical staff serve as advisors, consultants, medical directors, faculty, or investigators and for which any remuneration is received.

Procedure

It shall be the responsibility of the chief executive of the Practice, on an annual basis, to distribute to each physician and administration a copy of the Conflict of Interest and Declaration Policy. Included as part of this policy is the "Conflict of Interest and Declaration Statement and Attestation" ("Declaration"), which is to be returned to the chief executive completed and signed. Any physician or member of administration who begins employment outside the annual process will complete this declaration as part of his or her employment process.

Upon receipt of all signed declarations, the chief executive shall report to the chair of the board and president of the Practice, in writing, a summary of any relationships disclosed, together with the declarations.

It shall be the responsibility of the president of the Practice or his or her designee to distribute and have returned a copy of the Conflict of Interest and Declaration Policy to all members of the medical staff and administration.

These three (3) individuals shall review all potential conflicts that may exist or may influence future transactions or decisions within the Practice or an affiliated organization.

Continues next page

Conflict of Interest Statement (continued)

Further, at such time as any matter comes before the Practice, its administration, any functioning committee of the Practice or its management, its board of directors, or any affiliated organization of the Practice, the effected person shall make known the potential conflict, whether or not disclosed by his or her written declaration, and after answering any questions that may be asked, remove himself or herself from the discussion and decision-making.

Definitions

Immediate Family Member: A spouse, child, parent (natural or adoptive), sibling, grandparent, grandchild, spouse of grandparent or grandchild, stepparent, stepchild, stepbrother, stepsister, or any in-laws (father, mother, son, daughter, brother, sister).

Financial Relationship: Any ownership interest in or a compensation arrangement with any entity shall constitute a financial relationship. The ownership interest in an entity may be through equity, debt, or other means and may be held directly or indirectly. Compensation arrangements include most transfers of remuneration to and from an entity.

Individual Physician: ______________________
President: _______________________________
Original Issue Date: __________
Review Month: __________
Revised Date: __________
Reviewed Date: __________

Discharge Letter

Dear [PATIENT NAME]:

It is necessary to inform you that I can no longer act as your physician because [PROVIDE REASON. FOR EXAMPLE, YOU HAVE PERSISTED IN REFUSING TO FOLLOW MY MEDICAL ADVICE AND TREATMENT]. Since your condition requires medical attention, I suggest that you promptly choose another physician either inside or outside of the Practice.

If you wish assistance in this, there are several options: We can try to arrange to have you transferred to another member of my department; we can supply you with a list of other physicians who practice in [CITY OF PRACTICE, COUNTY]; or we can transfer your records to a physician of your choosing whom you personally contact.

Please let us know if we can help. Otherwise, effective [DATE], I will no longer be your physician except for emergency medical care.

Sincerely,

[PHYSICIAN/STOCKHOLDER NAME AND SIGNATURE]

Disruptive Physician: Common Behaviors

Inappropriate anger or resentments, including:

- Intimidation;
- Abusive language;
- Blaming or shaming others for possible adverse outcomes;
- Unnecessary sarcasm or cynicism; or
- Threatening violence, retribution, or litigation.

Inappropriate words or actions directed toward another person, including:

- Sexual comments or innuendoes;
- Sexual harassment;
- Seductive, aggressive, or assaultive behavior;
- Racial, ethnic, or socioeconomic slurs; or
- Lack of regard for personal comfort and dignity of others.

Inappropriate response to patient needs or staff requests, including:

- Late or unsuitable replies to pages or calls;
- Unprofessional demeanor, uncooperative conduct, or a defiant approach to problems; or
- Rigid, inflexible responses to requests for assistance or cooperation.

Disruptive Physician: Incident Report Form

Instructions

This form must be completed and signed by the complainant and signed by the medical director or hospital administrator when an employee, patient, or visitor reports an incident involving a threat, act of intimidation, violence, or other unacceptable behavior committed by a physician. Please use additional sheets of paper as needed. Once completed, please send this report to [PRACTICE NAME, ADDRESS, NAME OF BUSINESS MANAGER OR APPROPRIATE CONTACT].

1. Complainant's name: ______________________

   Date: ________

   ☐ Employee

   ☐ Patient

   ☐ Visitor
2. Complainant's home address: ______________________________________
3. Home telephone number: _______________

   Work telephone number: _______________
4. Department: _______________
5. Complainant's work location: ______________________________________
6. Incident date: ________
7. Incident time: ________
8. Incident location: ________
9. Type of incident: (check one):

   ☐ Assault

   ☐ Robbery

   ☐ Harassment

   ☐ Disorderly conduct

   ☐ Sex offense

   ☐ Other (please specify) ________
10. Were you injured?

    ☐ Yes

    ☐ No
11. If yes, please specify your injuries and the location of any treatment:

    ____

    ____
12. Did police respond to the incident?

    ☐ Yes

    ☐ No
13. Which police department responded to the incident? ______________________
14. Was a police report filed?

    ☐ Yes

    ☐ No

Continues next page

Disruptive Physician: Incident Report Form (continued)

15. Was your supervisor notified?
    ☐ Yes
    ☐ No
16. Supervisor's name: ______________________________
17. Was any action taken? (Please specify.)
    ____
    ____
18. Alleged physician's name: ______________________________
19. Please briefly describe the incident:
    ____
    ____
    ____
    ____
20. Were you alone when the incident occurred?
    ☐ Yes
    ☐ No
21. Provide information for all witnesses, including their names, departments, addresses, and telephone numbers.
    ____
    ____
    ____
    ____
22. Did the incident involve a weapon?
    ☐ Yes
    ☐ No
    Specify:
    ____
    ____
23. Were you unable to continue or report for work due to the incident?
    ☐ Yes
    ☐ No
    If so, for how long? __________
    Why?
    ____
    ____
    ____
24. Was the disruptive behavior or violence directed solely at you, or were others included?
    ____
    ____
    ____

Continues next page

Disruptive Physician: Incident Report Form (continued)

25. If others were included, please provide their name(s), department(s), address(es), and telephone number(s), if known.

____
____
____

26. Did you have any reason to believe that an incident might occur?
    - ☐ Yes
    - ☐ No

    Why?

____
____
____

27. Has this type of incident or similar incident(s) happened to you or your coworkers before?
    - ☐ Yes
    - ☐ No

    If so, please specify:

____
____
____

28. Was the alleged physician involved in previous incidents?
    - ☐ Yes
    - ☐ No
29. Have you had any counseling or support since the incident?
    - ☐ Yes
    - ☐ No

    If so, please specify:

____
____
____

30. What are your recommendations for avoiding such an incident?

____
____
____

31. Are there any measures in place to prevent similar incidents?
    - ☐ Yes
    - ☐ No

    If so, please specify:

____
____
____

Continues next page

Disruptive Physician: Incident Report Form (continued)

Complainant's signature: ______________________ Date: ________
Hospital administrator signature: ______________________ Date: ________
Medical director signature: ______________________ Date: ________

The following portion is to be completed by the Practice board of directors or its designee:

32. Has corrective action been taken?
    - ☐ Yes
    - ☐ No

    Specify:

    ____
    ____
    ____

33. Incident disposition (check all that apply):
    - ☐ No action taken
    - ☐ Arrest
    - ☐ Warning
    - ☐ Suspension
    - ☐ Reprimand
    - ☐ Termination
    - ☐ Other (please specify):

      ____
      ____
      ____

34. Comments:

    ____
    ____
    ____

    Action taken:

    ____
    ____
    ____

    Referred to ______________ for further action: ______________

    Interviewed all parties and investigated facts (if yes, attach memo detailing these investigations):
    - ☐ Yes
    - ☐ No

    Dismissed complaint because ______________________________

    Other ____

Director's signature: ______________________ Date: ________
Business manager's signature: ______________________ Date: ________

Disruptive Physician: Verbal Warning Report Form

We recommend that at least two Practice board members meet with the physician when giving a verbal warning.

Physician name: ______________________________

Nature of the offense:

____

____

____

Date warning issued: __________
Expected behavior change: __________
Time frame in which the change should occur: __________
Board of directors' signature: ______________________________ Date: __________
Board of directors' signature: ______________________________ Date: __________

Disruptive Physician: Written Warning Report Form

We recommend that at least two Practice board members meet with the physician when giving a written warning.

Physician name: ______________________________

Nature of the offense:

____

____

____

Date warning issued: __________
Expected behavior change: __________
Time frame in which the change should occur: __________
Length of time for suspension, if necessary: __________

- ☐ With pay
- ☐ Without pay

Board of directors' signature: ______________________________ Date: __________
Board of directors' signature: ______________________________ Date: __________

Employment Contract for Part-Time or Partially Retired Physician

[LETTERHEAD]
[DATE]
[PHYSICIAN NAME], MD

Re: Part-Time Employment (for the "Practice")

Dear __________:

We are pleased to offer you part-time employment on the following terms and conditions, for the term specified as follows.

1. **Duties and Time.** During the term of this agreement, you will actively engage in the practice of [SPECIALTY] for the Practice and will devote your best efforts and time and attention to such practice. You will maintain a time sheet reporting the hours that you work and submit the time sheet to accounting monthly. Your compensation is based on an average workweek of one (1) day per week.
2. **Term.** The term of this agreement shall commence on the date of this letter and end either by termination, as provided for herein, or upon an offer of full-time employment.
3. **Compensation.** During the term hereof, you will be paid $[X].00 per day at one (1) day per week. All applicable taxes and other required withholdings will be deducted from your pay.
4. **Other Benefits.** As a part-time employee, you will not be eligible for pension plan, 401K plan, profit-sharing plan, or other similar benefit plans, nor for group insurance plans or other employee benefits available to full-time employees of the Practice. You are also responsible for the cost of travel, food, lodging, and tuition for any professional development seminars or continuing education programs in excess of $[X].00 per year.
5. **Vacation and Leave.** As a part-time employee, no vacation benefit is provided for under this agreement.
6. **Confidential Information.** You further recognize and acknowledge that you have access to and the use of confidential information and trade secrets of the Practice related to its patients, referral sources, related ventures, hospital arrangements, and operations, which may include but are not limited to financial statements, internal memoranda, reports, patient lists, correspondence, referring physician lists, training, methods of operation, processes and other materials, procedures, or records of a proprietary nature. In order to protect this confidential information and these trade secrets, you agree that you will not, during your employment hereunder or anytime thereafter for so long as any such information and trade secrets remain confidential, secret, or otherwise wholly or partially protectable, use or disclose any such information or trade secrets for your own benefit to any other firm, person, corporation, association, or other entity for any reason or purpose whatsoever, without the prior written consent of the Practice to such use or disclosure. You acknowledge and agree that in the event of a breach or threatened breach of the provision of this paragraph 6, the Practice has no adequate remedy at law and that the injury suffered by the Practice would be irreparable in nature; therefore, the Practice shall be entitled to injunctive relief to prevent a breach and to secure enforcement. Nothing herein shall be construed as prohibiting the Practice from pursuing any other remedies available to it for such breach, including the recovery of damages, attorneys' fees, and court costs from you.
7. **Termination.** This agreement may be terminated by either party at any time upon forty-five (45) days' written notice to the other party. This agreement will terminate upon your death. In addition, your employment may be terminated for cause by the Practice immediately upon written notice to you. For this purpose, "cause" shall be defined to include the following events:
    a. You cease to be authorized to practice [SPECIALTY] in the state of [STATE];

Continues next page

Employment Contract for Part-Time or Partially Retired Physician (continued)

b. You, as a result of professional misconduct, are expelled, suspended, or otherwise disciplined by the final action of any professional organization;

c. You resign from any professional organization under threat of disciplinary action for professional misconduct;

d. You are convicted of a criminal offense involving moral turpitude;

e. You commit any dishonest or fraudulent act in the course of your relationship with the Practice;

f. You materially violate any obligations under this agreement;

g. You commit any act or omission that is materially detrimental to the image of the Practice or to the Practice's relationships with its patients, referral sources, healthcare colleagues, or to its business relationships or the like;

h. You fail to perform or carry out your duties as specified in this agreement;

i. You, through gross negligence or intentional conduct, subject the health or safety of a patient of the Practice to a material and unreasonable risk of harm;

j. You engage in substance abuse (including abuse of alcohol or use of illegal narcotics, and/or other drugs or substances); or

k. You fail and/or refuse to provide the Practice with any information reasonably requested by the Practice and necessary for the Practice to evaluate whether the you are in breach or violation of this agreement or have committed any other act or omission that might constitute a cause for termination hereunder.

Notwithstanding any termination of your employment, Paragraph 6 will remain in effect subsequent to such termination according to its terms.

8. **Notices.** All notices hereunder shall be in writing and sent by certified mail, return receipt requested, first-class postage prepaid, addressed to you at your last-known residence and to the Practice as follows:

   [PRACTICE NAME]

   [ADDRESS]

   [CITY], [STATE] [ZIP]

9. **Relationship of the Parties.** Our relationship is that of an employer and employee. You have no authority to enter into any contract binding the Practice or to create an obligation on behalf of the Practice without written authorization from the Practice.

10. **Miscellaneous.** This agreement (a) may not be assigned by either party without the written consent of the other; (b) may be modified or amended only by a writing signed by each party hereto; (c) shall be governed by and construed in accordance with the laws of the state of [STATE] and of the United States of America; (d) shall be deemed severable, and the invalidity or unenforceability of any one or more of the provisions shall not affect the validity and enforceability of the other provisions hereof; and (e) embodies the entire agreement and understanding between the parties with respect to the subject matter hereof, superseding all prior agreements, consents, and understanding relating to such matter. The captions in this agreement are for convenience only and shall be accorded no substantive meaning in the interpretation hereof.

If the foregoing accurately describes our agreement regarding your part-time employment with us, please signify by signing your name in the space provided below.

Sincerely,
The Practice
By: ______________________________ (MD, President)

ACCEPTED AND AGREED: __________

Letter to Pharmaceutical Representatives

To all Pharmaceutical Representatives:

The physicians at [PRACTICE NAME] appreciate your visits to our office to provide information about your products. Please keep in mind that the physicians and the medical assistants are very busy throughout the day with patient care and are limited in the amount of time they can spend with you.

When calling on our office, please adhere to the following protocols:

1. Check in at the receptionist desk downstairs.
2. Please make your visit brief.
3. Only one pharmaceutical company at a time will be admitted to the back office area. In addition, supervisors will not be allowed in the back office with the rep.
4. You may check the supply of your product in the cabinet, but leave your samples on the counter for the medical assistant to put away.
5. Do not remove or change the location of another company's product.
6. If a physician's signature is required, you will be asked to wait by the lab, and the medical assistant will notify you when the physician is available. Please do not visit with the medical assistants at their desks.
7. The physicians will not take detailed information from any reps during the hours they see patients. The only time allotted for detailing reps will be during luncheons.
8. Reps will not be admitted before noon on Mondays or after 4:00 p.m. any day of the week.

Your cooperation will assist us with the implementation of our Privacy Policies and compliance with HIPAA regulations. We appreciate your professional attitude toward our staff, patients, and other drug reps while at our office.

Sincerely,

[PRACTICE ADMINISTRATOR]

Outside Employment Form[1]

Physician name: ______________________________ Date: __________
Department: ______________________________ Date: __________
Job title: ______________________________
Supervisor: ______________________________
Practice employment date: __________

I have an interest in working in a second job. I understand that the Practice is my primary employer. I do not believe that this second job will be a conflict of interest or affect my current position.

Name of outside employer: ______________________________
Job title: ______________________________

Job duties and responsibilities:

____

____

Work schedule (list the exact work schedule and number of hours assigned each week):

____

____

Additional comments:

____

____

____

I understand that any changes occurring in my outside employment must be amended and recorded on a new form submitted to my supervisor. This form will become part of my physician record and is subject to review by the Practice.

Physician signature: ______________________________ Date: __________
Physician supervisor's signature: ______________________________ Date: __________

- ☐ Approved
- ☐ Disapproved

Comments:

____

____

____

____

1 Printed in *HR Policies and Procedures Manual for Medical Practices, 4th Edition,* by Courtney Price, PhD, and Alys Novak, MBA (Englewood, CO: Medical Group Management Association, 2007).

Patient Satisfaction Survey Form[2]

Physician: ______________________________
Date: __________

Our physician(s) and staff want to give you the best possible medical care. To do that, we need your feedback. Please let us know what you think we're doing right, and how we can improve, by filling out the following patient survey. All of your responses will be kept strictly confidential, and your signature is not required. Please use this opportunity to respond freely.

Please circle the number that best suits the criteria listed.

APPOINTMENT SCHEDULING				
	Poor	Fair	Good	Satisfactory
1. I was able to get an appointment easily.	1	2	3	4
2. I was able to get an appointment within a two-week period.	1	2	3	4
3. My appointment was scheduled at a convenient time.	1	2	3	4

Comments:

____
____
____

GREETING/REGISTRATION				
	Poor	Fair	Good	Satisfactory
1. Upon my arrival at the office, I was greeted in a courteous and timely manner.	1	2	3	4
2. The registration process was quick and easy.	1	2	3	4
3. The papers I had to complete were easy to read and understand.	1	2	3	4
4. I waited a short time to see the physician.	1	2	3	4

Comments:

____
____
____

Continues next page

2 Printed in *Star-Studded Service: 6 Steps to Winning Patient Satisfaction* by Kevin Sullivan and Meryl Luallin (Englewood, CO: Medical Group Management Association, 2007).

Patient Satisfaction Survey Form (continued)

APPEARANCE OF FACILITY				
	Poor	**Fair**	**Good**	**Satisfactory**
1. The waiting room was comfortable and neat.	1	2	3	4
2. There were not a lot of people waiting.	1	2	3	4
3. The exam room was clean.	1	2	3	4
4. The temperature of the room was comfortable.	1	2	3	4

Comments:

____

____

____

STAFF AND PHYSICIAN				
	Poor	**Fair**	**Good**	**Satisfactory**
1. The nurse and assistants were friendly and pleasant.	1	2	3	4
2. The staff showed concern for my problems.	1	2	3	4
3. The staff was professional and friendly.	1	2	3	4
4. The physician was professional and friendly.	1	2	3	4
5. The physician clearly explained my problem or condition.	1	2	3	4
6. The physician showed respect for and answered all of my questions.	1	2	3	4
7. Instructions regarding medication and/or follow-up care were clear and easy to understand.	1	2	3	4
8. I felt the doctor spent an appropriate amount of time with me.	1	2	3	4

Comments:

____

____

____

Continues next page

Patient Satisfaction Survey Form (continued)

OUR FACILITY	Poor	Fair	Good	Satisfactory
1. The hours of operation were convenient for me.	1	2	3	4
2. I felt comfortable finding and navigating the facility.	1	2	3	4
3. There was adequate parking available.	1	2	3	4
4. Facility signage and directions were easy to follow.	1	2	3	4

Comments:

___

___

___

BUSINESS OFFICE	Poor	Fair	Good	Satisfactory
1. The office personnel were courteous and knowledgeable regarding my account.	1	2	3	4
2. My bill arrangements and paperwork were handled efficiently and accurately.	1	2	3	4
3. My bill was sent promptly.	1	2	3	4

Comments:

___

___

___

OTHER QUESTIONS

1. How did you hear about our office?

My health insurance ______	Yellow Pages/phone book ______
Referred by friend ______ Friend's name ______	Internet ______ Website ______
Other ______	

2. Is this office convenient to where you live or work?

   ______ Yes ______ No

3. Are you under a managed care plan or HMO?

   ______ Yes ______ No

Continues next page

Patient Satisfaction Survey Form (continued)

4. How would you rate your visit overall at the office?

Poor	Fair	Good	Excellent
1	2	3	4

5. Have you visited any of our other affiliated clinics?

   ___________ Yes ___________ No

6. Would you recommend our office to a friend?

   ___________ Yes ___________ No

7. Would you see another physician in our office if your physician was not available?

   ___________ Yes ___________ No

Are there any comments or suggestions you would like to add that would make your next visit more comfortable?

____

____

____

Thank you for completing this survey!

If you would like our staff to call you and talk to you about your comments on this survey, please check here ____.

Name (optional): ______________________________

Phone: ______________________________

Some Information about You (Circle the Appropriate Number)					
GENDER		YOUR AGE		ARE YOU	
Male	1	Under 18	1	A new patient?	1
Female	2	18–30	2	A returning patient?	2
		31–40	3		
		41–50	4		
		51–64	5		
		65+	6		

Performance Appraisal Form

Assessment Criteria
Work ethic: Exhibits consistent effort and availability in the performance of associate physician responsibilities. Demonstrates a willingness to assume additional workload to enhance patient satisfaction and meet referring physician requirements. Manages time efficiently. Works cooperatively with staff to improve organizational performance.
Opportunities for improvement include: • • •
Patient-care productivity, efficiency, and outcomes: Practice throughput (patient-visit capacity) is equal to or exceeds associate goals. Resource utilization (e.g., direct overhead expenses, average length of stay (ALOS), and surgical efficiency) within normal benchmarks or budget. Clinical practices and surgical outcomes within expected range of community standards. Manages workload efficiently with appropriate delegation of work to support staff.
Opportunities for improvement include: • • •
Willingness and effectiveness in promoting the Practice: Represents the Practice at business development events and participates in assigned promotional activities. Presents Practice physicians and staff favorably to external groups, including referring physicians, patients, hospital staff, vendors, third-party payers, and community organizations.
Opportunities for improvement include: • • •
Acceptance of Practice assignments, work requirements, and responsibilities: Accepts clinic and coverage assignments and displays willingness to modify schedule to accommodate increased patient workload. Exhibits adequate preparation and competence in completing clinical responsibilities. Performs tasks consistent with organization policies and procedures.
Opportunities for improvement include: • • •
Continues next page

Performance Appraisal Form (continued)

Thirty- (30-) day plan or goal for development:
____
____
____

Twelve- (12-) month plan or goal for development:
____
____
____

Five- (5-) year plan or goal for development:
____
____
____

Employee signature: __________________________
Date: __________

Reviewed by: __________________________
Date: __________

Physician Compact: Basic Performance Expectations and Customer Service

1. Be on time every time.
2. Be professional in appearance, in clothing, and in grooming.
3. Wear your nametag, or at least make sure you introduce yourself clearly. Study after study shows that knowing the name of the physician greatly enhances a patient's feeling of connection and personal service.
4. Make sure you introduce yourself to surgeons and staff members whom you don't recognize; identify yourself as a physician of the Practice, and ask questions about how he or she wants the case or patient handled.
5. Allow real time for real questions. You must address real fears and answer questions. There are ways to do this quickly and efficiently — learn them.
6. This may be difficult, but if you can talk to patients without a mask or hair covering on, it will help more than you think! Patients like to see a face if possible.
7. Treat nurses and staff respectfully at all times. In general, behave appropriately at all times. Patients are more aware of what is going on around them in hallways than you think, and certainly your medical colleagues will appreciate professional behavior.
8. If you would like some business cards or general Practice information pamphlets to help with patient or other contacts, ask for them from the Practice administrator.

Physician Peer Review Form

Physician under review: ______________________________

Date of review: __________

Criteria	Score on a Scale of 1–10 (1 being difficult, 10 being easy)
1. Easy to work with	1 2 3 4 5 6 7 8 9 10
2. Relates to patients well (bedside manner)	1 2 3 4 5 6 7 8 9 10
3. Fund of knowledge	1 2 3 4 5 6 7 8 9 10
4. Conscientious in work habits	1 2 3 4 5 6 7 8 9 10
5. Has the interest of the Practice at heart	1 2 3 4 5 6 7 8 9 10

To be completed by administration and/or president:

Hospital attendance: __________ out of __________ = __________% attendance

Meeting attendance: __________ out of __________ = __________% attendance

CME credits earned last year: __________

QA reports: __________

Peer evaluation score: __________

Civic activities and community services provided in the last year:

1. ______________________________
2. ______________________________
3. ______________________________
4. ______________________________

Physician Satisfaction Survey Form

Survey Instructions

The following questions ask you about your satisfaction with the Practice.

Methodology

This survey will ask you questions regarding your satisfaction with the following areas:

- The profession of medicine;
- Your current practice environment;
- Time spent on patient care versus administrative tasks;
- Trade-off between income and hours worked;
- Income compared with comparable professions;
- Hours worked per week versus home life; and
- Level of services offered.

Depending on the question, the response scale ranges from “Very Rewarding” to “Very Unrewarding;” “Very Satisfied” to “Very Dissatisfied;” and “Very Competitive” to “Very Uncompetitive.”

When Completed

Please return your completed survey with all comments and/or feedback to [COMPLIANCE OFFICER]. Individual survey reports will be kept confidential, while a report will be made of overall scoring and ratings per question.

Thank you very much!

This survey is anonymous; please do not sign your name to the survey.

1. How would you rate the profession of medicine?
   - ☐ Very Rewarding
   - ☐ Rewarding
   - ☐ Neutral
   - ☐ Unrewarding
   - ☐ Very Unrewarding

   Additional Comments:

   ____
   ____
   ____

Continues next page

Physician Satisfaction Survey Form (continued)

2. Are you satisfied with the current practice environment?
   - ☐ Very Satisfied
   - ☐ Satisfied
   - ☐ Neutral
   - ☐ Dissatisfied
   - ☐ Very Dissatisfied

   Additional Comments:

   ____
   ____
   ____

3. Are you satisfied with the number of hours that you are able to spend on patient care versus administrative tasks?
   - ☐ Very Satisfied
   - ☐ Satisfied
   - ☐ Neutral
   - ☐ Dissatisfied
   - ☐ Very Dissatisfied

   Additional Comments:

   ____
   ____
   ____

4. Are you satisfied with the trade-off between your income and the number of hours you work?
   - ☐ Very Satisfied
   - ☐ Satisfied
   - ☐ Neutral
   - ☐ Dissatisfied
   - ☐ Very Dissatisfied

   Additional Comments:

   ____
   ____
   ____

Continues next page

Physician Satisfaction Survey Form (continued)

5. Compared to what you know about income in comparable professions, how do you rate your income?
   - ☐ Very Competitive
   - ☐ Competitive
   - ☐ Neutral
   - ☐ Uncompetitive
   - ☐ Very Uncompetitive

   Additional Comments:

   ____
   ____
   ____

6. Are you satisfied with the number of hours per week you work versus your ability to pursue a home life and/or personal interests?
   - ☐ Very Satisfied
   - ☐ Satisfied
   - ☐ Neutral
   - ☐ Dissatisfied
   - ☐ Very Dissatisfied

   Additional Comments:

   ____
   ____
   ____

7. Are you contemplating a career change because of the current practice environment?
   - ☐ Yes
   - ☐ No
   - ☐ N/A

   Additional Comments:

   ____
   ____
   ____

8. Are you satisfied with the level of service offered from the central billing office?
   - ☐ Very Satisfied
   - ☐ Satisfied
   - ☐ Neutral
   - ☐ Dissatisfied
   - ☐ Very Dissatisfied

   Additional Comments:

   ____
   ____
   ____

Continues next page

Physician Satisfaction Survey Form (continued)

9. Do you believe it is time for the Practice board of directors to change membership?
   - ☐ Yes
   - ☐ No

   Additional Comments:

   ____

   ____

   ____

10. Considering your current practice environment, would you choose medicine as a profession again?
    - ☐ Yes
    - ☐ No

    Additional Comments:

    ____

    ____

    ____

11. When do you plan to retire? (Check the answer closest to your goal.)
    - ☐ Next year
    - ☐ In 2 years
    - ☐ In 5 years
    - ☐ In 10–15 years
    - ☐ Not anytime soon

12. What are your ideas regarding future growth for the Practice?

    ____

    ____

    ____

Your primary specialty is: ______________________

Hours per weeks spent in direct patient care: __________

Thank you for completing this important survey!

Physician Statement on Fraud and Abuse

I understand and acknowledge that:

1. The Practice and its related organizations seek to comply fully with all federal and state laws and regulations applicable to providing medical services, especially those designed to prevent fraud and abuse;
2. I am required to do my part in helping the Practice comply with these laws by ensuring that all of my documentation (patient records, payroll records, expense and reimbursement reports, and all other materials submitted, prepared, or reviewed by me) is accurate, truthful, and free of any form of fraud;
3. If I learn of any activity that I believe involves fraud or abuse anywhere within the organization, it is my obligation to report it immediately to the chief executive officer;
4. I will not be disciplined, harassed, or retaliated against in any aspect of employment for any good faith disclosure made by me related to any actual or perceived fraud or abuse; and
5. My failure to comply with the rules and policies against fraud and abuse, or my failure to report any knowledge of fraud or abuse by others, will subject me to disciplinary action up to and including immediate termination from the Practice.

Physician name (print/type): ______________________________ Date: __________
Physician signature: ______________________________

Practice and Patient E-Communications Agreement

I, [PATIENT NAME], agree to engage in electronic (e-mail) correspondence with [PHYSICIAN/PRACTICE/STOCKHOLDER NAME] regarding nonurgent, nonemergency, and routine issues related to my healthcare and treatment, such as:

- Prescription refills;
- General medical advice after an initial face-to-face visit;
- Lab test results;
- Appointment requests for nonurgent problems;
- Simple treatment instructions; and
- Patient education to improve health literacy.

[PRACTICE NAME] personnel shall not compile patient e-mail addresses for marketing or fundraising purposes, or supply patient e-mail addresses to any third party for advertising, solicitations, or any other use.

DISCLAIMER: Please note that e-mail is not necessarily confidential and should be used for routine matters only. Urgent or emergent issues should be handled by telephone. E-mails may not be read in a timely manner if the physician is out of the office. If you have not received a response within two (2) business days, please contact [PRACTICE NAME] by phone at [PRACTICE PHONE NUMBER].

Resources

Medical specialty societies and state medical societies provide a wealth of physician policies and guidelines for medical practice. Following are several sites with special features noted.

American Medical Association (AMA)

www.ama-assn.org

- **Practice Management Center**

  Features sections on Medical Ethics, Legal Issues, and Clinical Practice Improvement and Patient Safety. Note the following features in this area of the AMA site:

  - **AMA's Code of Medical Ethics**
  - **Federation Repository of Ethics Documents Online (FRED Online)**

    A repository of links to full-text Codes of Ethics and ethics-related policies provided by state and specialty medical associations in the AMA's federation.

National Medical Specialty Society Websites

www.ama-assn.org/ama/pub/about-ama/our-people/the-federation-medicine/national-medical-specialty-society-websites.page

Provides links to major medical specialty sites. Noteworthy features of these organizations are highlighted below.

- **American Academy of Family Physicians (AAFP)**
  www.aafp.org

  See the sections on "Running a Practice" and "Policy and Advocacy" for physician policies relating to Family Practice.

- **American Academy of Orthopaedic Surgeons (AAOS)**
  www.aos.org
  This site features a "Quality Initiative" area and the following sections: E-prescribing, Physician Consortium for Performance Improvement, Quality Tools, and Evidence-based Medicine.

- **The American Academy of Pain Medicine**
  www.painmed.org
  The "Practice Management" area of this site offers a downloadable version of its Ethics Charter. Also, a Members-only section presents "Position Statements for Practice Management."

- **American Academy of Pediatrics (AAP) — AAP Policy Site**
  http://aappolicy.aappublications.org
  AAP Policy is an extensive collection of policy documents that gathers the following into one location: Policy Statements, Clinical Reports, Clinical Practice Guidelines, Technical Reports, Affirmation of Value, and Parent Pages. This site replaces the policy pages previously located on the AAP Website.

- **American College of Cardiology (ACC)**
  www.cardiosource.org/acc
  This site presents the Cardiovascular Leadership Institute, focusing on five areas of leadership training that include: Physician Executives, Early Career/Fellow-in-Training, College Leadership, Academic Leadership, and Inclusive Workforce.

- **American College of Emergency Physicians (ACEP)**
  www.acep.org/policystatements
  Located under Clinical and Practice Management, a robust section called "ACEP Policy Statements" highlights key issues in Emergency Medicine. These policies can be rank sorted by "most recent," "highest rated," or by title and are reviewed every seven years.

- **American College of Healthcare Executives (ACHE)**
  www.ache.org
  See the "Policy Statements" section for updated guidance on general issues and ethical behavior for healthcare executives, including physician executives.

- **American College of Physician Executives (ACPE)**
  www.acpe.org
  The Resources section of this site contains toolkits on Leadership, Physician Morale, Medical Errors, Disruptive Physician Behavior, and Ethical Behavior.

- **American College of Physicians (ACP)**
  www.acponline.org
  The site's section called "Running a Practice," features a topic area on Ethics and Professionalism. It presents an ethics manual, the full text for a physician's charter of medical responsibility, case studies, and other ethics resources.

- **American College of Radiology (ACR)**
  www.acr.org
  ACR offers a variety of guidance documents, such as Practice Guidelines, Technical Standards, Appropriateness Criteria, and other resources.

- **The American Congress of Obstetricians and Gynecologists (ACOG)**
  www.acog.org
  Members may access a "Compendium Online" which includes all ACOG Committee Opinions, evidence-based Practice Bulletins, Policy Statements, and Technology Assessments. Nonmembers may freely access the searchable Ethics Committee Opinions.

- **American Gastroenterological Association (AGA)**
  www.gastro.org/practice/medical-position-statements
  The "Practice" section offers an archive of medical position statements and guidelines developed under the aegis of the AGA Institute Clinical Practice and Quality Management Committee, which provides preferred approaches to specific medical problems or issues.

- **American Society of Anesthesiologists (ASA)**
  www.asahq.org
  The section titled "Standards, Guidelines, Statements and Other Documents" features an array of downloadable files providing guidance to improve decision-making and promote beneficial outcomes for the practice of anesthesiology.

- **College of American Pathologists (CAP) — "Transforming Pathologists" site**
  www.cap.org/apps/docs/membership/transformation/new/index.html
  This "sub-site" presents details of a multi-year, evidence-based program to "transform the specialty," fostering enhanced roles for the pathologist and greater recognition as a physician and a critical member of the patient care team.

State Medical Society Websites

www.ama-assn.org/ama/pub/about-ama/our-people/the-federation-medicine/state-medical-society-websites.page?

This provides links to major medical society sites. Several state societies provide in-depth information on their sites. Noteworthy are the following:

- **Iowa Medical Society**
  www.iowamedical.org
  The "Office of Legal Affairs" section offers an array of guidance, including Impaired Physicians/Physician Reporting and Medical Ethics, including several practice legal issues.

- **Louisiana State Medical Society**
  www.lsms.org/site/physicians
  This site provides separate sections addressing issues for both "Senior Physicians" (e.g., closing a practice, physician retirement) and "Young Physicians" (e.g., time management, negotiating contracts).

- **(Maryland) Med Chi: The Maryland State Medical Society**
  www.medchi.org

  Under the "Law and Advocacy" section, the Ethical Opinions area presents policies in PDF format for five key topics: Physician/Patient Relationship, Physician's Relationship with Health Care Professionals and Medical Office Staff, Physicians and Research, Corporate Medicine/Business Ventures, and Professional Income and Fees. Each section contains several related policies.

- **Massachusetts Medical Society**
  www.massmed.org

  The Physicians "Legal and Regulatory Issues" section contains physician self-governance model documents, links to "Law and Ethics" columns, the MMS Code of Ethics, and other guidelines.

- **Michigan State Medical Society**
  www.msms.org

  Presents work and findings from a task force on the "Future of Medicine," covering issues such as Administrative Simplification, Web 2.0, and Worksite Wellness. A downloadable policies manual is available to members of the society.

- **Minnesota Medical Association**
  www.mnmed.org

  The "Key Issues" section outlines resources and direction on an extensive list of relevant issues such as Alcohol Abuse, Physician Profiling, Physician Well-being, Scope of Practice, and many others.

- **Nevada State Medical Association**
  www.nsmadocs.org

  The "Policies" area of the site presents the "NSMA Policy Compendium," including resolutions passed since 1989 and cross-referencing AMA Policy Resolutions as appropriate.

- **(New York) The Medical Society of the State of New York**
  www.mssny.org

  Members of the society can access "Practice Guidelines," including both a "Physicians Guide" and "Professional Guidelines."

- **North Carolina Medical Society**
  www.ncmedsoc.org

  This very robust site features policies and guidance throughout its main menu sections on Practice Management, Government Affairs, and Payor Issues. A tabbed area on the home page highlights "priority issues" (e.g., "Physician-Hospital Issues").

- **Ohio State Medical Association**
  www.osma.org

  Located under the sections "Tools and Resources/Running a Practice," you will find several links to specific legal standards and guidelines from various areas of medicine.

- **Pennsylvania Medical Society**
  www.pamedsoc.org
  The PAMED "Better Health Network" facilitates sharing of ideas among physicians and other innovators who want to improve patient care. The Innovations section highlights new contributions in clinical care, health care teams, patient communication and engagement, and technology.

- **Rhode Island Medical Society**
  www.rimed.org
  This site sponsors a "Physician Health Program" that focuses on the well-being of a doctor, listing common warning signs such as changes in attitude, behavior, physical appearance, performance, and relationships; and outlines where physicians may find support.

- **(Virginia) Medical Society of Virginia**
  www.msv.org
  The "Policy and Regulatory" section features a Knowledgebase that contains a wealth of information on important topics that impact the practice of medicine in Virginia.

- **Washington State Medical Association**
  www.wsma.org
  WSMA features the "Center for Medical Professionalism," section which includes WSMA's "Principles of Medical Ethics," and sections on Quality Care/Best Practices, Leadership Development, Patient Safety, and other current issues.

- **Wisconsin Medical Society**
  www.wisconsinmedicalsociety.org/advocacy_and_policy/policy_compendium/2009
  The site's "Advocacy and Policy" section presents the complete compendium of society policies. Reviewed every five years, it includes Ethical/Judicial, Public Health, Access and Financing, Education, and Legal/Legislative issues, as well as Practice, Organizational, and Interprofessional issues.